Applied Econometrics

Applied Econometrics

Special Issue Editor
Chia-Lin Chang

MDPI • Basel • Beijing • Wuhan • Barcelona • Belgrade

MDPI

Special Issue Editor
Chia-Lin Chang
National Chung Hsing University
Taiwan

Editorial Office
MDPI
St. Alban-Anlage 66
4052 Basel, Switzerland

This is a reprint of articles from the Special Issue published online in the open access journal *Journal of Risk and Financial Management* (ISSN 1911-8074) from 2017 to 2019 (available at: https://www.mdpi.com/journal/jrfm/special_issues/applied_econometrics).

For citation purposes, cite each article independently as indicated on the article page online and as indicated below:

LastName, A.A.; LastName, B.B.; LastName, C.C. Article Title. *Journal Name* **Year**, *Article Number, Page Range.*

ISBN 978-3-03897-926-5 (Pbk)
ISBN 978-3-03897-927-2 (PDF)

Contents

About the Special Issue Editor

Chia-Lin Chang holds a PhD (Economics), 2004, Université Catholique de Louvain, Belgium, and is an elected Distinguished Fellow of the International Engineering and Technology Institute (DFIETI), and an elected Fellow of the Modelling and Simulation Society of Australia and New Zealand (FMSSANZ). Chia-Lin Chang is a University Distinguished Professor, Professor of Economics, Professor of Finance, and Director of the Agricultural and Natural Resources Research Centre (ANRRC) at the National Chung Hsing University, Taiwan, Distinguished Visiting Professor in the Faculty of Economic and Financial Sciences, the University of Johannesburg, South Africa, and Adjunct Professor, the Department of Economic Analysis and ICAE, the Complutense University of Madrid (founded 1293), Spain. Chia-Lin Chang has over 100 journal publications (most of which are in Web of Science Clarivate Analytics and Scopus, and chapters in books and edited and fully refereed conference proceedings volumes. Chia-Lin Chang is Executive Editor of the *Taiwan Journal of Applied Economics* (TJAE) (TSSCI), Co-Editor-in-Chief, *Journal of Reviews of Global Economics* (JRGE) (Scopus), Editor-in-Chief, *Journal of Medical and Health Economics* (JMHE), Co-Editor-in-Chief, *Journal of Management Information and Decision Sciences* (JMIDS), Co-Editor-in-Chief, *Journal of Big Data and Computational Science* (JBDCS), Senior Co-Editor in Chief, *Advances in Decision Sciences* (ADS) (Scopus), a member of the Editorial Boards of 20+ international journals, and has guest co-edited special issues of the following Web of Science Clarivate Analytics or Scopus journals: *Journal of Econometrics* (Elsevier), *Mathematics and Computers in Simulation* (Elsevier), *North American Journal of Economics and Finance* (Elsevier), *Annals of Financial Economics* (World Scientific), *Advances in Decision Sciences* (Hindawi), *Sustainability* (MDPI), *Energies* (MDPI), *Journal of Risk and Financial Management* (MDPI), *Risks* (MDPI), and *China Finance Review International* (Emerald). Chia-Lin Chang has been a visiting professor at the Econometric Institute, Erasmus School of Economics, Erasmus University Rotterdam, The Netherlands; Faculty of Economics and Faculty of Engineering, University of Tokyo, Japan; Institute of Economic Research, Kyoto University, Japan; Faculty of Economics, Yokohama National University, Japan; Department of Economics, University of Padova (founded 1222), Italy; and Department of Finance, Chinese University of Hong Kong, China; and Department of Mathematics, Hong Kong University of Science and Technology, China. Her research areas include applied econometrics, financial econometrics, applied statistics, quantitative finance, modeling risk, financial portfolio management, energy economics, energy finance, applied time series analysis, forecasting, technology and innovation, empirical industrial organization, health and medical economics, tourism research, tourism management, bibliometrics, and international rankings of journals and academics.

Preface to "Applied Econometrics"

This monograph is concerned with the broad topic of recent advances in "Applied Econometrics", and includes novel theoretical and empirical research associated with the application of econometrics in a broad range of disciplines associated with finance, risk modeling, portfolio management, optimal hedging strategies, economics, econometrics, and financial econometrics.

The interesting and innovative topics in the monograph include: Abnormal Returns or Mismeasured Risk? Network Effects and Risk Spillover in Stock Returns; the Effects of Global Oil Price on Exchange Rate, Trade Balance, and Reserves in Nigeria: A Frequency Domain Causality Approach; What Factors Affect Income Inequality and Economic Growth in Middle-Income Countries?; The Importance of the Financial Derivatives Markets to Economic Development in the World's Four Major Economies; Multivariate Student versus Multivariate Gaussian Regression Models with Application to Finance; Does the Misery Index Influence a U.S. President's Political Re-Election Prospects?; Limitation of Financial Health Prediction in Companies from Post-Communist Countries; Cash Use of the Taiwan Dollar: Is It Efficient?; The Relationship between Economic Freedom and FDI versus Economic Growth: Evidence from the GCC Countries; Systemic Approach to Management Control through Determining Factors; Nonlinear Time Series Modeling: A Unified Perspective, Algorithm and Application; How Informative Are Earnings Forecasts?; FHA Loans in Foreclosure Proceedings: Distinguishing Sources of Interdependence in Competing Risks; and Recovering Historical Inflation Data from Postage Stamps Prices.

Chia-Lin Chang
Special Issue Editor

Journal of
Risk and Financial Management

MDPI

Article

Abnormal Returns or Mismeasured Risk? Network Effects and Risk Spillover in Stock Returns

Arnab Bhattacharjee [1] and **Sudipto Roy** [2,*]

[1] Spatial Economics & Econometrics Centre, Heriot-Watt University, Edinburgh EH14 4AS, UK;
     a.bhattacharjee@hw.ac.uk
[2] Finlabs India Pvt. Ltd., Mumbai 400051, India
*   Correspondence: sudipto.r@finlabsindia.com; Tel.: +44-131-451-3482

Received: 4 February 2019; Accepted: 18 March 2019; Published: 29 March 2019

Abstract: Recent event study literature has highlighted abnormal stock returns, particularly in short event windows. A common explanation is the cross-correlation of stock returns that are often enhanced during periods of sharp market movements. This suggests the misspecification of the underlying factor model, typically the Fama-French model. By drawing upon recent panel data literature with cross-section dependence, we argue that the Fame-French factor model can be enriched by allowing explicitly for network effects between stock returns. We show that recent empirical work is consistent with the above interpretation, and we advance some hypotheses along which new structural models for stock returns may be developed. Applied to data on stock returns for the 30 Dow Jones Industrial Average (DJIA) stocks, our framework provides exciting new insights.

Keywords: Fama-French factor model; market microstructure; trading behavior; panel data factor model; social network model; risk spillover; abnormal returns

---

1. Introduction

In finance theory and empirics, stock returns are typically described by a factor model along the lines of Fama and French (1988, 1993, 2015) and Carhart (1997). However, despite the popularity of the Fama-French (FF) and FF-type models, substantial literature in the event study tradition, starting from Brown and Warner (1985) and Strong (1992), has pointed towards a failure of the FF model to adequately capture the relationship between risk and return; for recent literature, see Chiang and Li (2012) and Marks and Musumeci (2017), among others. Specifically, there are periods when stock returns are highly correlated (Kolari and Pynnönen 2010); this correlation leads to abnormal returns and mismeasured risk; see also Boehmer et al. (1991) and Kothari and Warner (2007).[1]

In this paper, we contrast the FF-type factor models for stock returns against the standard panel data factor model in contemporary econometrics. Then, recent developments in the econometrics of panel factor models with cross-section dependence suggest reasons why the FF-type model may be misspecified. To address such misspecifications, we propose modeling cross-correlations using a suitable structural model. Motivated by the recent clustering model (Nagy and Ormos 2018) and recursive model (Basak et al. 2018), we propose a social network dependence structure. Applied to data on stock returns for the 30 current DJIA stocks, we find evidence of network effects, the careful

---

[1] Abnormal return is defined in the event study finance literature as the difference between the actual return of a security (in our case, over a one week time horizon) and the expected return as calculated using a model; see, for example, Brown and Warner (1985). Thus, any misspecification in the underlying factor model implies mismeasurement of expected returns and the corresponding risk-return relationship and would be evident in substantial abnormal returns.

modeling of which addresses misspecification of the underlying factor model. This brings returns more in line with risks, and provides a structural understanding of risk spillovers.

Any model is necessarily an abstraction of reality, and will entail a certain degree of misspecification; understandably this is true of the FF model as well. Researchers have continued to improve upon the FF model with a larger collection of factors (FF-type models), and this has undoubtedly improved model fit and interpretation. Our contribution here lies in proposing quite a different extension. We consider trading activity and its structural interpretations more explicitly than the literature, which goes along the lines of structural interpretation of correlations that currently lies beyond the scope of the FF-type models. Then, together with the factors in the FF model, the proposed model provides substantial enhancement to our understanding and a better explanation of returns. We consider as benchmark a CAPM model (including only the market return factor) and an FF-type model including 6 factors: the 5 Fama and French (1988, 1993) factors, plus the momentum factor of Carhart (1997). Our results show that the base CAPM, together with network effects, has competitive explanatory power, and for some stocks offers substantial improvements relative to the above 6 factor model. This provides an alternate structural factor model for asset pricing, and develops avenues for new research.

Section 2 contrasts factor models in finance and econometrics and draws some insights into misspecification. Section 3 develops a social network model and estimates this using the DJIA stock returns. Structural interpretation of the model is discussed, together with alternate structural models. Section 4 concludes, with an appeal for further research on structural dependence in stock returns.

2. Factor Models in Finance and Econometrics

The FF and similar factor models in finance are typically expressed as:

$$y_{it} = \alpha_i + \beta_i m_t + \gamma_i' x_t + \varepsilon_{it}, \tag{1}$$

and estimated using time series data (t = 1, ..., T) on the returns, y_{it}, on n (i = 1, ..., n) stocks. Here m_t denotes the excess return on the market portfolio and β_i the corresponding beta-factor for stock i, x_t is a vector of returns on a finite number of firm-specific factors (typically called the Fama-French factors) and γ_i their corresponding factor exposures, α_i is a stock- (firm-) specific intercept that can be interpreted as a fixed effect, and ε_{it} is an idiosyncratic error term. Typically, the excess return on the market portfolio (m_t) is easily computed from market data and the time-varying returns (x_t) are reported in market research publications (French 2017). The original Fama and French (1993) factors SMB (Small Minus Big) and HML (High Minus Low) were extended to include Mom (momentum) in Carhart (1997) and further to RMW (Robust Minus Weak) and CMA (Conservative Minus Aggressive) in Fama and French (2015). Returns on these factors constitute x_t; see French (2017) for further details on concepts and computation.

2.1. Network Effects and Bias

Traditionally, the above FF model (1) is estimated by least squares, where the factor exposures β_i and γ_i are viewed as parameters to be estimated from the data. This estimation strategy raises issues that are well recognized in the literature; see, for example, Strong (1992), Kothari and Warner (2007) and Kolari and Pynnönen (2010). One important issue is that risk is not consistently estimated if there is either time-varying volatility or cross-section correlations in the errors ε_{it}. This renders inference on abnormal returns particularly challenging. This is really an estimation efficiency issue that is not in itself likely to cause bias in estimation of the factor model. However, there would be a more serious problem of endogeneity if, for some reason, there were network interdependencies between returns on different stocks. This will also lead to mismeasured risk and very likely biased estimates.

To understand the nature of the problem, consider for simplicity a CAPM type restricted factor model of the form

$$y_{it} = \alpha_i + \beta_i m_t + \varepsilon_{it}, \tag{2}$$

where the effect of additional FF firm-specific factors is not included. The above CAPM model (2) can imply a specific form of network architecture, known in the spatial econometrics literature as a social interactions model (Lee et al. 2010; Hsieh and Lee 2016; Bhattacharjee et al. 2018; Cohen-Cole et al. 2018; Doğan et al. 2018) or a farmer-district model (Case 1992; Robinson 2003; Gupta and Robinson 2015), whereby the units (here, stocks) are classified into several groups or social networks. Stocks in the same social network are related to each other, but not to stocks in the other networks. Further, the inter-network influences are symmetric across all directed pairs of stocks within the network and can be represented by an adjacency-based binary weights matrix. In turn, the membership of social networks is inferred either by cluster analysis (Bhattacharjee et al. 2016; Chakraborty et al. 2018; Nagy and Ormos 2018) or correlation analysis (Junior et al. 2015; Bailey et al. 2016) of the dependent variable, which in our case are stock returns.

Now, consider the clustering pattern implied by the above CAPM, assuming for simplicity that the parameter vector can take only one of two values, $(\alpha_i, \beta_i) \in \{(-\frac{1}{2}, 1), (\frac{1}{2}, 0)\}$, and these correspond to the two network classes. Likewise, assume for simplicity only two time periods, $t = 1, 2$. Then, if a scatterplot of returns is obtained along the axes given by $t = 1$ and $t = 2$, it is clearly seen that the loci of data points in the two network classes will be $\left(m_1 - \frac{1}{2}, m_2 - \frac{1}{2}\right)$ and $\left(\frac{1}{2}, \frac{1}{2}\right)$, with the random distribution of points around the loci determined solely by the idiosyncratic errors ε_{it}.

More generally, if the parameter vector takes values in a finite set $(\alpha_i, \beta_i) \in \{(a_1, b_1), (a_2, b_2), \cdots, (a_k, b_k)\}$, and we have data for $t = 1, ..., T$ time periods, then this would generate data points clustered around a corresponding set of k loci: $\{(a_j + b_j m_1, a_j + b_j m_2, \cdots, a_j + b_j m_T) : j = 1, \cdots, k\}$. Further, if there were no network interdependence between the stocks, the parameters can be recovered through time series least squares regressions based on (2) for each individual stock, since the observations are independent over time. Therefore, the loci of the clusters can also be precisely estimated as the number of time periods increase, that is, as $T \to \infty$. The same argument holds if we had additional FF firm-specific factors, in which case we would estimate a model of the Fama-French form (1). However, the endogenous network effects would lead to biased least squares estimation.

Let us now consider a simple extension to the CAPM type restricted factor model (2) to include network interdependence. Denote by $\underline{y}_t = (y_{1t}, y_{2t}, \cdots, y_{nt})\prime$ the vector of returns at time point t, and consider a standard spatial autoregressive (lag) network model of the form

$$\underline{y}_t = \rho W \underline{y}_t + \underline{\alpha} + \underline{\beta} m_t + \underline{\varepsilon}_t, \tag{3}$$

where $\underline{\alpha}$ and $\underline{\beta}$ are corresponding vectors of the CAPM parameters, $W_{(n \times n)}$ is a square matrix of network membership with zero diagonal elements and the off-diagonal elements are unit if two firms belong to the same network and zero otherwise, and ρ is the so-called spatial autoregressive or network dependence parameter ($|\rho| < 1$). Here, the network architecture follows exactly the social interactions or farmer-district model; see, for example, Lee et al. (2010). Further, we assume as before that the CAPM parameter vector takes values in a finite set

$$(\alpha_i, \beta_i) \in \{(a_1, b_1), (a_2, b_2), \cdots, (a_k, b_k)\},$$

and further that two stocks with the same parameters belong to the same network.

Now, without loss of generality, let the stocks in the first network have parameters (a_1, b_1) and come first in the ordering, followed by the second network with parameter values (a_2, b_2) and so on, we have the following block-diagonal equicorrelation structure for W:

$$W = \begin{pmatrix} W_1 & \cdots & 0 \\ \vdots & \ddots & \vdots \\ 0 & \cdots & W_k \end{pmatrix},$$

where the connection matrix for network j ($j = 1, \ldots, k$) is of order $(n_j \times n_j)$ and takes the form:

$$W_j = \begin{bmatrix} 0 & 1/(n_j - 1) & \cdots & 1/(n_j - 1) \\ 1/(n_j - 1) & 0 & \cdots & 1/(n_j - 1) \\ \vdots & \vdots & \ddots & \vdots \\ 1/(n_j - 1) & 1/(n_j - 1) & \cdots\cdots\cdots\cdots & 0 \end{bmatrix}_{(n_j \times n_j)},$$

with zero diagonal and row-standardised unit values everywhere else, and $n = n_1 + n_2 + \cdots + n_k$.

The equicorrelation form of the social interactions model clearly highlights why it may be useful to identify the network structure based on cross-section correlations, as in Lee et al. (2010) and mboxciteauthorB3-jrfm-450549 (2016). Then, the reduced form the network model (3) is:

$$\underline{y}_t = (I - \rho W)^{-1}\underline{\alpha} + (I - \rho W)^{-1}\underline{\beta} m_t + (I - \rho W)^{-1}\underline{\varepsilon}_t, \tag{4}$$

where

$$(I - \rho W)^{-1} = \begin{pmatrix} (I - \rho W_1)^{-1} & \cdots & 0 \\ \vdots & \ddots & \vdots \\ 0 & \cdots & (I - \rho W_k)^{-1} \end{pmatrix}.$$

This reduced form representation (4) clearly highlights how the network generates risk spillovers.

The structure of the reduced form in (4) has important implications for estimation and inference on the Fama-French model. First, additional FF-type firm-specific factors retain the same basic structure of the model, with slope parameters that are proportional to the underlying structural model at (3). Second, applied to data from the network interactions model (3), time series least squares regression based on individual stock returns will simply recover the reduced form intercept and slopes, rather than the underlying structural parameters (a_j and b_j); clearly this leads to biased and inconsistent inferences. Third, the reduced form least squares parameter estimates correctly recover the underlying network structure because the nature of clustering does not change. Specifically, the data points are still clustered around a set of k loci, which is a simple scale transformation of the original model without network dependence. Hence, the network structure can be accurately identified by cluster analysis of the underlying returns. In fact, within the context of the FF model (1) with network dependence as in (3), cluster analysis will typically recover the loci of the FF- firm specific factors as well. Fourth, simply accounting for the network structure does not help. True, the underlying network dependence can be identified by clustering; but under the network interactions model (3), if the CAPM (and FF) part of the model were ignored, this would provide biased inferences on the network dependence parameters. Hence, both parts of the model are important for accurate estimation and analyses of risk and return.

2.2. Comparison with Panel Data Factor Model

Cross-section dependence is well studied within the current literature in panel data econometrics. Here, the central factor model has the following form:

$$y_{it} = \delta_i' f_t + \theta_i' z_{it} + \varepsilon_{it}, \tag{5}$$

where f_t denotes a vector of time-specific *"factors"* with corresponding stock-specific loadings δ_i, z_{it} contains a collection of stock- and time-varying covariates, and ε_{it} are stationary but potentially cross-section dependent and autocorrelated regression errors; see, for example, Pesaran (2006). Some of the "factors" may be observed, and others latent. In particular, a factor taking unit value in each time period corresponds to fixed effects, denoted α_i in the FF model (1). The response variable (returns) y_{it} has cross-section dependence arising from two sources. First, there is the influence of common "factors" f_t, but potentially with effects heterogeneous across different stocks. Second, there are the cross-section dependent errors ε_{it}.

Pesaran (2006) points to an important distinction between cross-section strong and weak dependence (of returns on different stocks, in our case). The first arises from the effect of common factors, such as the market portfolio and the FF factor returns; the second is due to local interdependencies (spillovers) between firms and their stocks. Following from Pesaran (2006), an influential literature has spawned in this area; see, for example, Kapetanios and Pesaran (2007), Bai (2009), Pesaran and Tosetti (2009), and Bailey et al. (2016).

Pesaran (2006) developed two key results. First, least squares estimation of (5) with omitted latent factors provides inconsistent and biased estimates of θ_i in general. The only situation where credible inferences can be made is when the errors ε_{it} are stationary over time and granular across the cross-section. Pesaran (2006) and Pesaran and Tosetti (2009) provide technical definitions of cross-sectional granularity. This is conceptually akin to stationarity, but across the cross-section dimension, and implies that the degree of cross-section dependence is limited. Pesaran (2006) terms this case weak cross-section dependence, and Pesaran (2015) provided a statistical test based on average cross-section correlation of the residuals; see Bhattacharjee and Holly (2013) for an alternate test.

Second, Pesaran (2006) offers a large sample method to address strong dependence when both dimensions are large, that is, $n \to \infty$ and $T \to \infty$. In such situations, one can enrich the model by including cross-section averages of the dependent and independent variables as:

$$y_{it} = \delta_i'(\bar{y}_t, \bar{z}_t) + \theta_i' z_{it} + \varepsilon_{it}, \tag{6}$$

where the cross-section averages $(\bar{y}_t, \bar{z}_t)$ eliminate strong dependence from the model, leaving only weak dependence in the residuals. This model can then be consistently estimated by least squares. This methodology is called common correlated effects estimation because $(\bar{y}_t, \bar{z}_t)$ take these high cross-section correlations out of the data.

Let us now revert to a comparison with the FF model (1). The return on the market is akin to the average return in each period, and hence is very close to $\bar{y}_t$. Since temporal variation in the risk free rate is much lower than the market, the excess return on the market, m_t, is numerically almost the same cross-section average return less a constant.[2] Unfortunately, beyond $\bar{y}_t$, common correlated effects cannot be directly applied in (1), because there are no regressors with both cross-section and time variation, unlike z_{it} in (5). This key observation has two implications. First, one should always test the residuals from least squares estimation of (1) for potential strong dependence. Second, strong cross-section dependence needs to be modelled based on structural considerations of pricing in financial markets. We focus on this second issue in the next section.

---

[2] Over the period of our analysis, standard deviation of the risk free rate is only 0.15, as compared to 4.43 for the market return.

3. Structural Models of Asset Pricing Correlations

As discussed in Section 2, the lack of cross-section variation in the regressors precludes the opportunity to apply common correlated effects estimation in the FF model (1). This implies that any cross-section strong dependence (across the stocks) needs to be modelled explicitly using structural models of price formation in the market. This is where we turn to next. We first discuss a few structural models and the relevant literature, and propose an alternate model. Then, we illustrate our proposed structural model using data on monthly returns on the stocks currently included in the Dow Jones Industrial Average (DJIA).

3.1. Structural Models of Price Formation

Structural modelling of cross-section dependence is the domain of spatial and network econometrics. Within this literature, there is very little research on stock returns. However, one can draw some insights from the literature on other markets (for example, housing and labor markets) or to dependence across financial markets. A key result from this literature is that the underlying structural model is, in general, not fully identified from cross-section covariances and correlations (Bhattacharjee and Jensen-Butler 2013). Hence, one requires further structural assumptions, either from theory or from context specific research, to identify network effects.

One such admissible assumption is recursive structure under which information flows are sequential (but contemporaneous) through different segments of the market. Based on 25 portfolios formed on size and book-to-market (Fama and French 1996; French 2017), Basak et al. (2018) find substantial explanation for risk spillovers and abnormal returns, and the model outperforms reduced form VAR (vector autoregressive) factor models. Suppose risk neutral traders arrive sequentially and repeatedly at the market taking positions on preferred risk/return FF portfolios. Then, limit or market order mechanisms would generate such recursive ordering of the portfolios in terms of information flow, in turn leading to cross-portfolio correlations. This ties in with the recent market microstructure literature on limit orders; see, for example, Handa and Schwartz (1996), Parlour (1998), Foucault (1999), Mertens (2003) and Foucault et al. (2005).

Recursive ordering is often a feature of cross-market information flows, where the sequencing of opening and closing times of different markets produce the so-called 'meteor shower' phenomenon documented in volatility by Engle et al. (1990) and in returns by Hamao et al. (1990). Bhattacharjee (2017) find that return correlations across 19 markets worldwide are explained by recursive ordering, in combination with global factors capturing the dominance of major markets. We propose a different model in this paper, but recursive structural models hold good promise for the future.

Beyond recursive ordering, some other structural assumptions are also admissible. Bhattacharjee and Jensen-Butler (2013) show that network dependence structure is identified under the assumption of symmetric interdependence. There are three important special cases of symmetry. First, there are social network models where individuals in the same network share information or interact with each other, but not with members in other networks; see, for example, Lee et al. (2010) and Cohen-Cole et al. (2018). This model is also closely related to the farmer-district model (Case 1992; Robinson 2003). Cross-section dependent stock returns can well be represented by social network models, but in applications, the membership and identity of networks is seldom known *a priori*, and one still needs appropriate theory or clustering/LASSO methods (discussed below) to motivate these networks.

Second, there are models where interconnections are binary and reciprocal, as in the social networks model, but the networks can be overlapping. In the context where the network is sparse, but negative interactions are possible, Bailey et al. (2016) propose estimation of network structure based on multiple testing of estimated cross-section correlations. We will briefly consider a model of this type later. In the context of stock returns factor models, lack of any obvious structural interpretation of the network is obviously an impediment. Besides, one would expect network interdependence in the stock market to be fairly dense, and hence the sparsity assumption may also be somewhat tenuous.

The third class of models use either clustering or LASSO (least absolute shrinkage and selection operator; Tibshirani 1996) to identify social network or block structure from the data. However, an observed pattern of clustering does not necessarily imply clustering of the parameter vector, since the returns of different stocks may be similar because they share a network. This observation justifies current approaches of characterizing the underlying latent network structure using either spatial and spatio-temporal clustering (Bhattacharjee et al. 2016; Chakraborty et al. 2018) or an analysis of cross-section correlations (Junior et al. 2015; Bailey et al. 2016); Nagy and Ormos (2018) apply clustering across markets to study dependence. Lam and Souza (2016) provide a method to identify block structure using the LASSO and similar methods. Our structural model and empirical analysis are based mainly on this third approach. As discussed earlier, since the network structure can only contribute to weak dependence, the factor structure needs to be removed from the data a priori. As our analytical discussion in Section 2.1 shows, one can first estimate a FF-type factor model, identify the common factors that are associated with strong dependence, and then cluster the stocks based on the remaining weak-dependence factors. However, since the factors in the FF model are essentially returns on different types of risk, clustering can then be based on exposure to the corresponding risks.

The above approach is consistent with the following trading strategy. In the context of factor models (1) and (5), absence of cross-section variation in regressors for the FF-type model imply that subtle variations, over time, in the factor exposures for each stock are not captured in the data; hence, traders need to address this issue through diversification. Then, our structural model posits that, traders sort themselves on heterogenous risk preferences. Given a specific preference type over multiple risk factors, they then choose their preferred exposure to the risks and create a diversified portfolio of stocks with this risk exposure. This behavior generates interdependence across stock returns within this portfolio, but not beyond. Since the exposures are estimated by an FF-type factor model (1), the network can be identified by clustering the stocks on this estimated exposure vector.[3] The above trading model is structural, but its assumptions need validation. To highlight the promise that this approach holds, we now provide an illustrative application on the DJIA stock returns.

Our central argument is that, since the structural network effects are only partially identified from reduced form regressions (Bhattacharjee and Jensen-Butler 2013), inference requires structural assumptions underpinned by appropriate theory. Above, we have discussed three such lines of theory, emphasizing in particular one new structural model. There, traders choose their diversified portfolio with a preferred risk exposure; this trading behavior generates interdependence across stock returns within this portfolio, but not beyond. Since the exposures are estimated by an FF-type factor model, the network can be identified by clustering the stocks on this estimated exposure vector. This justifies our approach (in Section 3.2) of assuming that within cluster correlations dominate network effects across the clusters, which are then assumed to be absent.

Obviously, there are competing structural models where stocks belonging to different groups would be correlated, and we also discussed two such models: First, we refer to Basak et al. (2018), who developed a model where limit or market order mechanisms generate recursive ordering of the portfolios in terms of information flow, in turn leading to cross-portfolio correlations. This may be viewed as a model diametrically in opposition to the model developed in this paper. Second, unrestricted correlations can be modeled, and we also consider this approach. However, the unrestricted correlations model raises two further issues from a structural point of view. First, we need an assumption of sparsity (Bailey et al. 2016). Network interdependence in the stock market may be dense, and hence the sparsity assumption may be somewhat tenuous. Second, we do not currently have theory to justify sparse interactions, and lack of any obvious structural interpretation of the network is obviously an impediment. Nevertheless, we estimated such a model (Section 3.2)

---

[3] Alternate structural restrictions with asymmetric dependence, for example, tree-based nested dependence (Bhattacharjee and Holly 2013), sparsity (Ahrens and Bhattacharjee 2015; Lam and Souza 2018) and copulas (Liu et al. 2018) can also hold promise, but we do not consider these here.

and highlight that more work is required for structural understanding of the underlying trading mechanisms. We suggest this as an avenue for future research.

3.2. Data and Estimated Model

We collected daily stock returns data (adjusted for splits, dividends and distributions) from Yahoo Finance, on the stocks currently included in the Dow Jones Industrial Average (DJIA).[4] The period under analysis is January 2001 to December 2015.[5] Historical monthly factor returns on the Fama and French (1993, 2015) 5-factors and the Carhart (1997) momentum factor were collected from the web archive of French (2017). To make our stock returns data comparable with factor returns, stock returns are aggregated to the monthly level. These constitute our data under analysis.

First, we estimate by least squares a CAPM model (2) including only an intercept and excess return on the market. As discussed in Section 2.1, the network structure can be accurately identified by clustering on the vector (α_i, β_i). We also estimate a FF-type factor model including all the six factors: m_t, SMB, HML, RMW, CMA and Mom. The CAPM model exhibits spatial (network) strong dependence. Using the CD test of Pesaran (2015), the null hypothesis of weak dependence is strongly rejected. The test statistic evaluates to -4.026 with a *p*-value of 5.7×10^{-5}. However, the same is not true for the FF-type model with six factors; the CD test statistic is -1.775 with a *p*-value of 0.076.

Next, we apply cluster analysis to the estimated $(\hat{\alpha}_i, \hat{\beta}_i)$, and clearly identify 3 clusters: low alpha and low beta (13 stocks), low alpha and high beta (13 stocks) and high alpha (4 stocks). The membership of the clusters is reported in Table 1. Then, we construct a social network weighting matrix $W_{(n \times n)}$ based on membership of the above three clusters.

Finally, we estimate two spatial autoregressive (lag) network models, including only m_t but not the Fama and French (1993, 2015) or Carhart (1997) factors. In the first, a contemporaneous spatial lag $W\underline{y}_t$ is included; this is exactly the model in (3). Inclusion of the spatial lag introduces endogeneity in the model, and we estimate using a variant of the popular two stage least squares (2SLS) method in Kelejian and Prucha (1998). Like the application of common correlated effects, the above 2SLS method also presents challenges because there is no cross-section variation in the regressors. We use as instruments the omitted five FF-type factors, together with lagged residuals from the estimated CAPM model (2). The first stage estimation work well (with F-statistics much greater than 10 in all cases) and weak instruments issues are not apparent. However, 2SLS is known to have finite sample bias and there is loss of efficiency; for this reason, model comparison is based on root mean squared errors (RMSE). The second network model includes network effects as a time-lag, that is $W\underline{y}_{t-1}$. Here, we do not have contemporaneous endogeneity and the model can be estimated using least squares:

$$\underline{y}_t = \rho W \underline{y}_{t-1} + \underline{\alpha} + \underline{\beta} m_t + \underline{\varepsilon}_t, \qquad (7)$$

The spatial lag (3) and space-time lag (7) model would in general have different structural implications. However, in our specific context, they are similar since the time lag is one week, which is very long in financial markets. By this time lag, all stock specific temporal information is expected to already have been factored into prices, and this information is therefore not relevant for trading strategy based on portfolio construction. Under our proposed structural model discussed in Section 3.1, trading behavior generates network effects through the choice of portfolios which get updated at a much lower frequency. Hence, structural implications of the spatial autoregressive and time lag models

---

[4] The following 30 stocks are included (tickers in parentheses): 3M (MMM), American Express (AXP), Apple (AAPL), Boeing (BA), Caterpillar (CAT), Chevron (CVX), Cisco Systems (CSCO), Coca-Cola (KO), DowDuPont (DOW), ExxonMobil (XOM), Goldman Sachs (GS), The Home Depot (HD), IBM (IBM), Intel (INTC), Johnson & Johnson (JNJ), JPMorgan Chase (JPM), McDonald's (MCD), Merck & Company (MRK), Microsoft (MSFT), Nike (NKE), Pfizer (PFE), Procter & Gamble (PG), Travelers (TRV), UnitedHealth Group (UNH), United Technologies (UTX), Verizon (VZ), Visa (V), Walmart (WMT), Walgreens Boots Alliance (WBA), and Walt Disney (DIS).

[5] Data for Visa (V) are only from March 2008. Our methods are applicable to unbalanced panel data.

are literally the same in so far as network effect implications are concerned. In terms of econometric implications, estimation of the two models are different. The spatial lag model generates endogenous effects; hence, we use instrumental variables methods, while the space-time lag model has only lagged endogenous effects, and therefore, least squares estimation is employed.

Table 1. Clusters, Model Diagnostics and Relative Efficiencies.

Clusters (Network)	Ticker	Root Mean Squared Errors (RMSE)				Efficiency, Relative to	
		CAPM (2)	FF Model (1)	Contemporaneous Network (3)	Time-Lag Network (7)	CAPM (2)	FF Model (1)
Low alpha, low beta							
	PFE	4.757	4.596	**4.357**	4.744	−8.41%	−5.20%
	TRV	4.782	4.752	**4.633**	4.786	−3.11%	−2.50%
	MCD	4.764	4.700	**4.630**	4.777	−2.81%	−1.50%
	JNJ	3.697	3.445	**3.437**	3.660	−7.02%	−0.23%
	XOM	4.380	4.226	**4.224**	4.384	−3.55%	−0.03%
	KO	4.308	4.058	**4.066**	4.319	−5.61%	0.21%
	WMT	4.827	4.759	4.966	**4.819**	−0.17%	1.26%
	PG	3.927	3.720	**3.772**	3.932	−3.94%	1.39%
	WBA	6.515	6.325	6.788	**6.496**	−0.30%	2.71%
	MMM	4.431	4.263	4.524	**4.383**	−1.08%	2.81%
	CVX	4.807	4.603	**4.733**	4.798	−1.54%	2.84%
	MRK	6.489	5.939	6.329	**6.501**	−2.46%	6.56%
	VZ	5.536	4.969	5.570	**5.479**	−1.03%	10.27%
High alpha							
	V	6.217	5.894	5.490	**5.432**	−12.64%	−7.84%
	UNH	6.693	6.699	**6.658**	6.704	−0.52%	−0.61%
	NKE	5.681	5.657	6.508	**5.688**	0.14%	0.56%
	AAPL	9.143	8.929	9.906	**9.112**	−0.34%	2.05%
Low alpha, high beta							
	BA	6.340	6.262	6.316	**6.065**	−4.33%	−3.15%
	UTX	4.403	4.348	**4.322**	4.402	−1.82%	−0.58%
	DIS	4.760	4.688	4.708	**4.666**	−1.98%	−0.47%
	HD	5.680	5.698	5.767	**5.683**	0.05%	−0.28%
	MSFT	5.730	5.651	**5.696**	5.733	−0.58%	0.81%
	GS	5.938	5.856	5.946	**5.937**	−0.03%	1.38%
	INTC	7.283	6.887	7.224	**7.202**	−1.11%	4.56%
	CAT	6.501	6.201	6.518	**6.498**	−0.04%	4.78%
	IBM	5.303	4.937	5.322	**5.175**	−2.41%	4.83%
	CSCO	7.561	6.946	**7.395**	7.438	−2.19%	6.47%
	DOW	8.606	7.382	8.641	**8.540**	−0.76%	15.69%
	AXP	7.349	6.200	7.320	**7.255**	−1.27%	17.03%
	JPM	6.401	5.370	6.852	**6.418**	0.26%	19.52%

Between the two network models (3) and (7), we choose the one with lower RMSE; the model with better fit is indicated in bold in Table 1. Then, we apply the CD test to the correlation matrix of residuals. The test statistic is 1.458 with a p-value of 0.145. Hence, we are satisfied that weak dependence holds, and estimates of the network factor model are consistent. Finally, we report relative efficiency of the chosen network model, in terms of percent lower RMSE, relative to the CAPM model (1) and the FF-type model (2).

In terms of RMSE, the clustering network model improves upon the CAPM for all stocks except two (Nike and JPMorgan Chase). This is reassuring but not surprising because the network model includes one addition regressor, the spatial lag. However, it is remarkable that the network model improves upon the FF-type model with all six factors for 11 (out of the 30) stocks. This provides encouraging validation of the clustering structural model proposed in this paper. Understanding trading activity and pricing in financial markets is an important problem in finance. It is our belief that the work here takes an important step in this direction.

In Table 2, we report the estimated alphas (α) and betas (β) for the CAPM and network models. The distinction between the three estimated clusters is clear from the CAPM estimates. Further, as predicted by theory, there is strong correlation between the estimates from the two models; 0.68 for alpha and 0.76 for beta. However, also as expected from our theory, there is substantial bias in the CAPM model estimates; on average, positive bias in alpha is about 66% and 30% for beta. The FF-type model with 6 factors is qualitatively similar. Since the time-period under study is not too long, we assume that W and ρ is constant over time, but that ρ varies by stock (that is, ρ_i).

Table 2. Factor Model Estimates.

Clusters (Network)	Ticker	Estimated Network Model—(3) or (7)			Estimated CAPM	
		Alpha	Beta	Network (rho)	Alpha	Beta
Low alpha, low beta						
	PFE	−0.061	0.669	−0.147	−0.162	0.650
	TRV	0.463	0.787	−0.090	0.369	0.771
	MCD	0.746	0.660	0.013	0.670	0.649
	JNJ	0.515	0.484	−0.172	0.374	0.457
	XOM	0.329	0.582	−0.078	0.249	0.567
	KO	0.231	0.524	−0.032	0.179	0.515
	WMT	−0.224	−0.115	0.786	0.043	0.388
	PG	0.493	0.395	−0.064	0.409	0.380
	WBA	−0.033	0.044	1.222	0.305	0.779
	MMM	0.299	0.415	0.668	0.427	0.808
	CVX	0.247	0.298	0.703	0.410	0.721
	MRK	0.008	0.615	−0.080	−0.107	0.596
	VZ	0.254	0.696	−0.264	0.162	0.676
High alpha						
	V	0.698	0.414	0.355	1.410	0.785
	UNH	1.023	0.607	0.049	1.090	0.614
	NKE	0.060	0.223	0.608	1.133	0.762
	AAPL	0.716	0.248	1.423	2.612	1.252
Low alpha, high beta						
	BA	0.225	1.045	0.307	0.391	1.090
	UTX	0.311	0.976	0.055	0.329	0.981
	DIS	0.446	1.014	0.122	0.488	1.174
	HD	0.375	0.465	0.428	0.453	1.020
	MSFT	0.282	1.042	−0.062	0.430	1.059
	GS	−0.063	0.943	0.353	0.053	1.396
	INTC	−0.124	1.184	0.163	−0.015	1.402
	CAT	0.429	0.847	0.520	0.461	1.494
	IBM	−0.119	0.486	0.341	0.100	0.953
	CSCO	−0.173	1.599	−0.246	−0.319	1.563
	DOW	0.168	1.629	0.210	0.277	1.656
	AXP	−0.075	1.442	0.215	0.008	1.463
	JPM	0.025	1.367	0.025	0.152	1.388

In addition to the clustering model, we also applied the multiple testing procedure of Bailey et al. (2016) to construct a weighting matrix; in this case, the p-value of the CD test is 0.650, which is promising performance of this method in negating strong dependence. However, more work is required for structural understanding of the underlying trading mechanisms; this is also an avenue for future research.

We verify the robustness of our findings across several dimensions. First, we evaluate robustness in clustering. We use different starting clusters, and different algorithms, all of which provide consistent results. Further, we account for the uncertainty in estimated alpha and beta parameters by multiple imputation based on estimated confidence intervals, and the results are consistent as well. Second, we evaluate robustness in choice of factors by considering two traditional factor models. One is the CAPM with a single market return factor, and the other is a 6-factor model including the Fama and French (1988, 1993) and Carhart (1997) factors. We find that our model almost always provides an improvement over the CAPM (in terms of RMSE), but is also frequently better than the 6-factor model. Third, we consider several network models. One, a contemporaneous spatial lag model; two, a space-time lag model; and finally, a sparse network model with unrestricted interactions. The main implications of our results are consistent across all three specifications.

4. Conclusions

The Fama and French (1993) and similar factor models are important and popular in finance, and they provide good structural understanding of the risk, returns and price formation. Typically, the model is estimated as a time series regression separately for each stock (firm). Such estimation would provide consistent estimates if the data are independent across firms. However, if there were any network effects, such estimates can be inefficient or even inconsistent if the network effects are endogenous.

Indeed, persistent evidence of abnormal returns and cross-section correlations in stock returns points towards potential misspecification of the FF-type models. In this paper, we show that endogenous network effects create cross-section dependence that renders least squares estimation of FF-type factor models inconsistent; hence, computed returns and risk may both be erroneous.

Further, we argue that current econometric methods to deal with cross-section dependence are not applicable to the above factor models. This leads us to development of structural models to understand network effects better. We propose a social network model based on clustering and show that it lends itself to interesting structural interpretations. Applied to data on the 30 DJIA stocks, our model provides improved estimation of factor models and insightful new understanding of trading activity and price formation. How the information in improved relative efficiencies can be harnessed for trading is a matter of further research and practice, which we also retain for future work.

While our current evidence is limited to only the DJIA stocks, this work provides the basis for further empirical validation and development of theory, not to mention alternate structural models of trading activity as well. A larger temporal dimension would obviously be useful in highlighting the weaknesses of the FF model which ignores structural cross-sectional interactions that are highlighted from our findings. However, capturing such interactions requires a potentially strong assumption that the nature and strength of interactions is constant over time. Obviously, the validity of this assumption would become more tenuous with a larger sample, but can equally be verified using more data. The advantages of larger sample data would also be apparent with a larger cross-section dimension. The current paper is best viewed as a proof of concept that further research on structural network effects may be fruitful. Hence, our work provides several promising avenues for further research in the direction of market microstructure models and their applications.

Author Contributions: Both the authors were involved in conceptualization and writing. S.R. provided insights on trader behavior while A.B. developed insights from factor models and econometrics. A.B. provided contributions to methodology and formal analysis, as well as programming in the Stata software.

Funding: This research received no external funding.

Acknowledgments: We thank three anonymous reviewers and the Editorial team for encouragement and for numerous constructive comments. Their valuable, constructive and extensive comments allowed us to revise and improve the paper substantially. We also thank Nidhan Choudhuri, Andrea Eross, Boulis Ibrahim and Mustapha Waseja for helpful discussions, and Nidhan Choudhuri for help with data collection and interpretation of trading strategies. The usual disclaimer applies.

Conflicts of Interest: The authors declare no conflict of interest.

References

Ahrens, Achim, and Arnab Bhattacharjee. 2015. Two-step Lasso estimation of the spatial weights matrix. *Econometrics* 3: 128–55. [CrossRef]

Bai, Jushan. 2009. Panel data models with interactive fixed effects. *Econometrica* 77: 1229–79.

Bailey, Natalia, Sean Holly, and M. Hashem Pesaran. 2016. A Two-Stage Approach to Spatio-Temporal Analysis with Strong and Weak Cross-Sectional Dependence. *Journal of Applied Econometrics* 31: 249–80. [CrossRef]

Basak, Gopal K., Arnab Bhattacharjee, and Samarjit Das. 2018. Causal ordering and inference on acyclic networks. *Empirical Economics* 55: 213–32. [CrossRef]

Bhattacharjee, Arnab. 2017. Identifying the Causal Structure of Directed Acyclic Graphs (DAGs). Paper presented at the 40th International Panel Data Conference, Thessaloniki, Greece, July 7–8.

Bhattacharjee, Arnab, and Sean Holly. 2013. Understanding interactions in social networks and committees. *Spatial Economic Analysis* 8: 23–53. [CrossRef]

Bhattacharjee, Arnab, and Chris N. Jensen-Butler. 2013. Estimation of the spatial weights matrix under structural constraints. *Regional Science and Urban Economics* 43: 617–34. [CrossRef]

Bhattacharjee, Arnab, Eduardo A. Castro, Taps Maiti, and Zhen Zhang. 2016. Spatio-Temporal Patterns in Portuguese Regional Fertility Rates: A Bayesian Approach for Spatial Clustering of Curves. Mimeo. Available online: https://pureapps2.hw.ac.uk/ws/portalfiles/portal/10595008/POR_Demography_paper.pdf (accessed on 24 August 2018).

Bhattacharjee, Arnab, Sean Holly, and Jesus Mur. 2018. Contemporary developments in the theory and practice of spatial econometrics. *Spatial Economic Analysis* 13: 139–47. [CrossRef]

Boehmer, Ekkehart, Jim Masumeci, and Annette B. Poulsen. 1991. Event-study methodology under conditions of event-induced variance. *Journal of Financial Economics* 30: 253–72. [CrossRef]

Brown, Stephen J., and Jerold B. Warner. 1985. Using daily stock returns: The case of event studies. *Journal of Financial Economics* 14: 3–31. [CrossRef]

Carhart, Mark M. 1997. On Persistence in Mutual Fund Performance. *Journal of Finance* 52: 57–82. [CrossRef]

Case, Anne. 1992. Neighborhood influence and technological change. *Regional Science and Urban Economics* 22: 491–508. [CrossRef]

Chakraborty, Sayan, Arnab Bhattacharjee, and Taps Maiti. 2018. Structural Factorization of Latent Adjacency Matrix, with an application to Auto Industry Networks. Mimeo. Available online: https://www.researchgate.net/publication/324599853_Latent_Space_Linkages_of_Three_US_Auto_Manufacturing_Giants (accessed on 24 August 2018).

Chiang, Thomas C., and Jiandong Li. 2012. Stock returns and risk: Evidence from quantile. *Journal of Risk and Financial Management* 5: 20–58. [CrossRef]

Cohen-Cole, Ethan, Xiaodong Liu, and Yves Zenou. 2018. Multivariate choices and identification of social interactions. *Journal of Applied Econometrics* 33: 165–78. [CrossRef]

Doğan, Osman, Süleyman Taşpınar, and Anil K. Bera. 2018. Simple tests for social interaction models with network structures. *Spatial Economic Analysis* 13: 212–46. [CrossRef]

Engle, Robert F., Takatoshi Ito, and Wen-Ling Lin. 1990. Meteor Showers or Heat Waves? Heteroskedastic Intra-Daily Volatility in the Foreign Exchange Market. *Econometrica* 58: 525–42. [CrossRef]

Fama, Eugene F., and Kenneth R. French. 1988. Permanent and temporary components of stock prices. *Journal of Political Economy* 96: 246–73. [CrossRef]

Fama, Eugene F., and Kenneth R. French. 1993. Common risk factors in the returns on stocks and bonds. *Journal of Financial Economics* 33: 3–56. [CrossRef]

Fama, Eugene F., and Kenneth R. French. 1996. Multifactor explanations of asset pricing anomalies. *The Journal of Finance* 51: 55–84. [CrossRef]

Fama, Eugene F., and Kenneth R. French. 2015. A five-factor asset pricing model. *Journal of Financial Economics* 116: 1–22. [CrossRef]

Foucault, Thierry. 1999. Order flow composition and trading costs in a dynamic limit order market. *Journal of Financial Markets* 2: 99–134. [CrossRef]

Foucault, Thierry, Ohad Kadan, and Eugene Kandel. 2005. Limit order book as a market for liquidity. *The Review of Financial Studies* 18: 1171–217. [CrossRef]

French, K. R. 2017. Current Research Returns. Available online: http://mba.tuck.dartmouth.edu/pages/faculty/ken.french/data_library.html (accessed on 24 August 2018).

Gupta, Abhimanyu, and Peter M. Robinson. 2015. Inference on higher-order spatial autoregressive models with increasingly many parameters. *Journal of Econometrics* 186: 19–31. [CrossRef]

Hamao, Yasushi, Ronald W. Masulis, and Victor Ng. 1990. Correlations in price changes and volatility across international stock markets. *The Review of Financial Studies* 3: 281–307. [CrossRef]

Handa, Puneet, and Robert A. Schwartz. 1996. Limit order trading. *The Journal of Finance* 51: 1835–61. [CrossRef]

Hsieh, Chih-Sheng, and Lung-Fei Lee. 2016. A social interactions model with endogenous friendship formation and selectivity. *Journal of Applied Econometrics* 31: 301–19. [CrossRef]

Junior, Leonidas Sandoval, Asher Mullokandov, and Dror Y. Kenett. 2015. Dependency relations among international stock market indices. *Journal of Risk and Financial Management* 8: 227–65. [CrossRef]

Kapetanios, George, and M. Hashem Pesaran. 2007. Alternative approaches to estimation and inference in large multifactor panels: Small sample results with an application to modelling of asset returns. In *The Refinement of Econometric Estimation and Test Procedures: Finite Sample and Asymptotic Analysis*. Edited by Garry D. A. Phillips and Elias Tzavalis. Cambridge: Cambridge University Press, pp. 239–81.

Kelejian, Harry H., and Ingmar R. Prucha. 1998. A generalized spatial two-stage least squares procedure for estimating a spatial autoregressive model with autoregressive disturbances. *The Journal of Real Estate Finance and Economics* 17: 99–121. [CrossRef]

Kolari, James W., and Seppo Pynnönen. 2010. Event study testing with cross-sectional correlation of abnormal returns. *Review of Financial Studies* 23: 3996–4025. [CrossRef]

Kothari, Sagar P., and Jerold B. Warner. 2007. Econometrics of Event Studies. In *Handbook of Empirical Corporate Finance*. Edited by B. Espen Eckbo. Amsterdam: Elsevier/North-Holland, pp. 3–36.

Lam, Clifford, and Pedro C. L. Souza. 2016. Detection and estimation of block structure in spatial weight matrix. *Econometric Reviews* 35: 1347–76. [CrossRef]

Lam, Clifford, and Pedro C. L. Souza. 2018. Estimation and Selection of Spatial Weight Matrix in a Spatial Lag Model. *Journal of Business and Economic Statistics*. forthcoming.

Lee, Lung-Fei, Xiaodong Liu, and Xu Lin. 2010. Specification and estimation of social interaction models with network structures. *The Econometrics Journal* 13: 145–76. [CrossRef]

Liu, Guizhou, Xiao-Jing Cai, and Shigeyuki Hamori. 2018. Modeling the Dependence Structure of Share Prices among Three Chinese City Banks. *Journal of Risk and Financial Management* 11: 57. [CrossRef]

Marks, Joseph M., and Jim Musumeci. 2017. Misspecification in event studies. *Journal of Corporate Finance* 45: 333–41. [CrossRef]

Mertens, Jean F. 2003. The limit-price mechanism: In honour of Martin Shubik. *Journal of Mathematical Economics* 39: 433–528. [CrossRef]

Nagy, László, and Mihály Ormos. 2018. Friendship of Stock Market Indices: A Cluster-Based Investigation of Stock Markets. *Journal of Risk and Financial Management* 11: 88. [CrossRef]

Parlour, Christine A. 1998. Price dynamics in limit order markets. *The Review of Financial Studies* 11: 789–816. [CrossRef]

Pesaran, M. Hashem. 2006. Estimation and inference in large heterogeneous panels with a multifactor error structure. *Econometrica* 74: 967–1012. [CrossRef]

Pesaran, M. Hashem. 2015. Testing weak cross-sectional dependence in large panels. *Econometric Reviews* 34: 1089–117. [CrossRef]

Pesaran, M. Hashem, and Elisa Tosetti. 2009. Large panels with spatial correlations and common factors. *Journal of Econometrics* 161: 182–202. [CrossRef]

Robinson, Peter M. 2003. Denis Sargan: Some perspectives. *Econometric Theory* 19: 481–94. [CrossRef]

Strong, Norman. 1992. Modelling abnormal returns: A review article. *Journal of Business Finance & Accounting* 19: 533–53.

Tibshirani, Robert. 1996. Regression shrinkage and selection via the lasso. *Journal of the Royal Statistical Society Series B (Methodological)* 58: 267–88. [CrossRef]

Journal of
Risk and Financial Management

MDPI

Article

Effects of Global Oil Price on Exchange Rate, Trade Balance, and Reserves in Nigeria: A Frequency Domain Causality Approach

D. O. Olayungbo

Economics Department, Obafemi Awolowo University, Ile-Ife 220282, Nigeria; doolayungbo@oauife.edu.ng

Received: 2 January 2019; Accepted: 25 February 2019; Published: 13 March 2019

Abstract: This study investigated the relative Granger causal effects of oil price on exchange rate, trade balance, and foreign reserve in Nigeria. We used seasonally adjusted quarterly data from 1986Q4 to 2018Q1 to remove predictable changes in the series. Given the non-stationarity of our variables, we found cointegration to exist only between oil price and foreign reserve. The presence of cointegration implied the existence of long run relationship between the variables. The Granger causality result showed that oil price strongly Granger caused foreign reserve in the short period. However, no Granger causal relationships were found between oil price and trade balance and for oil price and exchange rate. The implication of the result is that Nigerian government should not rely solely on oil price to sustain her reserve but to diversify the economy towards non-resource production and export for foreign exchange generation.

Keywords: oil price; exchange rate; trade balance; cointegration; frequency domain causality; Nigeria

1. Introduction

Crude oil has been the largest component of the volume of export in Nigeria ever since in the 1970s when the non-renewable commodity was found in commercial quantities. Crude oil accounts for almost 83.5 percent of the total export in the country (Centre for Study of Economies of Africa 2018). Crude oil has been the major driver of the Nigerian economy and any changes in its price usually have significant effects not only on the structure but also the growth and welfare of the citizens. In spite of the abundance of oil in the country, Nigeria has become net importer of refined oil due to the underutilization of her existing refineries. The situation in the country is exportation of crude oil and importation of refined petroleum product at higher cost. This cost implication has a significant impact on the trade balance and the macroeconomic performance of the country.

As an oil dependent economy, Nigeria remains susceptible to the movements in global crude oil prices. During the periods of high oil price resulted from the macroeconomic and political conditions in the international market, the country usually experiences favorable trade balance, increase in foreign reserves, and exchange rate appreciation. On the contrary, when crude oil prices are low, occasioned by happenings in the international markets, the consequences are exchange rate depreciation, significant drop in the level of foreign exchange inflows, and reserve depletion that often result in budget deficit and slower growth. The drastic fall in the global oil price in 2008 and 2015 from over US$100 to below US$40 are great instances that led to the depreciation in exchange rate and deficit in the trade balance of the country. Similarly, the depreciation of the exchange rate from N231 per US$1 to N305 in the third quarter of 2016 has been associated with the fall in the global oil price, specifically below US$50.

As a result of the significance of the effects of oil prices on macroeconomic variables, many previous studies have attempted to examine the relationship among oil price, exchange rate, and trade balance. Some of these studies include Ozlale and Pekkurnaz (2010); Hassan and Zaman (2012); and Tiwari and Olayeni (2013). According Ozlale and Pekkurnaz (2010), oil price significantly affected trade balance. On the other hand, in the area of the effects of oil price on exchange rate, while Hassan and Zaman (2012) and Tiwari and Olayeni (2013) concluded that there are negative relationships between oil price and exchange rate for India. Studies such as Olomola and Adejumo (2006) and Aliyu (2009) found a positive relationship between oil price and exchange rate for Nigeria. Several other studies—such as Rautava (2004); Yousefi and Wirjanto (2004); Nikbakht (2010); Al-Ezzee (2011); and Benhabib et al. (2014)—have also examined causal relationships between oil price and exchange rate. Other studies—Rautava (2004); Yousefi and Wirjanto (2004); Nikbakht (2010); Al-Ezzee (2011)—found a significant relationship between oil price and exchange rate while Benhabib et al. (2014) found a negative relationship. In other words, apart from the inconclusiveness of the literature on the causal effects of oil price on exchange rate and trade balance, previous studies have employed causal analysis in the time domain which cannot analyze causality in the short-, medium-, and long-term but only at a point in time. Furthermore, the frequency domain analysis, on the other hand, provides the frequency and timing where causality exists. This identified shortcoming in this area motivates the use of frequency domain analysis. Studies that have applied the frequency domain causality in the literature are Breitung and Candelon (2006) for the United States (US); Croux and Reusens (2013) for G-7 countries; Yanfeng (2013) for the Japanese economy; Tiwari et al. (2015) for nine EU countries; Dergiades et al. (2015) for seven selected European Union (EU) countries; Bayat et al. (2015) for Czech Republic, Poland, and Hungary; Ozer and Kamisli (2016) for Turkey; Tiwari and Kyophilavong (2017) for India; and Bouri et al. (2017b) for China and India. A more recent study was done by Huang et al. (2018) for the US and nine EU countries. The frequency domain analysis has been known to provide time varying outcomes in terms of low and high frequency in the modeling of the relationship between financial and energy variables than the time domain approach. The frequency analysis is important for both the policy and decision makers in the energy sector as it enables them to know and plan ahead of time unlike in the time domain where causality is just assumed to exist without the knowledge of the period of timing and its frequency. Therefore, the decomposition of the frequency domain causality into different timings and frequencies gives a more in-depth understanding of economic phenomena than the time domain analysis. The objective of this study is to examine the dynamic effects of oil price on some selected macroeconomic variables in Nigeria. Our results show that short term causality exists from oil price to foreign reserve while causality is not found from oil price to trade balance and exchange rate, respectively. The rest of the paper is as follows. Section 2 gives the summary of the existing literature in tabular form, Section 3 has the descriptive statistics, the unit root tests, and the cointegration test. Section 4 describes the frequency domain causality, Section 5 provides the discussion of results, while Section 6 concludes and provides policy recommendations.

2. Literature Review

Tables 1–3 summarize the literature on the relationship between oil price, trade balance, and exchange rate in tabular form as follows:

Table 1. Summary of empirical Evidence on trade balance and exchange rate.

Author(s)	Country/Countries	Sample Period	Methodology	Results/Conclusion of the Study
Danmola and Olateju (2013)	Nigeria	1980 to 2010	OLS	Exchange rate volatility has a positive influence on GDP, FDI, and trade.
Shehu and Youtang (2012)	Sub-Sahara African countries with exclusive reference to Nigeria	1970 to 2009	Augmented Dickey Fuller (ADF), Granger causality test	The study concluded that the exchange rate has significant impact in influencing exports, imports, and economic growth.
Udoh et al. (2012)	Nigeria	1968 to 2010	Cointegration test, ECM	The study showed that exchange rate volatility reduces with external reserves, lending interest rate, and import.
Zheng (2012)	Thailand and China	1997 to 2011	GLS	The results indicated that the exchange rate volatility has a positive impact on the Thailand export to China and the exchange rate has no significant impact on GDP.
Joseph and Isaac (2011)	Nigeria	1970 to 2009	GARCH	The study showed indirect and insignificant relations between trade and exchange rate.
Ogbonna (2011)	Nigeria	1970 to 2005	OLS	The study revealed that there is no cointegration for trade balance model.
Oladipupo and Onotaniyohuwo (2011)	Nigeria	1970 to 2008	OLS	The study claimed that exchange rate has significant effects on balance of payments.
Olayungbo et al. (2011)	Sub-Sahara African countries	1986 to 2005	OLS and panel generalised method of moment	The result showed that exchange rate has positive effect on aggregate trade.
Ng et al. (2008)	Malaysia	1955 to 2006	VECM	The results concluded the existence of long run effects between trade balance and exchange rate.
Baak (2004)	East Asian countries	1981 to 2004	ECM	The study showed that exchange rate volatility had a significant short and long run effects on exports.
Rose (1990)	Organization for Economic Cooperation and Development countries (OECD)	Parametric and Non-parametric		The study concluded that exchange rate has insignificant impact on trade balance.

Notes: OLS—ordinary least square, ECM—error correction modeling, GLS—generalized least square, GARCH—generalized autoregressive conditional heteroscedasticity, VECM—vector error correction model.

Table 2. Empirical evidence on oil price and trade balance.

Author(s)	Country/Countries	Sample Period	Methodology	Results/Conclusion of the Study
Tiwari and Olayeni (2013)	India	1980 to 2011	Wavelet analysis	The study showed that oil price has negative effect on trade balance
Wu et al. (2013)	China and G7 countries	1975 to 2010	Panel smooth transition regression	The study affirmed that trade balance responded significantly to the changes in income, oil price, and import.
Hassan and Zaman (2012)	Pakistan	1975 to 2010	ARDL	The result showed that there is a significant negative effect of oil price on both exchange rate and trade balance.
Qiangian (2011)	China	1999 to 2008	VECM	The study revealed that there exists a long-term equilibrium relationship among oil price and output, inflation, trade balance, and money supply.
Ozlale and Pekkurnaz (2010)	Turkey	1999 to 2009	VAR	The study affirmed that oil price has significant effects on trade balance in the short run.
Tsen (2009)	Asian countries (Japan, Hong Kong, and Singapore)	1960 to 2016	VAR	The study showed that the variables of term of trade and oil price shock affect the trade balance both in the long run and short run.

Notes: ARDL—autoregressive distributed lag, VECM—vector error correction model, VAR—vector autoregression.

Table 3. Empirical evidence on oil price and exchange rate.

Author(s)	Country/Countries	Sample Period	Methodology	Results/Conclusion of the Study
Shafi et al. (2013)	France	1971 to 2012	ECM	The study concluded that the impact of oil price on exchange rate is positive in the long run.
Benhabib et al. (2014)	Algeria	2003 to 2013	VAR	The study indicated that oil price has impacted Algerian currency.
Al-Ezzee (2011)	Bahrain	1980 to 2005	VECM	The study affirmed the existence of a long run relationship between real GDP growth, global oil price, and exchange rate.
Nikbakht (2010)	OPEC members	2000 to 2007	Panel cointegration test	The result showed that oil price may have a dominant share of real exchange rate movement.
Aliyu (2009)	Nigeria	1986 to 2007	VAR	The study suggested the diversification of both the infrastructure and the economy.
Coudert et al. (2008)	US	1974 to 2004	VECM	The relationship between the dollar real exchange rate and oil price seems to be transmitted through US international investment position.
Chen and Chen (2007)	G7 countries	1992 to 2005	Panel co-integration	The study found that there is a link between oil price and exchange rate.
Gounder and Bartleet (2007)	New Zealand	1989 to 2006	VAR	Oil price has substantial effect on inflation and exchange rate in New Zealand.
Habib and Kalamova (2007)	Russia, Norway, and Saudi –Arabia	1980 to 2006	VAR	There is no significant evidence to maintain that the diverse exchange rate regimes of the countries may account for the different empirical results on the impact of oil price.
Olomola and Adejumo (2006)	Nigeria	1970 to 2003	VAR	The findings showed that while oil price significantly influenced exchange rate, it did not have a significant effect on output and inflation in Nigeria.
Rautava (2004)	Russia	1995 to 2001	VAR	The study found that the economy was influenced significantly by fluctuations in both long run equilibrium and short run direct impact.
Youseti and Wirjanto (2004)	OPEC Countries	1970 to 1999	Novel empirical approach	The study revealed that regional price correlations appeared to be indicative of segmentation within the OPEC market structure.

Notes: VECM—vector error correction model, VAR—vector autoregression.

In summary, from the empirical literature, the results from the review show different evidence regarding the issue of trade balance, oil price, reserve, and exchange rate. Firstly, it can be observed that extensive studies have been done on trade balance and exchange rate, oil price and exchange rate in both developed and less developed countries. Most of the literature highlighted made use of time domain analysis and studies that have applied frequency domain analysis were mainly on developed countries with few on developing countries. This study, therefore, contributes to the existing literature by applying the frequency domain causality on oil price and macroeconomic variables in Nigeria.

3. Data Analysis

This section presents the definition of variables used, their data sources, descriptive statistics of variables used, the unit root tests and the cointegration test employed in this study.

3.1. Variable Definition and Data Sources

The data used for this study is from the period of 1986Q4 to 2018Q1. The choice of a single country study and period are informed by data availability. Apart from these limitations, the sample country is the largest exporter of oil in Africa and her economy is largely driven by oil price. The variables used are oil price, trade balance, exchange rate, and trade balance. Trade balance is the volume of aggregate export of goods and services minus aggregate import of goods and services measured in naira. Oil price, on the other hand, is the price at which Brent crude oil is sold per barrel at each quarter measured in US dollar in the international oil market. The exchange rate is the relative price of exchange of the units of naira to the units of dollar. Lastly, foreign reserve is measured as the financial assets held in the form of US dollars in the country's treasury. The trade balance, reserve, and exchange rate were sourced from the Central Bank of Nigeria Statistical Bulletin (2018) while the oil prices sourced from the Energy Information Administration, US Federal Statistical System (2018). It should be noted that the data employed have been adjusted from their sources of any predictable changes that can overstate their true values.

3.2. Descriptive Analysis

The description of the data used in this study as presented in Table 4 shows the average value of $43.58 for oil price; $97.79 for exchange rate; $19,163 billion for reserve; and ₦168,856 billion for trade balance for the period of study. The exchange rate measured in US dollars has fluctuated widely over the study period given the maximum value of $306.4 to ₦1 and the minimum value of $1 to ₦1 during the study period. The volatility change is also true of the oil price with a maximum value of $123.78 and minimum value of $12.93 over the study period. The movement is correlated with both reserve and trade balance with maximum values of $60,875 billion and ₦718,742 billion respectively and minimum value of $913 million and ₦142 million respectively. The relationship in the movement of the variables shows the response of the selected macroeconomic variables to oil price over the study period.

Table 4. Descriptive statistics.

Statistics	Exchange Rate	Oil Price	Reserve	Trade Balance
Mean	97.79	43.58	19,163	168,856
Median	116.04	28.92	9101.47	79,865.46
Maximum	306.4	123.78	60,875.24	718,742
Minimum	1	12.93	913	141.59
Std-dev	80.96	29.62	17,121.85	198,198
Jacque-Bera	9.38	18.33	14.53	25.11
Prob.	0.00	0.00	0.00	0.00
observation	129	129	129	129

3.3. Unit Root Tests

The unit root tests of augmented Dickey–Fuller (ADF, Dickey and Fuller 1981) and the Phillips–Perron (PP, Phillips and Perron 1988) are carried out to ensure the stationarity of the variable of interest. From Table 5, it can be observed that all the variables are stationary at first difference with both ADF and PP except trade balance which is stationary at first difference with ADF but not with PP. The stationarity of the variables is important for the application of the frequency domain causality.

Table 5. Augmented Dickey–Fuller and Phillip–Perron.

Variables	Levels	First Diff.	Variables	Level	First Diff.
Exchange rate	0.637	−8.9128 ***	Exchange rate	1.0743	−8.8182 ***
Oil price	−1.5666	−9.5175 ***	Oil price	−1.4847	−8.9468 ***
Reserve	−1.0742	−4.0827 ***	Reserve	−0.9562	−8.0429 ***
Trade Balance	−2.6008	−15.4233	Trade Balance	−3.5938	-

The critical values are −3.4824, −2.8843, and −2.5790 at 1%, 5%, and 10% respectively. *** signifies 1% significance level.

3.4. Cointegration Tests

The next step is to verify if cointegration exists between the non-stationary variables of interest using the Johansen (1988) multivariate cointegration test. We conducted a bivariate cointegration test separately between oil price and each of the other three variables in order to ensure consistency with the bivariate frequency domain causality approach. This cointegration test compares the Eigenvalue and the trace statistics with their critical values to determine the presence of cointegration. The null hypothesis is the rejection of cointegration if the Eigen or trace statistics is greater than the critical value. From Table 6, the cointegration between oil price and reserve, $r = 0$ is rejected at 5 percent significance level with the value of 14.76 of the Eigen statistics greater than the critical value of 14.26. However, the null hypothesis of no cointegration cannot be rejected for $r \leq 1$ because the Eigen statistics value of 0.68 is less than the critical value of 3.84. The same for the trace statistics. We therefore conclude that there is at least one cointegrating relationship between oil price and foreign reserve. However, the test of cointegration between oil price and trade balance, $r = 0$ is rejected for both the Eigen and the trace statistics, because their values of 11.6 and 13.43 are less than there critical values of 14.26 and 15.49. The same is true for the cointegrating relationship between oil price and exchange rate. We therefore conclude that there is no long run relationship between oil price and trade balance on one hand and no long run relationship exists between oil price and exchange rate on another. Long run cointegration exists only between oil price and foreign exchange reserves. In other words, the study found the bivariate cointegration system to exist only for oil price and reserve in the study period.

Table 6. Johansen unrestricted bivariate cointegration results.

Coint. Rank	Eigen Value	Critical Value	Prob.	Trace Stat.	Critical Value	Prob.
Oil price and reserve						
$r = 0$	14.76	14.26	0.04 **	15.45	15.49	0.05 *
$r \leq 1$	0.68	3.84	0.41	0.68	3.84	0.41
Oil price and trade balance						
$r = 0$	11.6	14.26	0.13	13.43	15.49	0.10
$r \leq 1$	1.82	3.84	0.18	1.82	3.84	0.18
Oil price and exchange rate						
$r = 0$	11.49	15.49	0.18	10.61	14.26	0.17
$r \leq 1$	0.88	3.84	0.35	0.87	3.84	0.35

** and * denote the rejection of the null hypothesis of no cointegration at 5 and 10 percent significance level.

4. Methodology

In this study, we propose the granger causality in the frequency domain following Croux and Reusens (2013) as opposed to the usual time domain causality test. Many previous studies have applied frequency domain causality to wide areas of economic research. In earlier years, Breitung and Candelon (2006) investigated the predictive content of the yield spread for future output growth using United State (US) quarterly data. Also, Yanfeng (2013) applied the frequency domain causality on the dynamic effects of oil prices on the Japanese economy. In recent years, Dergiades et al. (2015) examined the effects of social media (Twitter, Facebook, and Google blogs) and web search intensity (Google) on financial markets with the use of frequency domain causality for Greece, Ireland, Italy, Portugal, and Spain and separately for two Euro countries, France, and The Netherlands. In addition, Bayat et al. (2015) investigated causal relationship between oil price and exchange rates in Czech Republic, Poland, and Hungary by employing frequency domain causal approach. In the same manner, Ozer and Kamisli (2016) used the frequency domain causality analysis to study the interactions between financial markets in Turkey. Likewise, Tiwari and Kyophilavong (2017) studied the relationship between exchange rate and international reserves for India using a frequency domain analysis. Bouri et al. (2017b) also adopted frequency domain causality to investigate the short-, medium-, and long-run causal relations among crude oil, wheat, and corn markets in the US. In another paper, Bouri et al. (2017a) used implied volatility indices with frequency domain analysis to examine the short and long-term causality dynamics between gold and stock market in China and India. In a more recent paper, Huang et al. (2018) investigated oil price effect on tourist arrivals to explain oil price effects on tourism-related economic activities for US and nine EU countries using frequency analyses. The modeling of the bivariate frequency domain starts from the time domain model as

$$\Delta X_t = \alpha_0 + \sum_{i=1}^{n} \alpha_i \Delta X_{t-i} + \sum_{i=1}^{n} \lambda_i \Delta Y_{t-i} + \varepsilon_{1t}$$

$$\Delta Y_t = \beta_0 + \sum_{i=1}^{n} \beta_i \Delta X_{t-i} + \sum_{i=1}^{n} \omega_i \Delta Y_{t-i} + \varepsilon_{2t} \tag{1}$$

The vector autoregression (VAR) in the time domain is then modified to frequency domain by Geweke (1982) to a bivariate and two-dimensional causal form of two stationary variables X_t and Y_t as

$$\Theta(L) \begin{pmatrix} X_t \\ Y_t \end{pmatrix} = \begin{pmatrix} \Theta_{11}(L) & \Theta_{12}(L) \\ \Theta_{21}(L) & \Theta_{22}(L) \end{pmatrix} \begin{pmatrix} X_t \\ Y_t \end{pmatrix} = \begin{pmatrix} \varepsilon_{1t} \\ \varepsilon_{2t} \end{pmatrix} \tag{2}$$

where $\Theta(L) = 1 - \Theta_1 L - \Theta_2 L^2 - \cdots - \Theta_p L^p$ is a 2×2 lag polynomial of order ρ with $L^j X_t = X_{t-j}$ and $L^j Y_t = Y_{t-j}$. The vector of error, $\varepsilon_t = (\varepsilon_{1t}, \varepsilon_{2t})'$ is assumed to be stationary with $E(\varepsilon_t) = 0$ and $E(\varepsilon_{1t}, \varepsilon_{2t})' = \Sigma$, where Σ is positive definite and symmetric. Applying the Cholesky decomposition, $G'G = \Sigma^{-1}$, where G is a lower triangular matrix and G' is an upper triangular matrix, the MA representation of the model is expressed as

$$\begin{pmatrix} X_t \\ Y_t \end{pmatrix} = \Phi(L) \begin{pmatrix} \eta_{1t} \\ \eta_{2t} \end{pmatrix} = \begin{pmatrix} \Phi_{11}(L) & \Phi_{12}(L) \\ \Phi_{21}(L) & \Phi_{22}(L) \end{pmatrix} \begin{pmatrix} \eta_{1t} \\ \eta_{2t} \end{pmatrix} \tag{3}$$

where $\Phi(L) = \Theta(L)^{-1} G^{-1}$ and $(\eta_{1t}, \eta_{2t})' = G(\varepsilon_{1t}, \varepsilon_{2t})'$, so that $\text{cov}(\eta_{1t}, \eta_{2t}) = 0$ and $\text{var}(\eta_{1t}) = \text{var}(\eta_{2t}) = 1$. Equation (3) means that X_t is a sum of two uncorrelated MA processes. Specifically, it is the sum of an intrinsic component driven by past shocks in X_t and a component containing the causal component of the variable Y_t. The causal component of Y_t at each frequency ω can be derived by comparing the causal component of the spectrum with the intrinsic component at the frequency. Y_t does not granger cause X_t at frequency ω if the causal component of the spectrum of X_t at frequency ω is zero. According to Geweke (1982), the measure of causality is defined as

$$M_{y \to x}(\omega) = \log \left[1 + \frac{|\Phi_{12}(e^{-i\omega})|^2}{|\Phi_{11}(e^{-i\omega})|^2} \right] \tag{4}$$

This measure of causality is the ratio of the total spectrum divided by the intrinsic component of the spectrum. It is expressed as $M_{y \to x}(\omega) = 0$ if $|\Phi_{12}(e^{-i\omega})| = 0$. Hence, the term $|\Phi_{12}(e^{-i\omega})| = 0$ provides a condition of no granger causality at frequency ω. For simplicity, Breitung and Candelon (2006), show that condition of no granger causality at frequency ω can be represented in a set of linear restrictions on the coefficient of the components of the VAR model in Equation (2) as

$$X_t = \sum_{i=1}^{\rho} \Theta_{11i} X_{t-i} + \sum_{i=1}^{\rho} \Theta_{12i} Y_{t-i} + \varepsilon_{1t} \tag{5}$$

where Θ_{11i} and Θ_{12i} are the coefficients of the lag polynomials $\Theta_{11}(L)$ and $\Theta_{12}(L)$. The necessary and sufficient conditions for absence of granger causality at frequency ω can be written as

$$\begin{cases} \sum_{i=1}^{\rho} \Theta_{12i} \cos(i\omega) = 0 \\ \sum_{i=1}^{\rho} \Theta_{12i} \sin(i\omega) = 0 \end{cases} \tag{6}$$

The linear restriction in Equation (6) on the coefficients can be tested by a standard F-test. The F-statistics is distributed as $F(2, T - 2\rho)$. Where 2 is the number of restrictions and T is the number of observations used to estimate the VAR model of order ρ. In the same vein, the linear restrictions in Equation (6) can be tested by an incremental R-squared test, measuring the proportion of explained variability of X_t lost as a result of the imposition of the two restrictions in Equation (6). The incremental R-squared is the difference between the R-squared test R^2 of the unrestricted equation in Equation (5) and the R-squared test R^2 of the equation estimated in Equation (6). The incremental R-squared can be explicitly written as

$$\text{Incremental } R^2 = R^2 - R_*{}^2 \tag{7}$$

The incremental R-squared test is the strength of the granger causality from Y_t to X_t at frequency ω and it lies between 0 and 0.01 according to Equation (5). The plot of the incremental R-squared of the frequencies is between 0 and π. It describes the strength of the Granger causality in the frequency domain $(0, \pi)$. The null hypothesis of absence of Granger causality at the frequency ω is rejected at significance level α on the condition that

$$\text{Incremental } R^2 > F_{(2,T-2P,1-\alpha)} \frac{2}{T - 2\rho}(1 - R^2) \tag{8}$$

where $F_{(2,T-2\rho,1-\alpha)}$ is the α upper critical value of the F-distribution with 2 and $T - 2\rho$ degree of freedom (Croux and Reusens 2013). As regards the lag length, which is crucial to the causality test, the Schwarz information criterion (SIC) is chosen among the other criterion with the true lag length order of 3 is chosen for the causality between oil price and reserve, lag 2 for oil price and trade balance, and lag 1 for causality between oil price and exchange rate (Asghar and Abid 2007). The results of the lag length selection criteria are presented at the Appendix A.

5. Discussion of Results

The frequency domain causality is carried out after ensuring the stationarity of the variables to investigate the causal effects of oil price on reserve, trade balance, and exchange rate in Nigeria. The short term causality is assumed to be periodicities (frequency) less than 1.5, while the periodicity of 1.5 is the intermediate term and the long term causality is the frequency greater than 1.5. In this study, Equation (5) is estimated separately with oil price as exogenous variable to reserve, trade balance, and exchange rate. This is so modeled because oil price is exogenous to Nigeria's economy. The global oil prices are dictated by the economic conditions in the international market which are external to the sample country's economy. As a result, we perform separate Granger causality tests for Y_t on X_t. In the model; Y_t stands for oil price; while X_t represents reserve, trade balance, and exchange rate. The results of the granger causality tests are presented in Figure 1. The first figure shows that oil price granger causes reserve in Nigeria at 0.001 incremental R-squared, that is, 0.001% critical value with a frequency of value of 1.0. The 0.001 incremental R-squared can be interpreted to mean that there is 99.999% confidence level of causality between oil price and reserve in Nigeria. This means that oil price strongly determines the level of reserve in Nigeria in the short term with the 1.0 frequency value. The periodicity is calculated by $S = \pi/(2\omega)$, where S is the year of periodicity, π is 3.1416 and ω is 1.0 in this case. From the calculation, the periodicity is 18 months, equivalent to 1 year and 6 months. This implies that oil price usually has significant impact on reserves at every 1 year and 6 months and that the occurrence of causality is at every short period. The previous presence of cointegration between oil price and foreign reserve confirms the existence of frequency Granger causality between the two variables. Our result of short-term frequency causality from oil to reserve is in line with a previous study done by Yanfeng (2013) for Japanese, where oil prices was found to have causal effects on the Japanese economy at short term frequency. Our findings of short term causal relationship between oil price and reserve is consistent with Nigeria's experience. Higher oil price has always been associated with higher reserve while low oil price is linked to low reserve. For example, in 2008, oil price was around US$103 and Nigeria's reserve hit about US$60 billion. In the same vein, reserve fell to US$23 billion with a fall in oil price to US$37 in 2015. On the other hand, causality is not found from oil price to trade balance. The absence of cointegration between oil price and trade balance corroborates the result for the frequency granger causality test. The outcome of the causality may be as a result of recent increase in non-oil export, such as solid minerals, agricultural products, and manufactured exports. The recent exported agricultural products are cashew nuts, sesame, shrimps, soya beans, ginger, cocoa. Although oil still dominates exports in Nigeria, yet government is making concerted effort towards diversifying the economy away from oil as laid down in the Nigerian Economic Recovery and Growth Plan (NERGP) on zero oil agenda. The result of no causal relationship from oil price to trade balance supports a previous study carried out on US and nine EU countries by Huang et al. (2018) that also found no causal effects from oil price to tourism-related economic activities. Lastly, causality is also not found from oil price to exchange rate. The cointegration result is also in line with the granger causality result. The frequent use of foreign exchange to stabilize the exchange rate level by the central bank of Nigeria (CBN) periodically may explain the absence of causal effects of oil price on the exchange rate. Nigeria practices a managed floated exchange rate system. Such exchange rate policy intervention can greatly eliminate the effects of oil price on the exchange rate. Our findings supported a previous study conducted by Habib and Kalamova (2007) for Russia, Norway, and Saudi Arabia that no significant causal relationship exists between oil price and exchange rate for the oil rich countries. It is also in support of a more recent paper by Bayat et al. (2015) that oil price does not have causal effect on exchange rate in Hungary with frequency domain analysis.

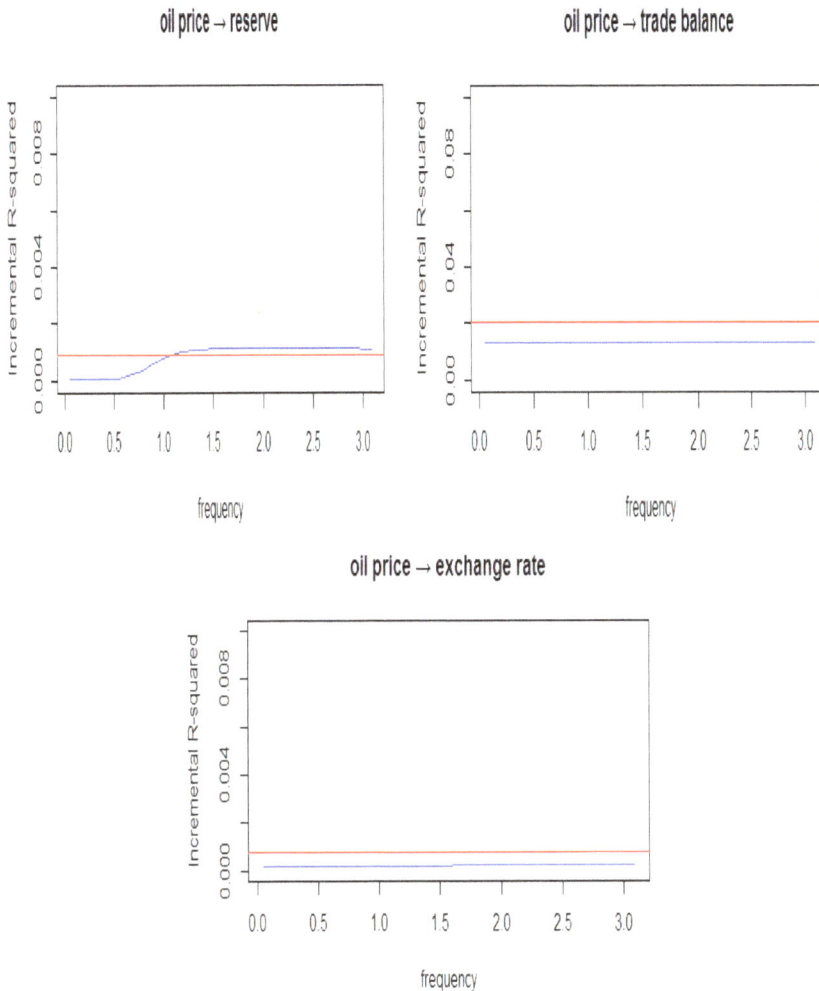

Figure 1. Granger causality of oil price effects on reserve, trade balance, and exchange rate in Nigeria.

6. Conclusions and Policy Recommendations

This study examined the causal effects of oil price on exchange rate, trade balance, and reserve in Nigeria between the periods of the fourth quarter of 1986 to the first quarter of 2018. We employed a frequency domain causality test as against the usual time domain causality to capture the possible short-, medium-, and long-term causal effects between the variables of interest. After performing the unit root tests and the cointegration test, we found short term causal effects of oil price on reserve. However, no causal effects were found from oil price to both exchange rate and trade balance.

The absence of causal effects suggests that oil price does not have any significant effect on Nigeria's exchange rate and trade balance. In other words, oil price does not matter for exchange rate and trade balance behavior in Nigeria. The short term causal effects running from oil price to reserve implies that movement in the global oil price plays a major role in reserve keeping in Nigeria in the short period. The findings suggest that short term energy policy would be appropriate for oil price-reserve relationship in Nigeria. The likely implication of the short predictor of oil price on reserve building is that reliance on oil price to build Nigeria's reserve can only be feasible in the short run and not over a long period of time. It further implies that Nigeria cannot not rely solely on the foreign exchange from oil price for her reserve building in the long run. The country currently has almost $42.34 billion in her reserve and increase in global oil price has been the major source of foreign exchange inflow into the reserve. Diversifying away from oil to other non-oil activities that would generate foreign exchange for reserve building, should be a continuous policy pursuit of the policy makers in the country. In addition, the country can attract other capital inflow apart from oil price for reserve building. Finally, the short run causal effects between oil price and reserve imply that policy makers should have short term and regular policy response to the interactions between the two variables.

Conflicts of Interest: The authors declare no conflict of interest.

Appendix A

Table A1. VAR lag order selection criteria. Endogenous variables: oil price and trade balance.

Lag	LogL	LR	FPE	AIC	SC	HQ
0	−1829.76	NA	4.83×10^{10}	30.28	30.32	30.3
1	−1539.23	566.67	4.24×10^{8}	25.54	25.68	25.6
2	−1527.29	22.89	3.72×10^{8}	25.41	25.64	25.5
3	−1514.97	23.2	3.24×10^{8} *	25.27 *	25.59 *	25.4 *
4	−1513.16	3.36	3.36×10^{8}	25.31	25.72	25.48
5	−1510.4	5.02	3.43×10^{8}	25.33	25.83	25.54
6	−1507.18	5.75	3.48×10^{8}	25.34	25.94	25.59
7	−1505.52	2.9	3.62×10^{8}	25.38	26.07	25.66
8	−1502.87	4.55	3.71×10^{8}	25.4	26.19	25.72

LR—likelihood ratio, FPE—final prediction error, AIC—Akaike information criterion, SC—Schwarz information criterion, HQ—Hannan–Quinn information criterion. * signifies optimal lag length.

Table A2. VAR lag order selection criteria. Endogenous variables: oil price and exchange rate.

Lag	LogL	LR	FPE	AIC	SC	HQ
0	−797.4	NA	1.88×10^{1}	13.21	13.26	13.23
1	−600.78	383.47	7.78×10^{1}	10.02	10.17 *	10.09
2	−583.03	34.05	6.20×10^{1}	9.80	10.03	9.90
3	−578.02	9.41	6.10×10^{1} *	9.79 *	10.11	9.92 *
4	−576.98	1.94	6.40×10^{1}	9.83	10.25	10.00
5	−573.23	6.81	6.43×10^{1}	9.84	10.35	10.04
6	−570.5	4.87	6.57×10^{1}	9.86	10.46	10.10
7	−569.51	1.74 *	6.91×10^{1}	9.91	10.6	10.19
8	−566.6	4.99	7.05×10^{1}	9.93	10.71	10.25

LR—likelihood ratio, FPE—final prediction error, AIC—Akaike information criterion, SC—Schwarz information criterion, HQ—Hannan–Quinn information criterion. * signifies optimal lag length.

Table A3. VAR lag order selection criteria. Endogenous variables: Oil price and exchange rate.

Lag	LogL	LR	FPE	AIC	SC	HQ
0	−1255.15	NA	3.63×10^3	20.78	20.83	20.8
1	−876.02	739.46	7.35×10^3	14.58	14.72 *	14.64
2	−869.03	13.39	7.00×10^3	14.53	14.76	14.62
3	−861.57	14.06	6.61×10^3 *	14.47 *	14.94	14.6 *
4	−860.89	1.26	6.99×10^3	14.53	15.08	14.7
5	−859.52	2.47	7.30×10^3	14.57	15.22	14.78
6	−858.64	1.59	7.69×10^3	14.62	15.22	14.87
7	−853.06	9.78 *	7.50×10^3	14.6	15.29	14.88
8	−851.47	2.72	7.82×10^3	14.64	15.42	14.95

LR—likelihood ratio, FPE—final prediction error, AIC—Akaike information criterion, SC—Schwarz information criterion, HQ—Hannan–Quinn information criterion. * signifies optimal lag length.

References

Al-Ezzee, Ibrahim. 2011. Real influences of Real Exchange rate and Oil price changes on the growth of real GDP: Case of Bahrain. Paper presented at International Conference of Management and Service Science IPEDR 8, Wuhan, China, August 12–14.

Aliyu, Shehu Usman Rano. 2009. Impact of Oil Price shock and Exchange Rate Volatility on Economic Growth in Nigeria: An Empirical Investigation. *Research Journal of International Studies* 11: 4–15.

Asghar, Zahid, and Irum Abid. 2007. Performance of Lag Length Selection Criteria in Three Different Situations. Paper No. 40042. Posted 13 July 2012. Available online: https://mpra.ub.uni-muechen.de/40042/MPRA (accessed on 5 December 2018).

Baak, SaangJoon. 2004. Exchange rate volatility and trade among the Asia pacific. *East Asian Economic Review* 8: 93–115. Available online: http://repec.org/esFEAM04/up.29293.1080736850.pdf (accessed on 7 December 2018). [CrossRef]

Bayat, Tayfur, Saban Nazlioglu, and Selim Kayhan. 2015. Exchange rate and oil price interactions in transition economics: Czech Republic, Hungary and Poland. *Panoeconomicus* 62: 267–85. [CrossRef]

Benhabib, Abderrezak, Si Mohammed Kamel, and Samir Maliki. 2014. The Relationship between Oil Price and the Algerian Exchange Rate. *Topics in Middle Eastern and African Economies* 16: 127–41.

Bouri, Elie, David Roubaud, Rania Jammazi, and Ata Assaf. 2017a. Uncovering frequency domain causality between gold and the stock markets of China and India: Evidence from implied volatility indices. *Finance Research Letters*. [CrossRef]

Bouri, Elie, Imad Kachacha, Donald Lien, and David Roubaud. 2017b. Short- and long-run causality across the implied volatility of crude oil and agricultural commodities. *Economics Bulletin* 37: 1077–88.

Breitung, Jörg, and Bertrand Candelon. 2006. Testing for short run and long run causality: A frequency domain approach. *Journal of Econometrics* 132: 363–78. [CrossRef]

Central Bank of Nigeria Statistical Bulletin. 2018. *Annual Publication*; Abuja: Central Bank of Nigeria.

Centre for Study of Economies of Africa. 2018. 4 Dep. Street off Danube Street, Maitama, Abuja, FCT, Nigeria. Available online: www.cseaafrica.org (accessed on 25 December 2018).

Chen, Shiu-Sheng, and Hung-Chyn Chen. 2007. Oil prices and real exchange rates. *Energy Economics* 29: 390–404. [CrossRef]

Coudert, Virginie, Valérie Mignon, and Alexis Penot. 2008. Oil Price and the Dollar. *Energy Studies Review* 15: 1–20. [CrossRef]

Croux, Christophe, and Peter Reusens. 2013. Do stock prices contain predictive power for the future economic activity? A Granger causality analysis in the frequency domain. *Journal of Macroeconomics* 35: 93–103. [CrossRef]

Danmola, Rasaq Akonji, and Adijat Olubunkola Olateju. 2013. The Impact of monetary policy on current Account Balance. *Journal of Humanities and Social Sciences* 7: 67–72.

Dergiades, Theologos, Costas Milas, and Theodore Panagiotidis. 2015. Tweets, Google trends, and sovereign spreads in the GIIPS. *Oxford Economic Papers* 67: 406–32. [CrossRef]

Dickey, David A., and Wayne A. Fuller. 1981. Distribution of the estimators for autoregressive time series with a Unit Root. *Journal of the American Statistical Association* 74: 427–31.

Energy Information Administration, US Federal Statistical System. 2018. Available online: http://www.eia.gov (accessed on 20 December 2018).

Geweke, John. 1982. Measurement of linear dependence and feedback between multiple time series. *Journal of American Statistical Association* 77: 304–24. [CrossRef]

Gounder, Rukmani, and Matthew Bartleet. 2007. Oil price shocks and economic growth: Evidence for New Zealand, 1989–2006. Paper presented at the New Zealand Association of Economist Annual Conference, Christchurch, New Zealand, June 27–29.

Habib, Maurizio Michael, and Margarita M. Kalamova. 2007. *Are There Oil Currencies? The Real Exchange Rate of Oil Exporting Countries*. Working Paper Series 839. Frankfurt: European Central Bank.

Hassan, Syeda Anam, and Khalid Zaman. 2012. Effect of oil prices on trade balance: New insights into the cointegration relationship from Pakistan. *Economic Modeling* 29: 2125–43. [CrossRef]

Huang, Xu, Emmanuel Silva, and Hossein Hassani. 2018. Causality between oil prices and tourist arrivals. *Stats* 1: 134–54. [CrossRef]

Johansen, Søren. 1988. Statistical analysis of cointegration vectors. *Journal of Economic Dynamics and Control* 12: 231–54. [CrossRef]

Joseph, Afolabi Ibikunle, and Akhanolu Isaac. 2011. An Empirical investigation of the link between exchange rate volatility and trade in Nigeria. *Journal of Emerging Trends in Economics and Management Sciences* 2: 175–83.

Ng, Yuen-Ling, Wai-Mun Har, and Geoi-Mei Tan. 2008. Real Exchange rate and trade balance relationship: An Empirical study on Malaysia. *International Journal of Business and Management* 3: 130–37. Available online: https://ssrn.com/abstract=1398329 (accessed on 23 December 2018). [CrossRef]

Nikbakht, Leili. 2010. Oil prices and exchange rate: The case of OPEC. *Business Intelligence Journal* 3: 88–92.

Ogbonna, BigBen Chukwuma. 2011. The impact of exchange rate variation on trade balance: Evidence from Nigeria, 1970–2005. *Journal of Research in National Development* 9: 393–403.

Oladipupo, Adesina Oladipupo, and Faith Ogheneovo Onotaniyohuwo. 2011. Impact of exchange rate on balance of payment in Nigeria. *African Research Review* 5: 73–88. [CrossRef]

Olayungbo, David Oluseun, Olalekan Yinusa, and Anthony Enisan Akinlo. 2011. Effect of Exchange Rate Volatility on Trade in Some Sub-Saharan African Countries. *Modern Economy* 2: 538. [CrossRef]

Olomola, Philip A., and Akintoye V. Adejumo. 2006. Oil price shock and macroeconomic Activities in Nigeria. *International Research Journal of Finance and Economics* 3: 28–34.

Ozer, Mustafa, and Melik Kamisli. 2016. Frequency domain causality analysis of interactions between financial markets of Turkey. *International Business Research* 9: 176–86. [CrossRef]

Ozlale, Ümit, and Didem Pekkurnaz. 2010. Oil price and current account: A structural analysis for the Turkish economy. *Energy Policy* 38: 4489–96. [CrossRef]

Phillips, Peter Charles Bonest, and Pierre Perron. 1988. Testing for a unit root in time series regressions. *Biometrica* 75: 335–46. [CrossRef]

Qiangian, Zhang. 2011. The impact of international oil price fluctuation on China's economy. *Energy Procedia* 5: 1360–64. [CrossRef]

Rautava, Jouko. 2004. The role of oil prices and the real exchange rate in Russia's economy—A Cointegration approach. *Journal of Comparative Economics* 32: 315–27. [CrossRef]

Rose, Andrew K. 1990. Exchange Rates and Trade Balance. Some evidence from developing countries. *Economic Letters* 34: 271–75. [CrossRef]

Shafi, Khuram, Liu Hua, and Nazeer Amna. 2013. Exchange rate volatility and oil price shocks. *International Journal of Academic Research in Business and Social Sciences* 5.

Shehu, Abba Abubakar, and Zhang Youtang. 2012. Exchange rate volatility, trade flows and economic growth in a small open Economy. *International Review of Business Research Paper* 8: 118–31.

Tiwari, Aviral Kumar, and Phouphet Kyophilavong. 2017. Exchange rate and international reserves in India: A frequency Domain Analysis. *South Asia Economic Journal* 18: 76–93. [CrossRef]

Tiwari, Aviral Kumar, and Olaolu Richard Olayeni. 2013. Oil price and trade balance: wavelet based analysis for India. *Economics Bulletin* 33: 2270–86.

Tiwari, Aviral Kumar, Süleyman Bolat, and Özgür Koçbulut. 2015. Revisit budget deficit and inflation: Evidence from time and frequency domain analyses. *Theoretical Economic Letters* 5: 357–69. [CrossRef]

Tsen, Wong Hock. 2009. Term-of-trade and trade balance: Some empirical evidence of Asian economies. *The International Trade Journal* XXIII: 422–57. [CrossRef]

Udoh, Edet Joshua, Sunday Brownson Akpan, Daniel Etim John, and Inimfon Vincent Patrick. 2012. Cointegration between exchange rate volatility and key macroeconomic fundamentals: evidence from Nigeria. *Modern Economy* 3: 846–55. [CrossRef]

Wu, Po-Chin, Shiao-Yen Liu, and Sheng-Chieh Pan. 2013. Nonlinear bilateral trade balance-fundamentals nexus: A panel regression approach. *International Review of Economics and Finance* 27: 318–29. [CrossRef]

Yanfeng, Wei. 2013. The dynamic relationships between oil prices and the Japanese economy: A frequency domain analysis. *Review of Economic &Finance* 3: 57–67.

Yousefi, Ayoub, and Tony S. Wirjanto. 2004. The empirical role of the exchange rate on the crude-oil Price formation. *Energy and Economics* 26: 783–99. [CrossRef]

Zheng, Yun. 2012. The Impact of Bilateral Exchange Rate on Trade between Thailand and China. Available online: http://eprints.utcc.ac.th/id/eprint/1340 (accessed on 12 December 2018).

Journal of
Risk and Financial Management

MDPI

Article

What Factors Affect Income Inequality and Economic Growth in Middle-Income Countries?

Duc Hong Vo *[iD], Thang Cong Nguyen[iD], Ngoc Phu Tran and Anh The Vo[iD]

Business and Economics Research Group, Ho Chi Minh City Open University, Ho Chi Minh 700000, Vietnam;
thang.ngc@ou.edu.vn (T.C.N.); tranphungoc91@gmail.com (N.P.T.); anh.vt@ou.edu.vn (A.T.V.)
* Correspondence: duc.vhong@ou.edu.vn

Received: 9 December 2018; Accepted: 19 February 2019; Published: 8 March 2019

Abstract: Income inequality in many middle-income countries has increased at an alarming level. While the time series relationship between income inequality and economic growth has been extensively investigated, the causal and dynamic link between them, particularly for the middle-income countries, has been largely ignored in the current literature. This study was conducted to fill in this gap on two different samples for the period from 1960 to 2014: (i) a full sample of 158 countries; and (ii) a sample of 86 middle-income countries. The Granger causality test and a system generalized method of moments (GMM) are utilized in this study. The findings from this study indicate that causality is found from economic growth to income inequality and vice versa in both samples of countries. In addition, this study also finds that income inequality contributes negatively to the economic growth in the middle-income countries in the research period.

Keywords: income inequality; economic growth; middle income countries; Granger causality test; system GMM

JEL Classification: O15; O47

1. Introduction

From the World Bank's classifications, middle-income countries (MICs) are nations with a per capita gross national income (GNI) between US$1005 and US$12,235. MICs, which are a very diverse group by region, size, population, and income level, can be broken up into lower-middle-income and upper-middle-income economies. Two MIC superpower economies—China and India—hold nearly one-third of humanity and continue to be increasingly influential players globally. The World Bank also considers that MICs are essential for continued global economic growth and stability. In addition, sustainable growth and development in MICs, including poverty reduction, international financial stability, and cross-border global issues including climate change, sustainable energy development, food and water security, and international trade, have positive spill-overs to the rest of the world[1].

Alvaredo et al. (2018) provided a comprehensive review of income inequality over the last 40 years and stressed a surge in income inequality in China, Russia, and India. Particularly, in China, it was found that in 2015 the top 10 percent of the population accounted for nearly 42 percent of the national income, but the bottom 50 percent only owned 15 percent of the national income; these groups both equally shared nearly one-third of the national income in 1978. During the same period, the urban–rural income gap has widened. Urban households earned twice as much as rural households in 1978. However, they earned a 3.5 times higher amount in 2015. Similarly, over the period from 1989 to

---

[1] See more at https://www.investopedia.com/terms/m/middle-income-countries.asp.

2015, the incomes of the top 1 percent and the bottom 50 percent have varied significantly in Russia. The share of the top 1 percent has increased from 25 percent to 45 percent of the national income compared to the share of the bottom 50 percent from 30 percent to 20 percent. In India, inequality has increased dramatically from the 1980s onwards, mostly due to economic reforms, leading to the share of the top 10 percent of the population accounting for nearly 60 percent of the national income.

It is widely noted that widening inequality has significant implications for growth and macroeconomic stability. Income inequality can lead to a suboptimal use of human resources, cause political and economic instability, and raise crisis risk[2].

The link between income inequality and economic growth and related issues has been extensively investigated in the literature. Typical studies are those by Forbes (2000) and Barro (2000), followed by various other studies (Fawaz et al. 2014; Wahiba and Weriemmi 2014; Huang et al. 2015; Madsen et al. 2018; Nguyen et al. 2019; Vo et al. 2019). The current study was conducted to provide additional empirical evidence on growth and income inequality for middle-income countries. To the best of our knowledge, most studies on income inequality and economic growth have utilized the Deininger and Squire (1996) "high-quality" data set, although this data set has recently been criticized for its accuracy, consistency, and comparability (Atkinson and Brandolini 2001; Galbraith and Kum 2005). As a result, using this data set might produce biased results (Malinen 2012). To address this issue, on the basis of Solt (2016) study, the data set was constructed to maximize comparability without losing the broadest coverage. In this paper, we contribute to the discussion by using the latest and most updated data set from World Development Indicator and Standardized World Income Inequality with a focus on middle-income countries, which have largely been ignored in previous studies.

The rest of the paper is structured as follows. Following the Introduction, Section 2 provides a comprehensive review of the relevant literature on the income inequality–economic growth nexus. The research methodology and data are presented in Section 3. Section 4 discusses empirical findings, followed by the Concluding Remarks in Section 5.

2. Literature Review

Although various studies have been conducted to investigate the relationship between income inequality and economic growth, thus far, modelling complexities have stood in the way of solid confirmation. The technical issues of endogeneity and of model specifications together with the diversified application of econometric techniques are considered to be the main factors (Fawaz et al. 2014).

The seminal study by Kuznets (1955) asserted that inequality was a consequence of economic growth. In this respect, inequality increases in the early stage of the economic development process before decreasing with further development. Since then, a large proportion of studies in the stock of documents relating inequality and economic growth have been conducted. Among them, various studies have supported a positive association (Rubin and Segal 2015; Wahiba and Weriemmi 2014; Lundberg and Squire 2003) while some analyses were in favor of a negative relationship (Majumdar and Partridge 2009; Nissim 2007). Some studies also offered a mixed result (Huang et al. 2015; Chambers 2010).

For example, Rubin and Segal (2015) presented that U.S. income inequality was positively related to economic growth in the period of 1953–2008. The data utilized in their study are income stream, which was defined as a total of wealth income and labor income; these were sensitive to economic growth and varied across income groups. Their empirical findings suggested that the sensitivity of income of the top 1 percent of the population was twice as much as that of the bottom 90 percent. In addition, empirical results also confirmed that the income of the top was more responsive to variation in market returns.

---

[2]   See more at https://www.imf.org/external/pubs/ft/sdn/2015/sdn1513.pdf.

Another illustration of Kuznets' hypothesis was also found in a study by Kozminski and Baek (2017). Using a data set compounding income inequality, income, and the population of Alaska over the period of 1963–2012, together with an autoregressive distributed lag (ARDL) approach to cointegration—a widely used estimation tool (see Stock and Watson 1993; Saikkonen 1991; Narayan 2004; Masih and Masih 1996; Hendry 1995; Forest and Turner 2013; Hayakawa and Kurozumi 2008; Bewley 1979)—the authors argued that income inequality was enhanced by economic growth after a certain turning point. Notably, the findings were not sensitive regardless of income measures (e.g., Gini coefficient, Theil's Entropy Index).

On the other hand, with the data set from the Standardized World Income Inequality and World Bank, Yang and Greaney (2017) concluded that the relationship between income inequality and economic growth followed the S-shape curve hypothesis in the context of South Korea, Japan, the U.S., and China in the long run, suggesting that economic growth had a significant impact on income inequality. Nevertheless, in the short run, the authors found no association between income inequality and economic growth except in Japan.

The realization that income inequality influences economic growth has been taken into consideration, together with the findings of Kuznets (1955). Yang and Greaney (2017) argued that on the one hand, inequality induced low-income people to work more to meet their requirements, leading to an increase of growth, and on the other hand, inequality interfered with the accumulation of human capital, which, in turn, impeded growth. Various studies have investigated whether inequality contributes to economic growth and have revealed a positive relationship (Li and Zou 1998; Forbes 2000) or a negative relationship (Cingano 2014; Wahiba and Weriemmi 2014).

For instance, Fawaz et al. (2014) confirmed a negative impact of income inequality on economic growth in low-income developing countries. Their conclusions emerged from using difference generalized method of moments (GMM) for a sample of 55 low-income developing countries and 56 high-income developing countries, proposed by World Bank's classification. Furthermore, in order to demonstrate that the empirical results were not arbitrary, the authors continued to use the difference GMM on a refined sample in which countries were categorized endogenously using the threshold procedure. In conclusion, they found no difference in the relationship across the two classifications.

In other views, a negative effect of income inequality on economic growth was also stressed in the work of Madsen et al. (2018). Specifically, the authors argued that at low levels of financial development, proxied by the credit to the non-banking sector/nominal GDP ratio, income inequality hindered growth. Their conclusions emerged from the application of the two-stage least squares (2SLS) approach over a sample of 21 selected Organisation for Economic Co-operation and Development (OECD) countries from 1870 to 2011. To ensure the results were not biased by the issue of causality from growth to income inequality, external communist influence was identified as an instrument variable due to a negative association between it and income inequality being identified in the study.

Findings from Kim (2016) also contributed to this line of research. From empirical results, economic growth was negatively related to income inequality. The study employed cross-sectional data for 40 countries in the Organisation for Economic Co-operation and Development (OECD) and in the European Union observed in the period of 2004–2011, together with a fixed effect model and GMM. The results consistently indicated that income inequality truly retarded economic growth in various subsamples, which were established by income level by the ratio of nonperforming loans to bank loans.

Intricacy also stemmed from the use of qualitative tools and/or the underlying measurement of income inequality. For the former, it was stated that income inequality was found to be positively correlated with economic growth using the GMM technique (Biswas et al. 2017; Fawaz et al. 2014; Forbes 2000). Inversely, income inequality was shown to impede economic growth via the use of OLS-FE and/or OLS-RE (Alesina and Rodrik 1994; Castelló-Climent 2004; Persson and Tabellini 1994). For the latter, empirical studies have been adopting various measures of inequality such as the Gini coefficient of inequality, Generalized Entropy measures, Atkinson's inequality measures, and the decile dispersion ratio[3]. Unfortunately, each measure by itself encounters some issues. Particularly, in relation to the Gini coefficient, the problem is the difference in the definition of welfare, together with the use of an equivalence scale among data sources.

3. Research Methodology and Data

3.1. Data

The data set was constructed from the Standardized World Income Inequality Database (SWIID), World Development Indicator (WDI), and Penn World Table (PWT). The PWT provides the latest observation at 2014. The data set is thus an unbalanced panel of data of 158 countries which were observed in the period of 1960–2014, or 2625 country–year observations. Moreover, this study also utilized country classifications by income level issued by World Bank to separate the original data set into subsamples. In total, there were four income groups including high income (47 countries), upper-middle income (45 countries), lower-middle income (41 countries), and low income (25 countries). That classification yielded 86 middle-income countries in the same time frame, or 1356 country–year observations. The variables used in the model are listed and explained in Table 1 in addition to a brief summary of statistics presented in Table 2. A list of countries included in the sample is reported in Tables A1 and A2 in the Appendix A.

Table 1. A brief summary of variables.

Variable	Definition	Source
$\dot{y}$	Annual growth of real GDP per capita.	WDI
$\dot{G}$	Percent change in the Gini coefficient.	SWIID
PPPI	Price level of investment.	PWT
%Agriculture	The proportion of employment in agriculture out of total employment.	WDI
%Industry	The proportion of employment in industry out of total employment.	WDI
%Service	The proportion of employment in service out of total employment.	WDI

Table 2. Descriptive statistics.

Variables	Observations	Mean	S.D.	Min	Max
Panel A: All countries (N = 158)					
$\dot{y}$	4046	2.05	4.78	−65.01	31.46
$\dot{G}$	4046	0.11	0.97	−6.50	8.74
PPPI	3917	45.86	28.30	0.15	165.16
%Agriculture	2672	30.49	26.10	0.12	92.84
%Industry	2672	20.82	8.88	1.97	49.55
%Service	2672	48.68	20.20	5.06	87.59
Panel B: Middle-income countries (N = 86)					
$\dot{y}$	1987	2.16	5.26	−60.37	28.54
$\dot{G}$	1987	0.02	0.78	−6.05	5.84
PPPI	1909	33.64	16.02	4.84	120.00
%Agriculture	1385	35.20	17.47	2.46	51.28
%Industry	1385	20.94	7.78	5.75	49.55
%Service	1385	43.85	13.84	12.01	78.34

In relation to the variable of interest—income inequality—this analysis employed data issued by SWIID among various sources such as the Luxembourg Income Study (LIS), the OECD Income Distribution Database, the Eurostat, and the World Bank. An explanation for the use of SWIID is its

---

[3]   See more at http://siteresources.worldbank.org/PGLP/Resources/PMch6.pdf.

sample coverage which is highly linked to the others. For instance, the Eurostat, through its mission, only provides statistics in Europe. LIS is another example as it only considers 50 countries around the world. Similarly, the OECD Income Distribution Database contains the Gini coefficient of 38 countries where the first observation was introduced in 2013.

In this line of research, one of the most used indices of income inequality is Deininger and Squire (1996) "high-quality" data set since various criteria were applied to standardize the inputs. However, the data set created by Deininger and Squire (1996) has been criticized for its accuracy, consistency, and comparability (Atkinson and Brandolini 2001; Galbraith and Kum 2005). Thus, studies relying on this kind of data set would encounter mistakes (Malinen 2012).

In response to the issues of coverage and comparability, Solt (2016) offered a standardized data set on income inequality which is normally referred to as the Standardized World Income Inequality Database (SWIID). The advantage of the data set is to maximize comparability without losing the broadest coverage. Since its first introduction in 2008, a number of studies have employed the data set to discuss inequality-related issues (Yang and Greaney 2017; De Haan et al. 2018).

The outcome of SWIID offered both inequality in disposable income and inequality in market income. We consider that the indicator of inequality in market income is more suitable because different countries have different tax systems.

3.2. Research Methodology

The data set contains a large number of countries (158 countries) and the time frame is quite long (1960–2014), so it is reasonable to believe that omitted variables could bias our estimates of the variables of interest. This endogeneity problem is considered due to omitted variables in the fixed effect panel data setting, including country dummies and time dummies. The model can be written as follows:

$$\dot{y}_{i,t} = \theta_0 + \theta_1 \dot{G}_{i,t-1} + \sum_{i=1}^{n} \delta_i X_{i,t-1} + \gamma_t + \alpha_i + \varepsilon_{i,t} \tag{1}$$

where $\dot{y}_{i,t} = \Delta \ln(GDP_{i,t})$ is the annual growth of the real GDP per capita in country i at time t. θ_0 is the intercept. $\dot{G}_{i,t-1}$ is the logarithmic changes in the Gini coefficient. $X_{i,t-1}$ is the vector of explanatory variables, including $PPPI$, $\%Agriculture$, $\%Industry$, and $\%Service$, and $\varepsilon_{i,t}$ is a stochastic error. Following Forbes (2000), we included the $PPPI$ variable to account for the price level of investment, which is widely used in the open economy literature.

To account for the endogenous issue of economic growth and the reversed effect running from economic growth to income inequality, we used the dynamic panel data setting. The following model was considered:

$$\dot{y}_{i,t} = \theta_0 + \theta_1 (\dot{y}_{i,t-1}) + \theta_2 (\dot{G}_{i,t-1}) + \sum_{i=1}^{n} \delta_i X_{i,t-1} + \varepsilon_{i,t} \tag{2}$$

Given the presence of the first-order lagged dependent variable in the model, the assumption of strictly exogenous variable seems not to hold for the lagged dependent variable containing observations from 2 to T on y and the residual term is a collection of observations from 1 to T, leading to a correlation between the regressor and the error terms. Thus, the application of regression techniques based on ordinary least squares (OLS) would potentially lead to a bias in the estimate of the lagged dependent variable, even in the case of infinite individuals (Hsiao 2014). To rectify this, a typical approach, which was suggested by Arellano and Bond (1991) and is normally referred to as the difference generalized method of moments (GMM), is taking the first difference, and then using lagged levels of the dependent variable as instruments for endogenous variables in the first-difference equation.

However, several years later, Arellano and Bover (1995) and Blundell and Bond (1998) argued that those instruments were likely to be poor, so such an approach would be weak if the dependent variable was close to a random walk and the panel data was short. As such, Blundell and Bond (1998) developed another estimation technique which is known as system GMM. Technically, together with the first-difference equation adopted in the difference GMM, the system GMM allows us to employ additional level equations and then uses first-difference lagged levels as instruments. In this paper, for the transformed equation, the lagged level dated at $t - 2$ was used as an instrument variable. For the level equation, the first difference dated at $t - 1$ was employed.

4. Result and Discussion

4.1. Granger Causality Test

According to the discussed studies in Section 2, it is worthy to note that there is a causal relationship between income inequality and economic growth. Nevertheless, this does not necessarily imply a causality running from income inequality to economic growth and from economic growth to income inequality in our sample. As such, we employed a procedure developed by Dumitrescu and Hurlin (2012) to test for Granger causality (see Granger 1969, 1980) in our panel data set. The following model was employed:

$$y_{i,t} = \alpha_i + \sum_{k=1}^{K} \beta_{ik} y_{i,t-k} + \sum_{k=1}^{K} \varphi_{ik} x_{i,t-k} + \varepsilon_{i,t}$$

where $x_{i,t}$ and $y_{i,t}$ are considered variables (i.e., income inequality and economic growth in this case). The inclusion of lagged values of x implies that if past values of x significantly explain variation in the current values of y when accounting for its preceding ones, x will have a causal effect on y. In doing so, an F-test was considered with following null hypothesis:

$$H_0 : \varphi_{i1} = \varphi_{i2} = \ldots = \varphi_{ik} = 0$$

If H_0 is rejected at a given significant level, there is causality running from x to y. In other words, the alternative hypothesis is accepted that there is a causality running from x to y in at least one panel. One of the assumptions of the Granger causality test, proposed by Dumitrescu and Hurlin (2012), is the stationarity of the considered variable. As such, to address the issue, we used the recently developed technique proposed by Pesaran (2007). Compared to a series of stationarity tests (Breitung 2000; Harris and Tzavalis 1999; Im et al. 2003), it takes the problem of cross-sectional dependence into account, which produces reliable results in the presence of both heterogeneity across panels and cross-sectional dependence. The findings are presented in Table 3. In the subsample of middle-income countries, all variables were stationary at their levels. Similarly, in the sample of all countries, except for the %*Industry* and %*Service* variables, all other variables were stationary. In summary, the stationarity, especially for the annual growth of GDP per capita and income inequality, allows us to examine the impact of income inequality on growth in the presence of feedback from the dependent variable using the GMM method.

Table 3. Unit root tests.

Sample	$\dot{y}$	$\dot{G}$	PPPI	%*Agriculture*	%*Industry*	%*Service*
All countries	−7.33 *** (0.00)	−3.96 *** (0.00)	−3.024 *** (0.00)	−2.44 *** (0.00)	0.81 (0.79)	−1.21 (0.11)
Middle-income countries	−4.75 *** (0.00)	−1.40 * (0.08)	−3.07 *** (0.00)	−2.57 *** (0.00)	−3.24 *** (0.00)	−1.87 ** (0.03)

p-value in parentheses. *** $p < 0.01$, ** $p < 0.05$, * $p < 0.1$.

In the next step, we examined the income inequality–economic growth causality nexus in the two samples. In the sample of all countries, the empirical findings in Panel A indicate the presence of unidirectional causality running from income inequality to economic growth. Similarly, in relation to the Panel B, the null hypothesis that economic growth does not Granger cause income inequality is rejected, suggesting that a causality from economic growth to income inequality exists. Overall, there is a bidirectional causality between income inequality and economic growth. The same conclusions can be reached for the sample including the middle-income countries. Particularly, the $\widetilde{Z}$ statistics are significant at the level of 1 percent in both Panel A and Panel B, as presented in Table 4. To put it differently, a bidirectional causality between income inequality and economic growth was found in the sample. The optimal number of lags was selected using the Akaike's information criterion (AIC).

Table 4. Granger causality test.

Sample	All Countries	Middle-Income Countries
Panel A		
	$H_0:\dot{G} \nrightarrow \dot{y}$	
$\widetilde{Z}$	7.02 ***	4.79 ***
$p(\widetilde{Z})$	0.00	0.00
Number of lags (AIC)	4	4
Panel B		
	$H_0:\dot{y} \nrightarrow \dot{G}$	
$\widetilde{Z}$	6.01 ***	5.27 ***
$p(\widetilde{Z})$	0.00	0.00
Number of lags (AIC)	4	1

p-value in parentheses. *** $p < 0.01$.

4.2. Empirical Analysis

In this section, the empirical analysis on the impact of independent variables on the dependent variable is presented.

Table 5 presents the system GMM estimations[4]. The coefficient of income inequality, denoted by $\dot{G}_{i,t-1}$, is negative and significant at the level of 1 percent, suggesting that income inequality decreases economic growth. The magnitude is somewhat larger for the middle-income countries sample than for the full sample. This finding is also consistent with those of previous studies (Halter et al. 2014; Castelló-Climent 2004; Deininger and Olinto 1999).

Among the explanatory variables, firstly, the PPPI, measuring market distortion on the price of investment, is also significantly negatively correlated with economic growth for both samples. This finding was also found in other studies (Fawaz et al. 2014; Forbes 2000; Perotti 1996). Secondly, *Industry* is negatively correlated to economic growth. Although the result is unexpected and contradicts growth theory, this finding is consistent with a finding from Szirmai and Verspagen (2015). With a significant and negative estimate for the all countries sample and for the system GMM estimation, the size effect of *Industry* is small. Finally, in contrast to the negative contribution of the variables above, positive impacts from *Agriculture* and *Service* on economic growth were found, which implies a positive effect of labor force on growth (Yang and Greaney 2017).

Table 5 also reports some statistics related to the system GMM. They are in relation to the Arellano and Bond test of second-order autocorrelation of the first-differenced residuals and the Hansen test of being exogenous of instrument variables. The results suggest that the null hypothesis of no second-order correlation failed to be rejected and that instruments are exogenous, which supports the validity of the GMM model.

---

[4] In addition to the system GMM estimation, we also estimated the effect of inequality on growth specified in Equation (1) using the fixed effects model. The results reveal a significant negative relationship between income inequality and economic growth. The estimates using fixed effects are higher than the GMM estimation above. Various studies have documented fixed effects estimators systematically producing higher effects (Neves et al. 2016; De Dominicis et al. 2008). Results will be available on request.

Table 5. Estimation results.

Variable	All Countries	Middle-Income Countries
	GMM	GMM
$\dot{y}_{i,t-1}$	0.32 ***	0.47 ***
	(0.09)	(0.06)
$\dot{G}_{i,t-1}$	−0.45 *	−0.97 **
	(0.25)	(0.46)
$PPPI_{i,t-1}$	−0.04 ***	−0.04 **
	(0.00)	(0.02)
$\%Agriculture_{i,t-1}$	0.01 *	0.04 *
	(0.00)	(0.02)
$\%Industry_{i,t-1}$	−0.07 *	−0.06
	(0.04)	(0.05)
$\%Service_{i,t-1}$	0.10 ***	0.06 *
	(0.02)	(0.03)
Observations	2625	1356
Arellano-Bond test for AR (1)	$Z = -3.02$ $p > Z = 0.00$	$Z = -4.08$ $p > Z = 0.00$
Arellano-Bond test for AR (2)	$Z = 1.30$ $p > Z = 0.19$	$Z = 1.39$ $p > Z = 0.16$
Hansen test	$H\chi^2 (211) = 134.69$ $p > \chi^2 = 1.00$	$H\chi^2 (211) = 68.12$ $p > \chi^2 = 1.00$

Robust standard errors in parentheses. *** $p < 0.01$, ** $p < 0.05$, * $p < 0.1$.

5. Concluding Remarks

Over the last 50 years, the impact of income inequality on economic growth has been extensively investigated. However, findings are mixed. It is argued that previous studies utilized suboptimal econometric techniques and imperfect data on income inequality. As such, this study was conducted to provide additional empirical findings on the inequality–growth nexus puzzle using a sample including only middle-income countries, which have largely been ignored in the literature. While previous studies utilized data on income inequality proposed by Deininger and Squire (1996) which have since then been considered imperfect and incomplete, this study employed a highly regarded data set on income inequality developed by Solt (2016).

Considering both cross-sectional and time dimensions, our empirical findings confirm a negative impact of income inequality on economic growth, implying that an increase in income inequality leads to a decrease in economic growth. These findings hold for both fixed effects panel model and dynamic panel model settings and for two samples—the full sample and the sample including only middle-income countries.

In addition, findings from this study confirm a positive contribution of labor force participation in agricultural and service sectors to economic growth, which is implied in the economic growth theories.

The findings of this empirical study also offer additional empirical evidence for governments in middle-income countries to formulate and implement their economic and social policies. Economic growth is generally associated with income inequality; thus, a disparity in income will, in turn, decrease the national output, leading to a reduction in economic growth. As such, policies which focus on a redistribution of economic achievement to the people, especially to those at the bottom of the income distribution, are required. Economic achievements will allow them to invest in human capital or physical capital, which offers a high rate of return. Also, policies to alleviate—though not necessarily eliminate—the capital–market imperfection through the development of financial intermediaries should be implemented. In addition, efficiency of capital allocation is required. In addition, policies to increase minimum wage or to support accumulating assets for working families can also narrow the income gap. Further, it is recommended for policy-makers to take into consideration friendly working environment-related regulations, so that low-paid workers can make their best effort to work and earn.

Author Contributions: Conceptualization, D.H.V.; Methodology, D.H.V.; T.C.N.; Software, T.C.N.; N.P.T.; Validation, D.H.V.; Formal Analysis, T.C.N., A.T.V.; Investigation, D.H.V.; Resources, D.H.V.; Data Curation, D.H.V.; Writing-Original Draft Preparation, D.H.V.; Writing-Review & Editing, D.H.V.; Visualization, T.C.N.; Supervision, D.H.V.; Project Administration, D.H.V.; Funding Acquisition, D.H.V.

Funding: This research is funded by Vietnam's National Foundation for Science and Technology Development (NAFOSTED) under grant number 502.01-2018.38.

Conflicts of Interest: The authors declare no conflict of interest.

Appendix A

Table A1. All countries in the study.

Countries				
Afghanistan	Costa Rica	Italy	Namibia	St. Kitts and Nevis
Albania	Croatia	Jamaica	Nepal	St. Lucia
Algeria	Cyprus	Japan	Netherlands	Sudan
Angola	Czech Republic	Jordan	New Zealand	Suriname
Argentina	Denmark	Kazakhstan	Nicaragua	Swaziland
Armenia	Dominica	Kenya	Niger	Sweden
Australia	Dominican Republic	Korea	Nigeria	Switzerland
Austria	Ecuador	Kosovo	Norway	Tajikistan
Azerbaijan	El Salvador	Laos	Pakistan	Tanzania
Bangladesh	Estonia	Latvia	Panama	Thailand
Barbados	Ethiopia	Lebanon	Papua New Guinea	Timor-Leste
Belarus	Fiji	Lesotho	Paraguay	Togo
Belgium	Finland	Liberia	Peru	Tonga
Belize	France	Lithuania	Philippines	Trinidad and Tobago
Benin	Georgia	Luxembourg	Poland	Tunisia
Bhutan	Germany	Macedonia	Portugal	Turkey
Bolivia	Ghana	Madagascar	Puerto Rico	Turkmenistan
Bosnia and Herzegovina	Greece	Malawi	Qatar	Tuvalu
Botswana	Grenada	Malaysia	Romania	Uganda
Brazil	Guatemala	Maldives	Russia	Ukraine
Bulgaria	Guinea	Mali	Rwanda	United Kingdom
Burkina Faso	Guinea-Bissau	Malta	Samoa	United States
Burundi	Guyana	Mauritania	Senegal	Uruguay
Cambodia	Haiti	Mauritius	Serbia	Uzbekistan
Cameroon	Honduras	Mexico	Seychelles	Vanuatu
Canada	Hungary	Micronesia	Sierra Leone	Venezuela
Central African Republic	Iceland	Moldova	Singapore	Vietnam
Chad	India	Mongolia	Slovenia	Yemen
Chile	Indonesia	Montenegro	Solomon Islands	Zambia
China	Iraq	Morocco	South Africa	Zimbabwe
Colombia	Ireland	Mozambique	Spain	
Comoros	Israel	Myanmar	Sri Lanka	

Source: World Bank.

Table A2. Middle-income countries with GNI per capita > 1045 US$ in the study.

Countries		
Albania	India	Paraguay
Algeria	Indonesia	Peru
Angola	Iraq	Philippines
Armenia	Jamaica	Romania
Azerbaijan	Jordan	Samoa
Bangladesh	Kazakhstan	Senegal
Belarus	Kenya	Serbia
Belize	Kosovo	Solomon Islands
Bhutan	Laos	South Africa
Bolivia	Lebanon	Sri Lanka
Bosnia and Herzegovina	Lesotho	St. Lucia
Botswana	Macedonia	Sudan
Brazil	Malaysia	Suriname
Bulgaria	Maldives	Swaziland
Cameroon	Mauritania	Tajikistan
China	Mauritius	Thailand
Colombia	Mexico	Timor-Leste
Costa Rica	Micronesia	Tonga
Dominica	Moldova	Tunisia
Dominican Republic	Mongolia	Turkey
Ecuador	Montenegro	Turkmenistan
El Salvador	Morocco	Tuvalu
Fiji	Myanmar	Ukraine
Georgia	Namibia	Uzbekistan
Ghana	Nicaragua	Vanuatu
Grenada	Nigeria	Vietnam
Guatemala	Pakistan	Yemen
Guyana	Panama	Zambia
Honduras	Papua New Guinea	

Source: World Bank.

References

Alesina, Alberto, and Dani Rodrik. 1994. Distributive politics and economic growth. *The Quarerly Journal of Economics* 109: 465–90. [CrossRef]

Alvaredo, Facundo, Lucas Chancel, Thomas Piketty, Emmanuel Saez, and Gabriel Zucman, eds. 2018. *World Inequality Report 2018*. Cambridge: Belknap Press of Harvard University Press.

Arellano, Manuel, and Stephen Bond. 1991. Some tests of specification for panel data: Monte Carlo evidence and an application to employment equations. *The Review of Economic Studies* 58: 277–97. [CrossRef]

Arellano, Manuel, and Olympia Bover. 1995. Another look at the instrumental variable estimation of error-components models. *Journal of Econometrics* 68: 29–51. [CrossRef]

Atkinson, Anthony B., and Andrea Brandolini. 2001. Promise and pitfalls in the use of "secondary" data-sets: Income inequality in OECD countries as a case study. *Journal of Economic Literature* 39: 771–99. [CrossRef]

Barro, Robert Joseph. 2000. Inequality and Growth in a Panel of Countries. *Journal of Economic Growth* 5: 5–32. [CrossRef]

Bewley, Ronald A. 1979. The direct estimation of the equilibrium response in a linear dynamic model. *Economics Letters* 3: 357–61. [CrossRef]

Biswas, Siddhartha, Indraneel Chakraborty, and Rong Hai. 2017. Income Inequality, Tax Policy, and Economic Growth. *The Economic Journal* 127: 688–727. [CrossRef]

Blundell, Richard, and Stephen Bond. 1998. Initial conditions and moment restrictions in dynamic panel data models. *Journal of Econometrics* 87: 115–43. [CrossRef]

Breitung, Jörg. 2000. The local power of some unit root tests for panel data. In *Advances in Econometrics, Volume 15: Nonstationary Panels, Panel Cointegration, and Dynamic Panels*. Edited by Badi H. Baltagi, Thomas B. Fomby and R. Carter Hill. Bingley: Emerald Group Publishing Limited, pp. 161–77.

Castelló-Climent, Amparo. 2004. *A Reassessment of the Relationship between Inequality and Growth: What Human Capital Inequality Data Say?* València: Instituto Valenciano de Investigaciones Económicas.

Chambers, Dustin. 2010. Chambers, Dustin. 2010. Does a rising tide raise all ships? The impact of growth on inequality. *Applied Economics Letters* 17: 581–86. [CrossRef]

Cingano, Federico. 2014. *Trends in Income Inequality and Its Impact on Economic Growth*. OECD Social, Employment and Migration Working Papers. Paris: OECD Publishing. [CrossRef]

De Dominicis, Laura, R. J. Florax, and H. L. De Groot. 2008. A meta-analysis on the relationship between income inequality and economic growth. *Scottish Journal of Political Economy* 55: 654–82. [CrossRef]

De Haan, Jakob, Regina Pleninger, and Jan Egbert Sturm. 2018. Does the impact of financial liberalization on income inequality depend on financial development? Some new evidence. *Applied Economics Letters* 25: 313–16. [CrossRef]

Deininger, Klaus, and Pedro Olinto. 1999. *Asset Distribution, Inequality, and Growth*. World Bank Policy Research Paper 2375. Washington, DC: World Bank.

Deininger, Klaus, and Lyn Squire. 1996. A New Data Set Measuring Income Inequality. *World Bank Economic Review* 10: 565–91. [CrossRef]

Dumitrescu, Elena Ivona, and Christophe Hurlin. 2012. Testing for Granger non-causality in heterogeneous panels. *Economic Modelling* 29: 1450–60. [CrossRef]

Fawaz, Fadi, Masha Rahnama, and Victor J. Valcarcel. 2014. A refinement of the relationship between economic growth and income inequality. *Applied Economics* 46: 3351–61. [CrossRef]

Forbes, Kristin J. 2000. A Reassessment of the Relationship between Inequality and Growth. *American Economic Review* 90: 869–87. [CrossRef]

Forest, J. James, and Paul Turner. 2013. Alternative estimators of cointegrating parameters in models with nonstationary data: An application to US export demand. *Applied Economics* 45: 629–36. [CrossRef]

Galbraith, James K., and Hyunsub Kum. 2005. Estimating the inequality of household incomes: A statistical approach to the creation of a dense and consistent global data set. *Review of Income and Wealth* 51: 115–43. [CrossRef]

Granger, Clive W. J. 1969. Investigating causal relations by econometric models and cross-spectral methods. *Econometrica* 37: 424–38. [CrossRef]

Granger, Clive W. J. 1980. Testing for causality: a personal viewpoint. *Journal of Economic Dynamics and Control* 2: 329–52. [CrossRef]

Halter, Daniel, Manuel Oechslin, and Josef Zweimüller. 2014. Inequality and growth: the neglected time dimension. *Journal of Economic Growth* 19: 81–104. [CrossRef]

Harris, Richard D. F., and Elias Tzavalis. 1999. Inference for unit roots in dynamic panels where the time dimension is fixed. *Journal of Econometrics* 91: 201–26. [CrossRef]

Hayakawa, Kazuhiko, and Eiji Kurozumi. 2008. The role of "leads" in the dynamic OLS estimation of cointegrating regression models. *Mathematics and Computers in Simulation* 79: 555–60. [CrossRef]

Hendry, David Forbes. 1995. *Dynamic Econometrics*. Oxford: Oxford University Press on Demand.

Hsiao, Cheng. 2014. *Analysis of Panel Data*, 3rd ed. Cambridge: Cambridge University Press.

Huang, Ho Chuan, WenShwo Fang, Stephen M. Miller, and Chih-Chuan Yeh. 2015. The effect of growth volatility on income inequality. *Economic Modelling* 45: 212–22. [CrossRef]

Im, Kyung So, Mohammad Hashem Pesaran, and Yongcheol Shin. 2003. Testing for unit roots in heterogeneous panels. *Journal of Econometrics* 115: 53–74. [CrossRef]

Kim, Jong-Hee. 2016. A Study on the Effect of Financial Inclusion on the Relationship Between Income Inequality and Economic Growth. *Emerging Markets Finance and Trade* 52: 498–512. [CrossRef]

Kozminski, Kate, and Jungho Baek. 2017. Can an oil-rich economy reduce its income inequality? Empirical evidence from Alaska's Permanent Fund Dividend. *Energy Economics* 65: 98–104. [CrossRef]

Kuznets, Simon. 1955. Economic Growth and Income Inequality. *American Economic Review* 45: 1–28.

Li, Hongyi, and Heng-fu Zou. 1998. Income inequality is not harmful for growth: Theory and evidence. *Review of Development Economics* 2: 318–34. [CrossRef]

Lundberg, Mattias, and Lyn Squire. 2003. The simultaneous evolution of growth and inequality. *The Economic Journal* 113: 326–44. [CrossRef]

Madsen, Jakob Brochner, M. Rabiul Islam, and Hristos Doucouliagos. 2018. Inequality, financial development and economic growth in the OECD, 1870–2011. *European Economic Review* 101: 605–24. [CrossRef]

Majumdar, Shibalee, and Mark D. Partridge. 2009. Impact of economic growth on income inequality: A regional perspective. Paper presented at the Agricultural and Applied Economics Association, Milwaukee, WI, USA, July 26.

Malinen, Tuomas. 2012. Inequality and growth: Another look with a new measure and method. *Journal of International Development* 25: 122–38. [CrossRef]

Masih, Rumi, and Abul Mansur Masih. 1996. Stock-Watson dynamic OLS (DOLS) and error-correction modelling approaches to estimating long-and short-run elasticities in a demand function: New evidence and methodological implications from an application to the demand for coal in mainland China. *Energy Economics* 18: 315–34. [CrossRef]

Narayan, Paresh Kumar. 2004. Do public investments crowd out private investments? Fresh evidence from Fiji. *Journal of Policy Modeling* 26: 747–53. [CrossRef]

Neves, Pedro Cunha, Óscar Afonso, and Sandra Silva. 2016. A Meta-Analytic Reassessment of the Effects of Inequality on Growth. *World Development* 78: 386–400. [CrossRef]

Nguyen, Cong Thang, Vo The Anh, Pham Ngoc Thach, Do Thanh Trung, and Vo Hong Duc. 2019. Gender-Based Attitudes toward Income Inequality in the Asia-Pacific Region. *Emerging Markets Finance and Trade*. [CrossRef]

Nissim, Ben-David. 2007. Economic growth and its effect on income distribution. *Journal of Economic Studies* 34: 42–58. [CrossRef]

Perotti, Roberto. 1996. Growth, income distribution, and democracy: What the data say. *Journal of Economic Growth* 1: 149–87. [CrossRef]

Persson, Torsten, and Guido Tabellini. 1994. Is Inequality Harmful for Growth? *The American Economic Review* 84: 600–621.

Pesaran, M. Hashem. 2007. A simple panel unit root test in the presence of cross-section dependence. *Journal of Applied Econometrics* 22: 265–312. [CrossRef]

Rubin, Amir, and Dan Segal. 2015. The effects of economic growth on income inequality in the US. *Journal of Macroeconomics* 45: 258–73. [CrossRef]

Saikkonen, Pentti. 1991. Asymptotically efficient estimation of cointegration regressions. *Econometric Theory* 7: 1–21. [CrossRef]

Solt, Frederick. 2016. The Standardized World Income Inequality Database. *Social Science Quarterly* 97: 1267–81. [CrossRef]

Stock, James H., and Mark W. Watson. 1993. A simple estimator of cointegrating vectors in higher order integrated systems. *Econometrica: Journal of the Econometric Society* 61: 783–820. [CrossRef]

Szirmai, Adam, and Bart Verspagen. 2015. Manufacturing and economic growth in developing countries, 1950–2005. *Structural Change and Economic Dynamics* 34: 46–59. [CrossRef]

Vo, Hong Duc, Nguyen Van Phuc, Nguyen Minh Ha, Vo The Anh, and Nguyen Cong Thang. 2019. Derivatives market and economic growth nexus: Policy implications for emerging markets. *North American Journal of Economics and Finance*. [CrossRef]

Wahiba, Nasfi Fkili, and Malek El Weriemmi. 2014. The Relationship Between Economic Growth and Income Inequality. *International Journal of Economics and Financial Issues* 4: 135–43.

Yang, Yiwen, and Theresa M. Greaney. 2017. Economic growth and income inequality in the Asia-Pacific region: A comparative study of China, Japan, South Korea, and the United States. *Journal of Asian Economics* 48: 6–22. [CrossRef]

Journal of
Risk and Financial Management

MDPI

Article

The Importance of the Financial Derivatives Markets to Economic Development in the World's Four Major Economies

Duc Hong Vo [1,*], Son Van Huynh [1], Anh The Vo [1] and Dao Thi-Thieu Ha [2]

[1]   Business and Economics Research Group, Ho Chi Minh City Open University,
       Ho Chi Minh City 722000, Vietnam; huynhvanson266@yahoo.com (S.V.H.); anh.vt@ou.edu.vn (A.T.V.)
[2]   International Economics Faculty, Banking University Ho Chi Minh City, Ho Chi Minh City 700000, Vietnam;
       daohtt@buh.edu.vn
*   Correspondence: duc.vhong@ou.edu.vn

Received: 28 December 2018; Accepted: 1 February 2019; Published: 14 February 2019

Abstract: Over the past three decades, China and India have attained economic power close to that of Japan and the U.S. During this period, the importance of the derivatives market within the financial market has been widely recognized. However, little supporting evidence is available on its economic effects. This paper investigates the dynamic relationship between the derivatives markets and economic development in these four large economies, which we consider together as the CIJU (China, India, Japan, and the U.S.) group. We use a Granger-causality test in the framework of a vector error correction model (VECM) to examine this causal and dynamic relation with data for the period 1998Q1 to 2017Q4. Derivative markets are found to positively contribute to economic development in the short run in the U.S., Japan, and India, but the effect disappears in the long run. In China, the derivatives market has a negative effect on economic development in the short run. However, in the long run, we observe a positive effect from the derivatives market on economic development based on two long-run estimation techniques, namely, dynamic ordinary least squares and fully modified ordinary least squares. Also, the development of derivative markets causes growth volatility in India, both in the short run and long run.

Keywords: derivatives market; economic development; Granger-causality tests; vector error correction model (VECM); DOLS; FMOLS

JEL Classification: C32; G10; G23; O16

---

1. Introduction

The development of the derivatives market has long been a topic of interest among researchers, policy makers, and financial agencies. It directly plays a vital role in a financial system and greatly contributes to various aspects of an economy as a whole. Lien and Zhang (2008) summarize the roles and functions of the derivatives market in emerging economies, in both theoretical and empirical studies. First, the derivatives market offers an effective mechanism that facilitates the sharing of price risks for commodities traded on the market, helping producers deal with price volatility. Also, it serves as a key role in smooth hedging and risk management by enhancing capital inflows in emerging and developing countries, but it has a negative impact on financial systems by introducing more unpredictable crisis dynamics and is a driver of contagion. Second, it is widely accepted that the derivatives market functions as a channel of risk reduction and redistribution, a means of price discovery and a price stabilizer. Various derivative instruments appear to suit the risk preference of different agents, such as hedgers or spectaculars. The derivatives market is expected to increase information flows in the market. Information about future prices is more likely to reflect future demand, thus influencing production and storage decisions and eventually reducing spot price volatility. Atilgan et al. (2016) offer an updated survey on the literature on derivatives in emerging countries, dividing empirical studies into groups according to the function of the derivatives market. In addition to updating the function of the derivatives market on hedging and risk management as well as price discovery in the spot market, they explore issues regarding market structure and efficiency, as well as risk and price measurement.

The crucial role played by the derivatives market in the financial system is indispensable with a vast amount of research having been conducted, both theoretically and empirically. However, a debate over its effects on economic development has arisen because of a lack of supporting evidence. To the best of our knowledge, few theoretical studies mention the impact of the development of the derivatives market on economic growth (Haiss and Sammer 2010). Some contemporary studies illustrate a link between risk and economic growth, indirectly implying one of the main roles of the derivatives market. Acemoglu and Zilibotti (1997) propose a model in which undiversified agent risks affect aggregate volatility and economic growth through the relocation of funding; agents tend to invest in higher-return projects that appear to have better diversification opportunities. Krebs (2003) reveals that the elimination of idiosyncratic risk leads to a decline in the ratio of physical to human capital and an increase in the degree of investment returns and welfare. In summary, having advanced financial tools fosters a better distribution of resources, both human and financial, to more productive activities, thus enhancing economic growth.

Our research investigates the dynamic relationship among the development of derivatives markets, economic growth, volatility, and other macroeconomic variables, namely, trade openness and interest rates. We consider the world's four large economies with large derivatives markets—China, India, Japan, and the U.S.—which we consider jointly as the CIJU countries. The U.S. is the biggest economy with a real gross domestic product (GDP) of about $17 trillion. China has experienced remarkable growth in its real GDP over the past two decades, now about $8.5 billion, making it the world's second-largest economy. Although its real GDP currently has the slowest increase, Japan is still one of the largest economies, with real GDP of around $6 trillion. India has increased its real GDP more than threefold over this period (approximately $2.5 trillion). The growth in real GDP is accompanied by an increase in GDP per capita in these countries (see Table 1).

Table 1. Real GDP and real GDP per capita in selected countries.

Country	Real GDP ($ Billion)			Real GDP per Capita ($)		
	1998	2007	2016	1998	2007	2016
China	1915	4596	8505	1542	3488	6894
India	710	1333	2466	699	1130	1862
Japan	5217	5848	6053	41,277	45,687	47,661
United States	11,667	15,055	16,920	42,293	49,979	52,319

Source: (World Bank. n.d. n.d.).

Our study contributes to the literature by focusing on the CIJU countries, which have had mature derivatives markets examining both the short- and long-run effects of the derivatives market, the trade openness, and interest rate on economic development, as well as economic growth volatility using several time-series econometric techniques that offer an analytical approach that is appropriate for the available data, and addressing potential endogeneity problems in the regression.

The remainder of the paper is organized as follows. Following this Introduction, Section 2 reviews the relevant literature in terms of theoretical and empirical studies. Section 3 offers an overview of the derivatives market in the CIJU countries. Then, we employ various econometric techniques to examine the nature of stationarity and co-integration of the data in Section 4. Next, we present the data and discuss our empirical results in Section 5. Finally, we present concluding remarks and policy implications in Section 6.

2. Literature Review

A great deal of effort has been expanding in investigating the important influence of the development of the derivatives market on various aspects of financial systems. Haiss and Sammer (2010) explore the role of derivatives in the nexus between finance and growth via three channels: volume, efficiency, and risk. First, in the volume channel, the development of derivatives markets influences the financial market and economic growth by facilitating and increasing the accumulation of capital. It enhances the allocation of resources into investment activities at higher rates of return with the help of the mobility of savings and the higher potential of investment in an enormous range of risky projects. Second, the efficiency channel is a summary of several functions, such as an efficient substitute for cash market trade, resource movement across time and space, and an information provider for risk management and price strategy. It is therefore beneficial for such agents as firms, financial institutions, and the government to have a larger combination of funding sources at lower costs. Third, the risk channel is concerned with the negative impact of derivatives market development on the financial market and economic growth. It may raise speculation about underlying assets, making the financial markets more volatile and adding more uncertainty to the economy. However, using derivatives as hedging instruments could be beneficial for firms and agents (see e.g., Allayannis and Ofek 2001; Bartram et al. 2009; Hammoudeh and McAleer 2013; Huang et al. 2017; Tanha and Dempsey 2017).

Şendeniz-Yüncü et al. (2018) mention that a well-functioning derivatives market makes it possible for firms to share risks efficiently and allows them to conduct projects with higher risk and consequently to boost economic growth. At the same time, agents, such as investors, consumers, and producers, can rely on the derivatives market as an information channel that reflects equilibrium prices so that they can make the right decisions, fostering the efficiency of resource distribution and consequently resulting in economic growth.

The causal relation between the futures market and economic growth in both developed and developing countries is highlighted in Şendeniz-Yüncü et al. (2018)'s study based on time-series data. They find that, in 29 out of the 32 countries studied, the two variables of concern have a long-run relationship and that middle-income countries have a Granger-causality effect from the futures market to economic growth while in high-income countries the effect is reversed. These authors distinguish these opposite unidirectional causations between futures market development and economic growth. On the one hand, the direction starts with futures market development to economic growth in most countries with relatively low real GDP per capita. On the other hand, in countries with a relatively high real per capita GDP, economic growth tends to lead to the development of a futures market. Like Khan et al. (2017) using a panel vector autoregressive method and the Granger causality approach, Vo et al. (2019) show the existence of bidirectional Granger causality between the derivatives market and economic growth, although the causal relation differs between high- and middle-income countries.

The empirical studies focus on the links between economic growth and financial market development, rather than the derivatives market. Various research has approached economic growth via the development of financial intermediaries, such as banking sector development (Beck et al. 2000; King and Levine 1993; Levine et al. 2000; Levine 2005; Menyah et al. 2014; Pradhan et al. 2014; Chaiechi 2012), stock market development (Tsouma 2009; Ang and McKibbin 2007; Huang et al. 2000), and bond market development (Coşkun et al. 2017; Thumrongvit et al. 2013).[1] Pradhan et al. (2014) conduct an analysis on paired relations among four economic components—including the banking sector, stocks, and economic growth—and macro variables, such as foreign direct investment (FDI), trade openness, inflation rate, and government consumption and expenditure. Of these selected variables, the financial

---

[1] Ang (2008) conducts a thorough survey of the literature in relation to the development of finance and growth.

sector, banking, and the derivatives market are found to boost economic growth, whereas the macro variables, namely FDI and trade openness, seem to spur economic activities through the stock market and the banking channel.

Theoretical and empirical research has discussed on the role of these macroeconomic variables in the link between economic growth and financial development or the capital market, which obviously includes the derivatives market. The use of macroeconomic determinants could be either separated (Kim et al. 2010) or simultaneous (Coşkun et al. 2017; Gries et al. 2009; Menyah et al. 2014; Pradhan et al. 2014; Rousseau and Wachtel 2002). Kim et al. (2010) discussed how trade openness influences the development of financial market whereas Menyah et al. (2014) and Coşkun et al. (2017) considered the interlink between financial development, trade openness, and economic growth. In addition, Pradhan et al. (2014) revealed that a combination between a mature financial sector and a macroeconomic policy of keeping inflation rate under control would result in a higher growth rate based on a large sample of Asian countries over more than four decades. Thumrongvit et al. (2013) and Ruiz (2018) also use varieties of macroeconomic factors as control variables in the investigation the effects of financial development on economic growth. Bowdler and Malik (2017) find a statically significant effect of trade openness on inflation volatility.

3. Overview on the Derivatives Market in the CIJU

A derivative product can be defined as a financial instrument whose value depends on, or is derived from, the value of an underlying variable, and it can be traded in derivative markets, traded either on the exchange or over the counter (OTC). The underlying variable often refers to the price of traded assets. The derivatives market has been successful because not only has it attracted many types of agents from hedgers and speculators to arbitrageurs, but it has also brought a great deal of liquidity. The derivatives market is often divided into two small groups: commodity and financial derivatives, which have different instruments, both simple and complex. The four simple instruments are forwards, futures, options, and swaps, whereas the more complex ones include those called exotic and credit derivatives, as well as weather, energy, and insurance derivatives. Details on the roles and the application of these instruments are discussed in Hull (2005) and Sundaram (2012).

Two important components of the derivatives market are futures and options, which are widely traded all around the world. They are divided into ten groups including equity index, individual equity, interest rates, currency, energy, precious metals, non-precious metals, and agriculture. Figure 1 depicts the volume trading over the past decade in the exchanged-traded market, showing an increase in the volume of these types of derivatives traded after the global financial crisis, from around 17.5 billion in 2008 to its peak of 25 billion in 2011. Over the next three years after its peak in 2011, the volume of exchange-trade futures and options dropped considerably, before recovering to its highest level in 2015. An increase in the volume traded after the crisis may imply that corporates or agents have turned into derivative instruments for their hedging purposes.

Among the CIJU countries, Japan and the U.S. have the most long-standing derivatives markets, with the first futures exchange set up in the Dojima Rice Exchange in Osaka, Japan, in 1730. The Chicago Board of Trade opened in the U.S. in 1848 (Sundaram 2012). In contrast, the derivatives market in China began recently, with the opening of the China Financial Futures Exchange in Shanghai in September 2006 and later an OTC derivatives market called the Shanghai Clearing House in November 2009. However, according to a recent overview on derivatives trade in China by Zhou (2016), the country has one of the world's largest commodity markets based on the amount of trade and its growth rate. The China Securities Regulatory Commission (CSRC) reported that trading on the commodity market in China has been at world levels for five years, as the cumulative volume of the future market was around $2.5 billion and its cumulative turnover was approximately $292 trillion. As in India, the country's derivatives market has emerged and grown in recent years with a significantly high use of derivatives instruments. The wave of globalization and liberalization in different parts of the world made risk management more important than ever before (Vashishtha and Kumar 2010). This view is supported by a dramatic increase in the daily turnover on the OTC, for both foreign exchange instruments and interest rate derivatives markets, as indicated in Table 2.

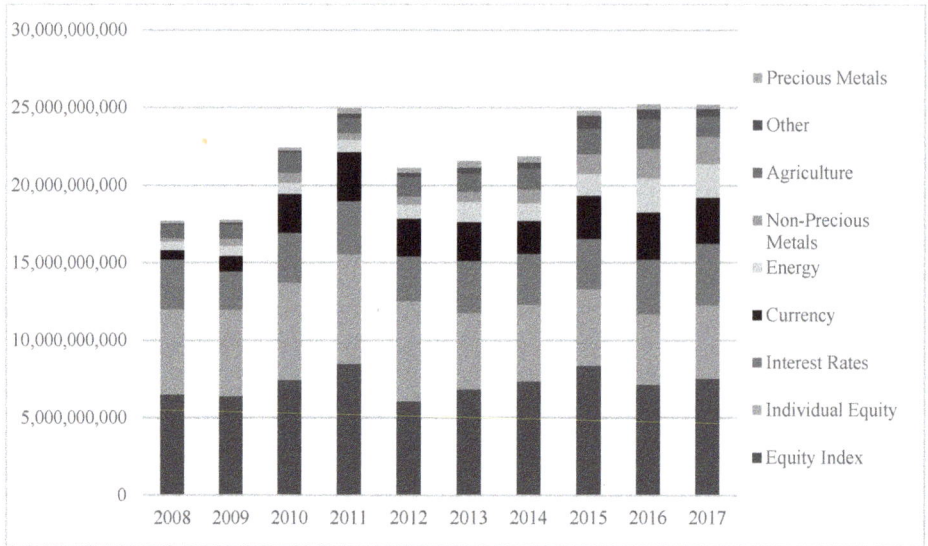

Figure 1. Annual volume of exchange-traded futures and options by category. Source: (Future Industry Association. n.d. n.d.).

Table 2. The daily average OTC turnover.

Country	Foreign Exchange Instruments			Interest Rate Derivatives		
	1998	2007	2016	1998	2007	2016
China	211	9288	72,833			4086
India	2445	38,365	34,330		3395	1858
Japan	146,268	250,223	399,028	31,623	76,357	55,910
United States	383,358	745,202	1,272,122	58,447	525,011	1,240,774

Source: (Bank for International Settlements (BIS)).

4. Methodology

We address the impact of the derivatives market on economic growth and growth volatility in four economies using time-series analysis in the short and long run. First, the short-run impact was considered via the impulse response function (IRFs) through either a vector error correction model (VECM), if a long-run relationship exists, or a vector autoregression (VAR) model. The appearance of the cointegration relationship allowed us to trace the long-run effect with dynamic ordinary least squares (DOLS) and fully modified least squares (FMOLS), so that we could take the endogeneity problem into account. Second, we accessed the causal relationship between the derivatives market, macroeconomic variables, and economic growth, as well as growth volatility with the application of a causality test. Finally, based on our results, we offer policy implications for countries on the path of promoting their derivatives market, especially in emerging and developing areas with underdeveloped financial systems.

4.1. Model Specification

Based on our extensive review of the literature on financial development and economic growth as well as empirical studies on this link, we constructed an analytical framework consisting of the derivatives market, economic growth, and two macroeconomic factors, the interest rate and trade openness, which act as control variables. Our initial goal was to develop a proper procedure for estimating the link between these variables. The regression specification is as follows:

$$LnGDPR_t^i = \alpha_0 + \alpha_1 LnDERR_t^i + \alpha_2 INTR_t^i + \alpha_3 LnOPEN_t^i + \varepsilon_t^i \qquad (1)$$

where i and t represent the sample country ($i = 1, \ldots, 4$) and the time series, respectively. $GDPR_t^i$ is the real gross domestic product (GDP) at time t in country i, and $DERR_t^i$ is the real value of derivatives trading of exchange rate market. The nominal values of GDP and derivatives trading are converted into real terms using the consumer price index (CPI). $INTR_t^i$ is the real interest rate, which is calculated by subtracting the nominal interest rate from inflation rate. $OPEN_t^i$ is the ratio of total exports and imports to GDP. Finally, ε_{it} is the error term, and Ln denotes the logarithm.

A concerning issue is that the excessive development in the derivatives is associated with higher volatility in economic growth as it may increase high uncertainty in the economy. To address this issue, we incorporated the derivatives market, growth volatility, and two macroeconomic factors, the interest rate and trade openness into an integrated framework in which the growth volatility (VOL) took the role of the economic growth as the dependent variable in Equation (1). In other words, we derived the estimated equation as follows:

$$VOL_t^i = \alpha_0 + \alpha_1 LnDERR_t^i + \alpha_2 INTR_t^i + \alpha_3 LnOPEN_t^i + \varepsilon_t^i \qquad (2)$$

where VOL_t^i is the volatility of real growth rate in countries i at year t, measured by the standard deviation of growth rate of four preceding quarters.

The study covered the four major economies in the world, namely, China, India, Japan, and the United States. The timeframe varied across countries, starting in 2006Q3 for China, 2007Q2 for India, and 1998Q1 for Japan and the U.S. Data for the analysis were collected from various sources. Information on the derivatives market originates in the Bank for International Settlements (BIS) database. It is difficult to define a good measure for the derivatives market, which has a wide variety of products. In this paper, we proxy it by total outstanding notation amounts of exchange-traded derivatives.[2] For the remaining variables, we obtained data from the International Monetary Fund (IMF) International Financial Statistics (IFS). Table 3 describes the data for the variables.

Table 3. Data description.

Variable	Obs.	Mean	Std. Dev.	Min	Max
			China		
LnGDPR	46	14.36	0.36	13.60	14.90
VOL	41	0.44	0.28	0.09	1.25
LnDERR	46	1.74	2.23	(1.68)	5.38
INRT	46	5.46	1.24	3.63	7.91
LnOPEN	46	3.79	0.21	3.47	4.22

---

[2] We assumed that the currency used for trading derivatives is that of the country formally issuing it. The total outstanding notation amounts of exchange-traded derivatives in terms of U.S. dollars are listed for the U.S. and the other countries in the sample.

Table 3. *Cont.*

Variable	Obs.	Mean	Std. Dev.	Min	Max
		India			
LnGDPR	42	12.87	0.09	12.74	13.06
VOL	38	0.59	0.57	0.07	1.97
LnDERR	43	2.03	2.80	(4.41)	4.50
INRT	43	9.86	3.92	5.75	18.07
LnOPEN	42	3.55	0.16	3.29	3.81
		Japan			
LnGDPR	78	13.99	0.13	13.70	14.33
VOL	75	0.12	0.05	0.02	0.23
LnDERR	80	9.18	0.73	7.82	10.41
INRT	77	1.65	0.34	0.96	2.29
LnOPEN	78	3.15	0.23	2.68	3.56
		United States			
LnGDPR	80	15.11	0.10	14.91	15.29
VOL	75	0.11	0.04	0.01	0.22
LnDERR	80	12.48	0.59	11.18	13.22
INRT	78	5.81	3.02	2.97	11.97
LnOPEN	80	3.01	0.11	2.78	3.22

4.2. Unit-Root Tests

To investigate how the development of the derivatives market, especially the trading of exchange rates, affects economic growth in the short and long run, we estimated Equations (1) and (2) for each individual country. Using time-series techniques, we began by testing whether the variables were stationary and whether they had a cointegrated relationship. First, to consider the stationarity, we adopted the Dickey–Fuller generalized least squares (DFGLS) unit-root test proposed by Elliott et al. (1996). The DFGLS test is perceived to generate better results with a small sample and has significantly greater power than the previous version of the augmented DF test. The time series was transformed via a generalized least squares (GLS) regression before the test was performed. Moreover, with the long period of about 80 quarters, the data series could exhibit structural breaks due to, for example, the dotcom crash and the 2008 global financial crisis. We also applied the ZA unit-root test by Zivot and Andrews (1992), which takes the existence of structural shifts in the series into account.

4.3. Cointegration Test

The next step is to examine the long-run relationship among four selected variables. The study employs the bound testing approach to cointegration by Pesaran et al. (2001).[3] Two proposed tests, standard F- and t-statistics, were performed on the basis of the conditional error correction mechanism using the autoregressive distributed lag (ARDL) model. Equations (1) and (2) is expressed in terms of the error correction version of the ARDL model as follows:

$$\Delta LnGDPR_t^i = \gamma_0 + \sum_{j=1}^{n} \gamma_{1j}\Delta LnGDPR_{t-j}^i +$$
$$\sum_{j=0}^{n} \gamma_{2j}\Delta LnDERR_{t-j}^i + \sum_{j=0}^{n} \gamma_{3j}\Delta INTR_{t-j}^i + \sum_{j=0}^{n} \gamma_{4j}\Delta LnOPEN_{t-j}^i + \delta_1 LnGDPR_{t-1}^i + \delta_2 LnDERR_{t-1}^i + \quad (3)$$
$$\delta_3 INTR_{t-1}^i + \delta_4 LnOPEN_{t-1}^i + \varepsilon_t^i$$

---

[3] The choice of a bound testing approach to cointegration has advantages. Not only does it do well in a small sample like ours, but it also ignores the problem of testing the long-run relationship between a dependent variable and a set of regressors irrespective of whether the regressors are I(0) or I(1). For more details on its advantages and application (see e.g., Pesaran et al. 2001; Narayan and Smyth 2005; Nguyen and Vo 2019).

$$\Delta VOL_t^i = \alpha_0 + \sum_{j=1}^n \alpha_{1j} \Delta VOL_{t-j}^i + \sum_{j=0}^n \alpha_{2j} \Delta LnDERR_{t-j}^i +$$
$$\sum_{j=0}^n \alpha_{3j} \Delta INTR_{t-j}^i + \sum_{j=0}^n \alpha_{4j} \Delta LnOPEN_{t-j}^i + \theta_1 LnGDPR_{t-1}^i + \theta_2 LnDERR_{t-1}^i + \theta_3 INTR_{t-1}^i + \quad (4)$$
$$\theta_4 LnOPEN_{t-1}^i + \varepsilon_t^i$$

where Δ denotes the first difference of a variable.

The bound test cointegration consisted of two steps. First, the dependent variable was regressed on a set of regressors with the ARDL model using the ordinary least squares (OLS) technique. Before the bound test was applied in the next step, the error term should be tested to ensure it was serially uncorrelated and homoskedastic. The second step was to confirm the presence of cointegration by tracing whether all the estimated coefficients of the lag level equaled zero with the F- and t-statistics. That is, the t-statistics tested the null hypothesis $\delta_1 = 0$ against the alternative $\delta_1 \neq 0$, while the F-statistics tested the null hypothesis $\delta_i = 0$ $(i = \overline{1,4})$ against the alternative of at least $\delta_i \neq 0$ $(i = \overline{1,4})$, provided that four lags were used. If the estimated F-statistics were smaller than the lower-bound critical value, larger than the upper-bound value, and between the lower- and upper-bound value, the null hypothesis was not rejected, rejected, and inconclusive, respectively. The lower- and upper-bound critical values are presented in Pesaran et al. (2001). The rejection of the null hypothesis means that a set of time series was cointegrated, implying the existence of a long-run relationship. Also, we applied the method by Gregory and Hansen (1996) to test for the presence of a structural break as a robustness test.

4.4. Granger-Causality Test

Equations (1) and (2) might show a causal relationship between the independent and dependent variables. A similar equation could be proposed, with each current independent variable acting as a dependent variable in turn. Therefore, we employed a causality test to clarify the direction of the variables concerned. Without the existent of the long-run link among the variables in Equations (1) and (2), we performed the traditional causality test proposed by Engle and Granger (1987) on the VAR model.

To investigate the uni- or bidirectional causal link between economic growth, growth volatility, and derivatives market development in view of the appearance of a long-run relationship, we depicted the Granger-causality test using a VECM framework in the following equation:

$$\Delta Z_t = \Pi Z_{t-1} + \Gamma_1 \Delta Z_{t-1} + \Gamma_2 \Delta Z_{t-2} + \cdots + \Gamma_{p-1} \Delta Z_{t-p+1} + \varepsilon_t \quad (5)$$

where $\Pi = -\left(I_m - \sum_{i=1}^p A_i\right)$ and $\Gamma_i = -(1 - \sum_{j=1}^i A_j)$ for $i = 1, \ldots, p-1$. The matrix $\Pi \,(= \alpha\beta')$ includes both the speed of adjustment to the equilibrium (α) and long-run information (β).

For investigating the causal relationship between economic growth and derivatives markets based on Equation (1), the vector Z consists of $\Delta Z_t = [\Delta LnGDPR, \Delta LnDERR, \Delta INTR, \Delta LnOPEN]'$, and for the case of growth volatility based on Equation (2), the vector Z comprises of $\Delta Z_t = [\Delta VOL, \Delta LnDERR, \Delta INTR, \Delta LnOPEN]'$.

The testing for Granger-causality was based on the null hypothesis that the coefficients (Γ_i) on the lagged values of independent variables were not statistically different from zero simultaneously, using F-statistics (Wald test). In cases of the rejection of the null hypothesis, a conclusion was that the independent variable did cause the dependent variable, and both the independent and dependent variables had a stable relationship in the long run.

5. Empirical Results

5.1. Unit Root Tests and Cointegration Tests

To determine the relation between the development of a derivatives market, economic growth, and macroeconomic variables in the short- and long-run, we first checked the stationarity of all these variables. The advanced DFGLS test by Elliott et al. (1996) and the ZA test by Zivot and Andrews (1992) are performed and presented in Table 4. The DFGLS revealed that some variables were stationary, such as the interest rate in China and trade openness in the United States while others contained unit roots. As in the DFGLS test, most variables in these four countries were found to have unit roots based on the ZA test.[4] Seven out of eight unit root tests confirmed the variable of growth volatility to be stationary at an at least 10 per cent significance level. Thus, a conclusion was that some were integrated I(0), and most series were I(1), depending on the type of stationarity test. This characteristic is quite normal for macroeconomic variables.

Table 4. Results of unit-root tests.

	China	India	Japan	United States
	DFGLS			
LnGDPR	−1.68	−2.24	−1.59	−1.25
VOL	−2.69	−2.91 *	−3.66 ***	−2.97 *
LnDERR	−1.54	−1.47	−1.37	−1.33
INTR	−2.90 *	−1.16	−1.9	−2.84 *
LnOPEN	−2.53	−1.37	−2.37	−2.91 *
	ZA			
LnGDPR	−4.28	−3.3	−4.07	−5.17 **
VOL	−4.69 *	−5.70 ***	−4.67 *	−4.83 **
LnDERR	−3.82	−10.40 ***	−3.89	−3.37
INTR	−3.58	−3.41	−5.19	−3.67
LnOPEN	−3.92	−4.11	−3.93	−3.72

Notes: ***, **, and * denote significance at the level of 1%, 5%, and 10%, respectively. For the Elliott et al. (1996) DFGLS test, critical values for 1%, 5%, and 10% were −3.58, −3.03, and −2.74, respectively. For Zivot and Andrews (1992) ZA test, critical values for 1%, 5%, and 10% were −5.34, −4.80, and −4.58, respectively.

To consider whether the long-run relationship existed among selected variables in each country, we performed two types of cointegration tests: the ARDL bounds tests by Pesaran et al. (2001), and the GH test by Gregory and Hansen (1996) to check the sensitivity of the conclusion.

Results of the cointegration tests are shown in Table 5. Equation (3) with the real GDP being the dependent variable is shown in Panel A while the case of growth volatility in Equation (4) is presented in Panel B. From Panel A, according to the computed *F*-statistics and *t*-statistics, it had a high likelihood of rejecting the null hypothesis of no cointegration at the 1 per cent significance level in China. Based on the *F*-statistics, the null hypothesis was rejected in Japan, but this conclusion was not supported by the *t*-statistics. In the two remaining countries (India and United States), no evidence rejected the null at even the 10% significance level. The GH tests appeared to support the findings from the ARDL bounds tests, with additional information on a structural break in each country. More specifically, a structural break was found in China and the United States in 2008, and in India and Japan in 2011 and 2013, respectively. Based on the cointegration tests, we therefore came to the conclusion that a long-run relationship among variables existed in China, but not India, Japan, and the United States. For the growth volatility, Panel B of Table 5 illustrates that both the bound test and GH test failed to reject the null hypothesis of no cointegration for the case of China, Japan, and the United States, while India experienced the long run relationship among the growth volatility, derivatives market, trade openness, and interest rate.[5]

---

[4] The two types of unit-root tests rejected the null hypothesis that each variable contains unit roots in all countries when the variables were in terms of difference. To conserve space, the results are available upon request.

[5] As the sample was relatively small, we use the critical values for the bound tests proposed by Narayan (2005). With 40 observations included in the estimation with an unrestricted intercept and unrestricted trend, the upper bound of the critical values were 5.64 and 3.76 at the significance level of 5% and 10%, respectively. Our results also confirmed the cointegration relationship in China for the case of economic growth and in India for the case of economic volatility.

Table 5. Results of Cointegration tests.

	China	India	Japan	United States
Panel A				
	Bound test			
F-statistics	13.32 ***	2.82	6.73 ***	1.43
t-statistics	−5.24 ***	−1.47	−2.77	−1.86
	GH test			
z-statistics	−7.84 ***	−4.76	−4.42	−5.50 *
Period break	2008Q2	2011Q4	2013Q3	2008Q3
Panel B				
	Bound test			
F-statistics	−2.41	−5.38 ***	4.44	2.69
t-statistics	−1.51	−2.07	−3.94	−3.27
	GH test			
z-statistics	−5.16	−6.04 **	−5.50	−4.89
Period break	2007Q4	2010Q1	2011Q3	2001Q2

Notes: ***, **, and * denote significance at the level of 1%, 5%, and 10%, respectively. The bound tests was based on Pesaran et al. (2001) and the GH test on Gregory and Hansen (1996).

5.2. Effect of Derivatives Market Development on Economic Growth and Volatility

With the presence of cointegration among derivatives, trade openness, and interest rate and economic growth in China, as well as growth volatility in India, we analyzed its long-run relationship further. We estimated Equation (1) for China and (2) for India using two long-run estimations, DOLS and FMOLS, and present the results in Table 6. First, in addition to revealing the significantly positive effect on economic growth of the interest rate in the long run, these two methods showed the positive influence of the derivatives market on economic growth. Our results provided supporting evidence for an abundance of theoretical and empirical studies on the impact of the general development of financial markets to economic growth in the long run (Ang 2008; Beck et al. 2000; Levine 2005; Levine et al. 2000). In particular, our findings appear to support the theory of Baluch and Ariff (2007), who underline the role of liquidity level of derivatives markets in facilitating economic growth. Also, Zhou (2016) statistically indicates the founding and development of China's derivative market have contributing effects to the country's massive import, fast economic growth, and gradual maturity of financial structure. Second, we found the negative impact of the financial market on growth volatility in India. This implies that an excessive increase in the development of derivatives market can have unfavorable effects in the long run for India. The similar pattern was recorded with trade openness in India.

Table 6. Long-run impact of the derivatives markets on economic growth and growth volatility.

	Dependent Variable: *LnGDPR*				Dependent Variable: *VOL*			
	China				India			
	DOLS		FMOLS		DOLS		FMOLS	
LnDERR	0.120 ***	(0.0228)	0.048 *	(0.0253)	−0.887 ***	(0.0593)	−0.581 ***	(0.0404)
LnOPEN	−0.107	(0.5363)	−1.830 ***	(0.5229)	−1.844 ***	(0.1815)	−1.036 ***	(0.1310)
INTR	0.135 **	(0.0662)	0.199 **	(0.0840)	0.033	(0.0206)	0.027	(0.0157)
Constant	13.967 ***	(0.8823)	20.176 ***	(1.6764)	5.089 ***	(0.4062)	2.905 ***	(0.3849)

Notes: ***, **, * denote significance at the level of 1%, 5%, and 10%, respectively. Standard deviation is in parentheses. The estimation includes a dummy for the structural break.

We then examined the short-run relationship among GDP growth, derivatives market development, trade openness, and the interest rate. Because of the presence of cointegration, it was better to use VECM rather than VAR. Therefore, we applied the former approach regarding China and adopt the latter method for the other countries using Equation (5), with the variables in first difference. We carried out impulse response functions (IRFs) and depict the results in Figure 2. Graphical representations of the IRFs can illustrate the dynamic relationship, as they show the response of a variable to a shock to itself and to other variables over time. In particular, a response to GDP growth is positively affected by its own shock, with the largest magnitude experienced in China. A response to GDP growth from trade openness was much more significant in China than in the other three countries, and the response among the countries in reaction to the interest rate showed a mixed pattern. Economic growth in China tended to be positively influenced by the derivatives market in the first year but this effect turned negative over time, and the other three countries had a positive response although with a moderate magnitude.

We show the IRFs for the relationship between growth volatility and other variables in Figure 3. The IRFs were based on the VECM for the case of India and the VAR for China, Japan, and United States due to the results from the cointegration tests. Volatility shocks were recorded to be positively affected itself in China but the effect gradually declined over time while volatility in Japan had an increasingly cumulative effect by itself over the period. Shocks in the derivatives market were found to have a positive effect on the growth volatility in India and Japan, but this effect was persistent overtime. The volatility in the growth rate in United States was marginally affected by shocks in the derivatives market while no effect was found for the case of China. When it comes to the effect of the shocks of trade openness, only India experienced a negative effect associated with growth volatility and the three remaining countries had almost no effect. The similar pattern was observed for China where growth volatility was related to shocks in interest rates.

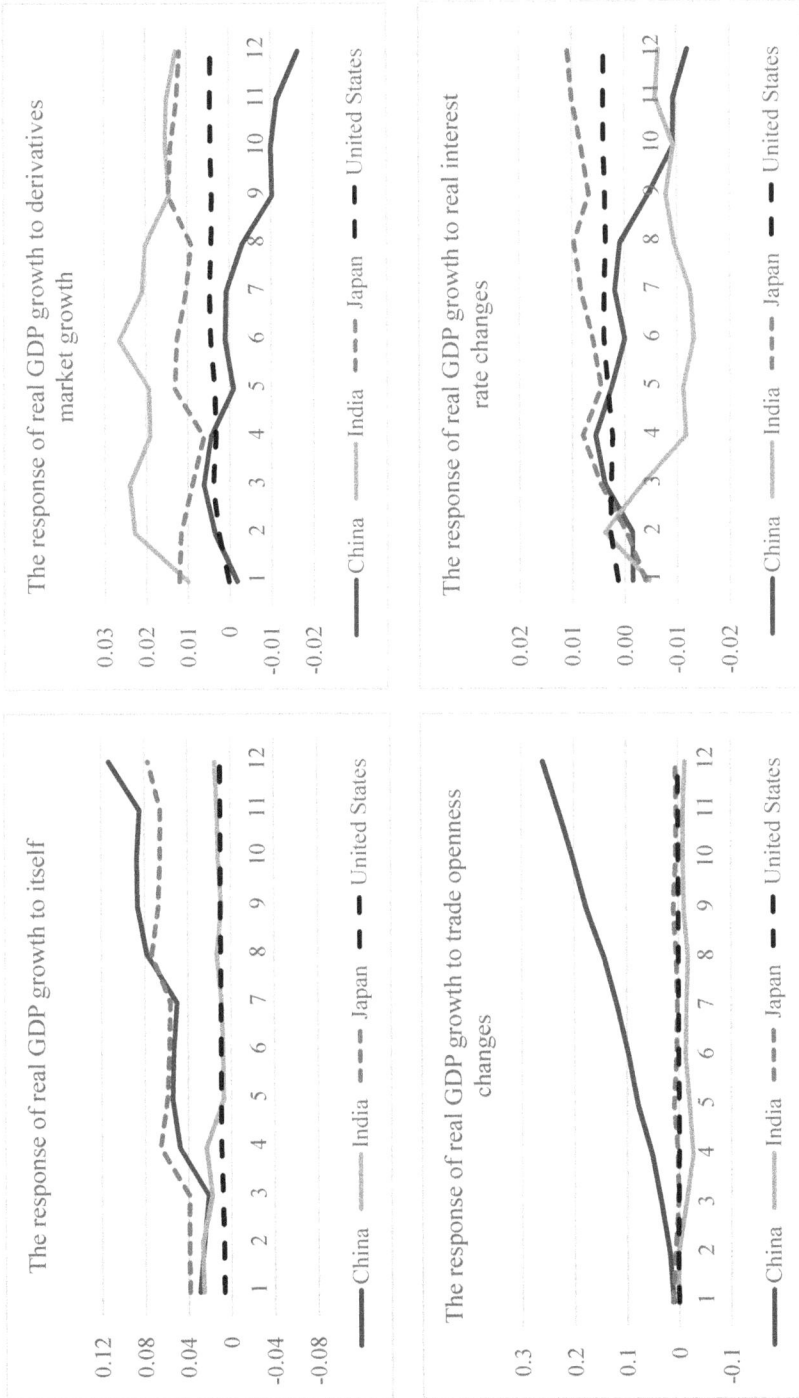

Figure 2. Cumulative orthogonalized impulse response function (the model includes GDP growth).

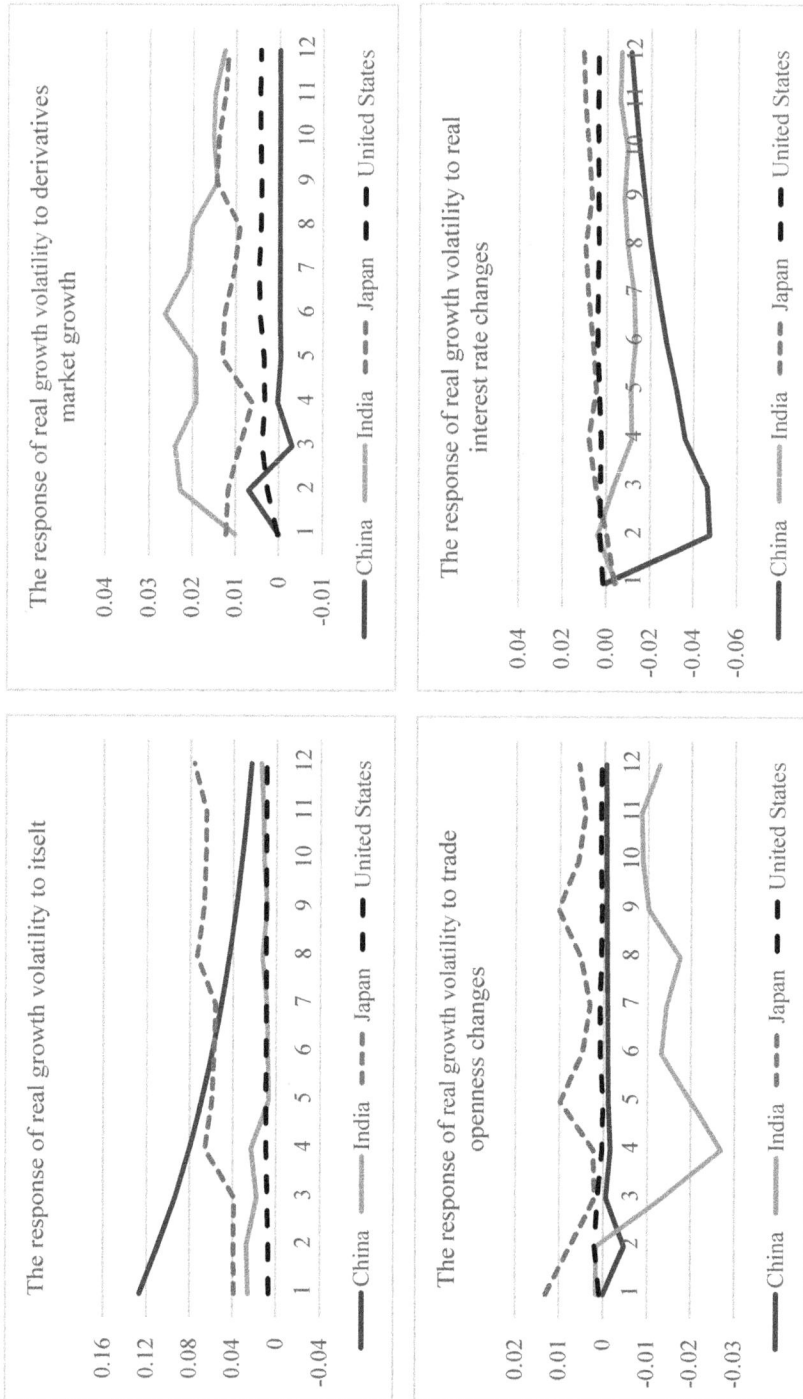

Figure 3. Cumulative orthogonalized impulse response function (the model include the volatility of GDP growth).

to

5.3. Granger Causality Effect of Derivatives Market Development on Economic Growth and Volatility

Finally, we performed a Granger-causality test to reveal any causal relations among variables. Reported in Table 7 are the results pertaining to the model that includes economic growth with several interesting findings. First, we found no causal link between economic growth and the derivatives market in China and Japan. Meanwhile, a unidirectional impact of economic growth on the derivatives market was found in India, and the reverse was observed in the United States. Second, economic growth tended to be closely associated with trade openness, as a bidirectional causal relation was found in India and Japan, and a unidirectional impact from economic growth on trade openness was seen in Japan. Its relation with the interest rate was less significant, with a unidirectional relationship found only in Japan and China. Third, when it came to a causal relation between the derivatives markets and the two remaining variables, India had the most active reaction, as the derivatives market was found to have a bidirectional relation with the interest rate and a unidirectional impact on trade openness. Japan had a unidirectional impact on the derivatives market on both the interest rate and trade openness, whereas it was unidirectionally affected by trade openness in the United States. Our findings in relation to the causality relationship were quite different from the recent studies. Vo et al. (2019) show the bidirectional Granger-causality between derivatives markets and economic growth internationally using the panel vector autoregressive (PVAR) method, while Şendeniz-Yüncü et al. (2018) illustrate the unidirectional causality in high-income countries from economic growth to the development of a futures market, a fraction of the general derivative market.

Table 7. Causality tests (the model includes GDP growth).

Null Hypothesis	China	India	Japan	United States
Δ*LnGDPR* does not Granger-cause Δ*LnDERR*	5.91	10.79 **	5.07	2.14
Δ*LnDERR* does not Granger-cause Δ*LnGDPR*	3.91	7.62	1.85	12.7 ***
Δ*LnGDPR* does not Granger-cause Δ*LnOPEN*	3.92	13.84 ***	13.38 ***	13.52 ***
Δ*LnOPEN* does not Granger-cause Δ*LnGDPR*	1.67	9.29 **	7.78 *	3.09
Δ*LnGDPR* does not Granger-cause Δ*INTR*	2.53	9.88 **	9.20 *	3.37
Δ*INTR* does not Granger-cause Δ*LnGDPR*	4.06	5.94	1.92	6.13
Δ*LnDERR* does not Granger-cause Δ*LnOPEN*	9.96 **	9.84 **	9.77 **	5.62
Δ*LnOPEN* does not Granger-cause Δ*LnDERR*	1.69	6.46	1.47	6.87 *
Δ*LnDERR* does not Granger-cause Δ*INTR*	3.60	40.51 ***	11.68 **	0.32
Δ*INTR* does not Granger-cause Δ*LnDERR*	2.78	9.57 **	1.16	2.64
Δ*LnOPEN* does not Granger-cause Δ*INTR*	4.39	7.78 *	3.57	2.16
Δ*INTR* does not Granger-cause Δ*LnOPEN*	5.18	4.77	0.23	9.77 **

Notes: ***, **, * denotes significance at the level of 1%, 5%, and 10%, respectively. The Wald test, which tests the joint significance of the lagged values of the independent variable is reported. The Wald test followed a chi-square distribution. Granger-causality results were based on a vector error correction model (VECM) for China and a vector autoregressive model (VAR) for India, Japan, and the United States. China, India, and Japan were regressed based on four lags, and the United States was based on three lags. Δ indicates the variable is in the first different form while *Ln* denotes the variable is in terms of logarithm.

Table 8 reports the causal relationship pertaining to the model that based on growth volatility and other variables. Generally, variables had more Granger-causal links to each other in the case of India rather than any other countries, namely, China, Japan, and United States. Specifically, India had experienced the bidirectional Granger link among growth volatility, derivatives market, and the interest rate. India had also experienced the unidirectional Granger effect from the derivatives market to growth volatility. This unfavorably potential effect empirically suggested a warning concern that the development of derivatives markets may generate an uncertainty to the domestic economy as raised by (Haiss and Sammer 2010). In China, the interest rate was found to have a unidirectional effect on both trade openness and growth volatility. On the contrary, United States had experienced the unidirectional impact of the derivatives market and interest rate on trade openness. There was a unidirectional influence from the development in the derivatives markets on interest rate.

Table 8. Causality tests (the model include the volatility of GDP growth).

Null Hypothesis	China	India	Japan	United States
ΔVOL does not Granger-cause $\Delta LnDERR$	0.02	9.69 **	1.18	0.00
$\Delta LnDERR$ does not Granger-cause ΔVOL	1.42	30.36 ***	1.68	0.15
ΔVOL does not Granger-cause $\Delta LnOPEN$	2.23	5.42	2.63	0.12
$\Delta LnOPEN$ does not Granger-cause ΔVOL	0.75	2.56	0.17	0.08
ΔVOL does not Granger-cause $\Delta INTR$	1.75	90.55 ***	0.83	0.02
$\Delta INTR$ does not Granger-cause ΔVOL	4.67 **	14.45 ***	0.62	0.56
$\Delta LnDERR$ does not Granger-cause $\Delta LnOPEN$	0.64	9.50 **	0.09	9.8 ***
$\Delta LnOPEN$ does not Granger-cause $\Delta LnDERR$	1.62	1.12	0.05	0.07
$\Delta LnDERR$ does not Granger-cause $\Delta INTR$	0.04	146.63 ***	3.24 *	0.10
$\Delta INTR$ does not Granger-cause $\Delta LnDERR$	1.32	12.80 ***	0.03	0.01
$\Delta LnOPEN$ does not Granger-cause $\Delta INTR$	0.81	42.39 ***	1.27	0.00
$\Delta INTR$ does not Granger-cause $\Delta LnOPEN$	13.31 ***	2.77	0.21	3.39 *

Notes: ***, **, * denote significance at the level of 1%, 5%, and 10%, respectively. The Wald test, which tests the joint significance of the lagged values of the independent variable is reported. The Wald test followed a chi-square distribution. Granger-causality results were based on the VAR model for China, Japan, and the United States using one lag, and India was based on the VECM with four lags. Δ indicates the variable is in the first different form while Ln denotes the variable is in terms of logarithm.

6. Concluding Remarks

The development of the derivatives market has played an increasingly important role in the financial market, serving not only as an effective hedging instrument but also as a useful provider of immediate information, thus boosting the efficiency of financial market operations. Recent interest focuses on how the development of derivatives markets influences the economy as a whole. Some research has theoretically suggested that the derivatives market positively affects economic growth by accelerating capital accumulation, making investment more efficient by offering more diversity in highly risky projects and reducing uncertainty in the economy as a risk hedging tool. However, insufficient empirical studies have been conducted on this important relation.

We study the relation between economic growth, volatility, and the derivatives market, as well as other macroeconomic variables: trade openness and the interest rate. We selected the four major economies (China, India, Japan, and the U.S.), which have a mature derivatives market, for our analysis using time-series econometric methods on an updated dataset up to the last quarter of 2017. The application of time-series techniques varies across countries because of the nature of the data. As such, several advanced, appropriate, and robust econometric techniques are used in this study.

The derivative market in China was found to have a significantly negative impact on economic growth in the short term, but this impact turns positive in the long run. The three remaining countries (India, Japan, and the U.S.), the results also reveal no long-run impact of the derivatives market on economic growth, but a positive impact was found in the short run. Moreover, the causality test indicates that India has a unidirectional effect from the derivatives market to economic growth whereas the reverse pattern is observed in the U.S., and no causality effect was found between these two variables in China and Japan. Also, India had experienced the bidirectional causal relationship India among growth volatility, the derivatives markets, and the interest rate.

We concluded that development of the derivatives markets had a positive effect on economic growth in the short run, as indicated in India, Japan, and the U.S., although it may gradually turn negative, as in China. However, it was found to generate an unexpected effect on growth volatility in India. In light of these findings, this research supports the theory on the favorable effect of the derivatives market on economic growth. As such, we suggest that any strategy for enhancing or boosting the size of the derivatives market should be encouraged, especially in emerging and developing countries so as to boost economic development, although it is important to have a proper regulatory framework in order to prevent unintended consequences, such as creating a negative impact in the short run as seen in China, causing the growth volatility as observed in India.

A limitation of the current paper is that the sample sizes including four selected countries covered approximately 80 observations and the applications of VAR or VECM required time lags for all variables, leading to a significant reduction of the number of the degrees of freedom. As a consequence, it raised a concern in relation to the biased coefficients in the estimation. In our future studies, a more comprehensive inclusion of dynamic panel data models, unit root tests, or cointegration analysis will be applied to ensure that empirical findings are more robust.

Author Contributions: D.H.V., S.V.H., A.T.V., and D.T.-T.H. have contributed jointly to all of the sections of the paper.

Funding: This research was funded by Ho Chi Minh City Open University grant number E2019.13.1.

Acknowledgments: We would like to thank the two anonymous referees for their helpful comments and suggestions. We also thank the participants at the 4th International Conference on China's Rise and Internationalization (Ningbo University, Ningbo, China, 7–8 December 2018). The authors are responsible for any remaining errors or shortcomings.

Conflicts of Interest: The authors declare no conflict of interest.

References

Acemoglu, Daron, and Fabrizio Zilibotti. 1997. Was Prometheus unbound by chance? Risk, diversification, and growth. *Journal of Political Economy* 105: 709–51. [CrossRef]

Allayannis, George, and Eli Ofek. 2001. Exchange rate exposure, hedging, and the use of foreign currency derivatives. *Journal of International Money and Finance* 20: 273–96. [CrossRef]

Ang, James. B. 2008. A survey of recent developments in the literature of finance and growth. *Journal of Economic Surveys* 22: 536–76. [CrossRef]

Ang, James B., and Warwick J. McKibbin. 2007. Financial liberalization, financial sector development and growth: Evidence from Malaysia. *Journal of Development Economics* 84: 215–33. [CrossRef]

Atilgan, Yigit, K. Ozgur Demirtas, and Koray D. Simsek. 2016. Derivative markets in emerging economies: A survey. *International Review of Economics and Finance* 42: 88–102. [CrossRef]

Bank for International Settlements (BIS). n.d. Available online: https://www.bis.org/statistics/ (accessed on 25 September 2018).

Bartram, Söhnke M., Gregory W. Brown, and Frank R. Fehle. 2009. International evidence on financial derivatives usage. *Financial Management* 38: 185–206. [CrossRef]

Beck, Thorsten, Ross Levine, and Norman Loayza. 2000. Finance and the sources of growth. *Journal of Financial Economics* 58: 261–300. [CrossRef]

Baluch, A., and Mohamed Ariff. 2007. *Derivative Markets and Economic Growth: Is There a Relationship?* Working Paper Series 13/2007; Australia: Bond University, Globalization & Development Centre, Available online: https://library.bond.edu.au/ (accessed on 10 September 2018).

Bowdler, Christopher, and Adeel Malik. 2017. Openness and inflation volatility: Panel data evidence. *North American Journal of Economics and Finance* 41: 57–69. [CrossRef]

Chaiechi, Taha. 2012. Financial development shocks and contemporaneous feedback effect on key macroeconomic indicators: A post Keynesian time series analysis. *Economic Modelling* 29: 487–501. [CrossRef]

Coşkun, Yener, Ünal Seven, H. Murat Ertuğrul, and Talat Ulussever. 2017. Capital market and economic growth nexus: Evidence from Turkey. *Central Bank Review* 17: 19–29. [CrossRef]

Elliott, Graham, Thomas J. Rothenberg, and James H. Stock. 1996. Efficient tests for an autoregressive unit root. *Econometrica* 64: 813–36. [CrossRef]

Engle, Robert F., and Clive WJ Granger. 1987. Co-integration and error correction: Representation, estimation, and testing. *Econometrica* 55: 251–76. [CrossRef]

Future Industry Association. n.d. Available online: https://fia.org/ (accessed on 25 September 2018).

Gregory, Allan W., and Bruce E. Hansen. 1996. Residual-based tests for cointegration in models with regime shifts. *Journal of Econometrics* 70: 99–126. [CrossRef]

Gries, Thomas, Manfred Kraft, and Daniel Meierrieks. 2009. Linkages between financial deepening, trade openness, and economic development: Causality evidence from Sub-Saharan Africa. *World Development* 37: 1849–60. [CrossRef]

Haiss, Peter, and Bernhard Sammer. 2010. The Impact of Derivatives Markets on Financial Integration, Risk, and Economic Growth. Available online: http://dx.doi.org/10.2139/ssrn.1720586 (accessed on 4 October 2018).

Hammoudeh, Shawkat, and Michael McAleer. 2013. Risk management and financial derivatives: An overview. *North American Journal of Economics and Finance* 25: 109–15. [CrossRef]

Huang, Bwo-Nung, Chin-Wei Yang, and John Wei-Shan Hu. 2000. Causality and cointegration of stock markets among the United States, Japan and the South China Growth Triangle. *International Review of Financial Analysis* 9: 281–97. [CrossRef]

Huang, Pinghsun, M. Humayun Kabir, and Yan Zhang. 2017. Does corporate derivative use reduce stock price exposure? Evidence from UK firms. *Quarterly Review of Economics and Finance* 65: 128–36. [CrossRef]

Hull, John C. 2005. *Options, Futures, and Other Derivatives*. Upper Saddle River: Pearson Education.

Khan, Habib Hussain, Ali M. Kutan, Iram Naz, and Fiza Qureshi. 2017. Efficiency, growth and market power in the banking industry: New approach to efficient structure hypothesis. *North American Journal of Economics and Finance* 42: 531–45. [CrossRef]

Kim, Dong-Hyeon, Shu-Chin Lin, and Yu-Bo Suen. 2010. Dynamic effects of trade openness on financial development. *Economic Modelling* 27: 254–61. [CrossRef]

King, Robert G., and Ross Levine. 1993. Finance and growth: Schumpeter might be right. *The Quarterly Journal of Economics* 108: 717–37. [CrossRef]

Krebs, Tom. 2003. Growth and welfare effects of business cycles in economies with idiosyncratic human capital risk. *Review of Economic Dynamics* 6: 846–68. [CrossRef]

Levine, Ross. 2005. Finance and growth: Theory and evidence. *Handbook of Economic Growth* 1: 865–934.

Levine, Ross, Norman Loayza, and Thorsten Beck. 2000. Financial intermediation and growth: Causality and causes. *Journal of Monetary Economics* 46: 31–77. [CrossRef]

Lien, Donald, and Mei Zhang. 2008. A survey of emerging derivatives markets. *Emerging Markets Finance and Trade* 44: 39–69. [CrossRef]

Menyah, Kojo, Saban Nazlioglu, and Yemane Wolde-Rufael. 2014. Financial development, trade openness and economic growth in African countries: New insights from a panel causality approach. *Economic Modelling* 37: 386–94. [CrossRef]

Narayan, Paresh Kumar. 2005. The saving and investment nexus for China: Evidence from cointegration tests. *Applied Economics* 37: 1979–90. [CrossRef]

Narayan, Paresh Kumar, and Russell Smyth. 2005. Electricity consumption, employment and real income in Australia evidence from multivariate Granger causality tests. *Energy Policy* 33: 1109–16. [CrossRef]

Nguyen, Phuc Van, and Duc Hong Vo. 2019. Macroeconomics Determinants of Exchange Rate Pass-Through: New Evidence from the Asia-Pacific Region. *Emerging Markets Finance and Trade*, 1–16. [CrossRef]

Pesaran, M. Hashem, Yongcheol Shin, and Richard J. Smith. 2001. Bounds testing approaches to the analysis of level relationships. *Journal of Applied Econometrics* 16: 289–326. [CrossRef]

Pradhan, Rudra P., Mak B. Arvin, John H. Hall, and Sahar Bahmani. 2014. Causal nexus between economic growth, banking sector development, stock market development, and other macroeconomic variables: The case of ASEAN countries. *Review of Financial Economics* 23: 155–73. [CrossRef]

Rousseau, Peter L., and Paul Wachtel. 2002. Inflation thresholds and the finance–growth nexus. *Journal of International Money and Finance* 21: 777–93. [CrossRef]

Ruiz, Jose L. 2018. Financial development, institutional investors, and economic growth. *International Review of Economics and Finance* 54: 218–24. [CrossRef]

Şendeniz-Yüncü, İlkay, Levent Akdeniz, and Kürşat Aydoğan. 2018. Do stock index futures affect economic growth? Evidence from 32 countries. *Emerging Markets Finance and Trade* 54: 410–29. [CrossRef]

Sundaram, Rangarajan K. 2012. *Derivatives in Financial Market Development*. London: International Growth Centre, p. 39.

Tanha, Hassan, and Michael Dempsey. 2017. Derivatives usage in emerging markets following the GFC: Evidence from the GCC countries. *Emerging Markets Finance and Trade* 53: 170–79. [CrossRef]

Thumrongvit, Patara, Yoonbai Kim, and Chong Soo Pyun. 2013. Linking the missing market: The effect of bond markets on economic growth. *International Review of Economics and Finance* 27: 529–41. [CrossRef]

Tsouma, Ekaterini. 2009. Stock returns and economic activity in mature and emerging markets. *Quarterly Review of Economics and Finance* 49: 668–85. [CrossRef]

Vashishtha, Ashutosh, and Satish Kumar. 2010. Development of financial derivatives market in India—A case study. *International Research Journal of Finance and Economics* 37: 15–29.

Vo, Duc Hong, Phuc Van Nguyen, Ha Minh Nguyen, Anh The Vo, and Thang Cong Nguyen. 2019. Derivatives market and economic growth nexus: Policy implication for emerging markets. *North American Journal of Economics and Finance*. [CrossRef]

World Bank. n.d. Available online: https://data.worldbank.org/.

Zhou, Tianying. 2016. Overview on derivatives trade in china. *European Scientific Journal* 12: 153–62. [CrossRef]

Zivot, Eric, and Donald W. K. Andrews. 1992. Further evidence on the great crash, the oil price shock, and the unit root hypothesis. *Journal of Business and Economic Statistics* 10: 251–70.

Journal of
Risk and Financial Management

MDPI

Article

Multivariate Student versus Multivariate Gaussian Regression Models with Application to Finance

Thi Huong An Nguyen [1,2,†], Anne Ruiz-Gazen [1,*,†], Christine Thomas-Agnan [1,†] and Thibault Laurent [3,†]

[1]   Toulouse School of Economics, University of Toulouse Capitole, 21 allée de Brienne, 31000 Toulouse, France; huongan.nguyen@tse-fr.eu (T.H.A.N.); christine.thomas@tse-fr.eu (C.T.-A.)
[2]   Department of Economics, DaNang Architecture University, Da Nang 550000, Vietnam
[3]   Toulouse School of Economics, CNRS, University of Toulouse Capitole, 31000 Toulouse, France; thibault.laurent@tse-fr.eu
*   Correspondence: anne.ruiz-gazen@tse-fr.eu; Tel.: +33-561-12-8767
†   These authors contributed equally to this work.

Received: 29 December 2018; Accepted: 31 January 2019; Published: 9 February 2019

Abstract: To model multivariate, possibly heavy-tailed data, we compare the multivariate normal model (N) with two versions of the multivariate Student model: the independent multivariate Student (IT) and the uncorrelated multivariate Student (UT). After recalling some facts about these distributions and models, known but scattered in the literature, we prove that the maximum likelihood estimator of the covariance matrix in the UT model is asymptotically biased and propose an unbiased version. We provide implementation details for an iterative reweighted algorithm to compute the maximum likelihood estimators of the parameters of the IT model. We present a simulation study to compare the bias and root mean squared error of the ensuing estimators of the regression coefficients and covariance matrix under several scenarios of the potential data-generating process, misspecified or not. We propose a graphical tool and a test based on the Mahalanobis distance to guide the choice between the competing models. We also present an application to model vectors of financial assets returns.

Keywords: multivariate regression models; heavy-tailed data; Mahalanobis distances; maximum likelihood estimator; independent multivariate Student distribution; uncorrelated multivariate Student distribution

---

1. Introduction

Many applications involving models for multivariate data underline the limitations of the classical multivariate Gaussian model, mainly due to its inability to model heavy tails. It is then natural to turn attention to a more flexible family of distributions, for example the multivariate Student distribution.

In one dimension, the generalized Student distribution encompasses the Gaussian distribution as a limit when the number of degrees of freedom or shape parameter tends to infinity, allowing for heavier tails when the shape parameter is small. As we will see, a first difficulty in higher dimensions is that there are several kinds of multivariate Student distributions; see for example Johnson and Kotz (1972) and more recently Kotz and Nadarajah (2004). A nice summary of the properties of the multivariate Student distribution that we will use later on in this paper, and its comparison with the Gaussian multivariate, can be found in Roth (2013).

Before going further, let us mention that it is not so easy to have a clear overview of the results in terms of Student regression models for at least three reasons. The first reason is that this topic is scattered, with some papers in the statistical literature and others in the econometrics literature, sometimes without cross-referencing. The second reason is that the word "multivariate" is sometimes misleading since, as we will see, the multivariate Student is used to define a univariate regression model. At last, the distinction between models UT and IT (see below) is not always clearly announced in the papers. Other miscellaneous reasons are that some authors just fit the distribution without covariates and finally that some authors consider the degrees of freedom as fixed, whereas others estimate it. Our first purpose here is to lead the reader through this literature and gather the results concerning the maximum likelihood estimators of the parameters in the multivariate UT and IT models with a common notation. In the present paper, we consider a multivariate dependent vector and a linear regression model with different assumptions on the error term distribution. The most common and convenient assumption is the Gaussian distribution. For a Gaussian vector, the assumption of independent coordinates is equivalent to the assumption of uncorrelated coordinates. Such an equivalence is no longer true when considering a multivariate Student distribution. We thus consider two cases: uncorrelated (UT) on the one hand and independent Student (IT) error vectors on the other hand.

The purpose of this paper is to contribute to the UT and IT models as well as to their comparisons. First of all, for the UT model, we extend to the multivariate case the results of Zellner (1976) for the derivation of the maximum likelihood estimators and Zellner's formula (Zellner (1976)) for the bias of the covariance matrix estimator, and we prove that it does not vanish asymptotically. For the multivariate IT model, in the same spirit as Lange and Sinsheimer (1993), we provide details for the implementation of an iterative reweighted algorithm to compute the maximum likelihood estimators of the parameters. We devise a simulation study to measure the impact of misspecification on the bias, variance, and mean squared error of these different parameters' estimates under several data-generating processes (Gaussian, UT, and IT) and try to answer the question: what are the consequences of a wrong specification? Finally we introduce a new procedure for model selection based on the knowledge of the distribution of the Mahalanobis distances under the different data-generating processes (DGP).

One application attracted our attention in the finance literature. The work in Platen and Rendek (2008) identified the Student distribution with between three and five degrees of freedom, with a concentration around four, as the typical distribution for modeling the distribution of log-returns of world stock indices. They embedded the Student t in the class of generalized hyperbolic distributions, itself a subclass of the normal/independent family. For bivariate returns, the work in Fung and Seneta (2010) compared a multivariate Student IT model with an alternative model obtained by a more complex mixing representation from the point of view of asymptotic tail dependence. The work in Hu and Kercheval (2009) insisted on the fact that the choice of distribution matters when optimizing the portfolio. They found that the Student UT model performs the best in the class of symmetric generalized hyperbolic distributions. The work in Kan and Zhou (2017) advocated using a multivariate IT model for fitting the joint distribution of stock returns for a few fixed values of the degrees of freedom parameter and showed that this model outperforms the multivariate Gaussian.

In Section 2, after recalling the univariate results, we extend the results of Zellner (1976) for the derivation of the maximum likelihood estimators and its properties in the UT model and propose an iterative implementation for the IT model. We present the results of the simulation study in Section 3 and of the model selection strategy in Section 4 using a toy example and a dataset from finance. Section 5 summarizes the findings and gives recommendations.

2. Multivariate Regression Models

2.1. Literature Review

In order to define a Student regression model, even in the univariate case (single dependent variable), one needs to use the multivariate Student distribution to describe the joint distribution of the vector of observations for the set of statistical units. There are mainly two options, which were described in Kelejian and Prucha (1985) for the case of univariate regression. Indeed, the property of the equivalence between the independence and uncorrelatedness for components of a Gaussian vector are not satisfied anymore for a multivariate Student vector. One option, which we will call the IT model (for independent *t*-distribution) in the sequel, considers that the components of the random disturbance vector of the regression model are independent with the same marginal Student distribution. The second option, which we will call the UT model (for uncorrelated *t*-distribution), postulates a joint multivariate Student distribution for the vector of disturbances. Note that in both models, the marginal distribution of each component still is Student univariate.

The work in Zellner (1976) introduced a univariate Student regression model of the type UT with known degrees of freedom and studied the corresponding maximum likelihood and Bayesian estimators (with some adapted priors). The work in Singh (1988) considered the case of univariate Student regression with the UT model and with unknown degrees of freedom and derived an estimator of the degrees of freedom and subsequent estimators of the other parameters. However, Fernandez and Steel (1999) showed that this estimator was not consistent. Using one possible representation of the multivariate Student distribution, Lange and Sinsheimer (1993) embedded univariate Student regression with the UT model in a larger family of regression models (with normal/independent error distributions) and developed EM algorithms to compute their maximum likelihood estimates, as in Dempster et al. (1978).

In the framework of the spherical error distribution, which includes the Student error model as a special case, the work in Fraser and Ng Kai (1980) proved an extension to the multivariate case of Zellner's result stating that inference about the parameters corresponds closely to that under normal theory. Motivated by a financial application, the work in Sutradhar and Ali (1986) used a multivariate UT Student regression model with moment estimators instead of maximum likelihood and allowing the degrees of freedom to be unknown.

The univariate IT model was introduced in Fraser (1979) and compared to the UT model in Kelejian and Prucha (1985).

Concerning multivariate IT Student distributions, there was first a collection of results or applications for the case without regressors. The work in McNeil et al. (2005) used a representation of the multivariate IT Student distribution to derive an algorithm of the EM type for computing the maximum likelihood parameter estimators. They used the framework of normal mixture distributions in which the Student distribution can be expressed as a combination of a Gaussian random variable and an inverse gamma random variable. More recently, the work in Dogru et al. (2018) proposed a more robust extension, replacing maximum likelihood by a kind of M-estimation method based on the minimization of a q-entropy criterion. For the multivariate Student IT model, the work in Prucha and Kelejian (1984) derived the normal equations for the maximum likelihood estimators and their asymptotic properties with known degrees of freedom in a framework that encompasses our multivariate Student regression case. The work in Lange et al. (1989) illustrated this multivariate IT model on several examples. The work in Lange and Sinsheimer (1993) considered the framework of normal/independent error distributions (same as normal variance mixtures) and derived the EM algorithm for the maximum likelihood estimators in a model with covariates. The works in Liu and Rubin (1995) and Liu (1997) developed extensions of the EM algorithm for the multivariate IT model with known or unknown degrees of freedom, with or without covariates and with or without missing data. The work in Katz and King (1999) fit a multivariate IT distribution to multiparty electoral data. The work in Fernandez and Steel (1999) attracted attention to the fact that maximum likelihood inference can encounter problems of unbounded likelihood when the number of degrees of freedom is considered unknown and has to be estimated. Before engaging in the use of the multivariate Student distribution, it is wise to read Hofert (2003), which explained some traps to be avoided. One difficulty indeed is to be aware that some authors parametrize the multivariate Student distribution using the covariance matrix, while others use the scatter matrix, sometimes with the same notation for either one.

We consider the following version of the Student p-multivariate distribution denoted by $\mathbf{T}_p(\boldsymbol{\mu}, \boldsymbol{\Sigma}, \nu)$ with $\boldsymbol{\mu}$ being the p-vector of means, $\boldsymbol{\Sigma}$ being the $p \times p$ covariance matrix, and $\nu > 2$ the degrees of freedom. It is defined, for a p-vector $\mathbf{z}$, by the probability density function:

$$p(\mathbf{z}|\boldsymbol{\mu}, \boldsymbol{\Sigma}, \nu) = \frac{f(\nu)}{\det(\boldsymbol{\Sigma})^{1/2}} \left[1 + \frac{1}{\nu - 2} (\mathbf{z} - \boldsymbol{\mu})^T \boldsymbol{\Sigma}^{-1} (\mathbf{z} - \boldsymbol{\mu}) \right]^{-(\nu+p)/2}, \tag{1}$$

where ^{T} denotes the transpose operator, $f(\nu) = \dfrac{\Gamma[(\nu + p)/2]}{\Gamma(\nu/2)(\nu - 2)^{p/2}\pi^{p/2}}$ and Γ is the usual Gamma function.

Note that the assumption $\nu > 2$ implies the existence of the first two moments of the distribution and that the above density function is parametrized in terms of the covariance matrix. In most of the literature on multivariate Student distributions, the density is rather parametrized as a function of the scatter matrix $((\nu - 2)/\nu)\boldsymbol{\Sigma}$. Using the covariance matrix parametrization facilitates the comparison with the Gaussian distribution. We first recall some results in the univariate regression context.

2.2. Univariate Regression Case Reminder

In the univariate regression case and for a sample of size n, we have a one-dimensional dependent variable $\mathcal{Y}_i$, $i = 1, \ldots, n$, whose values are stacked in a vector $\mathcal{Y}$, and K explanatory variables defining a $n \times (K + 1)$ design matrix $\mathcal{X}$ including the constant.

The regression model is written as $\mathcal{Y} = \mathcal{X}\boldsymbol{\beta} + \boldsymbol{\epsilon}$, where $\boldsymbol{\beta} = (\beta_0, \ldots, \beta_K)^T$ is a $(K+1)$-dimensional vector of parameters and the error term $\boldsymbol{\epsilon} = (\epsilon_1, \ldots, \epsilon_n)^T$ is an n-dimensional vector. If we consider that the design matrix is fixed with rank $K + 1$ or look at the distribution of $\boldsymbol{\epsilon}$ conditional on $\mathcal{X}$, the usual assumptions are the following. The errors ϵ_i, $i = 1, \ldots, n$, are independent and identically distributed (i.i.d.) with expectation zero and equal variance σ^2. In this context, it is well known that the least squares estimator of $\boldsymbol{\beta}$ is equal to:

$$\hat{\boldsymbol{\beta}} = (\mathcal{X}^T \mathcal{X})^{-1} \mathcal{X}^T \mathcal{Y} \tag{2}$$

while the classical σ^2 estimator is $\hat{\sigma}^2 = \hat{\mathbf{e}}^T \hat{\mathbf{e}} / (n - K - 1)$ where $\hat{\mathbf{e}} = \mathcal{Y} - \mathcal{X}\hat{\boldsymbol{\beta}}$. These estimators are unbiased. In the case of a Gaussian error distribution, the estimator $\hat{\boldsymbol{\beta}}$ coincides with the maximum likelihood estimator of $\boldsymbol{\beta}$, while the maximum likelihood estimator of σ^2 is equal to $\hat{\sigma}^2$ multiplied by $(n - K - 1)/n$ and is only asymptotically unbiased. In the Gaussian case, there is an equivalence between the ϵ_i being independent or uncorrelated. However, this property is no longer true for a Student distribution. This means that one should distinguish the case of uncorrelated errors from the case of independent errors. The case where the errors ϵ_i, $i = 1, \ldots, n$, follow a joint n-dimensional Student distribution with diagonal covariance matrix and equal variance is called the UT model, and its coordinates are uncorrelated, but not independent. Interestingly, the maximum likelihood method for the UT model with known degrees of freedom leads to the least squares estimator (2) of $\boldsymbol{\beta}$ (Zellner (1976)). This property is true for more general distributions as long as the likelihood is a decreasing function of $\mathbf{e}^T \mathbf{e}$. Concerning the error variance, the maximum likelihood estimator is $(n - K - 1)\nu \hat{\sigma}^2 / (n(\nu - 2))$ and is biased even asymptotically Zellner (1976). For the independent case, we assume that the errors ϵ_i, $i = 1, \ldots, n$, are i.i.d. with a Student univariate distribution and known degrees of freedom. The maximum likelihood estimators belong to the class of M-estimators, which are studied in detail in Chapter 7 of Huber and Ronchetti (2009). These estimators are defined through implicit equations and can be computed using an iterative reweighted algorithm.

In what follows, we consider the case of a multivariate dependent variable and propose to gather and complete the results from the literature. As we will see, the results derived in the multivariate case are very similar to their univariate counterpart. In particular, the maximum likelihood estimator of the error covariance matrix is biased for the uncorrelated Student model, while there is a need to define an iterative algorithm for the independent Student model.

2.3. The Multivariate Regression Model

Let us consider a sample of size n, and for $i = 1, \ldots, n$, let us denote the L-dimensional dependent vector by:

$$\mathcal{Y}_i = (y_{i1}, \ldots, y_{iL})^T.$$

For K explanatory variables, the design matrix is of size $L \times (K+1)L$ and is given by:

$$\mathcal{X}_i = I_L \otimes x_i^T$$

for $i = 1, \ldots, n$, with the $(K+1)$-vector $x_i = (1, x_{i1}, \ldots, x_{iK})^T$, I_L the identity matrix with dimension L, and $\otimes$ the usual Kronecker product. The parameter of interest is a $(K+1)L$ vector given by:

$$\beta = (\beta_1^T, \ldots, \beta_L^T)^T,$$

where $\beta_j = (\beta_{0j}, \ldots, \beta_{Kj})^T$, for $j = 1, \ldots, L$, and the L-vector of errors is denoted by:

$$\epsilon_i = (\epsilon_{i1}, \ldots, \epsilon_{iL})^T$$

for $i = 1, \ldots, n$. We consider the linear model:

$$\mathcal{Y}_i = \mathcal{X}_i \beta + \epsilon_i \tag{3}$$

with $\mathbb{E}(\epsilon_i) = 0$ and $i = 1, \ldots, n$. Using matrix notations, we can write Model (3) as:

$$\mathcal{Y} = \mathcal{X}\beta + \epsilon \tag{4}$$

with the nL-vectors:

$$\mathcal{Y} = (\mathcal{Y}_1^T, \ldots, \mathcal{Y}_n^T)^T,$$
$$\epsilon = (\epsilon_1^T, \ldots, \epsilon_n^T)^T$$

and the $nL \times (K+1)L$ matrix:

$$\mathcal{X} = (\mathcal{X}_1^T, \ldots, \mathcal{X}_n^T)^T.$$

In what follows, we make different assumptions on the distribution of ϵ and recall (for Gaussian and IT) or derive (for UT) the maximum likelihood estimators of the parameter β and of the covariance matrix of ϵ.

2.4. Multivariate Normal Error Vector

Let us first consider Model (4) with independent and identically distributed error vectors ϵ_i, $i = 1, \ldots, n$, following a multivariate normal distribution $\mathcal{N}_L(0, \Sigma)$ with an L-vector of means equal to zero and an $L \times L$ covariance matrix Σ. This model is denoted by N, and the subscript N is used to denote the error terms ϵ_{Ni}, $i = 1, \ldots, n$, and the parameters β_N and Σ_N of the model. The maximum likelihood estimators of β_N and Σ_N are:

$$\hat{\beta}_N = (\mathcal{X}^T \mathcal{X})^{-1} \mathcal{X}^T \mathcal{Y}, \tag{5}$$

$$\hat{\Sigma}_N = \frac{\sum_{i=1}^{n} \hat{\epsilon}_{Ni} \hat{\epsilon}_{Ni}^T}{n}, \tag{6}$$

where $\hat{\epsilon}_{Ni} = \mathcal{Y}_i - \mathcal{X}_i \hat{\beta}_N$ (see, e.g., Theorem 8.4 from Seber (2008)).

The estimator $\hat{\beta}_N$ is an unbiased estimator of β_N while the bias of $\hat{\Sigma}_N$ is equal to $-((K+1)/n)\Sigma_N$ and tends to zero when n tends to infinity (see, e.g., Theorems 8.1 and 8.2 from Seber (2008)).

For data such as financial data, it is well known that the Gaussian distribution does not fit the error term well. Student distributions are known to be more appropriate because they have heavier tails than the Gaussian. As for the univariate case, for Student distributions, the independence of coordinates is not equivalent to their uncorrelatedness, and we consider below two types of Student distributions for the error term. In Section 2.5, the error vector $\boldsymbol{\epsilon}$ is assumed to follow a Student distribution with nL dimensions and a particular block diagonal covariance matrix. More precisely, we assume that the error vectors $\boldsymbol{\epsilon}_i$, $i = 1, \ldots, n$, are identically distributed and uncorrelated but are not independent. In Section 2.6, however, we consider independent and identically distributed error vectors $\boldsymbol{\epsilon}_i$, $i = 1, \ldots, n$, with an L-dimensional Student distribution.

2.5. Uncorrelated Multivariate Student (UT) Error Vector

Let us consider Model (4) with uncorrelated and identically distributed error vectors $\boldsymbol{\epsilon}_i$, $i = 1, \ldots, n$, such that the vector $\boldsymbol{\epsilon}$ follows a multivariate Student distribution $\mathbf{T}_{nL}(\mathbf{0}, \boldsymbol{\Omega}, \nu)$ with known degrees of freedom $\nu > 2$ and covariance matrix $\boldsymbol{\Omega} = \mathbf{I}_n \otimes \boldsymbol{\Sigma}$. The $L \times L$ matrix $\boldsymbol{\Sigma}$ is the common covariance matrix of the $\boldsymbol{\epsilon}_i$, $i = 1, \ldots, n$. This model is denoted by UT, and the subscript UT is used to denote the error terms $\boldsymbol{\epsilon}_{UTi}$, $i = 1, \ldots, n$, and the parameters $\boldsymbol{\beta}_{UT}, \boldsymbol{\Omega}_{UT}$, and $\boldsymbol{\Sigma}_{UT}$ of the model. This model generalizes the model proposed by Zellner (1976) to the case of multivariate $\boldsymbol{\epsilon}_i$s. We derive the maximum likelihood estimators of $\boldsymbol{\beta}_{UT}$ and $\boldsymbol{\Sigma}_{UT}$ in Proposition 1 and give the bias of the covariance estimator in Proposition 2. The proofs of the propositions are given in the Appendix A.

Proposition 1. *The maximum likelihood estimators of $\boldsymbol{\beta}_{UT}$ and $\boldsymbol{\Sigma}_{UT}$ are given by:*

$$\hat{\boldsymbol{\beta}}_{UT} = \left(\boldsymbol{\mathcal{X}}^T \boldsymbol{\mathcal{X}} \right)^{-1} \boldsymbol{\mathcal{X}}^T \boldsymbol{\mathcal{y}},$$
$$\hat{\boldsymbol{\Sigma}}_{UT} = \frac{\nu}{\nu - 2} \frac{\sum_{i=1}^n \hat{\boldsymbol{\epsilon}}_{UTi} \hat{\boldsymbol{\epsilon}}_{UTi}^T}{n}, \tag{7}$$

where $\hat{\boldsymbol{\epsilon}}_{UTi} = \boldsymbol{\mathcal{y}}_i - \boldsymbol{\mathcal{X}}_i \hat{\boldsymbol{\beta}}_{UT}.$

The next proposition gives the bias of the maximum likelihood estimators and generalizes Zellner's result (Zellner (1976), p. 402) to the multivariate UT model. The maximum likelihood estimator of $\boldsymbol{\beta}_{UT}$ coincides with the least squares and with the method of moment estimators and is unbiased. This is no longer the case for the maximum likelihood estimator of $\boldsymbol{\Sigma}_{UT}$, which is biased even asymptotically. This gives an example of a maximum likelihood estimator that is not asymptotically unbiased in a context where the random variables are not independent. It illustrates that the independence assumption is crucial to derive the usual properties of the maximum likelihood estimators. Note that the method of moments estimator is a consistent estimator of $\boldsymbol{\Sigma}_{UT}$ (see Sutradhar and Ali (1986)).

Proposition 2. *The estimator $\hat{\boldsymbol{\beta}}_{UT}$ is unbiased for $\boldsymbol{\beta}_{UT}$. The estimator $\hat{\boldsymbol{\Sigma}}_{UT}$ is biased for $\boldsymbol{\Sigma}_{UT}$ even asymptotically. More precisely,*

$$\mathbb{E}(\hat{\boldsymbol{\Sigma}}_{UT}) = \frac{n - K}{n} \frac{\nu}{\nu - 2} \boldsymbol{\Sigma}_{UT}$$

A consequence of Proposition 2 is that an asymptotically unbiased estimator of $\boldsymbol{\Sigma}_{UT}$ is given by

$$\tilde{\boldsymbol{\Sigma}}_{UT} = \sum_{i=1}^n \hat{\boldsymbol{\epsilon}}_{UTi} \hat{\boldsymbol{\epsilon}}_{UTi}^T / n.$$

2.6. Independent Multivariate Student Error Vector

Let us consider Model (4) using the notations of Section 2.3 with i.i.d. $\boldsymbol{\epsilon}_i$, $i = 1, \ldots, n$, following a Student distribution with L dimensions and known degrees of freedom $\nu > 2$. We denote this model by IT and the parameters of the model by $\boldsymbol{\beta}_{IT}$ and $\boldsymbol{\Sigma}_{IT}$. The IT model is a particular case of Prucha and Kelejian (1984) where the B matrix in Expression (2.1) in Prucha and Kelejian (1984) is equal to zero.

Following Prucha and Kelejian (1984), we derive the maximum likelihood estimators for the IT model.

Proposition 3. *The maximum likelihood estimators of* $\boldsymbol{\beta}_{IT}$ *and* $\boldsymbol{\Sigma}_{IT}$ *in the IT regression model satisfy the following implicit equations:*

$$\hat{\boldsymbol{\beta}}_{IT} = \left(\sum_{i=1}^{n} \hat{w}_{ITi} \boldsymbol{X}_i^T \hat{\boldsymbol{\Sigma}}_{IT}^{-1} \boldsymbol{X}_i \right)^{-1} \sum_{i=1}^{n} \hat{w}_{ITi} \boldsymbol{X}_i^T \hat{\boldsymbol{\Sigma}}_{IT}^{-1} \boldsymbol{y}_i$$

$$\hat{\boldsymbol{\Sigma}}_{IT} = \frac{1}{n} \sum_{i=1}^{n} \hat{w}_{ITi} \hat{\boldsymbol{\varepsilon}}_{ITi} \hat{\boldsymbol{\varepsilon}}_{ITi}^T \qquad (8)$$

$$\text{with:} \quad \hat{\boldsymbol{\varepsilon}}_{ITi} = \boldsymbol{y}_i - \boldsymbol{X}_i \hat{\boldsymbol{\beta}}_{IT} \quad \text{and} \quad \hat{w}_{ITi} = \frac{\nu + L}{\nu - 2 + \hat{\boldsymbol{\varepsilon}}_{ITi}^T \hat{\boldsymbol{\Sigma}}_{IT}^{-1} \hat{\boldsymbol{\varepsilon}}_{ITi}}.$$

These estimators are consistent estimators of $\boldsymbol{\beta}_{IT}$ and $\boldsymbol{\Sigma}_{IT}$ (see Theorem 3.2 in Prucha and Kelejian (1984)). In order to compute them, we propose to implement the following iterative reweighted algorithm in the same spirit as in Huber and Ronchetti (2009) for the univariate case (see also Lange et al. (1989)).

Step 0: Let:

$$\hat{\boldsymbol{\beta}}_{IT}^{(0)} = (\boldsymbol{X}^T \boldsymbol{X})^{-1} \boldsymbol{X}^T \boldsymbol{y}$$

$$\hat{\boldsymbol{\varepsilon}}_{IT}^{(0)} = \boldsymbol{y} - \boldsymbol{X} \hat{\boldsymbol{\beta}}_{IT}^{(0)}$$

$$\hat{\boldsymbol{\Sigma}}_{IT}^{(0)} = \frac{1}{n} \sum_{i=1}^{n} \hat{\boldsymbol{\varepsilon}}_{ITi}^{(0)} \hat{\boldsymbol{\varepsilon}}_{ITi}^{(0)T}$$

Step $k \rightarrow$ Step $(k+1)$, $k > 0$:

$$\hat{w}_{ITi}^{(k+1)} = \frac{\nu + L}{\nu - 2 + \hat{\boldsymbol{\varepsilon}}_{ITi}^{(k)} \hat{\boldsymbol{\Sigma}}_{IT}^{(k)-1} \hat{\boldsymbol{\varepsilon}}_{ITi}^{(k)}}$$

$$\hat{\boldsymbol{\beta}}_{IT}^{(k+1)} = \left(\sum_{i=1}^{n} \hat{w}_{ITi}^{(k+1)} \boldsymbol{X}_i^T \hat{\boldsymbol{\Sigma}}_{IT}^{(k)-1} \boldsymbol{X}_i \right)^{-1} \sum_{i=1}^{n} \hat{w}_{ITi}^{(k+1)} \boldsymbol{X}_i^T \hat{\boldsymbol{\Sigma}}_{IT}^{(k)-1} \boldsymbol{y}_i$$

$$\hat{\boldsymbol{\varepsilon}}_{IT}^{(k+1)} = \boldsymbol{y} - \boldsymbol{X} \hat{\boldsymbol{\beta}}_{IT}^{(k+1)}$$

$$\hat{\boldsymbol{\Sigma}}_{IT}^{(k+1)} = \frac{1}{n} \sum_{i=1}^{n} \hat{w}_{ITi}^{(k+1)} \hat{\boldsymbol{\varepsilon}}_{ITi}^{(k+1)} \hat{\boldsymbol{\varepsilon}}_{ITi}^{(k+1)T}$$

The process is iterated until convergence. Note that this algorithm is given in detail in Section 7.8 of Huber and Ronchetti (2009) for a general class of univariate regression M-estimators. It is also sometimes called IRLS for iteratively-reweighted least squares and can be seen as a particular case of the EM algorithm (Dempster et al. (1978)).

Table 1 gathers the likelihoods and thus summarizes the three models of interest.

Table 1. Distribution of the error vector ϵ in the Gaussian, UT, and IT models.

Model	Distribution
$N(\epsilon_1,\ldots,\epsilon_n)$	$\mathcal{N}_{nL}(0, I_n \otimes \Sigma_N) = \prod_{i=1}^{n} \mathcal{N}_L(0, \Sigma_N)$
$UT(\epsilon_1,\ldots,\epsilon_n)$	$T_{nL}(0, I_n \otimes \Sigma_{UT}, \nu)$
$IT(\epsilon_1,\ldots,\epsilon_n)$	$\prod_{i=1}^{n} T_L(0, \Sigma_{IT}, \nu)$

3. Simulation Study

3.1. Design

This study aims at comparing the properties of the estimators of β and Σ as defined in the previous section for the multivariate Gaussian (N), the uncorrelated multivariate Student (UT), and the independent multivariate Student (IT) error distributions, under several scenarios for the DGP. Note that for the UT model, we used the asymptotically unbiased estimator $\tilde{\Sigma}_{UT}$ to estimate Σ_{UT}. We considered a variety of degrees of freedom ν_{DGP} for the Student IT and UT models with a focus on values between three and five. We used the function rmvt from the R package mvnfast to simulate the Student distributions. For a sample size $n = 1000$ and a number of replications $N = 10{,}000$, we simulated an explanatory variable $\mathcal{X}$ following a Gaussian distribution $\mathcal{N}(45, 10)$. The parameter vector β and the covariance matrix Σ are respectively chosen to be:

$$\beta = \begin{bmatrix} \beta_{01} \\ \beta_{11} \\ \beta_{02} \\ \beta_{12} \end{bmatrix} = \begin{bmatrix} 2 \\ 3 \\ 4 \\ -3 \end{bmatrix} ; \Sigma = \begin{bmatrix} \sigma_1^2 & \rho\sigma_1\sigma_2 \\ \rho\sigma_1\sigma_2 & \sigma_2^2 \end{bmatrix} = \begin{bmatrix} 2 & 0.5 \\ 0.5 & 1 \end{bmatrix}.$$

Note that similar results are obtained with other choices of parameters.

For each DGP, we calculate a number of Monte Carlo performance measures of the estimators proposed in Section 2. The performances are measured by the Monte Carlo relative bias (RB) and the mean squared error (MSE), which are defined for an estimator $\hat{\theta}$ of a parameter θ by:

$$\text{Bias}(\hat{\theta}) = \frac{1}{N}\sum_{i=1}^{n} \hat{\theta}^{(i)} - \theta$$

$$\text{RB}(\hat{\theta}) = 100\frac{\text{Bias}(\hat{\theta})}{\theta} \tag{9}$$

$$\text{MSE}(\hat{\theta}) = \frac{1}{N}\sum_{i=1}^{N} \left(\hat{\theta}^{(i)} - \theta\right)^2.$$

We also compute a relative root mean squared error (RRMSE) with respect to a baseline estimator $\tilde{\theta}$ as:

$$\text{RRMSE}(\hat{\theta}) = \left(\frac{\text{MSE}(\hat{\theta})}{\text{MSE}(\tilde{\theta})}\right)^{1/2}.$$

In our case, the baseline estimator is the maximum likelihood estimator (MLE) corresponding to the DGP. For example, in Table 2, the RRMSE of the $\hat{\beta}_{IT}$ for the Gaussian DGP is the ratio of the MSE of $\hat{\beta}_{IT}$ with the degrees of freedom ν_{MLE} and the MSE of $\hat{\beta}_N$. Note that if $\hat{\theta} = \tilde{\theta}$, then the RRMSE of $\hat{\theta}$ is equal to one.

Table 2. Relative bias and relative root mean squared error of the estimators of β ($\hat{\beta}_N$, $\hat{\beta}_{UT}$, $\hat{\beta}_{IT}$) for the corresponding DGP (Gaussian, UT, and IT).

DGP		N		UT ($\nu_{DGP} = 3$)		IT ($\nu_{DGP} = 3$)	
Methods	**Estimators**	**RB (%)**	**RRMSE**	**RB (%)**	**RRMSE**	**RB (%)**	**RRMSE**
	$\hat{\beta}_{01}$	−0.07	1.00	−0.06	1.00	−0.09	1.48
$\hat{\beta}_N, \hat{\beta}_{UT}$	$\hat{\beta}_{02}$	0.00	1.00	0.00	1.00	0.00	1.48
	$\hat{\beta}_{11}$	−0.02	1.00	−0.01	1.00	−0.07	1.46
	$\hat{\beta}_{12}$	−0.00	1.00	−0.00	1.00	−0.00	1.46
	$\hat{\beta}_{01}$	−0.09	1.04	−0.09	1.09	−0.03	1.00
$\hat{\beta}_{IT}(\nu_{MLE} = 3)$	$\hat{\beta}_{02}$	0.00	1.04	0.00	1.09	0.00	1.00
	$\hat{\beta}_{11}$	−0.04	1.07	−0.02	1.08	−0.03	1.00
	$\hat{\beta}_{12}$	−0.00	1.07	−0.00	1.08	−0.00	1.00

3.2. Estimators of the β Parameters

Table 3 reports the bias and the MSE of the Gaussian MLE estimator $\hat{\beta}_N$, the UT MLE estimator $\hat{\beta}_{UT}$ ($\nu_{DGP} = 3$), and the IT MLE estimator $\hat{\beta}_{IT}$ ($\nu_{DGP} = 3$) when the model is well specified, i.e., under the corresponding DGP. The bias and MSE of the estimators of β are small and comparable under the Gaussian and the UT DGP, but smaller for the IT DGP. Note that, in our implementation, the results of the algorithm for the IT estimators are very similar to those obtained using the function heavyLm from the R package heavy.

Table 3. Bias and MSE of the maximum likelihood estimators of β for the corresponding DGP (Gaussian, UT, and IT).

DGP	N		UT ($\nu_{DGP} = 3$)		IT ($\nu_{DGP} = 3$)	
Estimators	**Bias**	**MSE**	**Bias**	**MSE**	**Bias**	**MSE**
$\hat{\beta}_{01}$	-1.39×10^{-3}	4.57×10^{-2}	-1.27×10^{-3}	3.72×10^{-2}	6.65×10^{-4}	1.99×10^{-2}
$\hat{\beta}_{02}$	2.41×10^{-5}	2.18×10^{-5}	1.47×10^{-5}	1.76×10^{-5}	9.90×10^{-6}	9.50×10^{-6}
$\hat{\beta}_{11}$	-6.62×10^{-4}	2.16×10^{-2}	3.23×10^{-4}	2.05×10^{-2}	-1.02×10^{-3}	9.84×10^{-3}
$\hat{\beta}_{12}$	1.87×10^{-5}	1.02×10^{-5}	3.90×10^{-6}	9.60×10^{-6}	2.14×10^{-5}	4.70×10^{-6}

In Table 2, we start considering misspecifications and report the corresponding relative values RB and RRMSE of the same estimators and the same DGP as in Table 3 with all possible combinations of DGP and estimation methods. The results indicate that the RB of $\hat{\beta}$ are all very small. If the DGP is Gaussian and the estimator is IT, the RRMSE of coordinates of $\hat{\beta}$ is about 1.09. However, if the DGP is IT and the estimator is Gaussian, the RRMSE of coordinates of $\hat{\beta}$ is higher (from 1.46–1.48). Hence for the Gaussian DGP, we do not loose too much efficiency using the IT estimator $\hat{\beta}_{IT}$ with three degrees of freedom. Inversely, we loose much more efficiency when using $\hat{\beta}_N$ for the IT DGP with three degrees of freedom.

In order to consider more degrees of freedom (3, 4, and 5), we now drop the bias and focus on the RRMSE. Table 4 indicates that the RRMSE of $\hat{\beta}$ is very similar and close to one, with a maximum of 1.09, except for the case of the N estimator under the IT DGP, where it can reach 1.48. The work in Maronna (1976) provided theoretical asymptotic efficiencies of the Student versus the Gaussian estimators, the ratio of asymptotic variances being equal to $\dfrac{(v-2)(v+L+2)}{v(v+L)}$. The values obtained in Table 2 are very similar to these asymptotic values.

Table 4. The root relative mean squared errors of $\hat{\beta}$.

Methods	DGP	N	UT			IT		
	RRMSE		$\nu_{DGP} = 3$	$\nu_{DGP} = 4$	$\nu_{DGP} = 5$	$\nu_{DGP} = 3$	$\nu_{DGP} = 4$	$\nu_{DGP} = 5$
N	$\hat{\beta}_{01}$	1.00	1.00	1.00	1.00	1.48	1.22	1.14
	$\hat{\beta}_{02}$	1.00	1.00	1.00	1.00	1.48	1.23	1.14
	$\hat{\beta}_{11}$	1.00	1.00	1.00	1.00	1.46	1.22	1.13
	$\hat{\beta}_{12}$	1.00	1.00	1.00	1.00	1.46	1.22	1.13
IT ($\nu_{MLE} = 3$)	$\hat{\beta}_{01}$	1.04	1.09	1.09	1.08	1.00	1.00	1.01
	$\hat{\beta}_{02}$	1.04	1.09	1.09	1.08	1.00	1.00	1.01
	$\hat{\beta}_{11}$	1.07	1.08	1.10	1.08	1.00	1.00	1.01
	$\hat{\beta}_{12}$	1.07	1.08	1.09	1.09	1.00	1.00	1.01
IT ($\nu_{MLE} = 4$)	$\hat{\beta}_{01}$	1.02	1.07	1.06	1.06	1.00	1.00	1.00
	$\hat{\beta}_{02}$	1.01	1.06	1.06	1.05	1.00	1.00	1.00
	$\hat{\beta}_{11}$	1.04	1.06	1.07	1.06	1.00	1.00	1.00
	$\hat{\beta}_{12}$	1.04	1.05	1.07	1.06	1.00	1.00	1.00
IT ($\nu_{MLE} = 5$)	$\hat{\beta}_{01}$	1.00	1.05	1.05	1.04	1.01	1.00	1.00
	$\hat{\beta}_{02}$	1.00	1.05	1.05	1.04	1.01	1.00	1.00
	$\hat{\beta}_{11}$	1.03	1.04	1.05	1.05	1.01	1.00	1.00
	$\hat{\beta}_{12}$	1.03	1.04	1.05	1.05	1.01	1.00	1.00

Figure 1 shows the performances in terms of RRMSE of the IT estimators $\hat{\beta}_{12}^{IT}$ under different DGP as a function of the degrees of freedom of the IT estimator (ν_{MLE}). The considered DGP are the Gaussian, UT, and IT DGP with the degrees of freedom $\nu_{DGP} = 3$ (respectively, $\nu_{DGP} = 4$, $\nu_{DGP} = 5$) on the left (respectively, middle, right) plot. Overall, the RRMSE of $\hat{\beta}_{12}^{IT}$ for the IT DGP has a down trend and then an up trend, while for the Gaussian and the UT DGP, the RRMSE are decreasing when ν_{MLE} increases. The maximum RRMSE of $\hat{\beta}_{12}^{IT}$ is around 1.09 under the UT DGP and is around 1.08 under the Gaussian DGP. It decreases then to one when ν_{MLE} increases to twenty under the Gaussian and the UT DGP; thus, the risk under misspecification is not very high. The curve is U-shaped under the IT DGP with a minimum when $\nu_{MLE} = \nu_{DGP}$. The worst performance is when ν_{DGP} is small and ν_{MLE} is large. The RRMSE of $\hat{\beta}_{12}^{IT}$ with $\nu_{DGP} = 4$ is similar than the one with $\nu_{DGP} = 5$.

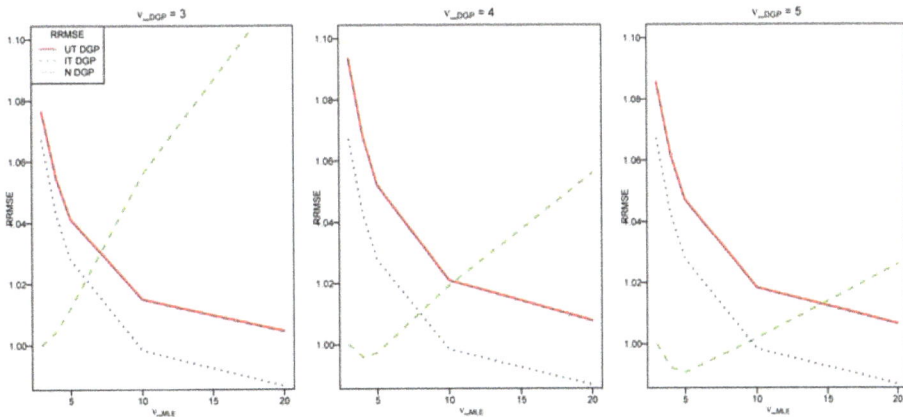

Figure 1. The RRMSE of the IT estimator of $\hat{\beta}_{12}$ for the UT DGP in solid line, for the IT DGP in dashed line, and for the Gaussian DGP in dotted line with $\nu_{DGP} = 3$ (respectively, $\nu_{DGP} = 4$, $\nu_{DGP} = 5$) on the left (respectively, middle, right) plot.

3.3. Estimators of the Variance Parameters

Table 5 reports the biases and the MSE of $\hat{\rho}$, $\hat{\sigma}_1^2$, $\hat{\sigma}_2^2$ for the Gaussian DGP, the UT ($v_{DGP} = 3$) DGP, and the IT ($v_{DGP} = 3$) DGP. The bias and the MSE of $\hat{\rho}$ are very similar and small for all cases. The MSE of the Gaussian estimators $\hat{\sigma}_1^2$ and $\hat{\sigma}_2^2$ are small under the Gaussian DGP, but they are higher under the UT and IT DGP. The biases and MSE of the IT estimator $\hat{\sigma}_1^2$ and $\hat{\sigma}_2^2$ are small under the IT DGP, but high under the Gaussian and the UT DGP. Besides, Table 5 also indicates that there is no method that estimates the variances well under the UT DGP.

Table 5. The bias and the MSE of $\hat{\rho}$, $\hat{\sigma}_1^2$, $\hat{\sigma}_2^2$.

Methods	DGP	N Bias	N MSE	UT ($v_{DGP}=3$) Bias	UT ($v_{DGP}=3$) MSE	IT ($v_{DGP}=3$) Bias	IT ($v_{DGP}=3$) MSE
N	$\hat{\rho}$	-4.85×10^{-4}	9.46×10^{-4}	-2.08×10^{-4}	7.68×10^{-4}	-3.99×10^{-3}	1.17×10^{-2}
	$\hat{\sigma}_1^2$	-3.89×10^{-3}	8.33×10^{-3}	-1.05×10^{-1}	58	6.94×10^{-3}	3.17
	$\hat{\sigma}_2^2$	-1.75×10^{-3}	2.01×10^{-3}	-5.17×10^{-2}	14.93	-1.77×10^{-2}	2.85×10^{-1}
IT $v_{MLE} = 3$	$\hat{\rho}$	-1.70×10^{-4}	8.94×10^{-4}	-2.18×10^{-4}	9.05×10^{-4}	-2.03×10^{-4}	1.07×10^{-3}
	$\hat{\sigma}_1^2$	2.00	4.06	1.80	244.87	-1.43×10^{-2}	1.54×10^{-2}
	$\hat{\sigma}_2^2$	1.00	1.02	0.91	64.75	-7.30×10^{-3}	3.94×10^{-3}

As before, we now consider misspecified cases and focus on relative bias in Table 6. We observe that the relative bias for $\hat{\rho}$ is negligible in all situations. The RB for $\hat{\sigma}_1^2$ and $\hat{\sigma}_2^2$ are also quite small (less than around 5%) when using the Gaussian estimator for all DGP. This is also true when using the IT estimator for the IT DGP with the same degrees of freedom $v_{MLE} = v_{DGP}$. There are some biases for $\hat{\sigma}_1^2$ and $\hat{\sigma}_2^2$ if the DGP is Gaussian or UT and the estimator is IT. For this estimator, the relative bias of $\hat{\sigma}_1^2$, $\hat{\sigma}_2^2$ is around 100% for the Gaussian DGP, 96% for the UT DGP with $v_{DGP} = 5$ and $v_{MLE} = 3$, and 22% for the UT DGP with $v_{DGP} = 5$ and $v_{MLE} = 5$. The RB for $\hat{\sigma}_1^2$ and $\hat{\sigma}_2^2$ are also quite high (up to 50%) for the IT estimator when the DGP is IT with $v_{MLE} \neq v_{DGP}$. To summarize, in terms of the RB of the variance estimators, the Gaussian estimator yields better results than the IT estimator.

Table 6. The RB of $\hat{\rho}$, $\hat{\sigma}_1^2$, $\hat{\sigma}_2^2$ with $v = 3, 4, 5$.

Methods	DGP RB (%)	N	UT $v_{DGP}=3$	UT $v_{DGP}=4$	UT $v_{DGP}=5$	IT $v_{DGP}=3$	IT $v_{DGP}=4$	IT $v_{DGP}=5$
N	$\hat{\rho}$	-0.14	-0.06	-0.06	-0.06	-1.13	-0.24	0.02
	$\hat{\sigma}_1^2$	-0.21	-5.23	-3.34	-2.31	0.35	-0.08	-0.12
	$\hat{\sigma}_2^2$	-0.18	-5.17	-3.33	-2.20	-1.77	-0.30	-0.09
IT, $v_{MLE} = 3$	$\hat{\rho}$	-0.05	-0.06	-0.06	-0.06	-0.06	-0.04	-0.02
	$\hat{\sigma}_1^2$	99.99	90.25	93.89	95.80	-0.72	32.79	50.12
	$\hat{\sigma}_2^2$	100.05	90.60	93.90	96.03	-0.73	32.79	50.13
IT, $v_{MLE} = 4$	$\hat{\rho}$	-0.05	-0.06	-0.06	-0.06	-0.06	-0.04	-0.01
	$\hat{\sigma}_1^2$	42.62	35.80	38.32	39.68	-24.66	-0.24	11.18
	$\hat{\sigma}_2^2$	42.66	36.01	38.34	39.85	-24.67	-0.23	11.19
IT, $v_{MLE} = 5$	$\hat{\rho}$	-0.06	-0.06	-0.06	-0.06	-0.06	-0.04	-0.00
	$\hat{\sigma}_1^2$	24.71	18.85	21.03	22.23	-31.75	-10.13	-0.14
	$\hat{\sigma}_2^2$	24.74	19.02	21.04	22.38	-31.76	-10.13	-0.14

Finally, Table 7 presents the RRMSE in the same cases. It shows that the RRMSE of $\hat{\rho}$ varies from 0.94–1.09 for all DGP except for the case of the IT DGP with the Gaussian estimator, which ranges between 1.42 and 3.21. Besides, if the DGP is Gaussian and the estimator is IT or if the DGP is IT and the estimator is Gaussian, the RRMSE of $\hat{\sigma}_1^2$ and $\hat{\sigma}_2^2$ are high in particular for $v_{DGP} = 3$ or $v_{MLE} = 3$: we loose a lot of efficiency in these misspecified cases. To conclude, we have seen from Table 6 that the RB of $\hat{\sigma}_1^2$ and $\hat{\sigma}_2^2$ are smaller for the Gaussian estimator than for the IT estimator. However, in terms of RRMSE, there is no clear advantage in using the Gaussian estimator with respect to the IT estimator.

It should be noted that for $v \leq 4$, the Student distribution has no fourth-order moment, which may explain the fact that the covariance estimators have large MSE.

Table 7. The RRMSE of $\hat{\rho}$, $\hat{\sigma}_1^2$, $\hat{\sigma}_2^2$ in the Gaussian DGP, the UT DGP ($v_{DGP} = 3, 4, 5$), and the IT DGP ($v_{DGP} = 3, 4, 5$).

Methods	DGP	N	UT			IT		
	RRMSE		$v_{DGP} = 3$	$v_{DGP} = 4$	$v_{DGP} = 5$	$v_{DGP} = 3$	$v_{DGP} = 4$	$v_{DGP} = 5$
N	$\hat{\rho}$	1.00	1.00	1.00	1.00	3.21	1.91	1.42
	$\hat{\sigma}_1^2$	1.00	1.00	1.00	1.00	14.33	2.65	1.64
	$\hat{\sigma}_2^2$	1.00	1.00	1.00	1.00	8.50	2.24	1.78
IT, $v_{MLE} = 3$	$\hat{\rho}$	0.97	1.09	1.09	1.09	1.00	1.00	1.01
	$\hat{\sigma}_1^2$	22.07	2.05	2.11	2.16	1.00	5.89	9.18
	$\hat{\sigma}_2^2$	22.45	2.08	2.11	2.16	1.00	5.77	9.13
IT, $v_{MLE} = 4$	$\hat{\rho}$	0.95	1.06	1.06	1.06	1.01	1.00	1.00
	$\hat{\sigma}_1^2$	9.49	1.46	1.47	1.48	4.04	1.00	2.31
	$\hat{\sigma}_2^2$	9.65	1.48	1.47	1.48	4.00	1.00	2.30
IT, $v_{MLE} = 5$	$\hat{\rho}$	0.94	1.05	1.05	1.05	1.01	1.00	1.00
	$\hat{\sigma}_1^2$	5.58	1.27	1.27	1.28	5.16	1.99	1.00
	$\hat{\sigma}_2^2$	5.68	1.28	1.28	1.27	5.10	1.95	1.00

In order to allow the reproducibility of the empirical analyses contained in the present and the following sections, some Supplementary Material is available at the following link: http://www.thibault.laurent.free.fr/code/jrfm/.

4. Selection between the Gaussian and IT Models

In this section, we propose a methodology to select a model between the Gaussian and independent Student models and to select the degrees of freedom for the Student in a short list of possibilities. Following the warnings of Fernandez and Steel (1999) and the empirical results of Katz and King (1999), Platen and Rendek (2008), and Kan and Zhou (2017), we decided to focus on a small selection of degrees of freedom and fit our models without estimating this parameter, considering that a second step of model selection will make the choice. Indeed, there is a limited number of interesting values, which are between three and eight (for larger values, the distribution gets close to being Gaussian). The work in Lange et al. (1989), p.883, proposed the likelihood ratio test for the univariate case. In what follows, we use the fact that the distribution of the Mahalanobis distances is known under the two DGP, which allows building a Kolmogorov–Smirnov test and using Q-Q plots. Unfortunately, this technique does not apply to the UT model for which the n observations are a single realization of the multivariate distribution. One advantage of this approach is that the Mahalanobis distance is a one-dimensional variable, whereas the original observations have L dimensions.

4.1. Distributions of Mahalanobis Distances

For an L-dimensional random vector $\mathbf{Y}$, with mean $\boldsymbol{\mu}$, and covariance matrix $\boldsymbol{\Sigma}$, the squared Mahalanobis distance is defined by:

$$d^2 = (\mathbf{Y} - \boldsymbol{\mu})^T \boldsymbol{\Sigma}^{-1} (\mathbf{Y} - \boldsymbol{\mu})$$

If $\mathbf{Y}_1, \ldots \mathbf{Y}_n$ is a sample of size n from the L-dimensional Gaussian distribution $\mathcal{N}_L(\boldsymbol{\mu}_N, \boldsymbol{\Sigma}_N)$, the squared Mahalanobis distance of observation i, denoted by d_{Ni}^2, follows a χ_L^2 distribution. If $\boldsymbol{\mu}_N$ and $\boldsymbol{\Sigma}_N$ are unknown, then the squared Mahalanobis distance of observation i can be estimated by:

$$\hat{d}_{Ni}^2 = (\mathbf{Y}_i - \hat{\boldsymbol{\mu}}_N)^T \hat{\boldsymbol{\Sigma}}_N^{-1} (\mathbf{Y}_i - \hat{\boldsymbol{\mu}}_N)$$

where $\hat{\boldsymbol{\mu}}_N = \tilde{\mathbf{Y}} = \dfrac{1}{n}\sum_{i=1}^{n}\mathbf{Y}_i$ and $\hat{\boldsymbol{\Sigma}}_N$ is the sample covariance matrix. The work in Gnanadesikan and Kettenring (1972) (see also Bilodeau and Brenner (1999)) proved that this square distance follows a Beta distribution, up to a multiplicative constant:

$$\frac{n}{(n-1)^2}(\mathbf{Y}_i - \hat{\boldsymbol{\mu}}_N)^T \hat{\boldsymbol{\Sigma}}_N^{-1}(\mathbf{Y}_i - \hat{\boldsymbol{\mu}}_N) \sim Beta\left(\frac{L}{2}, \frac{n-L-1}{2}\right)$$

where L is the dimension of $\mathbf{Y}$. For large n, this Beta distribution can be approximated by the chi-square distribution $d_{Ni}^2 \sim \chi_L^2$. According to Gnanadesikan and Kettenring (1972) (p. 172), $n = 25$ already provides a sufficiently large sample for this approximation, which is the case in all our examples below. If we now assume that $\mathbf{Y}_1, \ldots, \mathbf{Y}_n$ is a sample of size n from the L-dimensional Student distribution $\mathbf{Y}_i \sim \mathbf{T}(\boldsymbol{\mu}_{IT}, \boldsymbol{\Sigma}_{IT}, \nu)$, then the squared Mahalanobis distance of observation i, denoted by d_{ITi}^2 and properly scaled, follows a Fisher distribution (see Roth (2013)):

$$\frac{1}{L}\frac{\nu}{\nu-2}d_{ITi}^2 \sim \mathcal{F}(L, \nu)$$

If $\boldsymbol{\mu}_{IT}$ and $\boldsymbol{\Sigma}_{IT}$ are unknown, then the squared Mahalanobis distance of observation i can be estimated by:

$$\hat{d}_{ITi}^2 = (\mathbf{Y}_i - \hat{\boldsymbol{\mu}}_{IT})^T \hat{\boldsymbol{\Sigma}}_{IT}^{-1}(\mathbf{Y}_i - \hat{\boldsymbol{\mu}}_{IT}),$$

where $\hat{\boldsymbol{\mu}}_{IT}$ and $\hat{\boldsymbol{\Sigma}}_{IT}$ are the MLE of $\boldsymbol{\mu}_{IT}$ and $\boldsymbol{\Sigma}_{IT}$. Note that in the IT model, $\hat{\boldsymbol{\mu}}_{IT}$ is no longer equal to $\tilde{\mathbf{Y}}$. Up to our knowledge, there is no result about the distribution of $\hat{d}_{ITi}^2$.

In the elliptical distribution family, the distribution of Mahalanobis distances characterizes the distribution of the observations. Thus, in order to test the normality of the data, we can test whether the Mahalanobis distances follow a chi-square distribution. Similarly, testing the Student distribution is equivalent to testing whether the Mahalanobis distances follow the Fisher distribution. There are two difficulties with the approach. The first one is that the estimated Mahalanobis distances are not a sample from the chi-square (respectively, the Fisher) distribution because there is dependence due to the estimation of the parameters. The second one is that, in our case, we not only estimate $\boldsymbol{\mu}$ and $\boldsymbol{\Sigma}$, but we are in a regression framework where $\boldsymbol{\mu}$ is linear combination of regressors, and we indeed estimate its coefficients. In what follows, we will ignore these two difficulties and consider that, for large n, the distributions of the estimated Mahalanobis distances behave as if $\boldsymbol{\mu}$ and $\boldsymbol{\Sigma}$ were known.

We propose to implement several Kolmogorov–Smirnov tests in order to test different null hypothesis: Gaussian, Student with three degrees of freedom, and Student with four degrees of freedom. As an exploratory tool, we also propose drawing Q-Q plots of the Mahalanobis distances with respect to the chi-square and the Fisher distribution Small (1978).

4.2. Examples

This section illustrates some applications of the proposed methodology for selecting a model. We use a real dataset from finance and three simulated datasets with the same DGP as in Section 3.

The real dataset is the daily closing share price of IBM and MSFT, which are imported from Yahoo Finance from 3 January 2007–27 September 2018 using the quantmod package in R. It contains $n = 2955$ observations. Let $\mathbf{S}_t$, $t = 1, \ldots, n$ be the daily share price of IBM and MSFT and $\mathbf{Y}_t$ be the log-price increment (return) (see Fung and Seneta (2010)) over a day period, then:

$$\mathbf{Y}_t = \log \mathbf{S}_t - \log \mathbf{S}_{t-1}.$$

The three other datasets are simulated using the same model as in Section 3 with the Gaussian DGP, the IT DGP with $v_{DGP} = 3$, and the IT DGP with $v_{DGP} = 4$ and with sample size $n = 1000$. Figure 2 (respectively, Figure 3) displays the scatterplots of the financial data (respectively, the three toy data).

We compute the Gaussian and the IT estimators as in Section 3. We then calculate the squared Mahalanobis distances of the residuals and use a Kolmogorov–Smirnov test for deciding between the models. For the financial data, we have no predictor. We test the Gaussian (respectively the Student with three degrees of freedom, the Student with four degrees of freedom) null hypothesis. When testing one of the null hypotheses, we use the estimator corresponding to the null. Moreover, when the null hypothesis is Student, we use the corresponding degrees of freedom for computing the maximum likelihood estimator. We do reject the null hypothesis if the p-value is smaller than $\alpha = 5\%$. Note that we could adjust the level of α by taking into account multiple testing.

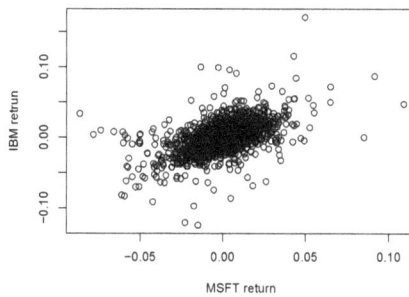

Figure 2. Financial data: scatterplot of returns.

Table 8 shows the p-values of these tests. For the simulated data, at the 5% level, we do not reject the Gaussian assumption when the DGP is Gaussian. Similarly, we do not reject the Student distribution with three (respectively, four) degrees of freedom when the DGP is the IT with degrees of freedom $v_{DGP} = 3$ (respectively, $v_{DGP} = 4$). For the financial data, we do not reject the Student distribution with three degrees of freedom, but we do reject the Gaussian distribution and the Student distribution with four degrees of freedom.

Table 8. All datasets: the p-values of the Mahalanobis distances tests with the null hypothesis and the corresponding estimators.

Hypothesis H_0		Toy DGP		Financial Data
Methods	N	IT, $v_{DGP} = 3$	IT, $v_{DGP} = 4$	
N	0.546	2.2×10^{-16}	2.2×10^{-16}	2.2×10^{-16}
IT, $v_{MLE} = 3$	2.2×10^{-16}	0.405	0.033	0.882
IT, $v_{MLE} = 4$	2.2×10^{-16}	0.023	0.303	0.049

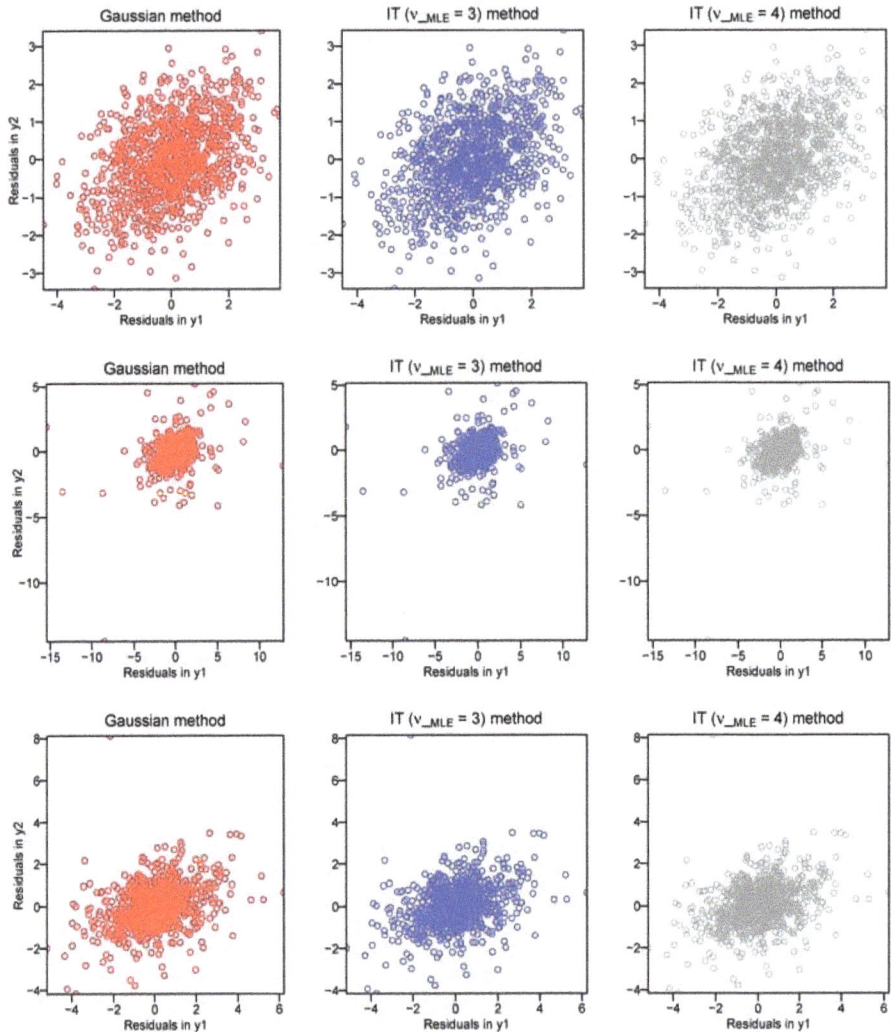

Figure 3. Toy data: scatterplots of residuals in the Gaussian DGP (respectively, the IT DGP with $v_{DGP} = 3$, the IT DGP with $v_{DGP} = 4$) on the first row (respectively, the second row, the third row).

Figure 4 shows the Q-Q plots comparing the empirical quantiles of the Mahalanobis distances for the normal (respectively, the IT ($v_{MLE} = 3$), the IT ($v_{MLE} = 4$)) estimators on the horizontal axis to the theoretical quantiles of the Mahalanobis distances for the normal (respectively, the IT ($v_{MLE} = 3$), the IT ($v_{MLE} = 4$)) on the vertical axis for the financial data. These Q-Q plots are coherent with the results of the tests in Table 8. The IT model with three degrees of freedom fits our financial data well.

Figure 5 displays the Q-Q plots for the toy DGP: the Gaussian DGP in the first column, the IT DGP with $v_{DGP} = 3$ in the second column, and the IT DGP with $v_{DGP} = 4$ in the third column. The first row compares the empirical quantiles to the normal case quantiles, the second to the Student case quantiles with $v_{DGP} = 3$, and the third row to Student case quantiles with $v_{DGP} = 4$. The Q-Q plots on the diagonal confirm that the fit is good when the model is correct. The other Q-Q plots outside the diagonal correctly reveal a clear deviation from the hypothesized model.

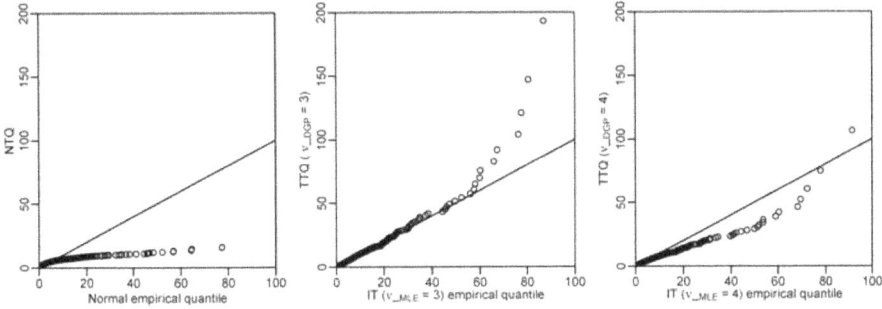

Figure 4. Financial data: Q-Q plots of the Mahalanobis distances for the normal, IT ($\nu_{MLE} = 3$), and IT ($\nu_{MLE} = 4$) estimators.

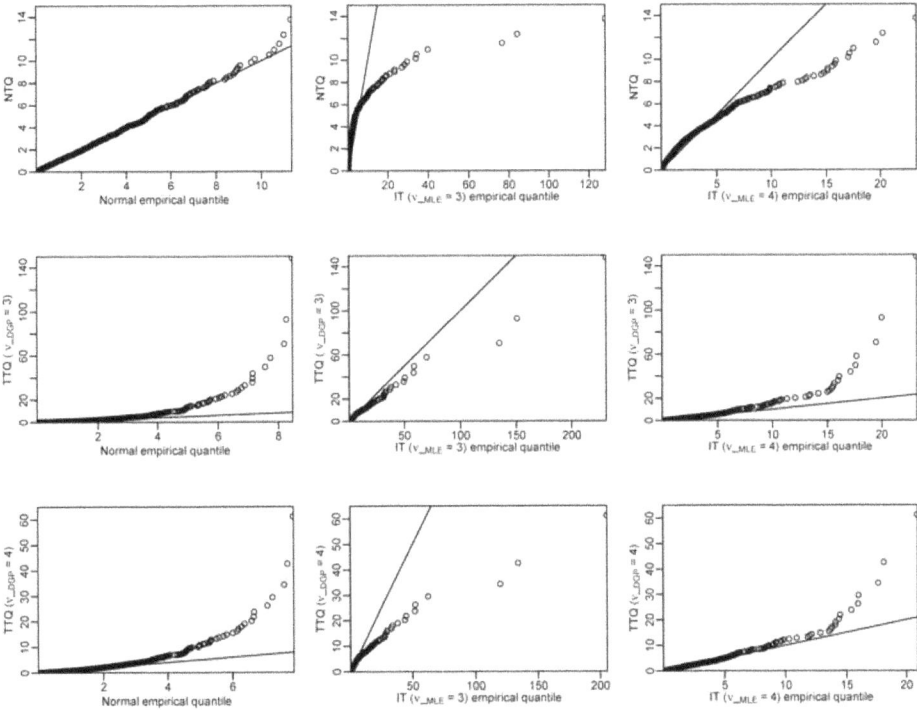

Figure 5. Toy data: Q-Q plots of the Mahalanobis distances of the residuals for the normal (respectively, the IT with $\nu_{DGP} = 3$, the IT with $\nu_{DGP} = 4$) case empirical quantiles against the normal (respectively, the IT with $\nu_{MLE} = 3$, the IT with $\nu_{MLE} = 4$) case theoretical quantiles in the first row (respectively, the second row, the third row).

To summarize the findings of this study, let us first say that there may be an abusive use of the Gaussian distribution in applications due to its simplicity. We have seen that considering the Student distribution instead is just slightly more complex, but feasible, and that one can test this choice. Concerning the two Student models, we have seen that the UT model is simpler to fit than the IT model, but has limitations due to the fact that it assumes a single realization, which restricts the properties of the maximum likelihood estimators and prevents the use of tests against the other two models.

5. Conclusions

We have compared three different models: the multivariate Gaussian model and two different multivariate Student models (uncorrelated or independent). We have derived some theoretical properties of the Student UT model and proposed a simple iterative reweighted algorithm to compute the maximum likelihood estimators in the IT model. Our simulations show that using a multivariate Student IT model instead of a multivariate Gaussian model for heavy tail data is simple and can be viewed as a safeguard against misspecification in the sense that there is more to loose if the DGP is Student and one uses a Gaussian model than in the reverse situation. Finally, we have proposed some graphical tools and a test to choose between the Gaussian and the IT models. The IT model fits our finance dataset quite well. There is still work to do in the direction of improving the model selection procedure to overcome the fact that the parameters are estimated and hence the hypothetical distribution is only approximate. Let us mention that it is also possible to adapt our algorithm for the IT model to the case of missing data. We intend to work in the direction of allowing different degrees of freedom for each coordinate. It may be also relevant to consider an alternative estimation method by generalizing the one proposed in Kent et al. (1994) to the multivariate regression case. Finally, another perspective is to consider multivariate errors-in-variables models, which allow incorporating measurement errors in the response and the explanatory variables. A possible approach is proposed in Croux et al. (2010).

Supplementary Materials: In order to allow the reproducibility of the empirical analyses contained in the present paper, some Supplementary Material is available at the following link: http://www.thibault.laurent.free.fr/code/jrfm/.

Author Contributions: T.H.A.N., C.T.-A. and A.R.-G., Methodology, analysis, review, and editing; T.H.A.N., writing, original draft preparation; C.T.-A. and A.R.-G. supervision and validation; T.L. and T.H.A.N., data curation.

Funding: This research received no external funding

Conflicts of Interest: The authors declare no conflict of interest.

Abbreviations

The following abbreviations are used in this manuscript:

EM	Expectation-maximization
MLE	Maximum likelihood estimator
N	Normal (Gaussian) model
IT	Independent multivariate Student
UT	Uncorrelated multivariate Student
RB	Relative bias
MSE	Mean squared error
RRMSE	Root relative mean squared error
DGP	Data-generating process

Appendix A

Proof of Proposition 1. Using Expression (1), the joint density function of $\hat{\boldsymbol{\epsilon}}_{UT}$ is:

$$p(\boldsymbol{\epsilon}_{UT}|\mathbf{0},\boldsymbol{\Omega}_{UT},v) = \frac{f(v)}{\det(\mathbf{I}_n \otimes \boldsymbol{\Sigma}_{UT})^{1/2}} \left[1 + \frac{1}{v-2}\boldsymbol{\epsilon}_{UT}^T(\mathbf{I}_n \otimes \boldsymbol{\Sigma}_{UT})^{-1}\boldsymbol{\epsilon}_{UT}\right]^{-\frac{v+nL}{2}}$$

$$= \frac{f(v)}{\det(\boldsymbol{\Sigma}_{UT})^{n/2}} \left[1 + \frac{1}{v-2}\boldsymbol{\epsilon}_{UT}^T(\mathbf{I}_n \otimes \boldsymbol{\Sigma}_{UT})^{-1}\boldsymbol{\epsilon}_{UT}\right]^{-\frac{v+nL}{2}}$$

$$= \frac{f(v)}{\det(\boldsymbol{\Sigma}_{UT})^{n/2}} \left[1 + \frac{1}{v-2}\sum_{i=1}^{n}\boldsymbol{\epsilon}_{UTi}^T\boldsymbol{\Sigma}_{UT}^{-1}\boldsymbol{\epsilon}_{UTi}\right]^{-\frac{v+nL}{2}}$$

Therefore, the logarithm of $p(\boldsymbol{\epsilon}_{UT}|0, \boldsymbol{\Omega}_{UT}, \nu)$ is:

$$\log p(\boldsymbol{\epsilon}_{UT}|0, \boldsymbol{\Omega}_{UT}, \nu) = \log f(\nu) - \frac{n}{2}\log \boldsymbol{\Sigma}_{UT} - \frac{\nu + nL}{2}\log\left[1 + \frac{1}{\nu-2}\sum_{i=1}^{n}\boldsymbol{\epsilon}_{UTi}^{T}\boldsymbol{\Sigma}_{UT}^{-1}\boldsymbol{\epsilon}_{UTi}\right]. \quad (A1)$$

In order to maximize $\log p(p(\boldsymbol{\epsilon}_{UT}|0, \boldsymbol{\Omega}_{UT}, \nu))$ as a function of $\boldsymbol{\beta}_{UT}$, we follow the same argument as in Theorem 8.4 from Seber (2008) for the Gaussian case and obtain that the minimum of $\sum_{i=1}^{n}\boldsymbol{\epsilon}_{UTi}^{T}\boldsymbol{\Sigma}_{UT}^{-1}\boldsymbol{\epsilon}_{UTi}$ is obtained for:

$$\hat{\boldsymbol{\beta}}_{UT} = \left(\boldsymbol{x}^{T}\boldsymbol{x}\right)^{-1}\boldsymbol{x}^{T}\boldsymbol{y}.$$

Besides, taking the partial derivative of (A1) as a function of $\boldsymbol{\Sigma}_{UT}$, we obtain:

$$\begin{aligned}\frac{\partial \log(p(\boldsymbol{\epsilon}_{UT}|0, \boldsymbol{\Omega}_{UT}, \nu))}{\partial \boldsymbol{\Sigma}_{UT}} &= -\frac{n\boldsymbol{\Sigma}_{UT}^{-1}}{2} - \frac{(\nu+nL)}{2}\frac{\partial \log(\nu - 2 + \sum_{i=1}^{n}\boldsymbol{\epsilon}_{UTi}^{T}\boldsymbol{\Sigma}_{UT}^{-1}\boldsymbol{\epsilon}_{UTi})}{\partial \boldsymbol{\Sigma}_{UT}} \\ &= -\frac{n\boldsymbol{\Sigma}_{UT}^{-1}}{2} - \frac{(\nu+nL)}{2}\frac{\partial(\nu - 2 + \sum_{i=1}^{n}\boldsymbol{\epsilon}_{UTi}^{T}\boldsymbol{\Sigma}_{UT}^{-1}\boldsymbol{\epsilon}_{UTi})/\partial \boldsymbol{\Sigma}_{UT}}{\nu - 2 + \sum_{i=1}^{n}\boldsymbol{\epsilon}_{UTi}^{T}\boldsymbol{\Sigma}_{UT}^{-1}\boldsymbol{\epsilon}_{UTi}}.\end{aligned}$$

Let:

$$w_{UT} = \frac{1}{\nu - 2 + \sum_{i=1}^{n}\boldsymbol{\epsilon}_{UTi}^{T}\boldsymbol{\Sigma}_{UT}^{-1}\boldsymbol{\epsilon}_{UTi}}. \quad (A2)$$

We have:

$$\begin{aligned}\frac{\partial \log(p(\boldsymbol{\epsilon}_{UT}|0, \boldsymbol{\Omega}_{UT}, \nu))}{\partial \boldsymbol{\Sigma}_{UT}} &= -\frac{n\boldsymbol{\Sigma}_{UT}^{-1}}{2} - \frac{(\nu+nL)w_{UT}}{2}\partial(\nu - 2 + \sum_{i=1}^{n}\boldsymbol{\epsilon}_{UTi}^{T}\boldsymbol{\Sigma}_{UT}^{-1}\boldsymbol{\epsilon}_{UTi})/\partial \boldsymbol{\Sigma}_{UT} \\ &= -\frac{n\boldsymbol{\Sigma}_{UT}^{-1}}{2} + \frac{(\nu+nL)w_{UT}}{2}\sum_{i=1}^{n}\boldsymbol{\Sigma}_{UT}^{-1}\boldsymbol{\epsilon}_{UTi}\boldsymbol{\epsilon}_{UTi}^{T}\boldsymbol{\Sigma}_{UT}^{-1}\end{aligned}$$

Solving $\dfrac{\partial \log(p(\boldsymbol{\epsilon}_{UT}|0, \boldsymbol{\Omega}_{UT}, \nu))}{\partial \boldsymbol{\Sigma}_{UT}} = 0$ and letting $\mathbf{E} = \sum_{i=1}^{n}\boldsymbol{\epsilon}_{UTi}\boldsymbol{\epsilon}_{UTi}^{T}$, we have:

$$\boldsymbol{\Sigma}_{UT}^{-1} = \frac{\nu + nL}{n}w_{UT}\sum_{i=1}^{n}\boldsymbol{\Sigma}_{UT}^{-1}\boldsymbol{\epsilon}_{UTi}\boldsymbol{\epsilon}_{UTi}^{T}\boldsymbol{\Sigma}_{UT}^{-1}$$

$$\boldsymbol{\Sigma}_{UT}\boldsymbol{\Sigma}_{UT}^{-1}\boldsymbol{\Sigma}_{UT} = \frac{\nu + nL}{n}w_{UT}\sum_{i=1}^{n}\boldsymbol{\Sigma}_{UT}\boldsymbol{\Sigma}_{UT}^{-1}\boldsymbol{\epsilon}_{UTi}\boldsymbol{\epsilon}_{UTi}^{T}\boldsymbol{\Sigma}_{UT}^{-1}\boldsymbol{\Sigma}_{UT}$$

$$\boldsymbol{\Sigma}_{UT} = (\nu + nL)w_{UT}\frac{\mathbf{E}}{n} \quad (A3)$$

The expression of w_{UT} in (A3) can be simplified by noting that:

$$\boldsymbol{\Sigma}_{UT}^{-1} = n((\nu+nL)w_{UT})^{-1}\mathbf{E}^{-1}$$

$$\sum_{i=1}^{n}\boldsymbol{\epsilon}_{UTi}^{T}\boldsymbol{\Sigma}_{UT}^{-1}\boldsymbol{\epsilon}_{UTi} = n((\nu+nL)w_{UT})^{-1}\sum_{i=1}^{n}\boldsymbol{\epsilon}_{UTi}^{T}\mathbf{E}^{-1}\boldsymbol{\epsilon}_{UTi}$$

$$= \frac{n}{(\nu+nL)w_{UT}}\mathrm{tr}\left(\sum_{i=1}^{n}\boldsymbol{\epsilon}_{UTi}\boldsymbol{\epsilon}_{UTi}^{T}\mathbf{E}^{-1}\right)$$

$$\sum_{i=1}^{n}\boldsymbol{\epsilon}_{UTi}^{T}\boldsymbol{\Sigma}_{UT}^{-1}\boldsymbol{\epsilon}_{UTi} = \frac{nL}{(\nu+nL)w_{UT}}. \quad (A4)$$

Replacing the expression of $\sum_{i=1}^{n} \boldsymbol{\epsilon}_{UTi}^{T} \boldsymbol{\Sigma}_{UT}^{-1} \boldsymbol{\epsilon}_{UTi}$ from (A4) into w_{UT}, we get:

$$w_{UT} = \frac{v}{(v-2)(v+nL)}.$$

Finally,

$$\hat{\boldsymbol{\Sigma}}_{UT} = \frac{v}{v-2} \frac{\sum_{i=1}^{n} \hat{\boldsymbol{e}}_{UTi} \hat{\boldsymbol{e}}_{UTi}^{T}}{n}.$$

☐

Proof of Proposition 2. The property $\mathbb{E}(\hat{\boldsymbol{\beta}}_{UT}) = \boldsymbol{\beta}_{UT}$ is immediate. In order to facilitate the derivation of the proof for $\hat{\boldsymbol{\Sigma}}_{UT}$, we write Model (4) as:

$$\mathbf{Y} = \mathbf{XB} + \boldsymbol{\varepsilon} \tag{A5}$$

where:

$$\mathbf{Y} = \begin{bmatrix} y_{11} & y_{12} & \cdots & y_{1L} \\ \vdots & \vdots & \vdots & \vdots \\ y_{n1} & y_{n2} & \cdots & y_{nL} \end{bmatrix}, \ \mathbf{X} = \begin{bmatrix} 1 & x_{11} & \cdots & x_{1K} \\ \vdots & \vdots & \vdots & \vdots \\ 1 & x_{n1} & \cdots & x_{nK} \end{bmatrix}, \ \mathbf{B} = \begin{bmatrix} \beta_{01} & \beta_{0L} \\ \beta_{11} & \beta_{1L} \\ \vdots & \vdots \\ \beta_{K1} & \beta_{KL} \end{bmatrix}$$

$$\boldsymbol{\varepsilon} = \begin{bmatrix} \varepsilon_{11} & \varepsilon_{12} & \cdots & \varepsilon_{1L} \\ \vdots & \vdots & \vdots & \vdots \\ \varepsilon_{n1} & \varepsilon_{n2} & \cdots & \varepsilon_{nL} \end{bmatrix}, \ \hat{\mathbf{B}}_{UT} = (\mathbf{X}^{T}\mathbf{X})^{-1}\mathbf{X}^{T}\mathbf{Y} \ \text{ and } \ \hat{\boldsymbol{e}}_{UT} = \mathbf{Y} - \mathbf{X}\hat{\mathbf{B}}_{UT}.$$

Let $\mathbf{E} = \hat{\boldsymbol{e}}_{UT}^{T}\hat{\boldsymbol{e}}_{UT}$ and $\mathbf{M} = \mathbf{I}_n - \mathbf{X}(\mathbf{X}^{T}\mathbf{X})^{-1}\mathbf{X}^{T}$. We have $\mathbf{MXB} = 0$, and following Seber (2008), Theorem 8.2,

$$\mathbf{E} = (\mathbf{Y} - \mathbf{X}\hat{\mathbf{B}}_{UT})^{T}(\mathbf{Y} - \mathbf{X}\hat{\mathbf{B}}_{UT}) = (\mathbf{MY})^{T}\mathbf{MY} = \mathbf{Y}^{T}\mathbf{MY}$$
$$= (\mathbf{Y} - \mathbf{XB})^{T}\mathbf{M}(\mathbf{Y} - \mathbf{XB}) = \boldsymbol{\varepsilon}^{T}\mathbf{M}\boldsymbol{\varepsilon} = \sum_{h}\sum_{i} M_{hi}\boldsymbol{\varepsilon}_{h}\boldsymbol{\varepsilon}_{i}^{T}.$$

Since $\mathbb{E}(\boldsymbol{\varepsilon}_{h}\boldsymbol{\varepsilon}_{i}^{T}) = \begin{cases} \boldsymbol{\Sigma} & \text{if } h = i \\ 0 & \text{otherwise} \end{cases}$, for $h, i = 1, \ldots, n$, $\mathbb{E}(\mathbf{E}) = \sum_{h} M_{hh}\boldsymbol{\Sigma} = tr(\mathbf{M})\boldsymbol{\Sigma} = (n-K)\boldsymbol{\Sigma}$

and:

$$\mathbb{E}(\hat{\boldsymbol{\Sigma}}_{UT}) = \mathbb{E}\left(\frac{v}{v-2}\frac{\mathbf{E}}{n}\right) = \frac{v}{v-2}\frac{\mathbb{E}(\mathbf{E})}{n} = \frac{v}{v-2}\frac{n-K}{n}\boldsymbol{\Sigma}_{UT}.$$

☐

References

Bilodeau, Martin, and David Brenner. 1999. *Theory of Multivariate Statistics (Springer Texts in Statistics)*. Berlin: Springer. ISBN 978-0-387-22616-3.

Croux, Christophe, Mohammed Fekri, and Anne Ruiz-Gazen. 2010. Fast and robust estimation of the multivariate errors in variables model. *Test* 19: 286–303. [CrossRef]

Dempster, Arthur P., Nan M. Laird, and Donald B. Rubin. 1978. Iteratively Reweighted Least Squared for Linear Regression when Errors are Normal/Independent distributed. *Multivariate Analysis V* 5: 35–37.

Dogru, Fatma Zehra, Y. Murat Bulut, and Olcay Arslan. 2018. Double Reweighted Estimators for the Parameters of the Multivariate t distribution. *Communications in Statistics-Theory and Methods* 47: 4751–71. [CrossRef]

Fernandez, Carmen, and Mark F. J. Steel. 1999. Multivariate Student t- Regression Models: Pitfalls and Inference. *Biometrika Trust* 86: 153–67. [CrossRef]

Fung, Thomas, and Eugene Seneta. 2010. Modeling and Estimating for Bivariate Financial Returns. *International Statistical Review* 78: 117–33. [CrossRef]

Fraser, Donald Alexander Stuart. 1979. *Inference and Linear Models*. New York: McGraw Hill. ISBN 9780070219106.

Fraser, Donald Alexander Stuart, and Kai Wang Ng. 1980. Multivariate regression analysis with spherical error. *Multivariate Analysis* 5: 369–86.

Gnanadesikan, Ram, and Jon R. Kettenring. 1972. Robust estimates, residuals, and outlier detection with multiresponse data. *Biometrics* 28: 81–124. [CrossRef]

Hofert, Marius. 2003. On Sampling from the Multivariate t Distribution. *The R Journal* 5: 129–36. [CrossRef]

Hu, Wenbo, and Alec N. Kercheval. 2009. Portfolio optimization for Student *t* and skewed *t* returns. *Quantitative Finance* 10: 129–36. [CrossRef]

Huber, Peter J., and Elvezio M. Ronchetti. 2009. *Robust Statistics*. Hoboken: Wiley. ISBN 9780470129906.

Johnson, Norman L., and Samuel Kotz. 1972. Student multivariate distribution. In *Distribution in Statistics: Continuous Multivariate Distributions*. Michigan: Wiley Publishing House. ISBN-13: 9780471443704.

Kan, Raymond, and Guofu Zhou. 2017. Modeling non-normality using multivariate t: implications for asset pricing. *China Finance Review International* 7: 2–32. [CrossRef]

Katz, Jonathan N., and Gary King. 1999. A Statistical Model for Multiparty Electoral Data. *American Political Science Review* 93: 15–32. [CrossRef]

Kelejian, Harry H., and Ingmar R. Prucha. 1985. Independent or Uncorrelated Disturbances in Linear Regression. *Economics Letters* 19: 35–38. [CrossRef]

Kent, John T., David E. Tyler, and Yahuda Vard. 1994. A curious likelihood identity for the multivariate t-distribution. *Communications in Statistics-Simulation and Computation* 23: 441–53. [CrossRef]

Kotz, Samuel, and Saralees Nadarajah. 2004. *Multivariate t Distributions and Their Applications*. Cambridge: Cambridge University Press. ISBN 9780511550683.

Lange, Kenneth, Roderick J. A. Little, and Jeremy Taylor. 1989. Robust Statistical Modeling Using the t-Distribution. *International Statistical Review* 84: 881–96. [CrossRef]

Lange, Kenneth, and Janet S. Sinsheimer. 1993. Normal/Independent Distributions and Their Applications in Robust Regression. *Journal of Computational and Graphical Statistics* 2: 175–98. [CrossRef]

Liu, Chuanhai, and Donald B. Rubin. 1995. ML estimation of the t distribution using EM and its extensions, ECM and ECME. *Statistica Sinica* 5: 19–39.

Liu, Chuanhai. 1997. ML Estimation of the Multivariate t Distribution and the EM Algorithm. *J. Multivar. Anal.* 63: 296–312. [CrossRef]

Maronna, Ricardo Antonio. 1976. Robust M-Estimators of Multivariate Location and Scatter. *The Annals of Statistics* 4: 51–67. [CrossRef]

McNeil, Alexander J., Rüdiger Frey, and Paul Embrechts. 2005. *Quantitative Risk Management: Concepts, Techniques and Tools*. Vol. 3. Princeton: Princeton University Press.

Platen, Eckhard, and Renata Rendek. 2008. Empirical Evidence on Student-t Log-Returns of Diversified World Stock Indices. *Journal of Statistical Theory and Practice* 2: 233–51. [CrossRef]

Prucha, Ingmar R., and Harry H. Kelejian. 1984. The Structure of Simultaneous Equation Estimators: A generalization Towards Nonnormal Disturbances. *Econometrica* 52: 721–36. [CrossRef]

Roth, Michael. 2013. *On the Multivariate t Distribution*. Report Number: LiTH-ISY-R-3059. Linkoping: Department of Electrical Engineering, Linkoping University.

Seber, George Arthur Frederick. 2008. *Multivariate Observations*. Hoboken: John Wiley & Sons. ISBN 9780471881049.

Singh, Radhey. 1988. Estimation of Error Variance in Linear Regression Models with Errors having Multivariate Student t-Distribution with Unknown Degrees of Freedom. *Economics Letters* 27: 47–53. [CrossRef]

Small, N. J. H. 1978. Plotting squared radii. *Biometrics* 65: 657–58. [CrossRef]

Sutradhar, Brajendra C., and Mir M. Ali. 1986. Estimation of the Parameters of a Regression Model with a Multivariate t Error Variable. *Communication Statistics Theory and Method* 15: 429–50. [CrossRef]

Zellner, Arnold. 1976. Bayesian and Non-Bayesian Analysis of the Regression Model with Multivariate Student-t Error Terms. *Journal of the American Statistical Association* 71: 400–5. [CrossRef]

Journal of
*Risk and Financial
Management*

MDPI

Article

Does the Misery Index Influence a U.S. President's Political Re-Election Prospects?

Bahram Adrangi [1] **and Joseph Macri** [2,*]

[1] R.B Pamplin School of Business Administration, University of Portland, Portland, OR 97203, USA;
    adrangi@up.edu
[2] Department of Economics, Macquarie University, North Ryde, Sydney, NSW 2109, Australia
* Correspondence: joseph.macri@mq.edu.au; Tel.: +612-9850-9469

Received: 12 December 2018; Accepted: 28 January 2019; Published: 1 February 2019

Abstract: We seek to determine whether a United States President's job approval rating is influenced by the Misery Index. This hypothesis is examined in two ways. First, we employ a nonlinear model that includes several macroeconomic variables: the current account deficit, exchange rate, unemployment, inflation, and mortgage rates. Second, we employ probit and logit regression models to calculate the probabilities of U.S. Presidents' approval ratings to the Misery Index. The results suggest that Layton's model does not perform well when adopted for the United States. Conversely, the probit and logit regression analysis suggests that the Misery Index significantly impacts the probability of the approval of U.S. Presidents' performances.

Keywords: Misery Index; inflation; unemployment; Probit and Logit models; Okun's law

JEL Classification: C13; C30; E32; E66

1. Introduction

"It's the economy, stupid", a statement famously coined by James Carville, campaign strategist to presidential candidate Bill Clinton's 1992 U.S. election campaign team, claimed that electoral success hinged on the performance of the United States economy. Are U.S. citizens better off now than 4 years ago? Is it relatively easier to find a job now than four years ago? Typically, questions of this nature resonate in the minds of constituents and political representatives that are seeking to run for public office. However, the performance of the economy in relation to the success, or otherwise, of the election or re-election of political representatives and or political parties is not new. The core "Misery Index", devised by Arthur Okun, who served as presidential advisor to United States President Lyndon B. Johnson's Council of Economic Advisers, is the sum of the inflation and unemployment rates, which was used as a core measure of economic discomfort. The Misery Index was used by policymakers and politicians as an "objective" measure of well-being. An accurate and objective measure of the "peoples" discomfort is typically perceived to influence politicians' likelihood of electoral success.

The objective of this paper is to determine whether U.S. Presidents' job approval ratings are influenced by the rates of inflation and unemployment—the Misery Index. Does the economy matter? Are the political fortunes of U.S. Presidents determined by changes in the components of the Misery Index? We are motivated to undertake this research for several reasons. First, it is of important policy interest to determine whether increases (or decreases) in unemployment and inflation rates decrease (or increase) the likelihood of electoral success of U.S. Presidents. Second, the period January 1973 through to November 2015, including the second term of the Obama administration, represents several significant economic and political events; the period of stagflation in the 1970s, world-wide recessions of 1981–1982, 1990–1991, the Iraq War, the 1997 Asian Financial Crisis, sub-prime crisis, and the Global Financial Crisis (GFC). Third, Layton (1992) estimated the degree that Australia's community welfare was affected by a number of macroeconomic variables that included unemployment, inflation rate, current account deficit, and the exchange rate. We extend this novel study by exploring the non-stationary properties of U.S. data and seek to determine whether the model adopted by Layton (1992) is robust to non-stationary tests and analysis. Fourth, we are not aware of any US study that has estimated the probability of electoral success of U.S. Presidents (as measured by their job approval rating) based on the Misery Index or its components and a set of "standard" macroeconomic variables using probit analysis. Fifth, it would be of policy interest to determine whether the impact of real economic variables matter to U.S. Presidents' approval ratings or is simply illusory and based upon perceptions, or non-economic factors. In particular, monitoring and managing the two components of the misery index, i.e., unemployment and inflation rates, are the congressional mandates of the Federal Reserve Bank.

This paper is organized in the following sections. Section 2 provides a review of the literature on the Misery Index. Section 3 describes the data and methodology employed in this paper. Section 4 reports the empirical findings. Section 5 is devoted to a short discussion of findings. Section 6 provides a summary of our findings.

2. Literature Review

The movement in the Misery Index, the sum of the levels of unemployment and inflation, has been used to monitor the movements in the level of macroeconomic welfare of a community. A decreasing (or increasing) value in the Misery Index is expected to improve (or deteriorate) well-being. In one paper, Layton (1992) employed a set of macroeconomic variables, namely, current account deficit, real wages, inflation, unemployment rate, rate of exchange rate between the Australian and US dollar ($US/$A), and an election dummy to examine the approval rating of the Prime Minister of Australia (dependent variable).

Many papers in the late 1970s addressed the relationship between the economy and the approval rate of U.S. presidents or votes they receive. Mueller (1970, 1973) led this line of research with his seminal work using Gallup aggregate approval ratings as the dependent variable in a number of regressions. His findings showed an asymmetric association between the state of the economy and presidential approval ratings. Specifically, the recessionary state of the economy was associated with declining presidential popularity, while positive economic trends did not show such association.

Other scholars explored the subject further. Kenski (1977, 1980), Fair (1978, 1982, 1988), and Rogoff and Sibert (1988), among others, are notable. The problem with many of these papers is that they relied on regression models that generally ignored the nonstationary time series. Ostrom and Smith (1992) are perhaps the first researchers that raised concerns about regression results regarding approval rates in the presence of nonstationary time series. It is well known that regression estimates in the presence of non-stationary variables produce spurious results.

Perhaps due to econometric issues, research prior to the mid-1990s failed to produce any consistent empirical verdict on the matter. Thus, even after decades since the first paper on the presidential approval rate, there is no clear consensus regarding the role of economic variables in the presidential approval rate. The literature tends to accept that the stance of the economy influences the popularity of the incumbent president. For example, Norpoth (1984, p. 266) states: "There can be little doubt that the economy matters for presidential popularity."

Researchers in recent years have examined the association of the misery index with several socioeconomic variables. For instance, Lorde et al. (2016), Nunley et al. (2011), Tang and Lean (2009), among others, studied the association of the crime rate and the misery index.

Given the econometric problems that beset most academic papers prior to 1990s, we focus our attention on papers that explore the association of the economy and the presidential performance approval in the post-1990 years.

Lean and Smyth (2011) show that the impact of positive aggregate demand shocks on misery index are temporary. Their findings would cast doubt that misery index and the presidential approval rate are associated over time.

Lovell and Tien (2000) investigate the association of the misery index with consumer confidence. Their findings indicate that there is a linear relationship between the two indices. Furthermore, they provide evidence that the frequency of the data may matter. For instance, the misery index that is the sum of annual rates of inflation and unemployment rate may be more useful in gauging consumer confidence. The unemployment rate is statistically significant in a comprehensive model of the relationship between the consumer sentiment and economic variables, while inflation rate is not.

Berlemann and Enkelmann (2014) offer an extensive survey of papers investigating the subject of the economy and presidential approval rate. They conclude that functional forms of equations that relate approval rate to economic variables, methods of estimation, presence of unit root in some time series, and the period of study, might have contributed to contradictory findings. However, they identify the inflation and unemployment rates as well as the budget deficit as economic factors that have been shown to influence presidents' approval ratings.

Berlemann et al. (2015), estimate popularity functions for the United States using semi-parametric estimation and flexible functional form, allowing for the data to determine the appropriate functional form. They prefer a flexible formulation form to linear models employed in most studies. Their estimation results offer statistical support for interaction of economic variables and non-linearities in the relationship between economic variables and presidential popularity. Allowing for the variable of time in office corroborates the common finding that presidential approval rate often declines toward the end of term in the office.

Choi et al. (2016) confirm that the relationship between the economy and the presidential approval is nonlinear. They employ a novel approach by estimating a nonlinear threshold model over quarterly data spanning the first quarter of 1960 through the second quarter of 2012. Impulse response functions track the impact of the shocks (rises) in unemployment and inflation rates on the presidential approval rate. Their impulse response functions show that presidential approval rate improves as the unemployment rate falls during the high unemployment periods, which is defined as above 7 percent. However, the impulse response of the approval rate is asymmetric and disappears if the unemployment rate is below the threshold rate of 7 percent.

Impulse responses of the presidential approval rate to inflation shocks also vary across the low to high unemployment rate conditions. They show that in periods of low unemployment rate (<7%), higher inflation shocks improve the approval rate, while the opposite occurs during high unemployment, at least in the first quarter. Given their findings on inflation and consumer sentiment shocks, Chi et al. believe further research is warranted.

Dickerson (2016) examines the association between the presidential performance approval rate in both directions. His approach is novel, which allows for feedback from the presidential approval to economic performance. This approach is based on the notion that the electorate uses economic information to confirm their existing political beliefs. His findings confirm the above notion by showing a stronger effect of presidential approval rate on economic perceptions than the other way around. His simultaneous equation estimation results suggest that recessionary economic periods may result in strong negative impact on presidential approval rate.

Ferreira and Sakurai (2013) investigate the relative importance of economic conditions versus other factors in determining the presidential approval rate. Specifically, do citizens consider macroeconomic conditions more important than personal attributes and charisma in forming their opinions of a president's performance rating? The analysis of the monthly data on Brazilian presidents' approval rates from 1999 to 2010 show that the economic and political indicators explain the variations in the presidential approval ratings in Brazil. Specifically, the unemployment rate and the minimum wage rate are the most important economic variables considered by citizens.

Edwards et al. (1995) suggest that saliency of issues for citizens may be the cornerstone of their rating of a president's performance. Salience of issues vary over time. For instance, while the Federal debt may take salience over other economic issues during some periods, the attention of the public may shift to inflation rate, and inflation may rise to salience for the public. Thus, depending on how a president performs in dealing with salient issues at the time, the presidential rating could respond accordingly. Edwards et al. (1995) analyze media coverage of issues. They estimate logit models of public opinion polls and time series regression of relationship between salient issues and their association with presidential approval. They confirm that the public perception of salient issues varies over time, and there is a direct relationship between issues of salience to the public and their approval rating of the presidential performance. The findings of Edwards et al. (1995) lend support to Berlemann and Enkelmann (2014), among others, who find that depending on the time period, presidential approval rate may respond to different economic variables.

The popular media continues to link the performance of a president to the economy. For instance, Langer (2018) suggests that the good economies do not necessarily make a president popular, and vice versa.

He considers the unemployment rate as a proxy for economic performance and identifies four tiers of unemployment rate from low to high rates. Tier 1 represents periods of unemployment of 4.5 percent or lower, generally considered full employment; Tier 2, 4.6 to 5.5 percent; Tier 3, 5.6 to 6.8 percent; and Tier 4, 6.9 percent unemployment or higher. Trumps presidency is currently enjoying unemployment rates below 4.5 percent, yet his approval rate is just 36-percent approval in the latest ABC News/Washington Post poll.

Langer (2018) provides correlation coefficient estimates. These estimates indicate that the correlation between unemployment rate and presidential approval rate is erratic, tenuous, and counterintuitive. He computes correlation coefficients between approval and unemployment for Gerald Ford (0.70), George H.W. Bush (0.71), Dwight Eisenhower (0.68), and Clinton (0.66), indicating that high unemployment rate was associated with high presidential approval rate. On the contrary, high employment rates were negatively associated with the approval of Truman (−0.65), Johnson (−0.90), John F. Kennedy (−0.49), and now Trump (−0.66). Kennedy, Jimmy Carter, Ronald Reagan, and Barack Obama all started with high approval despite higher than 6.9 percent unemployment. These findings would cast doubt on the relationship between the economy and the presidential approval rates. His conclusions are that a poor economy may make it difficult for a president to be popular. However, a better economy does not necessarily lead to popularity, though it may make it likely.

Cohn (2018) is another article in the popular media that discusses the association between presidential approval rate and the economy. He cites evidence that the stock market has surged. Unemployment is at 4.1 percent. ISIS has largely been vanquished from Iraq and Syria. However, Donald J. Trump's approval ratings are mired in the upper 30s. This is the lowest for any president at this stage of presidency since modern polling began more than three-quarters of a century ago. If the approval rating would be boosted by economic performance, Trump's approval rating should have been lifted into the 50s, based on the experience. Lyndon Johnson is the only other first-term president in the era of modern polling with an approval rating under 50 percent while the unemployment rate was below 5 percent.

The controversy regarding the relationship between the economy and the presidential approval rate is not resolved. Academic and popular research indicate that conclusions run the gamut from no to some relationship between the economy and the presidential approval rate. As Berlemann and Enkelmann (2014) and Choi et al. (2016) suggest, further research is in order. Given the importance of the unemployment and inflation rates, i.e., the components of the misery index for U.S. policy makers, including the Federal Reserve Bank, we address the issue differently from the previous studies. Specifically, we estimate the probability of the changes in the approval rate with respect to the components of the misery index.

3. Data and Methodology

The monthly observations on all variables are sourced from the Federal Reserve Bank of St. Louis database, FRED (https://fred.stlouisfed.org/). The current account balance is reported on a quarterly basis and converted to monthly observations by linear interpolation. This method assigns each value in the quarterly series to the first monthly observation associated with the low frequency period, then places all intermediate points on straight lines connecting these points.

The real hourly wage rate is deflated by the US Consumer Price Index (CPI). The exchange rate of the dollar is the effective rate, which is represented by the Trade-Weighted exchange rate of the US dollar. The presidential job approval rates are monthly averages for the period 1973:1 to 2015:11, and cover the Nixon presidency and the second Obama administration period. The raw data is derived from the database maintained by the University of California at Santa Barbara (http://www.presidency.ucsb.edu/data/popularity.php). The Election is a dummy variable that denotes one for election years and zero otherwise. The methodologies adopted are multivariate regressions following Layton's nonlinear functional form, and logit and probit regressions. We undertake tests for stationarity before estimating any regressions. Layton's (1992) empirical findings may be invalid as the time series variables may be non-stationary. However, it is important to note that the paper was completed when stationarity tests were in their infancy. We apply the ADF and PP tests of stationarity to test for variable stationarity. We initially proceed by adopting the Layton (1992) methodological approach, because previous research (see Berlemann and Enkelmann (2014)) indicates that a nonlinear functional form may be superior to linear models. However, as (Edwards et al. (1995)) indicates, the saliency of issues as perceived by citizens may shift unexpectedly. Therefore, it may be difficult for any functional formulation to capture a relationship that stems from almost random behavior by the citizens. This may also explain the divergence of empirical econometric results. We estimate the probability that approval rate may respond to economic factors rather than focusing on coefficient estimates. Thus, we estimate logit and probit models that provide econometrically robust estimates using the maximum likelihood methodology. Furthermore, they provide the marginal probabilities of the changes in the approval rate due to changes in unemployment and inflation rate.

4. Empirical Findings

The initial estimation is to adopt the methodological approach of Layton (1992). We estimate and report the results of Equation (1) from Layton's (1992) paper. The equation is estimated and expressed as follows:

$$APR = \alpha UR^{\beta_1} \inf^{\beta_2} mrg^{\beta_3} rhw^{\beta_4} twdol^{\beta_5} e^u \qquad (1)$$

The variable definitions are denoted follows:

APR = Monthly US President's Approval Rate
UR = Unemployment rate
Inflation = Change in Consumer Price Index (CPI)
MRG = Mortgage rate
RHW = Real Hourly Wages
TWDOL = Trade Weighted Exchange Rate of the US Dollar

The economic variables that determine the approval rate of a president are not concretely defined. Furthermore, while there is anecdotal evidence that some economic variables may be associated with a president's approval rate, the functional relationship is not obvious. Layton (1992) offers justification for including the above variables in his long-linear model. We also examine the linear functional form for probit and logit approach. Important variables that directly impact an electorate are unemployment and inflation because of their impact on household lives. Mortgage rates address housing accessibility, where higher mortgage rates make home ownership inaccessible, and vice versa. Real wage rates directly affect working people's purchasing power and well-being. The exchange rate of the dollar may affect the electorate's confidence in the economy, and thus, a president's approval rate. The components of the misery index, i.e., unemployment and inflation rates, are included as explanatory variables, as in Layton (1992). This allows us to investigate the impact of the disaggregated misery index on the APR and provide more granular information on these critical variables. Furthermore, the Federal Reserve Bank is mandated by the congress to maintain these two rates and the natural rate of unemployment, assumed to be 5 percent. We picked 5 percent as the natural rate of unemployment, however, the economists are not in total agreement on this rate, which is believed to be in the range of 4.7 to 5 percent. We also include an election dummy variable to capture the effects of election years on the incumbent US President's approval rate. This variable is equal to one in an election year and zero otherwise.

Table 1, column 1, presents the results that are based on Layton's estimated equation. Our findings, like Layton's findings, are not reassuring. Moreover, the results are likely to be spurious given that the APR is stationary or I (0) and all the explanatory variables are all I (1), which requires them to be differenced to render them stationary. Furthermore, autocorrelation is also present as shown by the significance of the Breusch-Godfrey test of autocorrelation, with two degrees of freedom for the chi-squared test.

Table 1. Estimation results of alternative formulations of Equation (1).

Functional Form 1	(1)	Functional Form 2	(2)	Functional Form 3	(3)
Dependent Variable: Natural Logarithm of Monthly Presidential Approval Rate					
Intercept	4.115 [a]	Intercept	4.471 [a]	Intercept	3.977 [a]
	(1.183)		(1.195)		(0.033)
LN (UR)	−0.264	LN(TWDOL)	1.055 [a]	DLN(TWDOL)	−0.93
	(0.400)		(−0.18)		(0.806)
LN(UR)(-1)	−0.206	LN(RHW)	−2.233 [a]	DLN(RHW)	−14.896 [b]
	(0.4)		(0.499)		(6.571)
LN(INF)	−0.008	LN(MRG)	−0.341 [a]	DLN(MRG)	0.033
	(0.012)		(0.075)		(0.358)
LN(INF)(-1)	−0.016	LN(URt-1)	-0.132	DLN(UR)	−0.244
	(0.01)		(0.393)		(0.496)
LN(MRG)	−0.299 [a]	LN(URt-2)	−0.044	DLN(CPI)	−20.717 [a]
	(0.078)		(0.217)		(8.363)
LN(RHW)	−2.036	LN(URt-3)	−0.406	ELECTION	−0.066
	(0.989)		(0.417)		(0.049)
LN(TWDOL)	1.010 [a]	ELECTION	−0.064 [c]		
	(−0.189)		(0.039)		
ELECTION	−0.066 [c]				
	(0.039)				
F	27.007 [a]		34.853 [a]		5.508 [a]
R^2	0.316		0.35		0.061
B-G	357.357 [a]		404.112 [a]		420.405 [a]

Notes: Columns (1) through (3) report the results of the variations of Equation (1) estimated by the Newy-West heteroscedastic and autocorrelation consistent methodology (HAC). (−1) stands for the lagged natural logarithm of a variable. B-G stands for the Breusch-Godfrey Lagrange Multiplier (LM) test of autocorrelation; D and LN, stand for the first difference and natural logarithm, respectively. [a] significant at 1% level, [b] significant at 5% level, [c] significant at 10% level.

The unemployment and inflation rates for the current and the previous months are negatively associated with the United States President's Approval rate, but are statistically insignificant. The Real Hourly Wages (RHW) may possibly capture the sentiment of the business world and employers who may view this as inflationary, consequently triggering cost-push inflation. Furthermore, rising RHW may signal that there may be a negative impact on corporate profits. This may have a negative impact on equity markets, which may have a negative impact on U.S. presidents' approval ratings. The signs on the mortgage rate and election year coefficients are consistent with expectations. The current account balance (CAB) was initially included but excluded due to its statistical insignificance. There may be a range of reasons why this variable may not be statistically significant in our analysis. First, it is not recorded monthly and it was therefore necessary to interpolate the monthly data. Second, the financial and news media do not focus on the CAB. It is typically examined by academics. Third, the United States has been running a CAB deficit since the mid-1960s. Therefore, it is assumed that the United States will have a current account deficit that may or may not improve on a monthly basis. We re-estimate a slight variation of Equation (1) by the Newey-West method so that we obtain the heteroscedastic and autocorrelation consistent standard deviations and t statistics. These are reported in Table 1, column 2.

Column 2 of Table 1 shows the estimation results after several iterations of the model was estimated. The results show that the unemployment rate is negatively associated with the APR. The inflation rate may be captured by the real wage rate. Importantly, the rising real wage may have two opposing effects. First, it could be a sign of improvements in the labor market, which should positively influence the approval rate of a president. Conversely, rising real wage rates may signal future inflationary periods and be negatively associated with U.S. Presidents' approval ratings. In this sample, the inflationary signal of rising real wage rates dominates.

The Augmented Dickey Fuller (ADF) and Phillips-Perron (PP) tests indicate that the dependent variable APR is stationary, while the remaining explanatory variables are nonstationary. Therefore, we estimate the model by first differencing the explanatory variables. The regression of the United States President's approval rating on the changes in the explanatory variables may still be informative. For example, changes in CPI, if positive, signal rising prices. If there are dramatic rises in price levels, the United States President's approval rating may decline. There may be ambiguous effects on U.S. Presidents' approval ratings if there is an appreciation of the United States dollar. The business community may view this as an indication of future declines in U.S. exports. Conversely, financial markets may view this as the strength of the United States economy and increase the demand for the United States dollar. The Newey-West estimation results of regressing U.S. Presidents' approval ratings on the first difference of the logarithm of the explanatory variables is reported in Table 1, Column 3.

Column 3, Table 1, reports mixed results. While inflationary signals, such as the change in the consumer price index or changes in real wages, are negatively associated with the United States President's approval rating, the unemployment rate and other model variables are statistically insignificant. The Ramsey regression model specification also indicates that there may be problems with model specification. We estimate several alternative specifications. However, we cannot find any robust or concrete relationship between U.S. Presidents' approval ratings and components of the misery index. Furthermore, autocorrelation continues to be a persistent problem, as indicated by the significance of the Breusch-Godfrey Lagrange Multiplier test of autocorrelation with two lags of residuals included in the test regression.

Therefore, our next stage of investigation explores the use of probit and logit models in seeking to rigorously establish a relationship between U.S. Presidents' approval ratings and the macroeconomic variables listed above. We decided to explore the logit and probit models for several reasons. First, the Maximum likelihood (ML) estimates of model coefficients are robust in the presence of various issues, such as autocorrelation and heteroscedasticity. Second, we can compute the marginal probability of U.S. President's approval ratings with respect to changes in unemployment and inflation rates when using the ML coefficient estimates. Third, the efficient allocation of campaign funds to highlight political goals of presidential candidates, as well as accomplishments of incumbents, is paramount for campaign managers and strategists. Measuring the changes in the probability of approval rates in response to changes in unemployment and inflation rates may offer a guide to the allocation of funds in political advertisements. The results from logit and probit models are qualitatively almost identical. Therefore, we report only the estimates of the probit model in Table 2, as well as the probability of U.S. President's approval ratings and the marginal probabilities with respect to the two variables of interest (i.e., unemployment rate and inflation).

Table 2. Maximum Likelihood estimation of the Probit Model.

Dependent Variable: Presidential Approval Rate = 1 if >0.4697, 0 Otherwise	
Intercept	−0.93
	(0.629)
CAB	0.003 [a]
	(0.001)
UR	−0.179 [a]
	(0.039)
INF	-0.024 [a]
	(0.073)
MRG	−0.083 [a]
	(0.03)
TWDOL	0.035 [a]
	(0.006)
ELECTION	0.267 [c]
	(0.143)
LR	78.805 [a]
Mc Fadden R^2	0.11
LL	−305.7
Restricted LL	−343.64

Notes: Probit model estimation. LL is the value of log likelihood function. LR is the likelihood ratio testing the null hypothesis restriction that all coefficients are statistically insignificant; [a] significant at 1% level, [c] significant at 10% level.

For logit and probit model estimation, the approval rate (APR) is set equal to one if the United States President's approval rating is greater than 46.97%, or 0 otherwise. We chose 46.97, even though the mean and median of approval rates are 51%, as based on Chebyshev's rule, 96% of time the United States President's approval rating is between 46.97 and 55%. The coefficient of the real hourly wage rate in all attempts, including the logit and probit estimation, behaved erratically with a counter-intuitive sign. Therefore, this variable is dropped in the remainder of the analysis. All coefficients in the probit model are collectively significant with a *p*-value of virtually zero for the loglikelihood ratio test. The test compares the value of the logarithm of the likelihood (LL) function from the model with the LL function from a restricted model, i.e., a model that sets all coefficients except the intercept equal to zero. McFadden's R-squared is 11%, which is consistent with the value of the log-likelihood ratio statistic. The McFadden's R-squared measure is derived from the value of the LL values, with and without restrictions that all explanatory variables are insignificant. It is usually lower than the R-squared derived from OLS and its variations. The coefficients of the current account balance, the exchange rate of the United States dollar, and the dummy variable for the election year are all positive and statistically significant. The interpretation of these signs is that as the current account balance improves, so does the United States President's approval rating. The same is also true of the effective exchange rate of the United States dollar. The election dummy variable is positively associated with the United States President's approval rating of the incumbent president. The unemployment and inflation and mortgage rates are negatively associated with the United States President's approval rating, as expected.

We estimate the United States President's approval rating based on the average of all explanatory variables, the United States Federal Reserve's inflation target rate, and the natural rate of unemployment of two and five percent, respectively. Based on the estimated coefficients, the United States President's approval rating is 75.86 per cent, which is significantly above the mean and median of 51 percent. This is a plausible outcome and suggests that if the inflation and unemployment rates are at their targets, i.e., 2 percent and 5 percent, respectively, the United States President's approval rating would be higher than the median and mean of all U.S. Presidents' approval ratings. This may suggest the importance of unemployment and inflation on a United States President's approval rating.

We compute the change in the probability of a United States President's approval rating, or the marginal probability with respect to changes in unemployment and inflation rates ($\frac{\partial APR}{\partial UR}$, $\frac{\partial APR}{\partial INF}$, respectively). For instance, using the chain rule and the fact that the derivative of the cumulative normal probability with respect to standard normal variable (z) is the standard normal density function, we have:

$$\frac{\partial APR}{\partial UR} = \frac{\partial \Phi}{\partial z} * \frac{\partial z}{\partial UR}$$
$$\frac{\partial APR}{\partial UR} = (\phi | z = X) * \hat{\beta}_{ur},$$

where Φ and ϕ represent cumulative standard normal probability and the standard normal density functions, respectively. X is the vector of average of all explanatory variables, and UR and INF are set at 5 and 2 percent, respectively. The estimated coefficient of the unemployment and inflation rates are $\hat{\beta}_{ur} = -0.179$ and $\hat{\beta}_{\text{inf}} = -0.024$, respectively.

The results suggest that for a one per cent increase in the unemployment rate, the probability of a US President receiving approval decreases by 3 percent. The probability that a US President receives performance approval decreases by a probability of 7 per cent for a one per cent increase in the inflation rate. The marginal probabilities, with respect to unemployment and inflation rates, confirm that the misery index could adversely affect the approval prospects of US Presidents. The inflation rate appears to have gained saliency for the electorate relative to the unemployment rate for the period of this study.

(a) $\frac{\partial APR}{\partial UR} = -0.03219$

(b) $\frac{\partial APR}{\partial INF} = -0.07018$

5. Discussion

Table 2 shows that the probit model estimation produces results that are intuitively plausible. Previous research has produced mixed results regarding the role of the economy in relation to presidential approval rate (see Berlemann and Enkelmann (2014)). Edwards et al. (1995) offer a cogent explanation for inconsistent findings by researchers. They show that saliency of issues for citizens changes over time in an unpredictable manner. Therefore, econometric models may be incapable of accounting for the unpredictable shifts. However, the probit model enables us to compute the probabilities of change in the presidential approval rate with respect to economic variable rather than significant versus insignificant coefficient estimates.

All coefficients in Table 2 have the expected signs and are statistically significant. Furthermore, the maximum likelihood estimation method ensures that the results are econometrically reliable. Based on these estimates, the electorate is sensitive to the misery index components. Specifically, the components of the misery index are statistically significant in determining the probability of a president performance approval. The electorate is more sensitive to changes in the inflation rate than the rate of unemployment. This could be due to the aging population in the United States and the rising number of retirees on a fixed income. This segment of the population tends to actively participate in the political process and elections and be sensitive to the loss of purchasing power due to rising inflation rates. They may tend to be less concerned with unemployment rate because of their retired status. Not only do the retired individuals enjoy free time to focus on political issues, they also tend to be members of various action groups, such as American Association of Retired persons (AARP). AARP, with its 38 million people memberships in 2018 (roughly 12 percent of the US population), keeps members informed of political and economic changes that may impact their lives. It is plausible that this segment of the population would be more likely to rate a president negatively due to rising inflation rate relative to the increases in the unemployment rate.

Our findings are consistent with findings of research in the past (see Berlemann and Enkelmann (2014)) confirming that unemployment and inflation rate are associated with the probability of changing citizens' view of presidents' performance approval inversely.

6. Conclusions

This paper's objective was to determine whether a United States President's job approval ratings are influenced by the Misery Index, using both the Layton's (1992) macroeconomic model and probit and logit regression analysis. Our paper differs from previous research in its emphasis on computing change in the probability of receiving performance approval rather than solely focusing on statistical significance of coefficients of the economic variables.

The results suggest that Layton's model, similar to many other researchers' (see Berlemann and Enkelmann (2014)), does not perform well for the United States when non-stationarity issues are considered. Conversely, we found that both the probit and logit regression analysis suggest that the unemployment and inflation rates significantly influence U.S. Presidents' electoral prospects. For example, a one per cent increase in the unemployment rate decreases the probability of a United States President receiving a positive approval rating by three percent. A one per cent increase in the inflation rate decreases the probability of a U.S. President's favorable approval rating by seven per cent. The marginal probabilities of approval of a president's performance with respect to unemployment and inflation rates confirm that the statement "it's the economy, stupid" may have relevance for politicians seeking to run for public office in the U.S.

Author Contributions: J.M. was the author behind the main idea and objectives of the paper. The authors jointly compiled and completed the data set for the research. Econometric work was jointly completed using Eviews software and authors met at conferences to discuss the findings and perform further econometric work. The analysis of the results was done jointly. J.M. completed the first finished draft of the paper. B.A. and J.M. jointly completed further econometric estimations and revised the paper twice.

Funding: This research received no external funding.

Acknowledgments: Authors are grateful for the extensive and constructive comments by two anonymous reviewers and the academic editor during the two rounds of revisions. Remaining errors are authors' responsibility.

Conflicts of Interest: The authors declare no conflict of interest.

References

Berlemann, Michael, and Sören Enkelmann. 2014. The economic determinants of US presidential approval: A survey. *European Journal of Political Economy* 36: 41–54. [CrossRef]

Berlemann, Michael, Sören Enkelmann, and Torben Kuhlenkasper. 2015. Unraveling the relationship between presidential approval and the economy: A multidimensional semiparametric approach. *Journal of Applied Econometrics* 30: 468–86. [CrossRef]

Choi, Seung-Whan, Patrick James, Yitan Li, and Eric Olson. 2016. Presidential approval and macroeconomic conditions: Evidence from a nonlinear model. *Applied Economics* 48: 4558–72. [CrossRef]

Cohn, Nate. 2018. Strong Economies Lift Presidents. Trump Seems an Exception. *New York Times*, January 8.

Dickerson, Bradley. 2016. Economic perceptions, presidential approval, and causality: The moderating role of the economic context. *American Politics Research* 44: 1037–65. [CrossRef]

Edwards, George C., III, William Mitchell, and Reed Welch. 1995. Explaining presidential approval: The significance of issue salience. *American Journal of Political Science* 39: 108–34.

Fair, Ray C. 1978. The Effects of Economic Events on Votes for President. *Review of Economics and Statistics* 60: 159–73. [CrossRef]

Fair, Ray C. 1982. The Effect of Economic Events on Votes for President: 1980 Results. *Review of Economics and Statistics* 10: 322–25. [CrossRef]

Fair, Ray C. 1988. The Effect of Economic Events on Votes for President: 1984 Update. *Political Behavior* 10: 168–79. [CrossRef]

Ferreira, Alex Luiz, and Sérgio Naruhiko Sakurai. 2013. Personal charisma or the economy?: Macroeconomic indicators of presidential approval ratings in Brazil. *EconomiA* 14: 214–32. [CrossRef]

Kenski, Henry. 1977. Inflation and Presidential Popularity. *The Public Opinion Quarterly* 41: 86–90. [CrossRef]

Kenski, Henry. 1980. Economic Perception and Presidential Popularity: A Comment. *The Journal of Politics* 42: 68–75. [CrossRef]

Langer, Gary. 2018. Presidential Approval: It's the Economy; Except When It's Not. Available online: https://thehill.com.

Layton, Allan. 1992. An Estimated Australian Macroeconomic Misery Index. *Economic Record* 68: 118–24. [CrossRef]

Lean, Hooi Hooi, and Russell Smyth. 2011. Will Obama's Economic Stimulus Package Be Effective? Evidence from the Misery Index. *Applied Economics Letters* 18: 493–95. [CrossRef]

Lorde, Troy, Mahalia Jackman, Simon Naitram, and Shane Lowe. 2016. Does Crime Depend on the 'State' of Economic Misery? *International Journal of Social Economics* 43: 1124–34. [CrossRef]

Lovell, Michael C., and Pao-Lin Tien. 2000. Economic Discomfort and Consumer Sentiment. *Eastern Economic Journal* 26: 1–8. [CrossRef]

Mueller, John E. 1970. Presidential popularity from Truman to Johnson. *American Political Science Review* 64: 18–34. [CrossRef]

Mueller, John E. 1973. *War, Presidents, and Public Opinion*. New York, NY, USA: Wiley, p. 53.

Norpoth, Helmut. 1984. Economics, politics, and the cycle of presidential popularity. *Political Behavior* 6: 253–73. [CrossRef]

Nunley, John M., Richard Alan Seals Jr., and Joachim Zietz. 2011. Demographic change, macroeconomic conditions, and the murder rate: The case of the United States, 1934–2006. *The Journal of Socio-Economics* 40: 942–48. [CrossRef]

Ostrom, Charles W., and Renee M. Smith. 1992. Error Correction, Attitude Persistence, and Executive Rewards and Punishments. A Behavioral Theory of Presidential Approval. *Political Analysis* 4: 127–83. [CrossRef]

Rogoff, Kenneth, and Anne Sibert. 1988. Elections and Macroeconomic Policy Cycles. *Review of Economic Studies* 55: 1–16. [CrossRef]

Tang, Chor Foon, and Hooi Hooi Lean. 2009. New Evidence from the Misery Index in the Crime Function. *Economics Letters* 102: 112–15. [CrossRef]

Journal of
Risk and Financial Management

MDPI

Article

Limitation of Financial Health Prediction in Companies from Post-Communist Countries

Adriana Csikosova *, Maria Janoskova and **Katarina Culkova**

Department of Earth sources Management, Faculty BERG, Technical University of Košice, 042 00 Košice,
Slovakia; maria.ria.janoskova@tuke.sk (M.J.); katarina.culkova@tuke.sk (K.C.)
* Correspondence: adriana.csikosova@tuke.sk; Tel.: +421-556-022-929

Received: 29 November 2018; Accepted: 15 January 2019; Published: 18 January 2019

Abstract: The financial health of a company can be seen as the ability to maintain a balance against
changing conditions in the environment and at the same time in relation to everyone participating
in the business. In the evaluation of financial health and prediction of financial problems of the
companies, various indexes are used that can serve as input for expert estimation or creation of
various models using, for example, multi-dimensional statistical methods. The practical application of
the proper method for evaluation of financial health has been analysed in post-communist countries,
since they have common historic experiences and economic interests. During the research we followed
up the following indexes: Altman model, Taffler model, Springate model, and the index IN, based on
multi-dimensional discrimination analysis. From the research results there is obvious a necessity to
combine available methods in post-communist countries and at least to eliminate their disadvantages
partially. Experiences from prediction models have proved their relatively high prediction ability,
but only in perfect conditions, which cannot be affirmed in post-communist countries. The task
remains to modify existing indexes to concrete situations and problems of the individual industries
in the chosen countries, which have unique conditions for business making.

Keywords: managing of financial health; risk of bankruptcy; prediction methods; post-communist
countries

1. Introduction

Idea of financial health can be seen as the ability of the company to maintain a balance against
changing conditions of the environment and at the same time in relation to everyone participating
in the business. A financial healthy company means a company that maintains its existence and is
able to evaluate invested capital to the measure that is demanded by shareholders. Results of financial
analysis are different in companies from various sectors, since companies have different property
and financial structures and also different structures of economic results. Financial health demands
achievement of sufficient profit, as well as long-term liquidity. Bankruptcy means a situation when a
given organization does not have the possibility to overcome bad financial health and this situation is
in accordance with available legislation in a given country. Such a situation is considered by experts as
a corporate failure or business failure.

In the evaluation of financial health and the prediction of financial problems of the companies,
various indexes are used that can serve as an input for expert estimation or creation of various
models by using, for example multi-dimensional statistical methods. The main disadvantage of such
approach based on chosen statistical methods is its limited time availability and the complexity of
model modification in changed conditions, conditioned by the availability of input data. The next
problem is the improper structure of the input file. We must be very careful during selection of a
proper method, construction of a correspondent model and also during interpretation, since this can

lead to considerable bad estimation of its predictive ability. But the advantage is its very good quality of prediction during the existence of a qualitative data file.

Approaches that are based on calculation of the total score of the company according to its values of financial indexes have advantages, but also disadvantages. The main advantage is the simplicity of realization and simple interpretation. The disadvantage is the determination of strict boundaries for interpretation. This can lead to a ranking of companies with almost identical values of financial indexes for various groups. A higher disadvantage of the approach is that it does not consider in most cases possible relations among indexes that are evaluated individually. This means that both approaches should be combined, while both approaches can be used and their disadvantages can be partially eliminated.

Our findings show that prediction indexes in individual sectors in post-communist countries record different results. Due to the poor index of payment disability, which evaluates financial health of the companies in V4, all models should be modified by this index. The findings encourage an evaluation of the accuracy of bankruptcy prediction models by examining a large sample of companies and evaluating the real benefits obtained from the acquired information.

Based on the finding we can state that before selection of the method for prediction of financial health, the economic conditions of an analysed subject must be considered. The findings could serve as a base for further research in other economic spaces.

2. Literature Review

Classical statistical methods were used for a long time for development of single dimensional discrimination analysis. The most used statistic method is the multi-dimensional discrimination analysis, followed up by logit analysis (Altman and Saunders 1997). The next classification methods are risk index models, probit analysis and linear probability models.

Beaver (1966) was one of the pioneers of models for bankruptcy prediction, based on financial rate indexes. He was the first author that applied a single dimensional model to results of financial rate indexes and compared individual results at prospering and non-prospering companies with a goal to define a model for bankruptcy prediction. The result of this method is often different from the practice, when a number of rate indexes has non-linear dependence on bankruptcy status (Keasey and Watson 1991). While using single dimensional model rate indexes, resulting from financial accounting, the evaluation of importance of one concrete index individually is very difficult, since a majority of indexes are connected. The single dimensional model is different from reality, when the financial situation of the company is seen as one unit, which cannot be evaluated only according one rate index. In reaction to Beaver (1966), Tamari (1966) understood that Beaver's analysis is not definite, since according to one index a company could be evaluated as prospering and according to another index a company could be ranked among non-prospering companies. Therefore, Tamari created so-called risk index model that presents very simple point system, including various rate indexes, which are generally accepted as indexes of the financial health of the company. The advantage of the risk index model is its intuitiveness and easy applicability, but on the other hand it can be considered also as its main disadvantage, since it means an index with rather subjective characteristics, due to for example subjective determination of individual weights in the Tamari index.

In 1968, Altman (1968) applied a technique of multi-dimensional statistical analysis (MDA) in connection with a prediction of bankruptcy and created a model, called the Z-score model. This method presents multi-dimensional discrimination analysis. Eisenbeis (1977) determined a final Z-score model, regarding also new standards of financial reporting for areas of business. Several authors emphasized the importance of first two limited assumptions and their possible mistakes, majority of studies about bankruptcy did not try to analyse if used data filled these assumptions. In practice, used data only rarely fill all three assumptions. MDA models are very often applied by improper way and conclusions are disputable. The first assumption of multivariate normally distributed (MND) models is often not observed (Deakin 1976). This can have the consequence of a bad picture of importance of tests and estimated measure of mistakes (McLeay and Omar 2000). It is necessary to mention that at the normal situation MND demands univariate normally distributed models (UND). Due to the mentioned some researchers test values only in UND conditions. Some authors amend UND and try to make UND transformation of indexes before their including to the model. Taffler (1983) and Altman et al. (1977) adapted values that do not correspond with UND through the transformation. A second assumption that must be tested before model development, based on MDA, is the assumption of dispersion matrixes equality. In case the assumption is violated, it tests importance of differences in variables between declined and prospering group of companies will be influenced. Third assumption mentions that during optimal score selection, deciding about the group, probability of mistaken evaluation should be considered in combination with costs of mistake type I and II (Zavgren 1983).

To date, when MDA where clear dominant method for models creation, this method has been replaced by less demanded statistic techniques, as for example logit analysis (LA), probit analysis (PA) and models of linear probability (LPM). By these methods were created evaluation models of conditioned probability (CPM) (Zavgren 1983). These models are constructed from a combination of variables that make the difference between group of prospering and non- prospering companies. Ohlson (1980) used LA to create his models. Zmijewski (1984) was on the other hand orientated to PA. Since then LA has been considered the most favourable method for bankruptcy prediction. Number of studies, using PA is less, since in comparing with LA it demands bigger number of calculations. CPM enables to estimate a probability of the unsuccessful situation in dependence on raw of company characteristics, mainly by non-linear estimation of maximal probability. Models are based on a certain assumption of probability distribution. Models based on LA, assume logarithmic distribution of probability (Maddala 1977). In models of linear probability, it is assumed that the relation between individual variables of the given model and probability of bankruptcy is linear. LA is in literature of company prediction the method of conditioned probability most used.

3. Materials and Methods

The use of bankruptcy indexes had been analysed in post-communist countries, since those countries have not only common historic experiences with communism, but also mentality, cultural background, traditions, as well as strategic economic interests and complex reforms and transitions to the market economy. We orientated the research mainly to the V4 group—Czech Republic, Slovakia, Hungary and Poland—since the situation in V4 was very similar also after the transformation to the market economy. V4 countries have very successful economic situation; all countries are growing rapidly than average in EU. But there is threat that after achievement of certain level the growth will be stopped (Onaran 2011). The main object of searching was chosen companies in individual industrial sectors from V4 countries.

3.1. The Data

The data for prediction of financial situation in chosen industrial companies was obtained as aggregate data available at the Ministry of Industry and Trade of the Czech Republic (Ministry of Industry and Trade CZ 2017) and Ministry of Economy in Slovakia (Ministry of Economy SR 2017), Hungarian Central Statistical Office (Hungarian Central Statistical Office 2017) and Ministry of Entrepreneurship and Technology Poland (Ministry of Entrepreneurship and Technology Poland 2017). Other necessary information to solve the research problem was data from the Register of financial statement (Register of Financial Statement SR 2017) and individual web sites of companies. Annual financial statements of 2007–2017 of investigated companies and industries had been analysed. Set of 30 financial statements had been acquired from companies that present representatives in individual industries.

3.2. Methods

Due to the research of prediction indexes used in post-communist countries we followed up the following indexes: Altman model, Taffler model, Springate model and Index IN, based on multi-dimensional discrimination analysis. We decided to follow up these indexes since the research of Kanapickiene and Kanapickiene and Marcinkevicius (2014) proved that the Taffler and Altman's Z" Score Model for emerging countries models are the least accurate. In multi-dimensional discrimination analysis, the financial situation of the company is predicted by various combinations of simple characteristics, which means by certain files of various indexes, to which various weights are given. Their task is to predict the financial situation through achieved results and with correspondent reliability to rank the company among prospering or non-prospering companies.

3.3. Altman Model

Altman improved the Beaver (1966) univariate method by establishment of a multi variant approach that reflects the financial situation of the company better. Altman analysed 66 companies and selected two groups of companies—one group before bankruptcy and a second group of excellent companies. By multivariable discrimination analysis he created weight of individual indexes and determined values for companies ranking to three groups. By this way he predicts future financial development of the company and the possibility of bankruptcy. Altman found out that following indexes reflect the best financial situation and its future development (Altman 2000).

By this way constructed discrimination function for the company in the following equation:

$$Z = 0.012X_1 + 0.014X_2 + 0.033X_3 + 0.006X_4 + 0.999X_5 \tag{1}$$

where:

X_1 = working capital/total assets,
X_2 = undivided profit/total assets,
X_3 = earnings before interest and taxes (EBIT)/total assets,
X_4 = market value of equity/debts,
X_5 = sales/total assets.

3.4. Index IN

Index IN presents next possibility of how to evaluate financial health of the company by bonity and bankruptcy models (Neumaierová and Neumaier 2002). By these indexes, we can determine with certain probability if acompany belongs among bonity or bankrupting companies, or if it is able to create value for its owners. Index IN is modified to several types according to time of their rising: index IN95, IN99, IN01, IN05, when Neumaier and Neumaierová (2005) are their authors. Index IN95 arose in 1995 according to data obtained in 1994. Data were obtained and elaborated for the industry as a whole, as well as for its individual sectors. Success of the index is over 70%. The index is created by six indexes with correspondent weights:

$$IN95 = 0.22X_1 + 0.11X_2 + 8.33X_3 + 0.52X_4 + 0.10X_5 - 16.8 X_6 \tag{2}$$

where:

X_1 = assets/debts,
X_2 = EBIT/interest costs,
X_3 = EBIT/assets,
X_4 = revenues/assets,
X_5 = floating assets/(short term liabilities + short term bank credits),
X_6 = unpaid liabilities/revenues.

Intervals of index IN95:

IN95 < 1   company in financial difficulty,

IN95 = 1–2   grey zone,

IN95 > 2   company without financial problems.

The given index is orientated to the ability of the company to pay its liabilities; it did not deal with the demands of owners for value creation. This regards the following index IN99. It reflects the demand of the owner; therefore, weights in IN95 are changed. Index IN99 is recommended to use in cases when it is not possible to state costs of equity for calculation of EVA index (economic value added). Success of the IN99 index is estimated at level over 85%.

3.5. Index Bonity B

The financial health of a company can be evaluated also from the view of financial management quality. This task can be fulfilled by index B, evaluating the bonity of the company, provided by qualified financial management.

$$B = 1.5X_1 + 0.08X_2 + 10X_3 + 5X_4 + 0.3X_5 + 0.1X_6 \tag{3}$$

where:

X_1 = cash flow/debts,
X_2 = total capital/debts,
X_3 = earnings before taxes (EBT)/total capital,
X_4 = EBT/total revenues,
X_5 = stocks/total assets,
X_6 = total revenues/total capital.

Evaluation scale: positive value means positive and healthy situation of the company. Negative values mean a negative and unhealthy situation, the lower the value, the worse the situation of the company.

4. Results

Using prediction indexes in company from post-communist countries show different results, as illustrated by Table 1.

Table 1. The example of prediction indexes using in company from post-communist country.

Method Used	Data Obtained	Evaluation
IN test	0.852	Rather not creating value
Z-score	1.5456	Bankruptcy threat
Index B	2.05348	Healthy situation
Overall evaluation		1. Profitable company
		2. Profitability is not sufficient
		3. Necessity to decrease debts

In spite of the positive bonity index, which means situation in the company is healthy, management of cash-flow can be evaluated positively, Z-score shows possible threat by bankruptcy, which demands a need for a detailed analysis, especially an analysis of debt management, etc. It is demanded also due to the unstable situation, given by IN test, which speak company does not create value. During the detailed analysis, we found the reason for such situation is high capital costs, which can be solved through improving of financial structure, using of debt management tools, decreasing of debts, etc. Prediction indexes of bonity in individual sectors in Slovakia recorded the following results given by Table 2.

Table 2. The Index B in Slovakian industrial sectors.

Negative Score	Positive Score
	Production of office equipment +0.978
Mining of iron ores −1.8	Production of construction materials +0.733
Ship construction −0.689	Beverage production +0.467
Steel production −0.372	Other mining +0.575
Automotive production −0.005	Production of dairy products +0.558

Due to the determined differences in bankruptcy indexes using in post-communist countries we found a necessity to provide during prediction following:

- To use for evaluation more than one index and to compare the results.
- To follow up indexes in time development.
- Further important fact that is necessary to consider during using of the indexes is working with data that are calculated in time horizon—one year, which means expression of performance per year.
- After finding a possible bankruptcy, to undertake a deeper analysis.
- To consider the undeveloped capital market in post-communist countries due to its short history existence.
- To count legislative restrictions, which can be overcome by common IFRS (international financial reporting standards), which due to the transition of several post-communist countries to the European Union (EU) (as for example Slovakia) are considered.
- To overcome insufficient preparation of financial managers to new models for financial health prediction.
- To make a comparison between the micro-economic and macro-economic environment of the company, since a possible bankruptcy is caused by internal, as well as external factors of the company.
- To count on shortages of existing methods, for example in post-communist countries due to the undeveloped capital market there is sometimes difficult to state capital values of calculated indexes and values are considered only as accounting values or values are determined by estimation.
- To consider new methods and their modification to concrete conditions, since most indexes for bankruptcy prediction are not created for conditions of companies from post-communist countries and must serve only as approximate orientation for prediction. Indexes must serve only as inspiration and financial analytics should make own indexes for post-communist countries.

The research of previous studies showed number of post-communist countries deals with the problem of payment ability in industries. The indexes were therefore modified in 1995, 1999 and 2001 to such problems, mainly to indexes, mentioned in following Figure 1.

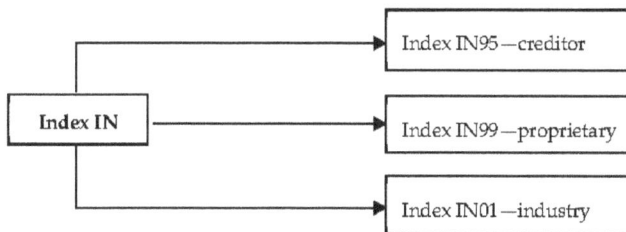

Figure 1. Modification of IN index in post-communist countries.

In 2000, the authors of IN95 and IN99 decided to construct the index that could connect the characteristics of both previous indexes and in this way evaluated the ability of the company to paid debts and at the same time to create value for owners. By discrimination analysis authors came to IN01, applied for industrial companies. While the IN test is from the view of the owner, the IN95 index for the creditor evaluates mainly a rating of the company.

$$IN95 = 0.22X_1 + 0.11X_2 + 8.33X_3 + 0.52X_4 + 0.10X_5 - 16.8X_6 \tag{4}$$

where:

X_1 = assets/total capital,
X_2 = EBIT/interest costs,
X_3 = EBIT/assets,
X_4 = revenues/assets,
X_5 = current assets/(current liabilities + current bank credits),
X_6 = liabilities after maturity/revenues.

Evaluation scale for IN95 is following:

IN95 > 2   financial healthy company, company is able to pay its liabilities,
IN95 < 1   company has financial hardship,
IN95 < 1–2 > financial health cannot be clearly evaluated.

4.1. Modification to Index IN99

With the aim of evaluating the financial ability of the company, not only the creation of value for the creditor but also for the owner, IN95 had been modified to IN99 by original authors, constructed according to data from 1698 post-communist companies. The calculation of the index is made by the following equation:

$$IN99 = -0.017X_1 + 4.573X_2 + 0.481X_3 + 0.015X_4 \tag{5}$$

Interpretation of IN99 is following:

IN99 > 2.070   company creates value (achieves net profit),
IN99 < 0.684   company creates negative value of net economic profit,
IN99 < 0.684–2.070 > creation of value cannot be clearly determined,

4.2. Modification to Index IN01

Next variant that connect both previous indexes (IN95 and IN99) presents IN01, determined for industrial sectors. Its calculation is as follows:

$$IN01 = 0.13X_1 + 0.04X_2 + 3.92X_3 + 0.21X_4 + 0.09X_5 \tag{6}$$

where:

X_1 = total capital/debts,
X_2 = EBIT/interest expenses,
X_3 = EBIT/total capital,
X_4 = revenues/total capital,
X_5 = current assets/short term liabilities (in broader sense).

Consequently, the interpretation of model results is given by following scale:

IN01 > 1.77   company creates the value,
IN01 < 0.75   company tends to bankruptcy,
IN01 < 0.75–1.77 >   future of the company is uncertain.

Considering the payment disability of companies in post-communist countries is made also in Altman, the Z-score was modified by Neumaier and Neumaierová (1995) to the following equation:

$$ZMOD = 1.2X_1 + 1.4X_2 + 3.3X_3 + 0.6X_4 + 1.0X_5 + 1.0X_6 \tag{7}$$

when:

X_6 = overdue liabilities/revenues.

At the same time, special conditions for business in companies from post-communist countries demand consideration of different weights during the indexes calculation. Table 3 gives an illustration of the weights for chosen industries in Slovakia and the Czech Republic.

Table 3. Weights of indexes in industries.

Industrial Sector	V_1	V_3	V_4	V_6
Agriculture	0.24	21.35	0.76	−14.57
Fishery	0.05	10.76	0.90	−84.11
Raw material mining	0.14	17.74	0.72	−16.89
Mining of energy sources	0.14	21.83	0.74	−16.31
Mining of other sources	0.16	5.39	0.56	−25.39
Processing industry	0.24	7.61	0.48	−11.92
Grocery industry	0.26	4.99	0.33	−17.36
Textile and clothing industry	0.23	6.08	0.43	−8.79
Leatherworking industry	0.24	7.95	0.43	−8.79
Wood industry	0.24	18.73	0.41	−11.57
Paper and printing industry	0.23	6.07	0.44	−16.99
Coke ovens and refineries	0.19	4.09	0.32	−20.26
Production of chemical products	0.21	4.81	0.57	−93.0
Rubber industry and plastics production	0.22	5.87	0.38	−17.06
Construction materials	0.20	5.28	0.55	−43.01
Production of metals	0.24	10.55	0.46	−9.74
Machinery	0.28	13.07	0.64	−6.36
Electro technique and electronics	0.27	9.50	0.51	−8.27
Production of transport vehicles	0.23	29.29	0.71	−7.46
Other industries	0.26	3.91	0.38	−17.62
Electricity, water, gas	0.15	4.61	0.72	−55.89
Construction	0.33	9.70	0.28	−28.32
Business and repair of automotive	0.33	9.70	0.28	−28.32
Catering and accommodation	0.35	12.57	0.88	−15.97
Transport and communication	0.07	14.35	0.75	−60.61
Economy of Slovakia	0.22	8.33	0.52	−16.80

Next, modification of the index IN presents the index IN05 that enables us to reach complex conclusions about performance of the company. The index consists of five indicators. Two of them characterize the ability of the company to create profit, and two of them characterize EBIT calculation. Weights, added to individual indexes, had been given by authors Neumaierová (2005) by discrimination analysis.

$$IN05 = 0.13X_1 + 0.04X_2 + 3.97X_3 + 0.21X_4 + 0.09X_5 \tag{8}$$

where:

X_1 = assets/debts,
X_2 = EBIT/interest costs,
X_3 = EBIT/assets,
X_4 = revenues/assets,
X_5 = floating assets/short term debts.

Such calculated values of the index IN05 divide the companies into individual intervals, while according to such calculations predicting future development of the company with high probability is possible. The intervals for companies ranking are as follows:

IN05 < 0.9   companies close to the bankruptcy,
0.9 ≤ IN05 < 1.6   companies in a grey zone,
IN05 ≥ 1.6   companies with financial health.

Through the index IN05, a user can answer several questions, for example, if the company is financially healthy, or if a company could be ranked to a certain group with sufficient probability and its future existence can be adapted to a first or second alternative. This is because the index was created and tested with data from big and middle industrial enterprises and due to the mentioned it has the best predictive ability for given enterprises.

- Moreover it is necessary to evaluate also possibilities of the company to grow.

Such possibility can be evaluated by an average growth of dividend g, which is added to index IN. In case of a negative index with the possibility of growth, a company would create value and overcome possible bankruptcy. The evaluation according to the growth is given by Table 4.

Table 4. Influence of growth possibility to index IN.

Index Value	Growth of Dividend g				
	Very Low	Low	Medium	High	Very High
	0–1%	1–2%	2–4%	4–7%	Over 7%
IN > 2.070	creating value	creating value	creating value	creating value	creating value
1.420 < IN < 2.070		creating value	creating value	creating value	creating value
1.089 < IN < 1.420			creating value	creating value	creating value
0.684 < IN < 1.089				creating value	creating value
IN < 0.684					creating value

- Using prediction indexes demands consideration of successful estimation of the financial situation of the company.

For example, a successful ranking of company by IN95% is 70%, success of ranking by IN99 is 84.62%. The Altman model can predict bankruptcy of the company relatively properly for two years in advance with approximating 70% probability for five years. Company with value IN01 over 1.77 with probability 67% would create value and on the other hand company with value IN01 under 0.75 will tend to bankruptcy with probability 86%.

- The success ranking of the company can be provided also by creation of more detailed evaluation scales, since a commonly uncertain situation can be very extensive.

More detailed scales have been created for the IN index, IN99 and Altman Z-score (see Tables 5 and 6).

Table 5. More detailed evaluation scale for IN index.

Scale for Evaluation	Index IN	Success of Ranking	
		Creates the Value	Does Not Create the Value
Creates value	IN > 2.070	84.62%	15.38%
More likely creation of value	1.420 < IN < 2.070	64.97%	35.03%
Cannot be predicted	1.089 < IN < 1.420	34.6%	65.40%
Rather not creating value	0.684 < IN < 1.089	10.08%	89.92%
Does not create the value	IN < 0.684	1.1%	98.90%

Table 6. Detailed evaluation scale for Altman Z-score.

Z = 0–1.8	Bankruptcy is strongly probable
Z = 1.81–2.675	Bankruptcy is weakly probable
Z = 2.675–2.99	Survival is weakly probable
Z over 2.99	Survival is strongly probable

- Increasing the success ranking of the company will be supported also by consideration of the legal form of business.

Financial experts together with E. I. Altman adapted the original model with regarding to the legal form of business by changes in area of financial management, capital markets and changing economic conditions. The actualized model Z-score for limited companies and other forms includes similar rate indexes as the original model, only in the fourth index the mainly market value of equity is replaced by accounting value. Also, weights of individual rate indexes are changed. Due to the mentioned changes criteria of evaluation is changed as well. The algorithm for the actualized model calculation is as follows (Altman 2000):

$$Z' = 0.717X_1 + 0.847X_2 + 3.107X_3 + 0.420X_4 + 0.998X_5 \tag{9}$$

where:

X_1 = net working capital/total assets,
X_2 = undivided profit/total assets,
X_3 = EBIT/total assets,
X_4 = accounting value of equity/debts,
X_5 = sales/total assets.

Altman (2000) defined for the model following classification conditions:

$Z > 2.90$ financial situation of the company is good,
$1.21 < Z < 2.89$ area of vague results (grey zone), bankruptcy is possible,
$Z < 1.20$ financial situation is critical, bankruptcy is very probable.

Companies that are ranked to the third group are serious candidates for bankruptcy. Companies in the first group are without problems. Finally, companies in the middle can develop in both directions and, therefore, need special attention.

But joint stock companies have a much higher business risk, which is considered in modification of Altman index as follows:

$$Z = 0.012X_1 + 0.014X_2 + 0.033X_3 + 0.006X_4 + 0.999X_5 \tag{10}$$

Evaluation scale for joint stock companies is due to the higher risk rather more strictly:

$Z > 2.99$ good financial situation of the company,
$1.81 < Z < 2.99$ area of uncertain future (possible bankruptcy),
$Z < 1.81$ financial situation of the company is critical, very probable bankruptcy.

- Next, modification of the Altman model is determined for production companies and it does not include a fifth parameter, which means sales to total capital.

In area of post-communist production companies the IN index for energetic companies—IN(E) is created:

$$IN (E) = -0.013X_1 + 4.166X_2 + 0.794X_3 + 0.025X_4 \tag{11}$$

where:

X_1 = debts/assets,
X_2 = EBIT/assets,
X_3 = revenues/assets,
X_4 = current assets/(current debts + current bank credits).

- Since non-productive companies do not have the same conditions for business in comparing with production enterprises, the modification can be as follows:

$$Z' = 6.56X_1 + 3.26X_2 + 6.72X_3 + 1.05X_4 \tag{12}$$

where:

X_1 = (current assets − bank accounts)/assets,
X_2 = EBT/assets,
X_3 = EBIT/assets,
X_4 = accounting value of priority and equity shares/debts,
Z' under 1.1 = bankruptcy,
Z' over 2.6 = prospering company.

- The model must also consider the firm size, which is ranked among key variables of the prediction.

This variable must be considered, since capital, assets, sales, etc. are different in small and medium enterprises (SMEs) in comparison with a big corporation. In most studies in this area, it is considered as the most important variable (Dang et al. 2018).

5. Discussion and Conclusions

For the prediction of bankruptcy of industrial companies in V4 countries by using selected methods, we obtained different results of ranking companies among prospering and non-prospering companies. To avoid such a situation, we needed to provide following conditions:

- necessity to combine available methods in post-communist countries;
- experiences from prediction models using proved relatively high prediction ability, but only in perfect conditions, which cannot be affirmed in post-communist countries;
- using prediction indexes in company from post-communist countries show different results according different models;
- there is a necessity to use more than one index and to compare the results and to follow them in trend development;
- one must consider an undeveloped capital market in post-communist countries due to its short history existence;
- count on legislative restrictions;
- making a comparison between the micro-economic and macro-economic environment of the company;
- indexes must serve only as an inspiration and financial analytics should make its own modification of indexes for post-communist countries, mainly modification by the biggest problem in post-communist countries, which means the problem of payment ability in industries;
- consideration of different weights during indexes calculation, considering possibilities of company growth and success of estimation;
- creation of more detailed evaluation scales, since the commonly uncertain situation can be very extensive;
- consideration of legal form of business;
- modification for production companies and non-productive companies;
- considering also the firm size, which is ranked among key variables of the prediction.

The present contribution distinguishes from previous similar studies from the view of the list of conditions necessary to obtain during the use of prediction models in post-communist countries. However, it must be noted that Altman models were several times verified by a single author, as well as other economists. Grice and Ingram (2001) tested the exactness of the model and compared their results with values obtained by Altman. They concluded that the relation between value of financial indexes and bankruptcy probability is changing over time. Their studies show that for their selected sample predictive ability of the model were significantly lower in comparison with the Altman results. At the same time, they found that in production companies the total accuracy of the model is higher (69.1%) in comparison with non-production companies (57.8%). Wu et al. (2010) compared the original Altman model with models where construction was based on discrimination analysis (for example Ohlson logit model), meaning that the Altman model has in comparison with other models lower reliability. Boritz et al. (2007) evaluated model reliability at the prediction of Canadian companies' bankruptcy. The model estimated 41.7% of bankruptcy. Russ et al. (2009) found the main disadvantage of the Altman model and his orientation to the industrial companies. In spite of the aforementioned, they concluded its accuracy is sufficient. They tested the model at the sample of several thousands of companies. The resulting mistakes were type I. (20.6%) and mistake II. (28.4%).

Due to the practical application of the models, the disadvantage is mainly that liabilities after the payment period are not publicly published data. But since they are obligatory part of notes to financial reports that is an available document, such problems can be easily solved. Also the fact that the index of payment disability evaluates financial health of the company from a short-term view does not present an obstacle, since financial analytics in our conditions evaluate regularly one accounting or annual period. Experiences with the Altman model showed its relatively high prediction ability. The model successfully predicts bankruptcy two years ahead of its realization; the distant future is statistically less reliable. Despite all objections, prediction models present a great tool for business bankruptcy avoiding the practical impacts that allows entrepreneurs and managers at enterprises to run their business better. The results of the research might be useful for both the executive managers of companies in individual industrial sectors, as well as for investors, who are looking to invest in the companies.

But it is still necessary to modify existing indexes to concrete situation and problems of the individual industries in chosen countries, which have unique conditions for business making. Such modification had been studied for example for conditions of the construction sector (Kanapickiene and Marcinkevicius 2014) and in the Slovakian agricultural sector (Gurčík 2002; Chrastinová 1998; Valášková et al. 2017). Next, modification must be done for all other industrial sectors in all other post-communist countries. The limitation of the study resides in the availability of the data in the register of financial statements. Therefore, further research could be focused on prediction, based on a larger amount of data.

Author Contributions: Conceptualization, K.C.; Methodology, K.C. and A.C.; Validation, K.C., A.C., and M.J.; Formal Analysis, M.J.; Investigation, K.C.; Resources, M.J.; Data Curation, K.C. and A.C.; Writing-Original Draft Preparation, K.C.; Writing-Review and Editing, M.J.; Visualization, M.J.; Supervision, A.C.; Project Administration, K.C. and M.J.; Funding Acquisition, M.J., and A.C.

Funding: This research was funded by VEGA grant number 1/0651/2018 "Research of institutional environment influence to the corporate social responsibility, consumers satisfaction and performance of the company" and grant number 1/0515/18 "The decision-making model of process of evaluating raw material policy of regions."

Conflicts of Interest: The authors declare no conflict of interest.

References

Altman, Edward I. 1968. Financial ratios, discriminant analysis and the prediction of corporate bankruptcy. *The Journal of Finance* 23: 589–609. [CrossRef]

Altman, Edward I. 2000. Predicting Financial Distress of Companies: Revisiting the Z Score and Zeta Models. Available online: http://pages.stern.nyu.edu/~ealtman/Zscores.pdf (accessed on 10 October 2018).

Altman, Edward I., and Anthony Saunders. 1997. Credit risk measurement: Development over the last 20 years. *Journal of Banking & Finance* 21: 1721–42. [CrossRef]

Altman, Edward I., Robert J. Haldeman, and Paul Narayanan. 1977. Zeta Analysis: A new model to identify bankruptcy risk of corporations. *Journal of Banking and Finance* 1: 39–54. [CrossRef]

Beaver, Wiliam H. 1966. Financial ratios predictors of failure. Empirical Research in Accounting: Selected Studies 1966. *Journal of Accounting Research* 4: 71–111. [CrossRef]

Boritz, Efrim J., Duane Kennedy, and Jerry Sun. 2007. Predicting business failures in Canada. *Accounting Perspectives* 6: 141–65. [CrossRef]

Chrastinová, Zuzana. 1998. *Methods of Economic Bonity Evaluation and Prediction of Financial Situation in Agricultural Companies*. Bratislava: VÚEPP. ISBN 80-8058-022-7. (In Slovak)

Dang, Chogyu D., Zhichuan F. Li, and Chen Yang. 2018. Measuring firm size in empirical corporate finance. *Journal of Banking and Finance* 86: 159–76. [CrossRef]

Deakin, Edward B. 1976. Distributions of Financial Accounting Ratios: Some Empirical Evidence. *The Accounting Review* 51: 90–96.

Eisenbeis, Robert A. 1977. Pitfalls in the Application of Discriminant Analysis in Business, Finance, and Economics. *Journal of Finance* 32: 875–900. [CrossRef]

Grice, John S., and Robert W. Ingram. 2001. Test of the generalizability of Altman's bankruptcy prediction model. *Journal of Business Research* 54: 53–61. [CrossRef]

Gurčík, Ľubomír. 2002. G-index–methods of financial situation prediction in agricultural companies. *Agricultural Economics* 48: 373–78. (In Slovak)

Hungarian Central Statistical Office. 2017. Available online: http://www.ksh.hu/docs/eng/imf/nsdp.html (accessed on 18 September 2018).

Kanapickiene, Rasa, and Rosvydas Marcinkevicius. 2014. Possibilities to apply classical bankruptcy prediction models in the construction sector in Lithuania. *Economics and Management* 19: 317–32. [CrossRef]

Keasey, Kevin, and Robert Watson. 1991. Financial distress prediction models: A review of their usefulness. *British Journal of Management* 2: 89–102. [CrossRef]

Maddala, G. S. 1977. *Econometrics*. New York: McGraw-Hill Book Co.

McLeay, Stuart, and Azmi Omar. 2000. The sensitivity of prediction models to the non-normality of bounded an unbounded financial rations. *The British Accounting Review* 32: 213–30. [CrossRef]

Ministry of Economy, Slovakia, Business Environment. 2017. Available online: https://www.mhsr.sk/podnikatelske-prostredie (accessed on 10 September 2018).

Ministry of Entrepreneurship and Technology Poland. 2017. Available online: http://www.miir.gov.pl/strony/zadania/ (accessed on 10 September 2018).

Ministry of Industry and Trade, Czech Republic. 2017. Financial Analysis of the Business Sphere. Available online: http://www.mpo.cz/cz/ministr-a-ministerstvo/analyticke-materialy/#category238 (accessed on 10 September 2018). (In Czech)

Neumaier, Ivan, and Inka Neumaierová. 1995. Try to calculate your index IN95. *Terno* 5: 7–10. (In Czech)

Neumaier, Ivan, and Inka Neumaierová. 2005. Index IN05. In *European Finance Systems: Proceedings from International Scientific Conference*. Brno: Masarykova univerzita v Brně, pp. 143–48. (In Czech)

Neumaierová, Inka. 2005. *Management of the Company Value, or Do Not Make Mystery from the Company*. Praha: Profess Consulting. ISBN 80-7259-022-7. (In Czech)

Neumaierová, Inka, and Ivan Neumaier. 2002. *Performance and Market Value of the Company*. Praha: GRADA Publishing. ISBN 80-247-0125-1. (In Czech)

Ohlson, James A. 1980. Financial ratios and the probabilistic prediction of bankruptcy. *Journal of Accounting Research* 18: 109–31. [CrossRef]

Onaran, Özlem. 2011. From transition crisis to the global crisis: twenty years of capitalism and labour in the Central and Eastern EU new member states. *Capital & Class* 35: 213–31. [CrossRef]

Register of Financial Statement, Slovak Republic. 2017. Available online: http://www.registeruz.sk/cruz-public/domain/accountingentity/search (accessed on 10 October 2018).

Russ, Robert W., Wendy Peffley, and Alfred C. Greenfield. 2009. The Altman Z-score revisited. *Journal of International Finance and Economics* 9: 59–73. [CrossRef]

Taffler, Richard J. 1983. The assessment of company solvency and performance using a statistical model. *Accounting and Business Research* 13: 295–307. [CrossRef]

Tamari, Meir. 1966. Financial ratios as a means of forecasting bankruptcy. *Management International Review* 6: 15–21.

Valášková, Katarína, Lucia Švábová, and Maroš Ďurica. 2017. Verification of prediction models in conditions of Slovakian agriculture sector. *Ekonomika Management Inovace* 9: 30–38. (In Slovak)

Wu, Yanhui, Clive Gaunt, and Stephen Gray. 2010. A comparison of alternative bankruptcy prediction models. *Journal of Contemporary Accounting and Economics* 6: 34–45. [CrossRef]

Zavgren, Christine. 1983. The prediction of corporate failure: The state of the art. *Journal of Accounting Literature* 2: 1–37.

Zmijewski, Mark E. 1984. Methodological issues related to the estimation of financial distress prediction models. *Journal of Accounting Research* 22: 59–82. [CrossRef]

Journal of
Risk and Financial Management

MDPI

Short Note
Cash Use of the Taiwan Dollar: Is It Efficient? [†]

Philip Hans Franses [*,‡] **and Max Welz**

Econometric Institute, Erasmus School of Economics, P.O. Box 1738, NL3000 DR Rotterdam, The Netherlands;
mwelz@student.eur.nl
* Correspondence: franses@ese.eur.nl; Tel.: +31-104-081-273
† The idea of this paper came up with the first author when he visited Taiwan in June 2018 and noticed that
  banknotes of 200 and 2000 NT$ did not seem to exist, while they do.
‡ As of June 2018, Honorary Chair Professor, Asia University, Taichung, Taiwan.

Received: 21 November 2018; Accepted: 12 January 2019; Published: 15 January 2019

Abstract: Two banknotes and two coins of the New Taiwan Dollar are infrequently (if at all) used in Taiwan when people make cash payments. This note examines the effect of this behavior on the efficiency of cash payments. The results are compared with the Euro, where the two highest and two lowest tokens are also rarely used. We find for Taiwan that inefficiency increases with 60.7%, while for the Euro it is only 25.3%. The main reason is that two of the rarely used coins and notes in Taiwan are in the middle of the denominational range, whereas for the Euro, these tokens concern the ends of that range.

Keywords: cash payments; efficiency; denomination range; E42; E58

1. Introduction

Central banks issue banknotes and coins. They do so in what is called a denominational range, where usually sequences of 1, 2, and 5 are used. For example, the Euro has banknotes 5, 10, 20, 50, 100, 200, and 500. Even though many people use credit cards or debit cards when making actual payments, the use of cash is still very popular (see for example, Van der Cruijsen et al. 2017). Research on cash payments concerns the costs of cash payments (see for example, Segendorf and Jansson 2012) and how people perceive various payment modes (Khan et al. 2015). Modern payment methods developed by fintech companies also attract much research, as well as studies on the bitcoin and the like, but there is also an interest in the link between payment methods and economic development, see for example, Hasan et al. (2012). Finally, research is done on the effects of 'removing zeroes' from notes and coins in times of high inflation. In the present paper, the focus is on what happens if the paying public does not use some of the notes and coins available, where we address the case of the New Taiwan Dollar and compare it with the Euro.

The currency in Taiwan is the New Taiwan Dollar (NT$). Its denominational range contains coins of NT$0.50, 1, 5, 10, 20, and 50 and the banknotes NT$100, 200, 500, 1000, and 2000. Personal observation, and also https://en.m.wikipedia.org/wiki/New_Taiwan_dollar, suggests that some coins and notes are not very popular in Taiwan. In particular the coins NT$0.50 and 20 and the notes NT$200 and 2000 are not often used by the Taiwanese public. In this note, we examine the consequences of these preferences for efficient payment behavior.

Efficient payment is defined as the smallest numbers of transactions involved in making a cash payment. The amount NT$10 is efficiently paid with a coin of NT$10. An inefficient payment for this amount would be to give a coin of NT$20 and to get a NT$10 coin in return. For each amount efficient payment schemes exist, and the number of efficient payments per amount can be computed. The algorithm to do this was developed in Cramer (1983), and a version has been presented in the Kippers et al. (2003). In this paper we provide a more complete version of the algorithm, and in Appendix A we give the relevant computer code that we used in our study.

In this note, we examine what happens with the number of efficient payments in case some notes and coins are dismissed. We first consider the case of Taiwan. Next, we compare our findings with those of the Euro. Indeed, also for the Euro there is a tendency to dismiss certain coins and notes. The Euro denominational range covers coins of 0.01, 0.02, 0.05, 0.10, 0.20, 0.50, 1, and 2, while it contains the banknotes 5, 10, 20, 50, 100, 200, and 500. The 200 and 500 notes are considered to be associated with criminal activities and hence rarely visibly used. In some European countries, like in the Netherlands, all amounts are rounded at 0.05 cents, and hence the coins 0.01 and 0.02 are effectively not used. A key difference between the payment behavior for the Euro and for the NT$ is that for the Euro it dismissed the 'end values' of the denominational range (0.01 and 0.02; 200 and 500), while in Taiwan the dismissed tokens are also midway the denominational range (like 20 and 200). We document that 60.7% more notes and coins are required to make efficient payments in Taiwan, while for the Euro this is just 25.3%. The dismissed coins and notes in Taiwan thus lead to substantial payment inefficiency.

2. Method

Denote with A the payment amount and with $N(A)$ the amount of tokens (notes and or coins) to be used for cash payment. The denomination range is given by the set $\{1, 2, \ldots, D\}$ and an element of this set is denoted by d. For Taiwan, this set is NT$0.50, 1, 5, 10, 20, and 50 for coins, and the country has the following banknotes, that is, NT$100, 200, 500, 1000, and 2000.

Denote with $N(A, d)$ the number of tokens of denomination d, so

$$N(A) = \sum_{d=1}^{D} N(A, d)$$

Finally, denote $v(d)$ as the value of denomination d.

The objective is now to minimize $n(A)$ by choosing the proper notes and coins out of the set $\{1, 2, \ldots, D\}$. More formally, one should solve

$$minimize \; n^*(A) = \sum_{d=1}^{D} |n(A, d)|$$

$$subject \; to \; \sum_{d=1}^{D} n(A, d)v(d) = A$$

Note that we consider the absolute value of $n(A, d)$ to allow for the possibility that notes and coins are returned as change.

The algorithm of Cramer to obtain all efficient payment schemes proceeds as follows. We take a range of payment amounts that are of potential interest, say NT$0.50 until NT$35,700, with intervals of NT$0.50. We choose for NT$35,700 as with the current exchange rate (November 2018) this amount is about equal to 1000 Euro. The algorithm seeks to find for each of these amounts the efficient combinations of notes and coins. A general pseudocode implementation of this algorithm can be found in Appendix A.

Step 1: The algorithm starts by taking all amounts that can be paid with only one note or one coin. For the New Taiwan Dollar, the amounts NT$0.50, 1, 5, 10, 20, 50, 100, 200, 500, 1000, and 2000 are now covered.

Step 2: All amounts that can be paid with two tokens, either two given by the individual as payment or one returned by someone else as change, are next to be computed. For example, NT$150 can be paid efficiently with notes of NT$100 and 50, but also with NT$200 and 50 as change. All such combinations that constitute an efficient payment for a given amount are stored. If we now observe an amount that was already covered with only one token in the previous step, we do not add this pair of two tokens to the list as these are obviously not efficient for this amount.

Step 3: To the pairs that were found efficient in the previous two steps, we add each token once, both with positive and negative sign, the latter indicating change. For example, to the NT$1000 and 500 notes we add a NT$20 coin, covering the amounts 1520 and 1480 (where in the last case the NT$20 is given as change). For a given pair in Step 2, this gives 2*D* extra combinations with an additional token each. Adding a token with a positive sign to a combination which has this same token with a negative sign (and vice versa) would yield a combination with less tokens and is therefore ignored.

Note that there are two restrictions which need to be taken into account, and it is here where the method of Kippers et al. (2003) is modified. First, we do not consider combinations which lead to infeasible amounts, that is, amounts that are lower or higher than the lowest or highest amounts that we consider. In our case, that would be amounts that are lower than NT$0.50 and higher than NT$35,700.

Second, duplicates may occur in this step. In different stages of this step, we may obtain the exact same combination multiple times, so we also do not consider such duplicates. Hence, each efficient payment scheme is unique.

Step 4: Repeat Step 3 by increasing each time the number of tokens until all amounts between NT$0.50 until NT$35,700 are covered.

When all tokens are considered the payment amount ranges from NT$0.50 to NT$35,700 with steps of NT$0.50. However, when tokens NT$0.50, 20, 200, and 2000 are excluded, the payment amount ranges from NT$1 to NT$35,700 with steps of NT$1.

A similar exercise is carried out for the Euro, now with amounts 0.01 to 1000 Euros. For the Euro we also consider the cases where the 200 and 500 Euro notes are not used, and where additionally the 0.01 and 0.02 Euro cents are dismissed.

3. Results

For Taiwan, the results of our exercise appear in Table 1. If all tokens are considered for all payment amounts until and including NT$35,700, we see that there are 195,659 efficient payment schemes. The average amount of tokens exchanged is 14.030, where the maximum amount is 25. When the tokens NT$0.5, 20, 200, and 2000 are excluded, we see that the number of efficient schemes reduces, but this is also due to the fact all amounts are now rounded at NT$1. A more important figure is the new average amount of tokens exchanged, which becomes 22.546. This entails an increase of inefficiency of 60.7%. The maximum number even increases to 43.

Table 1. Results for New Taiwan Dollar on efficient payment schemes (percentage increase, relative to the all tokens case) in parentheses.

Statistic	All Tokens	Excluded Tokens Are NT$0.50, 20, 200, and 2000
Amount of efficient schemes	195,659	47,073
Amount of tokens exchanged		
Average	14.030	22.546 (60.7%)
Median	13	22 (69.2%)
Minimum	1	1
Maximum	25	43 (72.0%)

Note: when all tokens are considered the payment amount ranges from NT$0.5 to NT$35,700 with steps of NT$0.5. When tokens are excluded the payment amount ranges from NT$1 to NT$35,700 with steps of NT$1.

To put these numbers in perspective, consider the results for the Euro in Table 2. For the range of 0.01 Euro to 1000 Euros, there are 577,066 efficient payment schemes. The average amount of tokens exchanged is 7.534. When we delete the 200 and 500 Euro notes, this average increases to 10.333 (a 37.2% increases of inefficiency), where when additionally the 0.01 and 0.02 cents are dismissed, the average of exchanged tokens across efficient payment schemes increases to 9.429. This latter increase of inefficiency is 25.3%.

Table 2. Results for Euro on efficient payment schemes (percentage increase, relative to the all tokens case) in parentheses.

Statistic	All Tokens	Excluded Tokens Are 200 and 500 Euro	Excluded Tokens Are 0.01, 0.02, 200, and 500 Euro
Amount of efficient schemes	577,066	365,910	
Amount of tokens exchanged			
Average	7.534	10.333 (37.2%)	9.429 (25.3%)
Median	6	10 (66.7%)	9 (50%)
Minimum	1	1	1
Maximum	11	17 (54.5%)	16 (45.5%)

Note: when all tokens are considered the payment amount ranges from 0.01 Euro to 1000 Euro with steps of 0.01 Euro. This also holds for the case where 200 and 500 Euro notes are dismissed. When additionally the 0.01 and 0.02 Euro cents are excluded the payment amount ranges from 0.05 Euro to 1000 Euro with steps of 0.05 Euro.

4. Conclusions

The overall conclusion of our exercise in this note is that excluding NT$0.50, 20, 200, and 2000 in Taiwan leads to a marked inefficiency in payment behavior, much more than the dismissal of Euro coins and notes implies. The main reason is that NT$20 and 200 are in the middle of the denominational range, whereas for the Euro the dismissed tokens appear at the end of the range.

Our exercise is a pure theoretical exercise, and it remains to be seen what happens when people make actual payments. Such empirical work involves tedious data collection, as is reported in Franses and Kippers (2007). The main reason is that the data collectors should also observe the wallet content of individuals, in order to see amongst which coins and notes the individuals can choose. In Franses and Kippers (2010), this tedious data collection is somewhat alleviated by making people play Monopoly games, where the wallet contents can be observed on the table. Further empirical research in Taiwan can lead to interesting insights.

Author Contributions: Conceptualization, P.H.F.; methodology, P.H.F. and M.W.; software, M.W.; writing—original draft preparation, P.H.F.; writing—review and editing, P.H.F. and M.W.; supervision, P.H.F.

Funding: This research received no external funding.

Acknowledgments: We thank two anonymous reviewers for helpful suggestions.

Conflicts of Interest: The author declares no conflicts of interest.

Appendix A Computer Code

We have listed the general program we wrote for our analysis as pseudocode here. The original MATLAB program can be provided on request, please contact the first author for such requests.

Initialize
D_set, A_set are column vectors that hold the currency denominations and amounts to be taken into account, respectively. P_mat is a three-dimensional array of zeros that will hold the efficient payment schemes in its columns. Each row corresponds to one token (from D_set, in that order), so each cell is a token counter, where negative numbers are change. Only the number of non-zero columns will correspond to the number of efficient payment schemes for a given amount.

Step 1:
for every amount in A_set:
>Cover all amounts that can be covered with only one token. Always start to fill the columns in the corresponding first column.

end(for)

Step 2:
for every amount in A_set:
>**if** the first column of this iteration's contains nonzero elements:
>>continue;
>
>**end(if)**
>
>**for** i,j in D_set:
>
>>\# All tokens given by customer:
>>**if** (D_set[i] + D_set[j] == amount):
>>>Increment corresponding token counters of this amount's matrix.
>>
>>**end(if)**
>>
>>\# Situation with change:
>>**if** (amount − D_set[i]) == D_set[j] * (−1)
>>>Increment or decrement (change) corresponding token counters of this amount's matrix.
>>
>>**end(if)**
>
>**end(for)**

end(for)
Replace all duplicate columns by zero columns.

Steps 3 and 4:
prv_tokens = 2; # number of tokens used in previous step, so 2 here.

while there is a first column in P_mat that holds only zeros:
>**for** every amount in A_set:
>>**if** there was no efficient number of tokens found in previous step:
>>>continue;
>>
>>**end(if)**
>>add_token_mat = zeros(D, 2D); # to hold the additional tokens
>>**for** every column that holds prv_tokens in P_mat:
>>>Add each token once, both with positive and negative sign to add_token_mat. Make sure to consider only valid columns of add_token_mat from here on (valid columns are columns that do not lead to an amount that is either lower or higher than the minimum or maximum, respectively, amount we consider).
>>>Find the corresponding amount of each valid column and add this column to that amount's matrix in P_mat provided that it is not already there.
>>
>>**end(for)**
>
>**end(for)**
>Update prv_tokens;

end(while)

Every nonempty column in P_mat will be unique and correspond to one efficient payment scheme.

References

Cramer, Jan S. 1983. Currency by denomination. *Economics Letters* 12: 299–303. [CrossRef]

Kippers, Jeanine, Erjen van Nierop, Richard Paap, and Philip Hans Franses. 2003. An empirical study of cash payments. *Statistica Neerlandica* 57: 484–508. [CrossRef]

Franses, Philip Hans, and Jeanine Kippers. 2007. An empirical analysis of euro cash payments. *European Economic Review* 51: 1985–97. [CrossRef]

Franses, Philip Hans, and Jeanine Kippers. 2010. How do we pay with euro notes when some notes are missing? Empirical evidence from Monopoly experiments. *Applied Financial Economics* 20: 459–64. [CrossRef]

Hasan, Iftekhar, Heiko Schmiedel, and Liang Song. 2012. Return from retail banking and payments. *Journal of Financial Services Research* 41: 163–95. [CrossRef]

Khan, Jashim, Russell W. Belk, and Margaret Craig-Lees. 2015. Measuring consumer perceptions of payment mode. *Journal of Economic Psychology* 47: 34–49. [CrossRef]

Segendorf, Bjorn, and Thomas Jansson. 2012. *The Cost of Consumer Payments in Sweden.* Sveriges Riksbank Working Paper No. 262. Stockholm: Sveriges Riksbank.

Van der Cruijsen, Carin, Lola Hernandez, and Nicole Jonker. 2017. In love with the debit card but still married to cash. *Applied Economics* 49: 2989–3004. [CrossRef]

Journal of
Risk and Financial Management

MDPI

Article

The Relationship between Economic Freedom and FDI versus Economic Growth: Evidence from the GCC Countries

Hichem Dkhili * and Lassad Ben Dhiab

College of Business Administration, Northern Border University, Arar 91431, Saudi Arabia;
Lassad.Dhiab@nbu.edu.sa
* Correspondence: hichem.dkhili@nbu.edu.sa; Tel.: +966-554-386-129

Received: 6 November 2018; Accepted: 18 November 2018; Published: 22 November 2018

Abstract: This study aims to explain the role of economic freedom in attracting foreign investments and thus raising the level of economic growth. Through a study based on a sample composed of the Gulf Cooperation Council (GCC) countries. A standard model consisting of GCC countries (Saudi Arabia, United Arab Emirates, Qatar, Kuwait, and Oman) was used during the period from 1995 to 2017. We based on the analytical descriptive and secondly, we used a multivariate analysis based on the panel unit root test, the cointegration and finally the regression Fully Modified Ordinary Least Squares (FMOLS) and Dynamic Ordinary Least Squares (DOLS) following the existence of a long-term integration, which includes the modern standard methods to determine the role of economic freedom in raising foreign direct investment and thus economic growth in the second stage. The research findings from GCC countries support the literature, suggesting that there are indeed some indications that greater levels of economic freedom support higher rates of economic growth in a country.

Keywords: economic growth; economic freedom; foreign direct investment; panel data

1. Introduction

The Gulf Cooperation Council (GCC) countries are generally characterized by the attractiveness of foreign direct investment (FDI) as they have advanced infrastructure and many energy sources. In recent years, these countries have improved their global ranking in the Ease of Doing Business Index for the World Bank, believing in the need to attract foreign investments due to the positive role of these investments in raising the productivity of enterprises and contributing to the transfer of technology and technical expertise. The flow of foreign direct investment has made many thinkers study the effects of these investments on a variety of economic phenomena such as economic growth as a beginning and the relationship with economic freedom later. In the context of encouraging policies to attract foreign investments and opening up to international markets, the importance of this research is considered a serious attempt based on a standard model to study the positive impact and negative impact of attracting foreign direct investment in the GCC countries compared to the economic growth index.

The FDI can even have opposite effects on the economic growth in an environment of trade limitation (Adams 2009) and (Ahmad et al. 2017). Borensztein et al. (1998) demonstrated that, in the host country, the scale of FDI depends on the availability of the stock of human capital. They add that this impact can be showed negative in countries endowed with a low level of human capital. Lamsiraroj (2016) showed that the effect of domination exercised by the foreign firms can discourage the local firms to develop their own activities of Rand. Another negative effect of the FDI can result from the excessive extraction of ores or the concentration of the production on one particular good which would engender a fall in export prices and a deterioration of the terms of exchange for the host country.

Sayari et al. (2018) and de Haan and Sturm (2000) studies the possibility of a long-run relationship between the Economic Freedom Index (EFI), foreign direct investment (FDI) and value added components of GDP in thirty Eastern, Central, and Western European countries. Their results indicate that there is a marginally significant and negative relationship between EFI and FDI in the random effects model.

In fact, foreign investments play a complementary role to the shortage that may exist in domestic capital. These investments are also important because of their role in the transfer of management, management, marketing and technology in general. These investments are usually accompanied by opportunities to train national cadres and acquire production, marketing and advanced management skills, thereby increasing employment opportunities and increasing the productivity of individuals and institutions.

The aim of this paper is to study the association between FDI, Economic Freedom (EF) and Economic growth (EG). For this reason, we have used data related to GCC countries during the period 1995–2017. In addition to the FDI as a financial variable, trade openness as a proxy of trade, we introduce in our model a proxy of infrastructure (air transport) to explain economic growth.

In this context, our problematic is: What are the determinants of the relationship between the index of economic freedom and foreign direct investment and economic growth?

Finally, this study will be based on the following scheme: First, a review of various modern literary views on economic freedom, foreign direct investment and economic development. Then we will try to give a glimpse of the realities of economic freedom, foreign direct investment and economic growth in the GCC countries through many statistics.

Second, a standard model will be developed to study the relationship between economic freedom, direct foreign investment and economic growth.

2. Literature Review

Foreign direct investment (FDI) exerts positive effects on economic growth through various direct and indirect channels. Economic Performance and economic growth of a country is influenced by multiple factors. Foreign direct investment has been observed and argued as a significant determinant. The role of FDI in economic development has been the subject of long debate. The FDI-growth literature has so far yielded mixed results on whether FDI contributes to economic growth.

Girma (2005), explores the effect of FDI on productivity growth by using recently developed threshold regression techniques.

The results mark the presence of nonlinear threshold effects: the productivity benefit from FDI increases with absorptive capacity until some threshold level beyond which it becomes less pronounced. Also, they conclude that there is also a minimum absorptive capacity threshold level below.

Nowak-Lehmann et al. (2012), analyze the relationship between per capita income and foreign aid. And found that foreign aid has a small positive impact on investment, but a significant negative impact on domestic savings (crowding out) and the real exchange rate.

Anwar and Nguyen (2014) study empirically the impact of foreign direct investment (FDI) and FDI generated spillovers on total factor productivity (TFP) in eight regions of Vietnam. Their results prove that the impact of FDI spillovers on TFP varies considerably across regions. In addition, the FDI spillovers generate a strong positive impact on the total factor productivity (TFP).

Ubeda and Pérez-Hernández (2017); Becker et al. (1990) and Doucouliagos and Ulubasoglu (2006) investigate the effect of foreign direct investment on productivity growth in the manufacturing industries of Spain. They advance a theoretical model to test nonlinear relationships between inward FDI and productivity improvement in domestic firms from 1993 to 2006. The results show that FDI is negatively on productivity growth.

The relationship between foreign direct investment and growth has been tested over several samples. Some studies have discussed this relationship overlarge samples, in fact Lee and Chang (2009) tested the interaction between FDI, financial development and economic growth in 37 countries for the period 1970–2002. Empirical results based on the panel Error Correction Model and the Granger Causality test reveals respectively evidence of a fairly strong long-run relationship and a weak short-run relationship. Overall, the findings underscore the potential gains associated with FDI when coupled with financial development in an increasingly global economy. Li and Liu (2004) investigated the association FDI-growth in a panel of 84 countries observed during the period of 1970–1999. Using both single equation and simultaneous equation system results show that there is a significant relationship between FDI and economic growth. FDI boosts economic growth directly and also indirectly via human capital, while that of FDI with the technology gap has a significant negative impact. The interaction between FDI and economic growth within the role of financial market has been analyzed, also, by Azman-Saini et al. (2010). Based on a data set for 91 countries over the 1975–2005 periods and applying the threshold regression model, results indicate that the benefit of FDI is non-existent.

Analyzing this relationship in the case of developed and developing countries, Borensztein et al. (1998) tested the effect of FDI on economic growth in 69 developing countries over the last two decades. Empirical results suggest that FDI is a strong mechanism for the transfer of technology, which positively affect growth more than domestic investment. FDI can promote economic growth only when a sufficient absorptive capability of the advanced technologies is available in the host economy. Aurangzeb and Thanasis (2014) examined the relationship between FDI and economic growth in a wide range of developing countries. The time period we cover in this study is from 1970 to 2001 and data for all other variables (real GDP, real gross domestic capital formation, real exports, population, and import price index) are obtained from the World Development Indicators (WDI) of the World Bank. By performing smooth coefficient semi-parametric approach, results show that countries with higher levels of FDI inflows experience higher productivity in the exports sector as compared with those with low level of FDI inflows.

In the case of Latin American countries Bengoa and Sanchez-Robles (2003) and Gwartney (2004) investigated the interaction between economic freedom, foreign direct investment (FDI) and economic growth in 18 countries for 1970–1999. Finding indicates that economic freedom is favorable for FDI inflows. Also, there is a positive correlation between foreign direct investment and economic growth in the host countries. This result can be explained as follow: the host country requires liberalized market, adequate human capital and economic stability to access to long-term capital.

For Asian countries the relationship between FDI and growth was treated. In fact, Chen and Zulkifli (2012) investigated the association between outward FDI and economic growth for Malaysia over the period 1980–2010. By performing a VECM, the results indicate that there exists a positive long-run relationship between FDI and growth as well as long-run bi-directional causation between them. However, there is no Granger-causality in the short-run between outward FDI and growth. For the case of China, Hong (2014) employed a Generalize Method of Moments GMM to analyze this relation in China for the period 1994–2010. The sample is composed from 254 cities in china. Findings indicate that there is a positive association between FDI and economic development.

From the case of the Middle East and North African countries (MENA), Hamdi et al. (2013a) examined the relationship between financial deepening, investment activities and growth for the Tunisian context over the period 1961–2010. In this study, they performed the cointegration method and the Vector Error Correction Model (VECM). Result of short run estimation shows that finance does not promote economic growth. However, there is a positive association between finance and growth in the long-run. In second study, Hamdi et al. (2013b) explored the nexus between FDI and growth in Tunisia over the period 1976–2010.

Cointegration and Vector Error Correction Model and Cointegration techniques reveal that FDI did not have significant impact on growth; however exports are the important source for growth in Tunisia. Belloumi (2014) analyzed the relationship between foreign direct investment (FDI), trade openness and growth in the Tunisian context. Based on the bounds testing (ARDL) approach over the period 1970 to 2008, findings confirm the existence of a long-run relationship between FDI and growth. However, FDI does not granger economic growth in the short run. The empirical results fail to confirm the widespread belief that FDI can generate positive externalities for the case of Tunisia.

For Gulf countries, Hussein (2009) examined the interaction between foreign direct investment FDI and economic growth in the six GCC countries[1] during the period 1996–2007. The econometric method used in this study is the Ordinary Least Square (OLS). Major findings indicate a weak relationship between FDI and growth for the sample of the GCC. Almfraji and Almsafir (2014) tested the FDI-growth association in an oil production country. For this end they collected dataset from 1990 to 2010 and they performed VAR Impulse Responses and the Granger Causality test. The result indicates that there a long-run relationship between FDI inflows and the economic growth in Qatar.

The main objective of the study of Al Khathlan (2013) is to empirically analyze the role of FDI in the economic growth of Saudi Arabia from 1980 to 2010. By using the famous Cobb–Douglas production function and performing a co-integration analysis finding indicates that FDI has a positive but insignificant role in economic growth in the country over the long term. However, the Granger causality test implies that domestic capital and government expenditure drive output growth in the economy. This result is also consistent with the IRFs over a time horizon of 10 years.

Bengoa and Sanchez-Robles (2003) explore the interplay between economic freedom, foreign direct investment and economic growth using panel data analysis for a sample of 18 Latin American countries for 1970–1999. And find that economic freedom in the host country is a positive determinant of FDI inflows. Our results also suggest that foreign direct investment is positively correlated with economic growth in the host countries. The host country requires, however, adequate human capital, economic stability and liberalized markets to benefit from long-term capital flows.

Borensztein et al. (1998) test the effect of foreign direct investment (FDI) on economic growth in a cross-country regression framework, utilizing data on FDI flows from industrial countries to 69 developing countries over the last two decades. Their results suggest that FDI is an important vehicle for the transfer of technology, contributing relatively more to growth than domestic investment. However, the higher productivity of FDI holds only when the host country has a minimum threshold stock of human capital. Thus, FDI contributes to economic growth only when a sufficient absorptive capability of the advanced technologies is available in the host economy.

Azman-Saini et al. (2010); Mogens (2008); Paakkonen (2010) and Pourshahabi et al. (2011) investigate the systemic link between economic freedom, foreign direct investment and economic growth in a panel of 85 countries. Their empirical results, based on the generalized method-of-moment system estimator, reveal that FDI by itself has no direct (positive) effect on output growth. Instead, the effect of FDI is contingent on the level of economic freedom in the host countries. This means the countries promote greater freedom of economic activities gain significantly from the presence of multinational corporations (MNCs).

Iamsiraroj and Ulubaşoğlu (2015) results that the FDI is positively affect economic growth. And found appropriate absorptive capacity indicators for positive growth are identified to be trade openness and financial development rather than schooling. Alguacil et al. (2011) contribute to the discussion on the role played by the absorptive capacities within host economies in their ability to grow and to exploit FDI efficiently. Alvarado et al. (2017), studies foreign direct investment and economic growth in Latin America and examines the effect of foreign direct investment (FDI) on economic growth in 19 Latin American countries.

By using panel data econometrics, they found that the effect of FDI on economic growth is not statistically significant in aggregated form. And they advance that FDI is not an adequate mechanism to accelerate economic growth in Latin America, with the exception of high-income countries.

The interest of the economic freedom study and its role in raising the volume of foreign direct investment and economic growth is especially in light of the new economic era that supports economic openness and globalization. The Apergis and Arusha (2017) study confirmed that FDI is positively correlated with economic growth in host countries which requires adequate human capital, economic

---

[1]   Saudi Arabia, United Arab Emirates, Oman, Qatar, Kuwait and Bahrain.

stability and market liberalization to capitalize on long-term capital flows. Goel et al. (2017) deals with economic freedom as an indicator of economic freedom. In this study it was ascertained that economic freedom contributes to economic growth. For the study of Azman-Saini et al. (2010), it touched on the investigation of linkages between business environment indicators (e.g., economic freedom) on the one hand, and foreign direct investment and economic growth on the other. The study was based on a sample of 85 countries and showed that countries that are interested in improving the business climate, such as promoting economic freedom, are the beneficiaries rather than the multinational companies. As for Saha et al. (2017) found a causal link between economic freedom and political inbound tourism for more than 110 countries during 1995–2012. In general, most studies confirm the importance and role of economic freedom in attracting foreign direct investment and raising the rate of economic growth. This is why we are concerned about this problem in the GCC (Saudi Arabia, United Arab Emirates, Qatar, Kuwait and Oman).

3. Empirical Analysis

3.1. Data and Methodology

We study the effect of FDI and economic freedom on economic growth in GCC countries. All papers have dealt with the issue of the relationship FDI/growth. So we take the initiative to address this issue. The second motivation comes from the fact that our target region is a set of countries whose economy is based on oil; and we are witnessing these years a drop in oil prices that has stabilized at \$ 30. This framework uses a standard model consisting of GCC countries (Saudi Arabia, United Arab Emirates, Qatar, Kuwait and Oman) during the period from 1995 to 2017. (2013) will be based on the analytical descriptive approach in the first stage and quantitative analytical approach, which includes the modern standard methods to determine the role of economic freedom in raising foreign direct investment and thus economic growth in the second stage. To study the relationship between economic freedom and the flow of foreign investment and economic growth of the GCC countries, the following standard model will be used:

$$\text{RGDPD}_{i,t} = \beta_0 + \beta_1 \text{FDI}_{i_{i,t}} + \beta_2 \text{FE}_{i_{i,t}} + \beta_3 \text{OPEN}_{i_{i,t}} + \beta_4 \text{GSAV}_{i_{i,t}} + \varepsilon_{i,t}$$

RGDPG: Represents the rate of economic growth
FDI: Is the ratio of foreign direct investment
EF: Is the index of economic freedom. Several indicators adopted by the World Bank can also be used.
OPEN: Represents the growth rate of economic openness
GSAV: Represents the gross savings rate.
Data are from model variables are collected from World Bank statistics World Development Indicators database—The Word Bank. The Freedom Economic Index data was collected from Heritage.

This model will be applied to a sample consisting of the GCC countries (Saudi Arabia, United Arab Emirates, Qatar, Kuwait, and Oman).

The empirical strategy is based on two approaches, panel data analysis and system GMM, to check the soundness of the results. The double dimensions, individual (countries) and temporal (years), of our sample oriented us towards the selection of panel data analysis. Panel data generally presents less multicollinearity than time series or cross section data. Also, it leads to more precise coefficient estimations.

Using panel data, the non-stationarity of time series and estimate errors seem to have been reduced (Baltagi 1995, 2001 and Ryan et al. 2011). Also, the GMM method has several advantages. It allows one to solve the problems of simultaneity bias, reverse causality and omitted variables which have weakened the results of previous studies. It also addresses the problem of the endogeneity of explanatory variables (Hansen 1982; Hansen and Singleton 1982; Tan 2015).

Our methodology is to conduct the panel data method over several stages. The first will be to test the effect of Economic Freedom (EF) and FDI on economic growth. At this level, we will use the global index of the EF. In the second step we will try to test the effect of the components of the EF

(6 components) on economic growth. In the third step, we will test the effect of EF and each component and its interaction with FDI on pattern-based economic growth.

As a result, we will have 7 models. In the fourth step, we will test the effect of EF components and their interactions with FDI on economic growth. At this level, we introduce all the variables together. In the last step, we will present the Results of Panel Fully Modified OLS (PFMOLS) and Dynamic Least Squares (DOLS) regressions.

The validity of the system GMM requires that three conditions be fulfilled. First, the Sargan test of over-identifying restrictions should provide no correlation between instruments and error term.

Second, for the second order correlation, there should be no serial correlation. System GMM results indicate that the Sargan and serial-correlation tests do not reject the null hypothesis of correct specification (p-value of Sargan test and p-value of AR(2) test of Arellano and Bond are larger than 5%), providing support for our estimation results. The p-value of the Sargan test of over-identifying restrictions is equal to 16% which is higher than 5%. Hence, we confirm the overall validity of the instruments. Also, the p-value of AR(2) is equal to 40.6% (more than 5%) which implies that there is no correlation.

Finally, we check the robustness of our results based from different test of Cointegration: the results of Pedroni Residual Cointegration Test, Kao Residual Cointegration Test and Johansen Fisher panel cointegration test.

3.2. Results and Interpretation

3.2.1. Pre-Estimation: Descriptive Statistics and the Correlation Matrix

Descriptive Statistics

Table 1 below summarizes descriptive statistics for our sample. Descriptive statistics are presented to describe the basic characteristics of the data used in this study. For each variable, we have the average value, the standard deviation, the minimum and the maximum values. The results of the descriptive statistics indicate that the average value of economic freedom index is (72.178). From these statistics, for the GDP growth per capita, descriptive statistics show that the average level of growth equal to (5.767%) with a minimum value of (−7.076%) and a maximum value of (+28.447%).

Table 1. Descriptive statistics. RDGPG: Represents the rate of economic growth; EF: Economic Freedom; FDI: foreign direct investment; OPEN: average value of trade openness.

	RGDPG	EF	FDI	OPEN	GDSAV
Mean	5.888	45.26	4.036	105.726	36.639
Median	4.861	66.700	2.936	95.584	33.431
Maximum	28.447	69.000	33.566	164.115	69.610
Minimum	−7.076	60.400	−1.315	56.474	7.342
Std. Dev.	5.422	1507.455	5.139	25.895	15.854
Skewness	1.521	3.674	2.853	0.311	0.401
Observations	114	114	114	114	114

	RGDPG	FDI	EF	OPEN	GDSAV
RGDPG	1.000				
FDI	0.329	1.000			
EF	0.146	−0.076	1.000		
OPEN	−0.091	−0.207	0.567	1.000	
GSAV	0.412	0.174	−0.244	−0.407	1.000

The average level of foreign direct investment net inflow (FDI) remains an average of 3.642%; having a maximum value of 33.566% while its minimum value is −1.315%. Contrary to foreign investment, the average value of domestic investment (INVES) seems to be satisfactory with a level of 46.355%; its maximum value is 75% while its minimum value is 30.000%. For gross domestic savings (GDSAV), the average value is 36.554%; its minimum value is 7.342% and 69.610% as its maximum value. Descriptive statistics indicate respectable values for trade openness. We find that the average value of trade openness (OPEN) is 105.726% and the maximum value is 164.115%.

3.2.2. FDI. Economic Freedom and Economic Growth in GCC Countries

Table 2 shows that Saudi knew a high rate of growth during the period 1970–1976. The RGDPC growth crossed from 12.03% in 1970 to reach 19.94% in 1971 and 12.72% in 1976. While the FDI inflow recorded negative values for the same period. FDI in % of PIB take a value of −1.64% in 1971 and −8.3 in 1974. The divergence trend of those indicators indicates that FDI did not well contribute to the growth of Saudi Arabia during this period. This country allows more importance to the oil revenue which is considered as the engine of growth.

Table 2. Economic Freedom and Economic Growth in Gulf Cooperation Council (GCC) countries.

Years	Index of Economic Freedom	FDI Inflow (in % of GDP)	Real GDP Growth (%)
1995	68.64	1.338	4.25
1996	69.02	6.388	3.93
1997	70.04	2.679	8.01
1998	68.52	2.286	3.93
1999	69.27	1.382	2.26
2000	68.25	2.464	6.82
2001	68.00	1.078	2.29
2002	68.47	1.289	3.68
2003	66.48	2.616	8.01
2004	65.70	4.208	10.62
2005	64.90	6.327	7.43
2006	64.75	9.297	10.62
2007	65.28	6.792	8.27
2008	66.77	5.843	7.54
2009	68.42	5.113	1.65
2010	69.33	3.189	5.02
2011	68.45	2.402	6.37
2012	68.67	2.277	4.16
2013	68.57	2.230	4.75
2014	69.33	3.189	5.02
2015	68.45	2.402	6.37
2016	68.25	2.464	6.82
2017	69.27	1.382	2.26

Source: Data related to economic Freedom are collected from www.heritage.org/index/ranking. Data related to FDI and Economic growth are collected from the World Bank Indicators.

Since 1977, the FDI net inflows begin to know positive values. Those positive values coincide with the development plan for 1975–1979 to encourage foreign direct investment. For example, we record a value of FDI of 1.06% in 1977. GDPpc growth continues to have positive value during the period 1977–1981 with respectively values of 7% and 4.69%. Since 1982, Saudi Arabia recorded negative rate of GDPpc growth. Those rates reach −11.1% in 1982 and −8.22% in 1983. GDPpc gets back to its positive values from 1988 and its fluctuations appear almost stable during the remaining period. Also, the FDI curve is constant during the period 1986–2004. However, it records very low values. Since 2005, the FDI net inflow follows a rising trend. It's crossed from 3.84% in 2005 to reach 9.68% in 2009.

3.2.3. Results of Correlation Matrix

The results of the matrix correlation in Table 3 demonstrate a strong correlation between the components of GDP and trade openness and the components of economic. The economic development literature has shown that industry adds to services, while the opposite is also true. The levels of correlation are 0.992, 0.518, and 0.502 for those pairs, respectively. There is also a strong negative correlation between the value added components of economic freedom and FDI. Also, a negative correlation between the values added components of economic freedom and the savings rate.

Table 3. Correlation Matrix.

	RGDPG	FDI	Gfc	OPEN	GDSAV	Fisf	Busf	Monf	Tradf	Invesf	Finanf	Fisfxfdi	Busfxfdi	Monfxfdi	Tradfxfdi	Invesfxfdi	Finafxfdi
RDGPG	1																
FDI	0.147	1															
Gfc	-0.203	0.119	1														
OPEN	-0.093	0.53	-0.081	1													
GDSAV	0.414	-0.239	-0.097	-0.4	1												
fisf	0.024	-0.163	0.257	-0.197	0.234	1											
busf	-0.212	-0.005	0.032	0.078	-0.361	0.235	1										
monf	-0.013	0.15	0.027	0.109	-0.303	-0.103	0.147	1									
tradf	0.043	-0.086	-0.002	0.158	0.308	0.56	0.071	-0.444	1								
invesf	-0.138	0.22	-0.306	0.37	-0.344	-0.557	0.001	-0.001	-0.171	1							
finanf	-0.091	0.329	-0.162	0.58	-0.422	-0.249	0.414	0.146	-0.08	0.57	1						
fisfxfdi	0.152	0.991	0.147	0.518	-0.212	-0.089	0.034	0.133	-0.026	0.184	0.316	1					
busfxfdi	0.095	0.964	0.113	0.502	-0.252	-0.093	0.164	0.162	-0.045	0.216	0.354	0.976	1				
monfxfdi	0.134	0.997	0.137	0.526	-0.259	-0.16	0.013	0.199	-0.099	0.221	0.335	0.989	0.969	1			
tradfxfdi	0.148	0.992	0.148	0.521	-0.226	-0.108	0.015	0.116	0.001	0.198	0.309	0.996	0.972	0.987	1		
invesfxfdi	0.092	0.971	0.068	0.541	-0.334	-0.247	0.03	0.173	-0.143	0.377	0.413	0.946	0.938	0.973	0.953	1	
finafxfdi	0.104	0.975	0.095	0.551	-0.285	-0.166	0.092	0.194	-0.113	0.275	0.461	0.966	0.959	0.975	0.961	0.971	1

Where: RGDPG: Represents the rate of economic growth. FDI: Is the ratio of foreign direct investment and (Fisfxfdi, Busfxfdi, Monfxfdi, Tradfxfdi, Invesfxfdi and Finafxfdi) are the components of the FDI. EF: Is the index of economic freedom. Fisf, Busf, Monf, Tradf, Invest and Finanf: Represents the components of the EF. OPEN: Represents the growth rate of economic openness. GSAV: Represents the Gross savings rate. Gfc: Represents the domestic investment.

3.3. Results of the Effect of Economic Freedom and FDI on Economic Growth

The results of the Effect of Economic Freedom (EF) and FDI (FDI) on economic growth (EG) are summarized in Table 4. The results showed that all the coefficients are positive except economic freedom and trade openness with a negative coefficient respectively equal (−0.263) and (−0.025).

Thereafter, we note that the coefficients of economic freedom and savings rate are statically significant. With a positive coefficient for the savings rate equal (0.176).

Results indicate that the effect of Effect of EF and FDI on economic growth (EG) is solid since its coefficient is negative and statistically significant at the 1% level for Economic Freedom and trade openness. Coefficients of FDI and savings rate are respectively positive and statistically significant.

Table 4. The effect of economic freedom (EF) and FDI on economic growth (EG).

Rgdpg	Coef.	Std. Err.	t	$p > t$
Ef	−0.263	0.157	−1.67	0.098 **
Fdi	0.200	0.118	1.70	0.092 **
Gfc	0.073	0.104	0.70	0.484
Gsav	0.176	0.032	5.50	0.000 ***
Open	−0.025	0.042	−0.60	0.550
_cons	23.621	11.758	2.01	0.047 **
chi2 haus	14.200	-	-	-
Prob	0.006	-	-	-
Fisher	2.030	-	-	-
Prob > F	0.097	-	-	-
N° Obs	104	-	-	-

** and *** denote level of significance respectively at 5% and 1%.

3.4. Results of the Effect of the Components of the EF (6 Components) on Economic Growth

We introduce the interactive relation between the components of the economic freedom with six components and economic growth in Table 5. Thus, the coefficient savings rate is more significant in spite of its positive sign. The coefficient trade openness is negative and statistically insignificant suggesting that the effects of economic freedom on economic growth are more apparent with a higher level of investment. This may be explained by a negative coefficient and significant of investment with a coefficient equal (−0.151), and with a positive and significant coefficient for the variable Gross save rating equal (0.176).

Table 5. Effect of the components of the EF (6 components) on EG.

RGDPG	Coef.	Std. Err.	t	$p > t$
FDI	0.140	0.118	1.180	0.240
Gfc	0.081	0.106	0.760	0.448
OPEN	−0.084	0.052	−1.610	0.111
Gsav	0.175	0.059	2.960	0.004 ***
Ef	−0.263	0.188	−1.400	0.166
Fisf	0.044	0.079	0.560	0.574
Busf	0.066	0.062	1.070	0.289
Monf	0.039	0.084	0.460	0.648
Tradf	0.013	0.092	0.140	0.891
Invesf	−0.151	0.062	−2.440	0.017 **
Finanf	0.001	0.074	0.010	0.993
_cons	17.611	19.156	0.920	0.361
chi2 haus	41.39	-	-	-
Prob	0.000	-	-	-
Fisher	2.17	-	-	-
Prob > F	0.0248	-	-	-
N° Obs	93	-	-	-

** and *** denote level of significance respectively at 5% and 1%.

3.5. Result of Panel Data Analysis on the Effect of Economic Freedom and FDI on the Economic Growth

We estimate regressions by including all the variables with all the components. The Coefficient EF and Trade openness are negative and insignificant. Results present in Table 6, coefficient (Invesf) is negative and significant, and one unit increase of the index decreases growth by 1.51%. The results devote a negative and significant correlation between economic freedom and foreign direct investment (FDI), also, we note a positive correlation between FDI and trade openness with a coefficient equal (0.433).

More concretely, access to credit leads to more investment which turns positively on the level of growth (Rajan and Zingales 1998; Guiso et al. 2004). However, our results have revealed negative relationships. These results indicate that the governments of GCC countries should adopt a more flexible but prudent credit policy to stimulate investment, especially in the private sector as an important key to boosting economic growth in this region. It's obvious that foreign direct investment (FDI) is an important factor in stimulating economic growth. Results of system GMM show a positive and significant association between FDI and GDPPC.

This finding supports the positive role of FDI as a channel of technological transfer and a factor for promoting employment and improving the productivity of local firms. However, these results are only significant at 10% and the coefficient is very weak at only 3.8%. This implies that GCC countries should put more effort into financial reform, business environment and fighting corruption to attract more foreign investment. It is better for foreign investment to be cleaner to protect the environment and more productive to absorb the high rate of unemployment. The positive association between FDI and GDPPC is in line with the findings of Sayari et al. (2018) and Borensztein et al. (1998). Like foreign direct investment, domestic investment (INVES) is recognized as an important key for economic growth. Domestic direct investment (DDI) is considered as a smarter capital. In China for example, DDI represents 40% of all investments. However, FDI is only about 3%. Our empirical findings indicate that there is a highly positive and significant association between domestic investment and economic growth.

Table 6. Result of Panel Data Analysis on the effect of Economic Freedom and FDI on the Economic Growth.

	EF		FISF		BUS		MONF		TRADF		INVESF		FINANF	
	Coeff	Z–Stat	Coeff	Z–Stat	Coeff	Z–Stat	Coeff	Z–Stat	Coeff	Z–Stat	Coeff	Z–Stat	Coeff	Z–Stat
RGDPG														
FDI	-0.008	-1.000	1.005	1.290	1.057	2.250**	4.330	3.110***	0.433	0.490	-0.186	-0.360	0.082	2.660***
Gfc	0.000	0.110	-0.102	-1.510	0.003	0.020	-0.118	-1.930	-0.091	-1.410	0.076	0.760	-0.108	-1.700
OPEN	0.001	0.310	-0.010	-0.410	-0.033	-0.700	-0.004	-0.180	-0.007	-0.300	-0.090	-1.910	-0.030	-1.130
Gsav	-0.003	-1.230	0.160	4.910***	0.137	2.710***	0.170	5.440***	0.163	4.660***	0.191	3.560***	0.157	4.960***
Ef	-0.085	-11.650***												
Efxfdi	0.015	155.500***												
Fisf			0.018	0.350										
Fisfxfdi			-0.008	-0.890										
Busf					0.074	1.140								
busfxfdi					-0.010	-1.830								
Monf							0.256	2.840***						
monfxfdi							-0.048	-2.900***						
Tradf									-0.034	-0.440				
tradfxfdi									-0.002	-0.150				
Invesf											-0.186	-2.790***		
invesfxfdi											0.008	0.720		
Finanf													0.082	1.660
finanfxfdi													-0.016	-2.100***
_cons	5.663	11.21***	0.409	0.07	-2.443	-0.33	-19.251	-2.29**	4.048	0.75	14.454	2.57***	-0.452	-0.11
chi2 haus	6.280		11.630		12.700		6.440		9.140		31.710		6.300	
Prob	0.393		0.070		0.048		0.375		0.165		0.000		0.390	
wald chi2	34.007		37.600		–		50.290		37.160		–		42.890	
Prob > chi2	0.000		0.000		–		0.000		0.000		–		0.000	
Fisher	–		–		2.630		–		–		3.650		–	
N° Obs	99		92		92		92		92		92		92	

** and *** denote level of significance respectively at 5% and 1%.

3.6. Effect of EF Components and Their Interactions with FDI on Economic Growth (EG)

From the results of the effect of EF components and their interactions with FDI on economic growth (EG) presented in Table 7, we remark that the components of the variable Economic Freedom exert a positive relation on the variable (FDI) with a positive coefficient (2.856), this positive correlation is stronger than the other correlation such as the correlation with savings rates (0.181).

Furthermore, the results shown in the table below show a very good whole model fit as remarked by the Wald chi-Square (34.007) and Hausman chi-Square respectively (6.280).

Table 7. Effect of EF components and their interactions with FDI on economic growth (EG).

RGDPG	Coef.	Std. Err.	z	$p > z$
FDI	2.856	3.328	0.860	0.391
gfc	−0.155	0.072	−2.140	0.032 **
OPEN	−0.012	0.034	−0.330	0.738
gsav	0.181	0.046	3.920	0.000 ***
fisf	0.002	0.081	0.020	0.984
busf	0.049	0.080	0.620	0.538
monf	0.166	0.122	1.360	0.173
tradf	−0.050	0.125	−0.400	0.690
invesf	−0.055	0.064	−0.850	0.393
finanf	0.077	0.065	1.180	0.236
fisfxfdi	0.004	0.022	0.160	0.870
busfxfdi	−0.009	0.012	−0.710	0.478
monfxfdi	−0.021	0.026	−0.810	0.419
tradfxfdi	0.004	0.022	0.190	0.847
invesfxfdi	0.005	0.017	0.280	0.781
finafxfdi	−0.014	0.010	−1.430	0.154
_cons	−13.006	13.899	−0.940	0.349
chi2 haus	6.280			
prob	0.393			
wald chi2	34.007			
Prob > chi2	0.000			
N° Obs	99			

** and *** denote level of significance respectively at 5% and 1%.

3.7. Panel Unit Root Test (PURT) and Panel Cointegration

We use the Augmented Dickey–Fuller (F-ADF) unit root tests to check the stationarity of each variable. The augmented Dickey–Fuller (ADF) statistic, used in the test, is a negative number. The more negative, it is, the stronger the rejection of the hypothesis that there is a unit roots. The results of the Augmented Dickey-Fuller (ADF) and Phillips–Perron (PP) tests for the four variables of the model are presented in Table 8.

Table 8. Results of Panel Unit Root Test (PURT).

Method	RGDPG		FDI		EF		OPEN		GSAV		Order of Integration
	LEVEL	FIRST	LEVEL	FIRST	LEVEL	FIRST	LEVEL	FIRST	LEVEL	FIRST	
LLC	−0.194	−3.946 ***	0.7978	−2.523 ***	−1.272	−2.237 **	−1.191	−5.469 ***	−1.234	−3.059 ***	I(1)
Breitung	−0.1846	−3.169 ***	−1.412	−2.714 ***	−0.247	−4.25 ***	−1.539	−5.032 ***	−1.312	−4.307 ***	I(1)
IPS	−0.0708	−3.761 ***	−0.962	−2.163 **	−0.187	−2.543 ***	−1.274	−2.758 ***	0.0647	−3.284 ***	I(1)
ADF	11.0234	36.229 ***	15.979	24.575 **	13.91	25.735 **	17.75	30.405 ***	10.922	23.795 **	I(1)
PP	16.3737	90.139 ***	18.658	54.88 ***	10.46	70.429 ***	10.913	51.978 ***	7.6922	53.781 ***	I(1)

** and *** denote level of significance respectively at 5% and 1%.

The results show that in the level, the null hypothesis cannot be rejected for all the variables for both the two-unit root test ADF and Phillips–Perron (PP) test. GDPPC, FDI, OPEN, EF, and GSAV are not stationary in the level. By testing through first difference, the results rejected the null hypothesis of non-stationarity. The unit roots tests confirm that each variable is integrated of order one.

Findings of the cointegration tests indicate that there exist relationships between variables. Therefore, all the variables are cointegrated.

3.8. Result of Panel Fully Modified OLS (PFMOLS) and Dynamic Least Squares (DOLS)

Two statistics are used in the cointegration test of Johansen (1988), they are Trace test and Max-Eigen value. The cointegration test aims to check whether it exist a long run relationship association.

Table 9 below presents the result of long-run association reveals that FDI acts positively and significantly on the economic growth. Although that the FDI in GCC countries transmitted by the multinational corporation have several welfare advantages, one of which is the technology transfer. FDI promotes economic growth by stimulating technological progress, which affect positively the economic growth (Borensztein et al. 1998). Foreign firms transfer new products or processes to the domestic market, domestic firms may benefit from the accelerated diffusion of new technology (Teece 1977). To fight the competition of foreign company, domestic firms try to increase their economic freedom. An increase of economic freedom can stimulate the growth economic. The trade openness acts positively and significantly on the economic growth and economic freedom. Also trade openness promotes the efficient allocation of resources through comparative advantage, allows the dissemination of knowledge and technological progress, and encourages competition in domestic and international markets. Our finding is consistent with the studies of Romer (1993); Grossman and Helpman (1991).

Table 9. Result of Panel Fully Modified Ordinary Least Square (FMOLS), Dynamic Least Squares (DOLS) Regression.

	FMOLS				DOLS			
RGDPG	**Coeff**	**Std. Err**	**t-Stat**	**Prob.**	**Coeff**	**Std. Err**	**t-Stat**	**Prob.**
FDI	0.001	0.000	2.014	0.047 **	0.006	0.001	4.797	0.000 ***
EF	0.371	0.128	2.890	0.004 ***	−0.537	0.396	−1.356	0.187
OPEN	−0.066	0.051	−1.300	0.197	0.256	0.097	2.653	0.013 **
GSAV	0.110	0.053	2.075	0.041 **	−0.198	0.064	−3.100	0.005 ***
R2		0.385				0.977		
Adjusted R2		0.318				0.918		
Durbin-Watson		1.759				–		
				Diagnostic tests				
Q-Stat		0.681				3.415		
Prob		0.711				0.065		
Squared Res		3.556				13.405		
Prob		0.168				0.000		

*** and ** denote level of significance at 1% and 5%.

The results suggest the existence of the long-run cointegrating relationship between economic freedom and economic growth that is statistically significant. It is approximately 0.371, meaning that, on average, a 1% change in GDP leads to a 0.371% change in economic freedom. Also positive relation between trade openness and economic growth, meaning that, on average, a 1% change in GDP leads to a 0.256% change in trade openness. The close values of long-run coefficients for all estimations confirm the robustness of the estimated results.

4. Robustness Tests Check

Lu and White (2014) study when and how one can infer structural validity from coefficient robustness and plausibility. And provide a straightforward new Hausman (1978) type test of robustness for the critical core coefficients, additional diagnostics that can help explain why robustness test rejection occurs, and a new estimator, the Feasible Optimally combined GLS (FOGLeSs) estimator, that makes relatively efficient use of the robustness check regressions.

The robustness tests tried to examine how certain "core" regression coefficient estimates behave when the regression specification is modified by adding or removing regressors. If the coefficients are plausible and robust, this is commonly interpreted as evidence of structural validity.

To check the model specification, or how robust the coefficients of economic freedom, FDI, Growth economic, trade openness and save ratings are to changes in the conditioning set of information, we apply the extreme bound analysis (Levine and Renelt 1992).

Robustness checks showed consistent results estimating the model with standard errors. For the Panel Fully Modified OLS (PFMOLS) and Dynamic Least Squares (DOLS) model, we also estimated standard errors.

Table 10 below summarizes the results from different test of Cointegration: the results of Pedroni Residual Cointegration Test, Kao Residual Cointegration Test and Johansen Fisher panel cointegration test.

We provide the results of seven panel cointegration tests suggested by Pedroni (1999, 2004) between dimensions are reported in Table 10. These seven tests are based on the estimated residuals.

The test results indicate that most statistics are statistically significant, and therefore the null hypothesis of no cointegration can be rejected at conventional levels, suggesting that the variables are cointegrated in both models. For the results of panel cointegration test, suggested by Kao (1999). The test results also indicate that variables between dimensions are panel cointegrated with 5% and 1% significance levels, respectively.

Finally, the results of panel cointegration test suggested Johansen Fisher panel cointegration test indicate that with the asymptotic *p*-values, the no cointegration null is rejected.

Table 10. Results of different test of Cointegration.

Pedroni Residual Cointegration Test				
		Weighted		
	Statistic	Prob.	Statistic	Prob.
Panel v-Statistic	−1.704	0.955	−1.857	0.968
Panel rho-Statistic	−0.406	0.342	−0.285	0.387
Panel PP-Statistic	−6.621	0.000 ***	−6.387	0.000 ***
Panel ADF-Statistic	−2.048	0.020 **	−2.665	0.003 **
Alternative hypothesis: individual AR coefs. (between-dimension)				
	Statistic	Prob.		
Group rho-Statistic	1.287	0.901		
Group PP-Statistic	−6.548	0.000 ***		
Group ADF-Statistic	−1.739	0.041 **		
Kao Residual Cointegration Test				
		t-Statistic	Prob.	
ADF		−4.650	0.000 ***	
Johansen Fisher panel cointegration test				
Hypothesized	Fisher Stat. **		Fisher Stat. **	
No. of CE(s)	(from trace test)	Prob.	(from max-eigen test)	Prob.
None	160.2	0.000 ***	126.2	0.000 ***
At most 1	79.06	0.000 ***	49.24	0.000 ***
At most 2	40.92	0.000 ***	33.26	0.000 ***
At most 3	16.48	0.036 **	11.99	0.151
At most 4	14.84	0.062	14.84	0.062

** and *** denote level of significance respectively at 5% and 1%.

5. Conclusions and Policy Remarks

This paper investigated the relationship between economic freedom, FDI and economic growth for a panel of GCC countries for the period 1995–2017.

We investigate the impact of economic freedom on economic growth and foreign direct investment (FDI). Our findings show a positive and significant relation between economic freedom and FDI and between economic freedoms an economic growth.

Theoretically there is a widespread belief that FDI generates positive externalities for host countries. To explore the linkage between FDI, economic freedom and growth, we had used a dataset related to GCC countries during the period 1995–2017. Data used in this paper are collected from the World Development Indicators (WDI) and for the Freedom Economic Index; the data was collected from the web site Heritage. The empirical approach used in this paper is based on three steps. The first one checks the stationarity of each variable. The second step, aimed to test the existence of a long-run cointegration between variables. This is performed by the Johansen methods. Thirdly, of Panel Fully Modified OLS (PFMOLS) and Dynamic Least Squares (DOLS) is used if all variables are integrated of order one I (1) and cointegrated.

Empirical results show that in long-run regression, FDI promotes economic growth in GCC countries. Also the long-run cointegrating relationship shows that there is a relation between FDI and growth and economic freedom. Findings indicate also that trade openness (LOPEN).

These results are confirming the results of Bengoa and Sanchez-Robles (2003); Azman-Saini et al. (2010) and Goel et al. (2017).

In fact, Bengoa and Sanchez-Robles (2003) found a significant and a positive relation between freedom, foreign direct investment (FDI) and economic growth in 18 countries for 1970–1999. In this context Goel et al. (2017) provide empirically that economic freedom contributes to economic growth. As far as study of Azman-Saini et al. (2010), they found a relation between economic freedom and foreign direct investment and economic growth on the other.

Finally, we perform a robustness tests check for our methodology, we used in this step the results of seven panel cointegration tests suggested by Pedroni (1999, 2004) between dimensions.

The results confirm that all variables are statistically significant, and therefore the null hypothesis of no cointegration can be rejected at conventional levels. The same results for the test proposed by Kao (1999).

This finding may be considered of great interest, the GCC countries should continue its efforts to attract foreign investors and to promote FDI by offering many investments incentives by promoting the economic freedom. Also, the GCC countries should encourage and support the FDI by developing the trade openness (LOPEN), which appears an important engine to stimulate the economic growth.

Author Contributions: The research problem was identified by H.D.; the Data Collection was fixed out by L.B.D.; the econometric model was performed by H.D.; both authors contributed to the specification of models and the interpretation of results; the paper was written and supervised by H.D. with collaboration from L.B.D.

Funding: This project was funded by deanship of Scientific Research, Northern Border University for their financial support under grant N°. (435/000). We are thankful to technical and financial support of the DSR who provided expertise that greatly assisted the research, and my completion of this project could not have been accomplished without him support.

Acknowledgments: We are grateful to two anonymous referees for their helpful suggestion. We are responsible for any remaining errors.

Conflicts of Interest: The authors declare no conflict of interest.

References

Adams, Samuel. 2009. Foreign direct investment, domestic investment, and economic growth in Sub-Saharan Africa. *Journal of Policy Modeling* 31: 939–49. [CrossRef]

Ahmad, Najid, Liangsheng Du, Jiye Lu, Jianlin Wang, Hong-Zhou Li, and Muhammad Zaffar Hashmi. 2017. Modelling the CO_2 emissions and economic growth in Croatia: Is there any environmental Kuznets curve? *Energy* 123: 164–72. [CrossRef]

Al Khathlan, Khalid. 2013. Foreign direct investment inflows and economic growth in Saudi Arabia: A co-integration analysis. *Review of Economics and Finance* 4: 70–80.

Alguacil, Maite, Ana Cuadros, and Vicente Orts. 2011. Inward FDI and growth: The role of macroeconomic and institutional environment. *Journal of Policy Modeling* 33: 481–96. [CrossRef]

Almfraji, Mohammad Amin, and Mahmoud Khalid Almsafir. 2014. Foreign Direct Investment and Economic Growth Literature Review from 1994 to 2012. *Procedia Social and Behavioral Sciences* 129: 206–13. [CrossRef]

Alvarado, Rafael, Maria Iñiguez, and Pablo Ponce. 2017. Foreign direct investment and economic growth in Latin America. *Economic Analysis and Policy* 56: 176–87. [CrossRef]

Anwar, Sajid, and Lan Phi Nguyen. 2014. Is foreign direct investment productive? A case study of the regions of Vietnam. *Journal of Business Research* 67: 1376–87. [CrossRef]

Apergis, Nicolas, and Cooray Arusha. 2017. Economic Freedom and Income Inequality: Evidence from a Panel of Global Economies—A Linear and a Non-Linear Long-Run Analysis. *The Manchester School* 85: 88–105. [CrossRef]

Aurangzeb, Zeb, and Stengos Thanasis. 2014. The role of Foreign Direct Investment (FDI) in a dualistic growth framework: A smooth coefficient semi-parametric approach. *Borsa Istanbul Review* 14: 133–44. [CrossRef]

Azman-Saini, W. N. W., Ahmad Zubaidi Baharumshah, and Siong Hook Law. 2010. Foreign direct investment. Economic freedom and economic growth: International evidence. *Economic Modelling* 27: 1079–89. [CrossRef]

Baltagi, Badi H. 1995. Editor's introduction: Panel data. *Journal of Econometrics* 68: 1–4. [CrossRef]

Baltagi, Badi H. 2001. *Econometric Analysis of Panel Data*, 2nd ed. New York: John Wiley and Sons.

Becker, Gary S., Kevin M. Murphy, and Robert Tamura. 1990. Human capital, fertility and growth. *Journal of Political Economy* 98: S12–37. [CrossRef]

Belloumi, Mounir. 2014. The relationship between trade, FDI and economic growth in Tunisia: An application of the autoregressive distributed lag model. *Economic Systems* 38: 269–87. [CrossRef]

Bengoa, Marta, and Blanca Sanchez-Robles. 2003. Foreign direct investment. Economic freedom and growth: New evidence from Latin America. *European Journal of Political Economy* 19: 529–45. [CrossRef]

Borensztein, Eduardo R., José R. De Gregorio, and Jongwha Lee. 1998. How does foreign direct investment affect economic growth? *Journal of International Economics* 45: 115–35. [CrossRef]

Chen, Jen-Eem, and Azreen Mohd Zulkifli. 2012. Malaysian Outward FDI and Economic Growth. *Procedia Social and Behavioral Sciences* 65: 717–22. [CrossRef]

de Haan, Jakob, and Jan-Egbert Sturm. 2000. On the relationship between economic freedom and economic growth. *European Journal of Political Economy* 16: 215–41. [CrossRef]

Doucouliagos, Chris, and Mehmet Ali Ulubasoglu. 2006. Foreign direct investment. Economic freedom and economic growth: International evidence. *European Journal of Political Economy* 22: 60–81. [CrossRef]

Girma, Sourafel. 2005. Absorptive Capacity and Productivity Spillovers from FDI: A Threshold Regression Analysis. *Oxford Bulletin of Economics and Statistics* 67: 281–306. [CrossRef]

Goel, Rajeev K., James W. Saunoris, and Friedrich Schneider. 2017. Growth in the shadows: Effect of the shadow economy on US economic growth over more than a century. *Contemporary Economic Policy*. [CrossRef]

Grossman, Gene, and Elhanan Helpman. 1991. Trade, knowledge spillovers, and growth. *European Economic Review* 35: 517–26. [CrossRef]

Guiso, Luigi, Sapienza Paola, and Zingales Luigi. 2004. Does Local Financial Development Matter? *Quarterly Journal of Economics* 119: 929–69. [CrossRef]

Gwartney, James. 2004. *Ten Consequences of Economic Freedom*. NCPA Policy Report No. 268. Dallas: NCPA Policy. ISBN #1-56808-137-5.

Hamdi, Helmi, Abdelaziz Hakimi, and Sbia Rashid. 2013a. Multivariate Granger Causality between Financial Development, Investment and Economic Growth: Evidence from Tunisia. *Journal of Quantitative Economics* 11: 111–29.

Hamdi, Helmi, Sbia Rashid, Abdelaziz Hakimi, and Wafa Khlaifia Hakimi. 2013b. Multivariate Granger causality between foreign direct investment and economic growth in Tunisia. *Economics Bulletin* 33: 1193–203.

Hansen, Lars Peter. 1982. Large Sample Properties of Generalized Method of Moments Estimators. *Econometrica* 50: 1029–54. [CrossRef]

Hansen, Lars Peter, and Kenneth Singleton. 1982. Generalized Instrumental Variables of Nonlinear Rational Expectations Models. *Econometrica* 50: 1269–86. [CrossRef]

Hausman, Jerry. 1978. Specification Tests in Econometrics. *Econometrica* 46: 1251–71. [CrossRef]

Hong, Liming. 2014. Does and How does FDI Promote the Economic Growth? Evidence from Dynamic Panel Data of Prefecture City in China. *IERI Procedia* 6: 57–62. [CrossRef]

Hussein, Muawya Ahmed. 2009. Impacts of foreign direct investment on economic growth in the Gulf Cooperation Council (GCC) Countries. *International Review of Business Research Papers* 5: 362–76.

Iamsiraroj, Sasi, and Mehmet Ali Ulubaşoğlu. 2015. Foreign direct investment and economic growth: A real relationship or wishful thinking? *Economic Modelling* 51: 200–13. [CrossRef]

Johansen, Soren. 1988. Statistical Analysis of Cointegration Vectors. *Journal of Economic Dynamics and Control* 12: 231–54. [CrossRef]

Kao, Chihwa. 1999. Spurious regression and residual-based tests for cointegration in panel data. *Journal of Econometrics* 90: 1–44. [CrossRef]

Lamsiraroj, Sasi. 2016. The foreign direct investment–economic growth nexus. *International Review of Economics and Finance* 42: 116–33. [CrossRef]

Lee, Chien-Chiang, and Chung.-Ping Chang. 2009. FDI, financial development, and economic growth: International evidence. *Journal of Applied Economics* 12: 249–71. [CrossRef]

Levine, Ross, and David Renelt. 1992. A Sensitivity Analysis of Cross-Country Growth Regressions. *The American Economic Review* 82: 942–63.

Li, Xiaying, and Xiaming Liu. 2004. Foreign Direct Investment and Economic Growth: An Increasingly Endogenous Relationship. *Worm Development* 33: 393–407. [CrossRef]

Lu, Xun, and Halbert White. 2014. Robustness checks and robustness tests in applied economics. *Journal of Econometrics* 178: 194–206. [CrossRef]

Mogens, K. Justesen. 2008. The effect of economic freedom on growth revisited: New evidence on causality from a panel of countries 1970–1999. *European Journal of Political Economy* 24: 642–60.

Nowak-Lehmann, Felicitas, Axel Dreher, Dierk Herzer, Stephan Klasen, and Inmaculada Martínez-Zarzoso. 2012. Does foreign aid really raise per capita income? A time series perspective. *Canadian Journal of Economics/Revue Canadienne D'économique* 45: 288–313. [CrossRef]

Paakkonen, Jenni. 2010. Economic freedom as driver of growth in transition. *Economic Systems* 34: 469–79. [CrossRef]

Pedroni, Peter. 1999. Critical Values for Cointegration Tests in Heterogeneous Panels with Multiple Regressors. *Oxford Bulletin of Economics and Statistics* 61: 653–70. [CrossRef]

Pedroni, Peter. 2004. Panel Cointegration: Asymptotic and Finite Sample Properties of Pooled Time Series Tests with an Application to the PPP Hypothesis. *Econometric Theory* 20: 597–625. [CrossRef]

Pourshahabi, Farshid, Davoud Mahmoudinia, and Ehsan Salimi Soderjani. 2011. FDI. Human Capital. Economic Freedom and Growth in OECD Countries. *Research Journal of International Studies* 19: 71–81.

Rajan, Raghuram G, and Luigi Zingales. 1998. Financial dependence and growth. *American Economic Review* 88: 559–86.

Romer, P. 1993. Idea gaps and object gaps in economic development. *Journal of Monetary Economics* 32: 543–73. [CrossRef]

Ryan, Compton, Daniel Giedeman, and Gary Hoover. 2011. Panel evidence on economic freedom and growth in the United States. *European Journal of Political Economy* 27: 423–35.

Saha, Shrabani, Jen-Je Su, and Neil Campbell. 2017. Does Political and Economic Freedom Matter for Inbound Tourism? A Cross-National Panel Data Estimation. *Journal of Travel Research* 56: 221–34. [CrossRef]

Sayari, Naz, Sari Ramazan, and Shawkat Hammoudeh. 2018. The impact of value added components of GDP and FDI on economic freedom in Europe. *Economic Systems* 42: 282–94. [CrossRef]

Tan, Yong. 2015. The impacts of risk and competition on bank profitability in China. *Journal of International Financial Markets, Institutions and Money* 40: 85–110. [CrossRef]

Teece, David. 1977. Technology Transfer by Multinational Firms: The Resource Cost of Transferring Technological Know-how. *Economic Journal* 87: 242–61. [CrossRef]

Ubeda, Fernando, and Francisco Pérez-Hernández. 2017. Absorptive Capacity and Geographical Distance Two Mediating Factors of FDI Spillovers: A Threshold Regression Analysis for Spanish Firms. *Journal of Industry, Competition and Trade* 17: 1–28. [CrossRef]

Journal of
Risk and Financial Management

MDPI

Article

Systemic Approach to Management Control through Determining Factors

Ionel Bostan [1,*] , Aliona Bîrcă [2], Viorel Țurcanu [2] and Christiana Brigitte Sandu [3]

[1]   Faculty of Law and Administrative Sciences, Stefan cel Mare University, Suceava 720229, Romania
[2]   Faculty of Accounting, Academy of Economic Studies of Moldova, Chișinău MD-2005, Moldova;
       birca.aliona1@gmail.com (A.B.); vturcanu@mail.ru (V.Ț.)
[3]   Faculty of Economics and Business Administration, Alexandru Ioan Cuza University, Iași 700506, Romania;
       christiana.balan@uaic.ro
*   Correspondence: ionel_bostan@yahoo.com or ibostan@fdsa.usv.ro

Received: 28 September 2018; Accepted: 17 October 2018; Published: 22 October 2018

Abstract: This article aimed to analyse the influence of the main factors on management control used in optimization activities, in order to reach the strategic goals of a company. Agency, transactional costs and contingency theories have been analysed from the traditional perspective. This study reviewed resource-based, institutional, planned behaviour and upper echelon theories, and underlined the main features of management control processes. Empirical evaluation was conducted using data collected from interviews of top management of the main and secondary segments of the Bucharest Stock Exchange. Consequently, we showed the specific features of the systemic approach to management control by means of its determining factors: control environment, management strategies and budgetary system, operational control and the performance appraisal system.

Keywords: control environment; budgetary system and strategies; operational control; company performance

1. Introduction

Dated back to antiquity, management control plays a significant role in ensuring the financial viability of a company, and economic stability in a country. The first empirical models of control in such big companies as Ford, General Motors, Du Pont Company, and later at General Electric, laid the foundation of the universal theory of scientific management, and later, other theories in the field. Also, it supported the research of R. Anthony and R. Simons, developed at Harvard Business School. A significant contribution was brought about by a set of laws adopted during specific stages of economic development, usually after economic crises—Companies Act of 1862, Securities Exchange Act of 1934, Sarbanes-Oxley Act of 2002. After analysing the causes that generated the need to implement these regulations, we observe that the first one appeared against a background of discontent of English colonists. The Securities Exchange Act of 1934 contributed to the elimination of deficiencies of the economic crises of 1929–1933, and the historical context of the SOX law originated in the wave of scandals around big companies around 2000.

New approaches in science focus on the relations between accounting and management using a set of notions of systemic value. Specific financial and accounting information are needed in order to make any decision. Cost calculation and distribution methods refer to the functions of managerial accounting, and their use in the decision-making process becomes a function of the executive management. Accounting through the range of information it provides is involved in managerial decision-making. It is no longer viewed only as a technical tool for providing information but rather as in-company decision making. So, considering that both theoretical and practical issues are company-driven, then the main idea stems from the following research question: What is the theoretical background, and which are the factors that influence management control processes?

The answer to theoretical grounding is provided by theory, and the pragmatic approach investigates the factors influencing management control. The existence of management control theories shows how deep the matter has been studied. We analysed from a traditional perspective the agency, transactional costs and contingency theories. The resource-based, institutional, planned behaviour and upper echelons theories refer to modern approaches to management control.

Behavioural theories are the newest approaches in science, investigating the relations among management control, management strategies and company performance. In addition, the systemic view generated the expansion of the field of study. Management control has been defined as all procedures implemented by the executive management to achieve its strategic goals. For this purpose, the empirical analysis of the degree of influence of various factors on management control should include the following factors: control environment, management strategies and budgetary system, operational control and company performance.

2. Literature Review

Over time, literature in the field confirmed that the issue of control has been one of the most researched topics. In antiquity, control was known as a verification of collections to the state budget. Later, there appeared to be a need to check the operations of big companies and colonies. Pragmatically, control has been first recorded in Ancient Greece, and theoretically, the first studies appeared during feudalism, and later in capitalism. At the beginning of the 20th century, significant changes occurred in its evolution. The results of the period were reflected in the studies of Taylor (1911), Fayol (1949) and in the research of other authors. Demartini (2014) presents control as the "central idea" of scientific management (Copley and Taylor 1923; Giglioni and Bedeian 1974; Person 1929). Therefore, Copley and Copley and Taylor (1923) and Locke (1982) believe that Taylor had introduced a system of accounting and costs back in 1893.

Even if at the beginning of the 20th century, management control was viewed as a centralised function of management (Demartini 2014; Lichtner 1924; Holden et al. 1941; Rowland 1947) together with other authors, the meaning of management control including the planned control was extended. H. Fayol in his treatise of 1916 (Fayol 1949) entitled: Administration industrielle et Générale, developed the universal theory of management. He included management control to the six company functions: technical, commercial, financial, security, accounting and management. He cautioned that the management function is executive and is included into the six functions of enterprise government that should not be confused with government (Dunlevy 1965).

Viewed as a reference author in the field of management control, Anthony (1988) used the notion of "management control". He formulated three definitions. In the version of 1988, management control was seen as: "the process by which managers influence other members of an organization to implement their strategies". Simons (1994, 2000) continued Anthony's initial research at Harvard Business School, defining management control as a set of mechanisms and instruments needed by the manager in decision-making and operations. Management control involves two dimensions: an economic and a strategic one. The first involves the selection and design of operating procedures needed for reaching the objectives. The second dimension refers to organizational and psycho-social factors by which individuals are guided in their actions complying with the operational standards (Cappelletti 2008).

Boisselier et al. (2013) observed the following lines of research in the evolution of management control:

- First (Anthony 1988) is a technical view oriented towards utility;
- second (Grenier 1990) is a larger view where the effects of control reflect a function of managerial behaviour.

Review of various theoretical approaches to management control underlines its significance in delivering information useful for managers and employees in managing the company. Also, we should observe that even if until the end of the 19th century management control had been studied form the perspective of accounting, starting with the 20th century, it should be viewed as an academic discipline having a pragmatic approach as it helps managers in implementing their strategies. Its efficiency, effectiveness and economy is related to the scarcity of resources that should be combined properly in order to reach the objectives.

The appearance of a wide range of management control theories was a good occasion to solve problems related to its disciplinary belonging: management or accounting. Most researchers state that the origins of management control are grounded in the neoclassical economic theory. Bouquin and Pesqueux (1999) noted two significant theories: agency and rational anticipation theory. Agency theory presents the life of homo economicus through shareholders and top management. Rational anticipation theory is newer and guarantees to the appointed executive manager the decision-making right, achieving a rational correlation between forecasts and pre-set objectives (Bouquin and Pesqueux 1999).

In reviewing organizational control theories, Demartini (2014) noted two main lines of research. The first one provides a socio-political and a corporate governance perspective, and the second one refers to company management behaviour at all levels. Moreover, Arrow's definition of organizational control (Arrow 1964) was interpreted by Cyert and March (1963) from two viewpoints: "operating rules" and "enforcement rules". Operational rules refer to the structure of the accounting computer system and affect all employees that have to do their tasks. Enforcement rules refer to behaviour of managers, and ways used to motivate them in reaching organizational objectives. In this sense, management control is seen as a combination of individual and organizational goals (Demartini 2014; Cyert and March 1963; Ouchi 1979; Flamholtz 1996). Therefore, Demartini (2014) divided organizational control theories into four categories: economic, sociological, psychological and behavioural. The first two refer to traditional approaches:

- Economic theories: agency and transactional cost theory;
- Sociological theories: contingency theory, general theory on systemic approach.

Psychological and behavioural theories have been viewed as elements of modern approaches.

Agency theory appeared in the late 60s and early 70s. Eisenhardt (1989) noted two types of problems that this theory wanted to solve. The first type aims to solve conflicts between the principal and the agent caused by different objectives and desires, as well as difficulties that appear when the agent is verified by the principal. The second type refers to risk-sharing when the principal and the agent have or practice different attitudes towards risk. Finally, Eisenhardt (1989) and Jensen (1983) stated that these problems lead to similar analysis underlining the two dimensions: principal-agent theory and the positivist theory.

In the early 70s of the 20th century, Williamson, in his research, tried to improve the flaws of the firm theory provided by neo-classicists. Dominated by the ideas of institutional economy, he started from research of Coase, Barnard and Commons stating that during 1940–1970, the firm was seen as a function of production. Using the contributions of Coase, Commons, Arrow and Chandler to legal issues in contracts, he brought his contribution to the development of transaction cost theory (Coriat and Weinstein 1995; Essoua 2006). However, Williamson's greatest contribution to science was the fact that he opted for hierarchical-functional structure of a firm in a multi-divisional M-form. It is characterised by a centralised structure for strategic planning, resource allocation and the control of autonomous operational divisions (Essoua 2006; Williamson 1994). The aim of M form is to reduce the discretionary power of department leaders that could generate negligence in operations, pursuing personal interests and compromises. By emphasizing the new hierarchical-functional structure of a firm, Williamson wanted to eliminate the flaws of U-form developed earlier by F. Taylor.

Coase carried out a set of studies on transaction cost theory, in which he stated that "the entrepreneur should fulfil his duties with the lowest cost considering that he should obtain factors of production at the lowest transaction cost on the market … as he can always return to the free market if he does not manage to get the best price" (Demartini 2014; Coase 1937). This suggests that a manager should be assessed by his ability to conclude contracts at lower prices than on the market. Also, he should be cautious as any time in case of failure, he should be able to return to the market. Demartini (2014) and Fama (1980) state that in investigating the transaction costs, the firm could be seen as a "nexus of contracts". Therefore, the notion of company property is irrelevant and is just a condition for the firm existence. The focus is placed on the executive manager who should take important decisions regarding allocation of resources. Also, we may note the separation of risk bearers from holders of decision-making rights, or business owners from decision-makers.

Contingency, agency and transaction costs theories were underlined in studies of Bruns and Waterhouse (1975) or Elgharbawy and Elgharbawy and Abdel-Kader (2013), as well as in the research of Gordon and Miller (1976). Known by its insight into the study of organizations, the contingency theory played an important role in empirical research of management accounting (Elgharbawy and Abdel-Kader 2013; Otley 1980; Fisher 1995; Cadez and Guilding 2008). The main idea of Otley (1980) concerning this theory is based on the fact that there is no single structure matching all companies without considering the environmental factors; and each organizational structure is a response to a contingency. Elgharbawy and Elgharbawy and Abdel-Kader (2013) emphasized the contribution of contingency theory to management control systems, especially the role of ABC and ABM (Anderson and Young 1999; Gosselin 1997) non-financial performance measures (Ittner and Larcker 1998), balanced scorecard (Davis and Albright 2004; Hoque and James 2000), and variation analysis–Emsley (2000), etc.

Probably, Otley in his studies was inspired by the ideas of Etzioni (1969) or Demartini (2014), who argued that social systems cannot function as a computer system, except in the case when their interests and values match. Similarly, Lawrence and Lorsch (1967) stressed out that company performance depends on the compatibility between organizational variables and environmental features. Most recent studies maintain Otley's main idea. For instance, in the analysis of factors influencing the structure of internal control, Jokipii (2010) foresaw four main features of contingency features: strategies, company size, organizational structure and perceived uncertainties about the environment.

Therefore, the agency, transaction cost and contingency theories are the traditional theoretical grounding of management control. Before the appearance of these theories, researchers faced a great number of problems related to the place of management control; some insisted that it is linked to management, whilst others believed it is a matter of accounting. The company is the core of these theories, and their theoretical foundation is centred around the relations among the main actors involved in reaching a company's goals. It is true that at the macroeconomic level, this approach has been scrutinized. Modern management control theories play the role of finding solutions at the macroeconomic level.

The tradition continues also in the 21st century but the mainstream research converges to other values. In this sense, we have presented resource-based, institutional, planned behaviour and upper echelon theories. According to Braganza et al. (2013), Wernerfelt (1984), Peteraf (1993) and Hart (1994), the resource-based theories look at management control from the performance perspective. The institutional theory has a broader scope, making reference to the macroeconomic level, and it appeared due to criticism made to macroeconomic theories. Herremans and Nazari (2016) proved that the institutional theory helps understand organizational behaviour in the context of cultural norms and cognitive structures scrutiny (Aupperle et al. 1985; McGuire et al. 1988). Also, other researchers divided institutional influences into three categories: regulatory, normative and cultural-cognitive. The regulating influence imposes specific pressure, the company being forced to handle its rules and behaviour in order to reach the highest standards. The normative influence is related to company's reaction to the pressure of clients, multitude of norms, and requirements of other companies. Some researchers argue that these three categories of influence operate separately, and contend that cognitive influence produce a transfer of "conscious to the unconscious" (Herremans and Nazari 2016; Aupperle et al. 1985; Donaldson and Preston 1995; Thornton and Ocasio 1999, 2008). Similarly, Herremans and Nazari (2016) and Thornton and Ocasio (1999, 2008) explain organizational influences based on organizational logic, stating that these operate rather together than separately. Therefore, organizations perceive messages in their own way, and respond differently to pressure due to differences in values and beliefs (Herremans and Nazari 2016; Thornton and Ocasio 1999, 2008; Friedland and Alford 1991; Herremans et al. 2009; Jackall 1988; Suddaby and Greenwood 2005).

The theory of planned behaviour was developed by Ajzen (1985, 1991) and Heinsman et al. (2006), being viewed as the successor of the theory of reasoned action (Heinsman et al. 2006; Fishbein and Ajzen 1975). According to the theory of reasoned action, human behaviour is influenced by the intention of people. These intentions are influenced by the attitudes towards that behaviour, and by the perceived social pressure. Starting from the ideology of the planned behaviour theory, understanding behaviour through control, easiness or perception, or difficulty to model behaviour, are the three determining factors of human behaviour (Heinsman et al. 2006; Ajzen and Fishbein 1980). Finally, the actual estimation of managerial skills should be made considering the following three elements (Heinsman et al. 2006):

- Positive or negative result of managerial skills appraisal (attitude);
- perception of social pressure in the use of managerial skills at the workplace (subjective norm);
- trust of the employee in his ability to use managerial skills (behaviour control). These together influence the actual foreseeing of managerial skills.

According to Hambrick and Hambrick and Mason (1984), the upper echelon theory is based on the fact that top management creates cognitive structures depending on their previous experience. These are of course based on limited rationality of Hambrick and Mason (1986), Seaton and Boyd (2007), being seen as the "software of the mind". This theory appeared against a background of problems generated by managers in the area of strategic decision-making. For example, executive directors were often selected due to their tough personality for the implementation of strategic aims, different to the aims of the board of directors. Moreover, the financial director was selected by the executive director to save money and make the company more efficient. These decisions are not accidental, and are based on well-structured strategic aims.

In the last two decades, new features have been added to company control due to provisions of SOX Law (2002), and the Committee of Sponsoring Organizations of the Treadway Commission (COSO) (McNally 2013). These require top management to write a report on the efficiency of control procedures, designed and implemented, taking into account the level of inherent risk. At the same time, Pfister and Hartmann (2009) and Simons (1994) show the system position of control on two levels. The first level refers to the decision-making process that includes the strategic and the managerial control system, with the focus on the company's external and internal environment, respectively. The second level plays a generalising role, called the internal control system, and it aims to ensure the quality of information in annual reports, and to protect company assets. As it may be observed, the systemic perspective is used for dealing with managerial control, seen as an element of internal control. So, recent studies link internal control to financial reporting and the culture of countries in which a company operates (Caban-Garcia et al. 2017), while managerial control is seen through the same systemic perspective, when it comes to budgets made from a creative perspective (Chen 2017).

In this study, views of different scholars have been combined with provisions of regulations by assessing the systemic value of control by means of such elements as control environment, managerial strategy, operational control and performance appraisal system.

3. Research Methodology

According to the "principle of doubt" of Descartes, there is a specific scepticism in science towards what is new or different from what is known. In this sense, the theoretical framework of the literature review was tested by means of quantitative methods by applying a statistical questionnaire. The studied sample includes top managers of companies listed on the regulated market and AeRO of the Bucharest Stock Exchange in 2017. Hypotheses were used to evaluate empirically the relations between management control and company control environment, managerial strategies and the budgetary system, and the operational control and the performance appraisal system. The questionnaire was applied to executive and financial directors, chief accountants and chartered accountants. A total 154 responses were obtained. Responses by each group have not been specified as no significant differences were recorded from one group to another.

For this purpose, we have formulated the following research hypotheses:

Hypotheses 1 (H1). *Company control environment exercises a significant influence on the structure of management control processes.*

Hypotheses 2 (H2). *Correspondence ratio between managerial strategies and the budgetary system has a significant impact on the efficiency of management control processes.*

Hypotheses 3 (H3). *In management control, the efficiency of operational control is estimated using the relation between the financial-accounting information and decision-making processes.*

Hypotheses 4 (H4). *Utility of performance appraisal system has a significant impact on the efficiency of management control processes.*

Testing and validation of research hypotheses were carried out using the answers of respondents collected in a questionnaire and processed by means of econometric modelling. The relations between the hypotheses are shown in Figure 1.

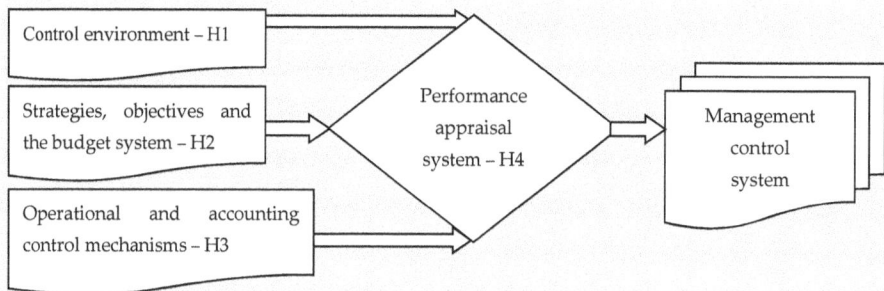

Figure 1. Relational scheme for the four research hypotheses. Source: own processing.

According to relations in Figure 1, the following independent variables (X) exercise influence on the management control system as a dependent variable (Y): Control environment (H1), strategies, objectives and the budgetary system (H2), operational and accounting control (H3), and performance appraisal system (H4). It is important to mention that the association between performance assessment and other variables has special features. So, performance appraisal in management control starts with company strategies and budgetary system, and ends with checking current operations specific to operational control.

The confidence analysis of answers was conducted by assessing the internal consistency or the consistency of results. For this purpose, the Cronbach's Alpha is the most well-known indicator for measuring the internal consistency of a scale.

Most questions in the questionnaire were established using a 5-point Likert scale. As the sets of analysed questions measure different questions, we carried out separate confidence analyses and calculated the value of Cronbach's Alpha coefficient separately for each set. The results of confidence analysis are presented in Table 1. Cronbach's Alpha coefficient indicates the six features in measuring each item. The variation limits of this coefficient are between 0 and 1. The higher the value of the coefficient, the more reliable the used scale is, or it is considered to be more consistent. If the Cronbach's Alpha coefficient is over 0.7, then the set of items measure the same concept, and therefore, the consistency of the measuring scale is good.

Table 1. Results of confidence tests for the instruments and scales used in the questionnaire.

Scale	Cronbach's Alpha Coefficient	Observations
1. Management control system and control environment (6 items)	0.714	The elimination of any item does not improve the Cronbach's Alpha coefficient
2. Management control system and strategic objectives (7 items)	0.763	The elimination of any item does not improve the Cronbach's Alpha coefficient
3. Management control system and budgetary system (7 items)	0.742	If 7.6 is eliminated, Cronbach's Alpha coefficient equals to 0.770, value that is not big enough to accept the improvement by item elimination.
4. Management control system and operational control (7 items)	0.780	The elimination of any item does not improve the Cronbach's Alpha coefficient
5. Management control system and company performance (7 items)	0.855	The elimination of any item does not improve the Cronbach's Alpha coefficient

Source: own processing based on questionnaire and SPSS 20.0.

Regression analysis was used to measure the effects of explanatory variables (independent variables) on management control (dependent variable). We applied a method for selecting independent variables with significant influence using Stepwise in SPSS 20.0. By estimating the four regression models, we obtained the regression coefficients between management control and the sets of items viewed as influence factors.

4. Analysis and Interpretation of Results

Correlation and regression coefficients were used to analyse statistically the relations between variables. Pearson correlation coefficient measures the intensity of the relation between the two quantitative and continuous normally distributed variables. The regressions reflect the degree of influence of factors or the identification of dominant factors by prediction of variable (Y) depending on other variables (X).

Pearson correlation coefficient was used to test the significance of the intensity of the relations between the dependent variable in your opinion, management control is an instrument of executive management for optimizing company performance and other questions viewed as independent variables. The answers to the main question mentioned above are presented in Table 2.

Table 2. Distribution of answers by main question related to the dependent variable.

	Totally Disagree	Disagree	Neither Agree, or Disagree	Agree	Totally Agree	Total
In your opinion, management control is an instrument of executive management for optimizing company performance?	1	4	22	55	72	154
	0.6%	2.6%	14.3%	35.7%	46.8%	100%

Source: own processing based on questionnaire and SPSS 20.0.

After the analysis of frequency distribution of answers in Table 2, we may observe that of the predominant favourable answers to the statements included in the questionnaire, 82.5 % of answers were "Agree" and "Totally agree".

Information from Table 3 shows statistically significant correlations for a significance threshold of 1%, between the variable system of management control and all items included into the set of questions of the statistical questionnaire.

Table 3. Correlations between the management control system and the internal control environment of the company.

	1.	1.1.	1.2.	1.3.	1.4.	1.5.	1.6.
1. Management control	1	0.337 **	0.410 **	0.406 **	0.257 **	0.258 **	0.372 **
1.1. Abilities, education, and skills o executive management	0.337 **	1	0.446 **	0.307 **	0.333 **	0.378 **	0.355 **
1.2. Commitment towards ethical values, and organizational culture	0.410 **	0.446 **	1	0.464 **	0.250 **	0.235 **	0.276 **
1.3. Overseeing responsibility of management, and development of spirit of responsibility in employees	0.406 **	0.307 **	0.464 **	1	0.174 *	0.217 **	0.127 *
1.4. Organizational structure based on centres of responsibility	0.257 **	0.333 **	0.250 **	0.174 *	1	0.246 **	0.181 *
1.5. Attitude towards internal audit and control	0.258 **	0.378 **	0.235 **	0.217 **	0.246 **	1	0.455 **
1.6. Leadership	0.372 **	0.355 **	0.276 **	0.127	0.181 *	0.455 **	1

Note: ** Correlation is significant starting with 0.01/ * Correlation is significant starting with 0.05 Source: own processing based on questionnaire and SPSS 20.0.

Values of linear Pearson correlation coefficient in Table 3 show whether there is or not an association between management control and each element of the control environment. The working hypotheses H_0: $\rho = 0$ and H_1: $\rho \neq 0$ were verified. Taking into account that this coefficient has values between $[-1; 1]$, the positive bold values in Table 3 mean the rejection of hypothesis H_0, and a direct proportional association between these variables.

The estimations of regression model coefficients, and the determination ratio are synthetically presented in Table 4. From the set of independent variables defining the internal control environment of the company presented in Table 3, we maintained in the model only those with significant statistical influence. In hierarchical order by values of standardized coefficients, factors with a positive impact on management control are presented below:

1.6. Leadership has a positive influence on the control environment of the company: b = 0.247, $t_{calculated}$ = 3.772, Sig = 0.000;

1.2. A favourable control environment shows commitment to ethical values and integrity: b = 0.217, $t_{calculted}$ = 2.891, Sig = 0.004;

1.3. In a favourable control environment, management has overseeing responsibilities, and employees develop a sense of responsibility: b = 0.181, $t_{calculted}$ = 2.297, Sig = 0.023.

Table 4. Regression coefficients of the model between management control and control environment.

	Coefficients [b]				
Model	Unstandardized Coefficients B	Std. Error	Standardized Coefficients Beta	t	Sig.
(Constant)	1.657	0.381		4.343	0.000
1.2. Commitment	0.217	0.075	0.240	2.891	0.004
1.6. Leadership	0.247	0.065	0.281	3.772	0.000
1.3. Responsibilities	0.181	0.079	0.184	2.297	0.023
R	0.510				
R Square	0.260				
Adjusted R Square	0.245				
F (ANOVA)	16.983	Sig. = 0.000			

Note: [b] Predictors: (Constant), Commitment, Leadership, Responsibility. Source: own processing based on questionnaire and SPSS 20.0.

Testing the parameters of the regression model was made using a Student's (t) test to find out the likelihood of each parameter to be null. Based on the data from Table 4, the working hypotheses H_0: $\beta = 0$ and H_1: β 0 were verified. In this sense, Sig. value less than 0.05 show that the slope of the regression line (β) is significant. The significant link between variables is shown through the following calculation formula:

1.2: H_0: $\beta_1 = 0$, H_1: $\beta_1 \neq 0$;

$$t = \frac{b_1}{s_{\hat{\beta}_1}} = \frac{0.217}{0.075} = 2.891, \text{ Sig } (t) = 0.004 < 0.05 \tag{1}$$

1.3: H_0: $\beta_2 = 0$, H_1: $\beta_2 \neq 0$;

$$t = \frac{b_2}{s_{\hat{\beta}_2}} = \frac{0.181}{0.079} = 2.297, \text{ Sig } (t) = 0.023 < 0.05 \tag{2}$$

1.6: H_0: $\beta_3 = 0$, H_1: $\beta_3 \neq 0$;

$$t = \frac{b_3}{s_{\hat{\beta}_3}} = \frac{0.247}{0.065} = 3.772, \text{ Sig } (t) = 0 < 0.05 \tag{3}$$

Determination ratio R Square (R^2) may have values between [0; 1]: if $R^2 = 0$, or a very small value, then the chosen regression model does not explain the link between variables, and if $R^2 = 1$, then all observations fall on the regression line, and the model explains perfectly the link between variables. So, this coefficient is used to verify if the model is specified correctly or not. The determination coefficient equals to 0.260, which means that 26% of the management control is due to the control environment.

Questions 2 and 3 in the questionnaire were used to verify the relationship between the management control system as a dependent variable, and management strategies, objectives and the budgetary system as independent variables. Information form Table 5 shows strong statistically significant links between the variable of the management control system and all other questions included in set no. 2 of the statistical questionnaire.

The values of the linear Pearson correlation coefficient in Table 5 prove the intensity of correlation between these variables. The statistical hypotheses H_0: $\rho = 0$ and H_1: $\rho \neq 0$ were verified, and the coefficients marked in bold in the table show positive values for questions 2.1, 2.2, 2.3, 2.5, 2.6, 2.7, and values differing from null for rejection of H_0 hypothesis.

In the regression model, there are only four significant factors defining the role of strategies and objectives in a company. The level of significance in testing regression coefficients is less than the threshold of 1% and 5%, respectively. The most important factor in question 2.3.—Are the biggest investments made in new technology?—has a positive effect on *management control* that is also valid for questions 2.2, 2.3 and 2.7, while question 2.4 has a negative effect ($b = -0.204$).

Values of correlation coefficient (R) is 0.488 in Table 6, which shows a link between management control, strategies and company objectives. Determination coefficient R Square (R^2) of 0.238 shows that 23.8% of management control variance is influenced by simultaneous variance of strategies and objectives.

Pearson coefficient measures the intensity of correlation between management control and items related to the budgetary system presented in Table 7.

Information in Table 7 shows that the budgetary system belongs to management control due to the following features: key instrument for performance control, feature of corporate governance, centres of responsibility, analysis of resource-intensive activities, and management control efficiency. We may note insignificant correlations between management control and decisions based on instinct (question 3.6), and the results of answers to question 3.7 show that ABC, ABB/ABM methods are less known to managers.

Table 8 presents estimated values of regression coefficients, standard errors, and significance levels of the Student's test. Only items 3.1 and 3.4 were kept in the model from the set of items defining the role of budget in strategy implementation, the inclusion of plans into figures and the verification of control procedures quality. The two factors have a positive influence on management control due to statistically significant influence, and Sig values less than the assumed risk of 1%.

Table 5. Correlations between management control and management strategies.

	2	2.1	2.2	2.3	2.4	2.5	2.6	2.7
2. Management control	1	0.326 **	0.358 **	0.389 **	0.075	0.247 **	0.208 *	0.216 **
2.1. Company strategies target new product development	0.326 **	1	0.499 **	0.548 **	0.117	0.411 **	0.351 **	0.204 *
2.2. Strategies target new product and current market development	0.358 **	0.499 **	1	0.462 **	0.063	0.315 **	0.315 **	0.294 **
2.3. Investments in new technology	0.389 **	0.548 **	0.462 **	1	0.195 *	0.517 **	0.409 **	0.261 **
2.4. Greater is the focus on strategy implementation, more decentralized is the company control	0.075	0.117	0.063	0.195 *	1	0.283 **	0.107	0.370 **
2.5. Sustainable strategies match the company's level of performance development	0.247 **	0.411 **	0.315 **	0.517 **	0.283 **	1	0.306 **	0.278 **
2.6. Assessment of resource consumption identifies new problems, and also contributes to solving current problems	0.208 *	0.351 **	0.315 **	0.409 **	0.107	0.306 **	1	0.290 **
2.7. The structure of management control system depends on the nature of strategies	0.216 **	0.204 *	0.294 **	0.261 **	0.370 **	0.278 **	0.290 **	1

Note: ** Correlation is significant starting with 0.01/* Correlation is significant starting with 0.05 Source: own processing based on questionnaire and SPSS 20.0.

Table 6. Regression coefficients between management control and management strategies.

Model	Coefficients		Standardized Coefficients	t	Sig.
	Unstandardized Coefficients B	Std. Error	Beta		
(Constant)	2.782	0.362		7.692	0.000
2.3. Investments in new technology	0.244	0.070	0.295	3.463	0.001
2.2. Product profitability	0.167	0.080	0.179	2.095	0.038
24. Decentralized control	−0.204	0.076	−0.215	−2.677	0.008
2.7. SCG structure	0.172	0.075	0.192	2.303	0.023
R	0.488				
R Square	0.238				
Adjusted R Square	0.216				
F	10.921	Sig. = 0.000			

Source: own processing based on questionnaire and SPSS 20.0.

Table 7. Correlation between management control and the budgetary system.

	3	3.1.	3.2.	3.3.	3.4.	3.5.	3.6.	3.7.
3. Management control	1	0.382 **	0.283 **	0.344 **	0.370 **	0.306 **	0.124	0.048
3.1. Budget—performance control instrument	0.382 **	1	0.625 **	0.502 **	0.459 **	0.428 **	0.115	0.173 *
3.2. Budget—feature of corporate governance	0.283 **	0.625 **	1	0.513 **	0.391 **	0.317 **	0.172*	0.079
3.3. Responsibility centres contribute to inclusion of objectives into budget figures	0.344 **	0.502 **	0.513 **	1	0.550 **	0.299 **	0.166 *	0.298 **
3.4. Budget analysis—summary of resource-intensive activities	0.370 **	0.459 **	0.391 **	0.550 **	1	0.407 **	0.164 *	0.203 *
3.5. Accuracy of budgetary forecasts is lower in companies with inefficient internal control	0.306 **	0.428 **	0.317 **	0.299 **	0.407 **	1	0.065	0.144
3.6. Frequency of decisions based on "instinct"	0.124	0.115	0.172*	0.166 *	0.164 *	0.065	1	0.417 **
3.7. Low-cost strategies means extension in use of ABC and ABB/ABM	0.048	0.173 *	0.079	0.298 **	0.203 *	0.144	0.417 **	1

Note: ** Correlation is significant starting with 0.01/ * Correlation is significant starting with 0.05 ** Source: own processing based on questionnaire and SPSS 20.0.

Table 8. Regression coefficients between management control and budgetary system.

	Coefficients [a,b]					
Model	Unstandardized Coefficients		Standardized Coefficients		t	Sig.
	B	Std. Error	Beta			
(Constant)	2.196	0.348			6.303	0.000
3.1. Control instrument	0.257	0.081	0.270		3.193	0.002
3.4. ERP summary	0.246	0.083	0.252		2.973	0.003
R	0.448					
R Square	0.201					
Adjusted R Square	0.190					
F	18.115	Sig. = 0.000				

Note: [a] Dependent variable: management control. [b] Predictors: (Constant), Control instrument, summary of activities. Source: own processing based on questionnaire and SPSS 20.0.

The value of correlation coefficient (R) de 0.488 in table no. 8 shows a link between management control and the budgetary system. Determination ratio R Square (R^2) is 0.201 and shows that 20% of the management control variance is influenced by simultaneous variance of the budgetary system.

Testing the parameters of the regression model were made using a Student's (t) test to find out the likelihood of each parameter to be null. Based on data from table no. 6 and 8, the working hypotheses H_0: $\beta = 0$ and H_1: β 0 were verified. In this sense, Sig = 0 Sig. should be less than 0.05 showing that the slope of the regression line (β) shows a significant link between variables, being verified for each question of the questionnaire:

2.2: H_0: $\beta_1 = 0$, H_1: $\beta_1 \neq 0$;

$$t = \frac{b_1}{s_{\beta_1}} = \frac{0.167}{0.080} = 2.095, \text{ Sig (t)} = 0.038 < 0.05 \tag{4}$$

2.3: H_0: $\beta_2 = 0$, H_1: $\beta_2 \neq 0$;

$$t = \frac{b_2}{s_{\beta_2}} = \frac{0,244}{0,070} = 3.463, \text{ Sig (t)} = 0.001 < 0.05 \tag{5}$$

2.4: H_0: $\beta_3 = 0$, H_1: $\beta_3 \neq 0$;

$$t = \frac{b_3}{s_{\beta_3}} = \frac{-0.204}{0.760} = -2.677, \text{ Sig (t)} = 0.008 < 0.05 \tag{6}$$

2.7: H_0: $\beta_4 = 0$, H_1: $\beta_4 \neq 0$;

$$t = \frac{b_4}{s_{\beta_4}} = \frac{0.172}{0.075} = 2.303, \text{ Sig (t)} = 0.023 < 0.05 \tag{7}$$

3.1: H_0: $\beta_1 = 0$, H_1: $\beta_1 \neq 0$;

$$t = \frac{b_1}{s_{\beta_1}} = \frac{0.257}{0.081} = 3.193, \text{ Sig (t)} = 0.002 < 0.05 \tag{8}$$

3.4: H_0: $\beta_2 = 0$, H_1: $\beta_2 \neq 0$;

$$t = \frac{b_2}{s_{\beta_2}} = \frac{0.246}{0.083} = 2.973, \text{ Sig (t)} = 0.003 < 0.05 \tag{9}$$

Verification of relationships between the management control system as a dependent variable, and costs needed for decision-making as independent variables, were tested by questions from item 4 of the questionnaire. The presentation in Table 9 of answers for each question aims to show the results of the statistical questionnaire.

Table 9. Correlation between management and operational control.

	4	4.1	4.2	4.3	4.4	4.5	4.6	4.7
4. Management control	1	0.396 **	0.315 **	0.070	0.002	0.149	0.140	0.203 *
4.1. Profit centres are used to design the organizational structure	0.396 **	1	0.409 **	0.270 **	0.190 *	0.247 **	0.328 **	0.368 **
4.2. Standard-cost method provides information needed for budgetary control	0.315 **	0.409 **	1	0.322 **	0.276 **	0.238 **	0.348 **	0.256 **
4.3. Cost-volume-profit method provides information needed for performance assessment	0.070	0.270 **	0.322 **	1	0.351 **	0.327 **	0.436 **	0.371 **
4.4. ABC/ABM methods aim to correct the flaws of traditional methods	0.002	0.190*	0.276 **	0.351 **	1	0.428 **	0.444 **	0.168 *
4.5. Innovation in accounting by: ABC, target costing, kaizen costing, TQM, JIT, WCM	0.149	0.247 **	0.238 **	0.327 **	0.428**	1	0.388 **	0.494 **
4.6. Relevant costs influence decisions to accept or not additional orders	0.140	0.328 **	0.348 **	0.436 **	0.444 **	0.388 **	1	0.488 **
4.7. Relevant costs influence decisions to reduce or outsource specific operations	0.203 *	0.368 **	0.256 **	0.371 **	0.168 *	0.494 **	0.488 **	1

Note: ** Correlation is significant starting with 0.01/ * Correlation is significant starting with 0.05** Source: own processing based on questionnaire and SPSS 20.0.

Table 9 shows positive and significant correlations between management control and profit centres (question 4.1), standard-cost method (question 4.2), and relevant costs (question 4.7); their correlation indicators appear in bold. The other factors have an insignificant influence on the management control system, while for questions 4.1, 4.2 and 4.7, the statistical hypothesis H_0: $\rho = 0$ was rejected, and H_1: $\rho \neq 0$ was accepted.

As calculations using the Pearson linear correlation regression show an association of three out of seven questions of item 4 of the questionnaire, we included in the model only items 4.1 and 4.2 from Table 9 with a significant influence on the management control system from the set of factors defining the importance of costs in taking management and management control decisions.

Data in Table 10 are used to verify working hypotheses H_0: $\beta = 0$ and H_1: $\beta\ 0$. In this sense, = 0.000 means that the slope of the regression line (β) shows a significant link between the variables. The hypotheses were verified for each question based on answers to questions 4.1 and 4.2:

4.1: H_0: $\beta_1 = 0$, H_1: $\beta_1 \neq 0$;

$$t = \frac{b_1}{s_{\beta_1}} = \frac{0.298}{0.081} = 3.697, \text{Sig (t)} = 0 < 0.05 \tag{10}$$

4.2: H_0: $\beta_2 = 0$, H_1: $\beta_2 \neq 0$;

$$t = \frac{b_2}{s_{\beta_2}} = \frac{0.191}{0.085} = 2.249, \text{Sig (t)} = 0.026 < 0.05 \tag{11}$$

Correlation ratio (R) of 0.417 in table no. 10 shows a link between management and operational control, including accounting control. Determination ratio R Square (R^2) of 0.147 shows that 14.7% of management control variance is explained by simultaneous variance of costs.

Overall, in questions related to the role of performance assessment system for management control, we observe that the highest share belongs to non-financial indicators in question 5.7—to which degree your company has been using its ability to respond immediately to client's demands as a non-financial instrument for assessing performance?

Correlation coefficients marked in bold in Table 11 show statistically significant associations (significance threshold of 1%) between the management control variable and all items defining performance assessment. The values of coefficients make us observe an association with all items of point 5 of the questionnaire, reject the working hypothesis H_0: $\rho = 0$, and accept hypothesis H_1: $\rho \neq 0$.

Table 10. Regression coefficients between management and operational control.

Model	Unstandardized Coefficients		Standardized Coefficients	t	Sig.
	B	Std. Error	Beta		
(Constant)	2.353	0.356		6.614	0.000
4.1. Profit centres	0.298	0.081	0.306	3.697	0.000
4.2. Standard-cost method	0.191	0.085	0.186	2.249	0.026
R	0.417				
R Square	0.147				
Adjusted R Square	0.163				
F	15.176	Sig. = 0.000			

Coefficients [a,b]

Note: [a] Dependent variable: management control. [b] Predictors: (Constant), Profit centres, Standard-cost method. Source: own processing based on questionnaire and SPSS 20.0.

Table 11. Correlations between management control and performance assessment.

	5.	5.1.	5.2.	5.3.	5.4.	5.5.	5.6.	5.7.
5. Management control	1	0.242 **	0.362 **	0.320 **	0.333 **	0.311 **	0.376 **	0.303 **
5.1. Financial performance directly influences company performance	0.242 **	1	0.508 **	0.139	0.177 *	0.191 *	0.236 **	0.233 **
5.2. Financial performance is a consequence of economic, social, and environmental performance	0.362 **	0.508 **	1	0.393 **	0.364 **	0.310 **	0.464 **	0.290 **
5.3. How often cash flow is used in performance assessment?	0.320 **	0.139	0.393 **	1	0.474 **	0.391 **	0.307 **	0.358 **
5.4. Balanced scorecard is the most efficient method for performance management	0.333 **	0.177 *	0.364 **	0.474 **	1	0.598 **	0.302 **	0.261 **
5.5. Balanced scorecard helps supervise the degree to which strategic objectives have been reached	0.311 **	0.191 *	0.310 **	0.391 **	0.598 **	1	0.339 **	0.229 **
5.6. Company's ability to respond immediately to client demands	0.376 **	0.236 **	0.464 **	0.307 **	0.302 **	0.339 **	1	0.294 **
5.7. To which degree your company has been using non-financial factors for assessing performance?	0.303 **	0.233 **	0.290 **	0.358 **	0.261 **	0.229 **	0.294 **	1

Note: ** Correlation is significant at the 0.01 level (2-tailed)./ * Correlation is significant at the 0.05 level (2-tailed). Source: own processing based on questionnaire and SPSS 20.0.

The estimations of regression model coefficients, and the determination ratio are synthetically presented in Table 12. From the set of independent variables defining the role of performance in management control, we kept in the model only those with significant statistical influence. All three factors have a positive impact on management control. In order of importance (hierarchy by standardized coefficients values), the influence factors are as follows:

5.1. How often the company uses cash flow to assess performance and projects? (ROI, RI)? (b = 0.238, $t_{calculated}$ = 3.229, Sig = 0.002);

5.6. Company's ability to react immediately to client demands? (b = 0.186, $t_{calculated}$ = 2.512, Sig = 0.013);

5.7. To which degree your company takes into account non-financial factors (product quality, market share, client satisfaction, etc) for assessing performance? (b = 0.173, $t_{calculated}$ = 2.213, Sig = 0.029).

Table 12. Regression coefficients between management control and performance assessment.

	Coefficients [a,b]				
Model	Unstandardized Coefficients		Standardized Coefficients	t	Sig.
	B	Std. Error	Beta		
(Constant)	1.828	0.368		4.965	0.000
5.3. Cash flow	0.238	0.074	0.266	3.229	0.002
5.6. Reaction to client demands	0.186	0.074	0.204	2.512	0.013
5.7. Non-financial factors	0.173	0.078	0.180	2.213	0.029
R	0.496				
R Square	0.246				
Adjusted R Square	0.230				
F	15.198	Sig. = 0.000			

Note: [a] Dependent variable: management control. [b] Predictors: (Constant), Cash flow, Reaction to client demands, Non-financial factors. Source: own processing based on questionnaire and SPSS 20.0.

Based on the data of Table 12, working hypotheses H_0: β = 0 and H_1: β 0 were verified, with Sig = 0.000, and the significant links between variables were verified for each question of item 3 in the questionnaire by using the following calculation formula:

5.3: H_0: β_1 = 0, H_1: $\beta_1 \neq 0$;

$$ t = \frac{b_1}{s_{\beta_1}} = \frac{0.238}{0.074} = 3.229, \text{ Sig (t)} = 0.002 < 0.05 \tag{12} $$

5.6: H_0: β_2 = 0, H_1: $\beta_2 \neq 0$;

$$ t = \frac{b_2}{s_{\beta_2}} = \frac{0.186}{0.074} = 2.512, \text{ Sig (t)} = 0.013 < 0.05 \tag{13} $$

5.7: H_0: β_3 = 0, H_1: $\beta_3 \neq 0$;

$$ t = \frac{b_3}{s_{\beta_3}} = \frac{0.173}{0.078} = 2.213, \text{ Sig (t)} = 0.029 < 0.05 \tag{14} $$

Correlation ratio (R) of 0.496 in Table 12 shows a link between management control and performance assessment. Determination ratio R Square (R^2) de 0.23 shows that 23% management control variance is influenced by performance variance.

5. Conclusions

In conclusion, theoretical and practical approaches to management control have been continuously developed. If in antiquity and in feudalism these were mainly practical, capitalism imposed new rigour. Diversity of traditional and modern theories on management control show how deep this matter has been researched. Also, it is a limitless source of inspiration for future generations of specialists in the field.

New approaches showed its status as a system and proved the difference between management control and accounting management. From this perspective, it was proven that accounting information does not include only past data but also data of prescriptive nature needed for benefitting from the company's strategic future. Management control has broadened its scope. To design its processes, it is important to take into account both the ratio between consumed resources and outcomes, its impact at the micro and macro levels, and also the human behaviour psychology of its main actors.

The empirical analysis of factors influencing the processes of management control showed that the company control environment depends on the attitude towards cultural and ethical values, and the development of a spirit of responsibility and leadership. Management strategies have been noted for investments in new technologies, growth of product profitability, and control decentralization. While budgetary control contributes to increasing performance control by means of the summary of resource-intensive activities for each centre of responsibility, the operational-accounting control uses standard-cost method and rational costs in managerial decision-making. Performance assessment is needed in each stage of control, and it should combine financial and non-financial performance.

As a result, managers make sure that their strategic and operational objectives are reached by using this type of control; public institutions accumulate and monitor financial means; and the population have a balanced and quiet daily life. Control penetrates into the essence of processes and facts, guides managers, provides opportunities to discover shortcomings, and helps prevent causes of their appearance.

We believe the research has the following limitations:

- theoretical approaches were studied using international literature, but the empirical analysis covers only national data;
- relationships with corporate governance have not been researched;
- factors at the macroeconomic level have not been considered.
- Future lines of research will be focused on:
- Unification of internal and management control by creating a system of company control;
- inclusion in the study of internal and financial audit;
- influence of management control on the economy of a country using the concept of sustainable corporate governance.

Author Contributions: Conceptualization, I.B. and A.B.; Methodology, A.B. and C.B.S.; Formal Analysis, I.B. and V.Ț.; Writing—Original Draft Preparation, A.B. and C.B.S.; Writing—Review & Editing, A.B. and I.B.

Funding: This research received no external funding.

Conflicts of Interest: The authors declare no conflict of interest.

References

Ajzen, Icek. 1985. From intentions to actions: A theory of planned behavior. In *Action Control: From Cognition to Behaviour*. Berlin: Springer, pp. 11–39.

Ajzen, Icek. 1991. The theory of planned behavior. *Organizational Behavior and Human Decision Processes* 50: 179–211. [CrossRef]

Ajzen, Icek, and Martin Fishbein. 1980. *Understanding Attitudes and Predicting Social Behaviour*. Englewood Cliffs: Prentice Hall.

Anderson, Shannon W., and S. Mark Young. 1999. The impact of contextual and process factors on the evaluation of activity-based costing systems. *Accounting, Organizations and Society* 24: 525–59. [CrossRef]

Anthony, Robert Newton. 1988. *The Management Control Function*. Boston: Harvard Business School Press.

Arrow, Kenneth J. 1964. Control in large organizations. *Management Science* 10: 397–408. [CrossRef]

Aupperle, Kenneth E., Archie B. Carroll, and John D. Hatfield. 1985. An Empirical Examination of the Relationship between Corporate Social Responsibility and Profitability. *Academy of Management Journal* 28: 446–63.

Boisselier, Patrick, Chalençon Ludivine, Doriol David, Jardin Philippe, Mard Yves, and Mayrhofer Ulrike. 2013. *Contrôle de gestion*. Paris: Magnard-Vuibert-Août, p. 666.

Bouquin, Henri, and Yvon Pesqueux. 1999. Vingt ans de contrôle de gestion ou le passage d'une technique à une discipline. *Comptabilité–Contrôle–Audit* 5: 93–105. [CrossRef]

Braganza, Ashley, Heather Stebbings, and Theodora Ngosi. 2013. The case of customer recruitment processes: Dynamic evolution of customer relationship management resource networks. *Journal of Marketing Management* 29: 439–66. [CrossRef]

Bruns, William J., and John H. Waterhouse. 1975. Budgetary control and organization structure. *Journal of Accounting Research* 13: 177–203. [CrossRef]

Caban-Garcia, Maria T., Carmen B. Ríos Figueroa, and Karin A. Petruska. 2017. The Impact of Culture on Internal Control Weaknesses: Evidence from Firms That Cross-List in the U.S. *Journal of International Accounting Research* 16: 119–45. [CrossRef]

Cadez, Simon, and Chris Guilding. 2008. An exploratory investigation of an integrated contingency model of strategic management accounting. *Accounting, Organizations and Society* 33: 836–63. [CrossRef]

Cappelletti, Laurent. 2008. Vers un contrôle de gestion intégré à la fonction commerciale: Cas d'expérimentation. *Management & Avenir* 2: 156–73.

Chen, Clara Xiaoling. 2017. Management Control for Stimulating Different Types of Creativity: The Role of Budgets. *Journal of Management Accounting Research* 29: 23–26. [CrossRef]

Coase, Ronald H. 1937. The nature of the firm. *Economica* 4: 386–405. [CrossRef]

Copley, Frank Barkley, and Frederick Winslow Taylor. 1923. *Father of Scientific Management*. New York: Harper & Row.

Coriat, Benjamin, and Olivier Weinstein. 1995. *Les nouvelles théories de l'entreprise*. Paris: Librairie Générale Française.

Cyert, Richard M., and James G. March. 1963. *A Behavioral Theory of the Firm*. New York: Prentice-Hall, p. 332.

Davis, Stan, and Tom Albright. 2004. An investigation of the effect of Balanced Scorecard implementation on financial performance. *Management Accounting Research* 5: 135–53. [CrossRef]

Demartini, Chiara. 2014. *Performance Management Systems, Contributions to Management Science*. Berlin and Heidelberg: Springer.

Donaldson, Thomas, and Lee E. Preston. 1995. The Stakeholder Theory of Corporation: Concepts, Evidence and Implications. *Academy of Management Review* 20: 65–91. [CrossRef]

Dunlevy, John H. 1965. *Management Control Systems: A short History from Fayol to Forrester*. Monterey: George Washington University.

Eisenhardt, Kathleen M. 1989. Agency Theory: An Assessment and Review. *Academy of Management Review* 14: 57–74. [CrossRef]

Elgharbawy, Adel, and Magdy Abdel-Kader. 2013. Enterprise governance and value-based management: A theoretical contingency framework. *Journal of Management and Governance* 17: 99–129. [CrossRef]

Emsley, David. 2000. Variance analysis and performance: Two empirical studies. *Accounting, Organizations and Society* 1: 33–47. [CrossRef]

Essoua, Benoît Ekoka. 2006. Cohérence logique entre le modèle stratégico-opérationnel en contrôle de gestion et la théorie de la firme-compétence foncière des économistes évolutionnistes: une lecture historique. *Comptabilité–Contrôle–Audit* 12: 139–61. [CrossRef]

Etzioni, Amitai. 1969. *The Semi-Professions and Their Organization*. London: Collier-Macmillan, p. 328.

Fama, Eugene F. 1980. Agency problems and the theory of the firm. *Journal of Political Economyn* 88: 288–307. [CrossRef]

Fayol, Henri. 1949. *General and Industrial Management*. Translated by Constance Storrs. London: Sir Isaac Pitman&Sons.

Fishbein, Martin, and Icek Ajzen. 1975. *Belief, Attitude, Intention and Behavior: An Introduction to Theory and Research*. Reading, Massachusestts Amherst: Addison-Wesley Publishing Company.

Fisher, Joseph. 1995. Contingency-based research on management control systems: Categorization by level of complexity. *Journal of Accounting Literature* 14: 24–53.

Flamholtz, Eric. 1996. Effective organizational control. A framework, applications, and implications. *European Management Journal* 14: 596–611. [CrossRef]

Friedland, Roger, and Robert R. Alford. 1991. Bringing society back in: Symbols, practices and institutional contradictions. In *The New Institutionalism in Organizational Analysis*. Edited by W. Powell and P. DiMaggio. Chicago: University of Chicago Press, pp. 232–63.

Giglioni, Giovanni B., and Arthur G. Bedeian. 1974. A conspectus of management control theory: 1900–1972. *Academy of Management Journal* 17: 292–305. [CrossRef]

Gordon, Lawrence A., and Danny Miller. 1976. A contingency framework for the design of accounting information systems. *Accounting for Management Control* 1: 59–70.

Gosselin, Maurice. 1997. The effects of strategy and organizational structure on the adoption and implementation of activity-based costing. *Accounting, Organizations and Society* 22: 105–22. [CrossRef]

Grenier, Claude. 1990. *Les pratiques et les recherches en contrôle de gestion: évolution et perspectives*. Sophia Antipolis: Travaux et Recherches du CERAM.

Hambrick, Donald C., and Phyllis A. Mason. 1984. Upper Echelons: The Organization as a Reflection of Its Top Managers. *Academy of Management Review* 9: 193–206. [CrossRef]

Hart, Ellen R. 1994. Strategic Change: Reconfiguring Operational Processes to Implement Strategy. Edited by L. Fahey and R. M. Randall. The Portable MBA in Strategy. New York: John Wiley, pp. 358–88.

Heinsman, Hanneke, Annebel H.B. de Hoogh, Paul L. Koopman, and Jaap J. van Muijen. 2006. Competency management: Balancing between commitment and control. *Management Revue* 17: 292–306. [CrossRef]

Herremans, Irene M., and Jamal A. Nazari. 2016. Sustainability Reporting Driving Forces and Management Control Systems. *Journal of Management Accounting Research American Accounting Association* 28: 103–24. [CrossRef]

Herremans, Irene M., M. Sandy Herschovis, and Stephanie Bertels. 2009. Leaders and laggards: The influence of competing logics on corporate environmental action. *Journal of Business Ethics* 89: 449–72. [CrossRef]

Hambrick, Donald C., and Phyllis A. Mason. 1986. *Cultures and Organizations: Software of the Mind*. New York: McGraw-Hill.

Holden, Paul Eugene, Fish Lounsbury Spaight, and Hubert L. Smith. 1941. *Top Management Organization and Control: A research Study of the Management Policies and Practices of Thirty Leading Industrial Corporations*. Stanford: Stanford University Press.

Hoque, Zahirul, and Wendy James. 2000. Linking Balanced Scorecard Measures to Size and Market Factors: Impact on Organizational Performance. *Journal of Management Accounting Research* 12: 1–17. [CrossRef]

Ittner, Christopher D., and David F. Larcker. 1998. Innovations in performance measurement: Trends and research implications. *Journal of Management Accounting Research* 10: 205–38.

Jackall, Robert. 1988. Moral mazes: The world of corporate managers. *International Journal of Politics, Culture, and Society* 1: 598–614. [CrossRef]

Jensen, Michael C. 1983. Organization theory and methodology. *Accounting Review* 56: 319–38. [CrossRef]

Jokipii, Annukka. 2010. Determinants and consequences of internal control in firms: A contingency theory based analysis. *Journal of Management Governance* 14: 115–44. [CrossRef]

Lawrence, Paul R., and Jay W. Lorsch. 1967. Differentiation and Integration in Complex Organizations. *Administrative Science Quarterly* 12: 1–30. [CrossRef]

Lichtner, William Otto. 1924. *Planned Control in Manufacturing*. New York: The Ronald Press Company.

Locke, Edwin A. 1982. The Ideas of Frederick W. Taylor: An Evaluation. *Academy of Management Review* 7: 14–24. [CrossRef]

McGuire, Jean B., Alison Sundgren, and Thomas Schneeweis. 1988. Corporate social responsibility and Firm financial performance. *Academy of Management Journal* 31: 854–72.

McNally, J. Stephen. 2013. The 2013 COSO Framework & Sox Compliance. Paper Presented at The Committee of Sponsoring Organizations of the Treadway Commission (COSO), Strategic Finance, Durham, NC, USA, June 1–8.

Otley, David T. 1980. The contingency theory of management accounting: Achievement and prognosis. *Accounting for Management Control* 5: 413–28.

Ouchi, William G. 1979. A conceptual framework for the design of organizational control mechanisms. *Readings in Accounting for Management Control* 25: 833–48.

Person, Harlow S. 1929. *The Origin and Nature of Scientific Management*. Edited by H.S. Person. Scientific management in American industry. New York: Harper & Brothers, pp. 1–22.

Peteraf, Margaret A. 1993. The Cornerstones of Competitive Advantage: A Resource-Based View. *Strategic Management Journal* 14: 179–92. [CrossRef]

Pfister, Jan, and Frank Hartmann. 2009. *Managing Organizational Culture for Effective Internal Control*. Berlin and Heideberg: Physica-Verlag, p. 245.

Rowland, Floyd H. 1947. *Business Planning and Control.* New York: Harper.

Seaton, L. Jeff, and Michael Boyd. 2007. The organizational leadership of the post baby boom generation: An upper. *Academy of Entrepreneurship Journal* 13: 69–77.

Simons, Robert. 1994. *Levers of Control: How Managers Use Innovative Control Systems to Drive Strategic Renewal.* Boston: Harvard Business School Press.

Simons, Robert. 2000. *Performance Measurement and Control Systems for Implementing Strategy.* New Jersey: Prentice Hall.

SOX Law. 2002. *Sarbanes-Oxley Act of 2002 Corporate Responsibility,* Public Law 107–204, Be it enacted by the Senate and House of Representatives of the United States of America in Congress assembled, July 30, 107th US Congress.

Suddaby, Roy, and Royston Greenwood. 2005. Rhetorical Strategies of Legitimacy. *Administrative Science Quarterly* 50: 35–67. [CrossRef]

Taylor, Frederick Winslow. 1911. *Principles of Scientific Management.* New York and London: Harper & Brothers Publishers.

Thornton, Patricia H., and William Ocasio. 1999. Institutional logics and the historical contingency of power in organizations: Executive succession in the higher education publishing industry, 1958–1990. *American Journal of Sociology* 105: 801–43. [CrossRef]

Thornton, Patricia H., and William Ocasio. 2008. Institutional logics. In *Handbook of Organizational Institutionalism.* Edited by R. Greenwood, C. Oliver, R. Suddaby and K. Sahlin-Andersson. Thousand Oaks and London: Sage Publications.

Wernerfelt, Birger. 1984. A Resource-Based View of the Firm. *Strategic Management Journal* 5: 171–80. [CrossRef]

Williamson, Oliver E. 1994. *Les institutions de l'économie.* Paris: InterEditions.

Journal of
Risk and Financial Management

MDPI

Article

Nonlinear Time Series Modeling: A Unified Perspective, Algorithm and Application

Subhadeep Mukhopadhyay [1,*] and Emanuel Parzen [2,†]

1   Department of Statistical Science, Temple University, Philadelphia, PA 19122, USA
2   Department of Statistics, Texas A&M University, College Station, TX 77843, USA; eparzen@tamu.edu
*   Correspondence: deep@temple.edu
†   Shortly after finishing the first draft of this paper, Manny Parzen passed away. Deceased 6 February 2016.

Received: 4 June 2018; Accepted: 3 July 2018; Published: 6 July 2018

Abstract: A new comprehensive approach to nonlinear time series analysis and modeling is developed in the present paper. We introduce novel data-specific mid-distribution-based Legendre Polynomial (LP)-like nonlinear transformations of the original time series $\{Y(t)\}$ that enable us to adapt all the existing stationary linear Gaussian time series modeling strategies and make them applicable to non-Gaussian and nonlinear processes in a robust fashion. The emphasis of the present paper is on empirical time series modeling via the algorithm LPTime. We demonstrate the effectiveness of our theoretical framework using daily S&P 500 return data between 2 January 1963 and 31 December 2009. Our proposed LPTime algorithm systematically discovers all the 'stylized facts' of the financial time series automatically, all at once, which were previously noted by many researchers one at a time.

Keywords: nonparametric time series modeling; nonlinearity; unified time series algorithm; exploratory diagnostics

---

1. Introduction

When one observes a sample $Y(t), t = 1, \ldots, T$, of a (discrete parameter) time series $Y(t)$, one seeks to nonparametrically learn from the data a stochastic model with two purposes: (a1) scientific understanding; (a2) forecasting (predict future values of the time series under the assumption that the future obeys the same laws as the past). Our prime focus in this paper is on developing a nonparametric empirical modeling technique for nonlinear (stationary) time series that can be used by data scientists as a practical tool for obtaining insights into (i) the temporal dynamic patterns and (ii) the internal data generating mechanism; a crucial step for achieving (a1) and (a2).

Under the assumption that the time series is stationary (which can be extended to asymptotically stationary), the distribution of $Y(t)$ is identical for all t, and the joint distribution of $Y(t)$ and $Y(t + h)$ depends only on lag h. Typical estimation goals are as follows:

(1) Marginal modeling: The identification of the marginal probability law (in particular, the heavy-tailed marginal densities) of a time series plays a vital role in financial econometrics. Notations: common quantile Q, inverse of the distribution function F, respectively denoted $Q(u; Y), 0 < u < 1$ and $F(y; Y)$. The mid-distribution is defined as $F^{\mathrm{mid}}(y; Y) = F(y; Y) - 0.5 \Pr(Y(t) = y)$.

(2) Correlation modeling: Covariance function (defined for positive and negative lag h) $R(h; Y) = \mathrm{Cov}[Y(t), Y(t + h)]$. $R(0; Y) = \mathrm{Var}[Y(t)]$, $\mu = \mathbb{E}[Y(t)]$ assumed zero in our prediction theory. Correlation function $\rho(h) = \mathrm{Cor}[Y(t), Y(t + h)] = R(h; Y)/R(0; Y)$.

(3) Frequency-domain modeling: When covariance is absolutely summable, define spectral density function $f(\omega; Y) = \sum R(h; Y) e^{-2\pi i \omega h}, -1/2 < \omega < 1/2$.

(4) Time-domain modeling: The time domain model is a linear filter relating $Y(t)$ to white noise $\epsilon(t)$, $\mathcal{N}(0,1)$ independent random variables. Autoregressive scheme of order m, a predominant linear time series technique for modeling conditional mean, is defined as (assuming $\mathbb{E}[Y(t)] = 0$):

$$Y(t) - a(1;m)Y(t-1) - \ldots - a(m;m)Y(t-m) = \sigma_m \epsilon(t), \tag{1}$$

with the spectral density function given by:

$$f(\omega;Y) = \frac{\sigma_m^2}{\left|1 - \sum_{k=1}^{m} a(k;m)e^{2\pi i \omega k}\right|^2}. \tag{2}$$

To fit an AR model, compute the linear predictor of $Y(t)$ given $Y(t-j), j = 1,\ldots,m$ by:

$$Y^{\mu,m}[t] = \mathbb{E}[Y(t) \mid Y(t-1),\ldots,Y(t-m)] = a(1;m)Y(t-1) + \cdots + a(m;m)Y(t-m). \tag{3}$$

Verify that the prediction error $Y[t] - Y^{\mu,m}[t]$ is white noise. The best fitting AR order is identified by the Akaike criterion (AIC) (or Schwarz's criterion, BIC) as the value of m minimizes:

$$\mathrm{AIC}(m) = 2\log \sigma_m + 2m/n.$$

In what follows, we aim to develop a parallel modeling framework for nonlinear time series.

2. From Linear to Nonlinear Modeling

Our approach to nonlinear modeling, called LPTime[1], is via approximate calculation of conditional expectation $\mathbb{E}[Y(t)|Y(t-1),\ldots,Y(t-m)]$. Because with probability one $Q(F(Y)) = Y$, one can prove that the conditional expectation of $Y(t)$ given past values $Y(t-j)$ is equal to (with probability one) the conditional expectation of $Y(t)$ given past values $F^{\mathrm{mid}}(Y(t-j))$, which can be approximated by linear orthogonal series expansion in score functions $T_k[F^{\mathrm{mid}}(Y(t-j))]$ constructed by Gram–Schmidt orthonormalization of powers of:

$$T_1 = \frac{F^{\mathrm{mid}}(Y(t);Y) - 0.5}{\sigma[F^{\mathrm{mid}}(Y(t);Y)]}, \tag{4}$$

where $\sigma[F^{\mathrm{mid}}(Y(t);Y)]$ is the standard deviation of the mid-distribution transform random variable given by $\sqrt{(1 - \sum_y p^3(y))/12}$ and $p(y)$ denotes the probability mass function of Y. This score polynomial allows us to simultaneously tackle the discrete (say count-valued) and continuous time series. Note that for Y continuous, T_1 reduces to:

$$T_1 = \sqrt{12}\left(F(Y(t)) - 0.5\right). \tag{5}$$

and all the higher order polynomials T_j can be compactly expressed as $\mathrm{Leg}_j[F(Y)]$, where $\mathrm{Leg}_j(u)$, $0 < u < 1$ denotes orthonormal Legendre polynomials. It is worthwhile to note that T_j are orthonormal polynomials of mid-rank (instead of polynomials of the original y's), which inject robustness into our analysis while allowing us to capture nonlinear patterns. Having constructed score functions of y denoted by T_j, we transform it into a unit interval by letting $y = Q(u;Y)$ and defining:

---

[1] The LP nomenclature: In nonparametric statistics, the letter L plays a special role to denote robust methods based on ranks and order statistics such as quantile-domain methods. With the same motivation, we use the letter L. On the other hand, P simply stands for Polynomials. Our custom-constructed basis functions are orthonormal polynomials of mid-rank transform instead of raw y-values; for more details see Mukhopadhyay and Parzen (2014).

$$S_j(u;Y) = T_j\big[F^{\text{mid}}(Q(u;Y))\big], \quad T_j(y;Y) = S_j\big[F^{\text{mid}}(Y(t))\big]. \tag{6}$$

In general, our score functions are custom constructed for each distribution function F, which can be discrete or continuous.

3. Nonparametric LPTime Analysis

Our LPTime empirical time series modeling strategy for nonlinear modeling of a univariate time series $Y(t)$ is based on linear modeling of the multivariate time series:

$$\text{Vec}(\text{YS})(t) = \big[\text{YS}_1(t), \ldots, \text{YS}_k(t)\big]^{\mathsf{T}}, \tag{7}$$

where $\text{YS}_k(t) = T_k[F^{\text{mid}}(Y(t))]$, our tailor-made orthonormal mid-rank-based nonlinear transformed series. We summarize below the main steps of the algorithm LPTime. To better understand the functionality and applicability of LPTime, we break it into several inter-connected steps, each of which highlights:

(a)   The algorithmic modeling aspect (how it works).
(b)   The required theoretical ideas and notions (why it works).
(c)   The application to daily S&P 500 return data between 2 January 1963 and 31 December 2009 (empirical proof-of-work).

3.1. The Data and LP-Transformation

The data used in this paper are daily S&P 500 return data between 2 January 1963 and 31 December 2009 (defined as $\log(P_t/P_{t-1})$, where P_t is the closing price on trading day t). We begin our modeling process by transforming the given univariate time series $\{Y(t)\}$ into multiple (robust) time series by means of special data-analytic construction rules described in Equations (4)–(6) and (7). We display the original "normalized" time series $\mathcal{Z}(Y(t)) = (Y(t) - \mathbb{E}[Y(t)])/\sigma[Y(t)]$ and the transformed time series $\text{YS}_1(t), \ldots, \text{YS}_k(t)$ on a single plot.

Figure 1 shows the first look at the transformed S&P 500 return data between October 1986 and October 1988. These newly-constructed time series work as a universal preprocessor for any time series modeling in contrast with other ad hoc power transformations. In the next sections, we will describe how the temporal patterns of these multivariate LP-transformed series $\text{Vec}(\text{YS})(t) = \{\text{YS}_1(t), \ldots, \text{YS}_k(t)\}$ generate various insights for the time series $\{Y(t)\}$ in an organized fashion.

3.2. Marginal Modeling

Our time series modeling starts with the nonparametric identification of probability distributions.

Non-Normality Diagnosis

Does the normal probability distribution provide a good fit to the S&P 500 return data? Figure 2a clearly indicates that the distribution of daily return is certainly non-normal. At this point, the natural question is how the distribution is different from the assumed normal one? A quick insight into this question can be gained by looking at the distribution of the random variable $U = G(Y)$, called the comparison density (Mukhopadhyay 2017; Parzen 1997), given by:

$$d(u;G,F) = \frac{f(Q(u;G))}{g(Q(u;G))}, \quad 0 \le u \le 1, \tag{8}$$

where $Q(u;G) = \inf\{x : G(x) \ge u\}$ is the quantile function. The flat uniform shape of the estimated comparison density provides a quick graphical diagnostic to test the fit of the parametric G to the true unknown distribution F. The Legendre polynomial-based orthogonal series comparison density estimator is given by:

$$d(u; G, F) = 1 + \sum_j LP[j; G, F] \, Leg_j(u), \ 0 < u < 1 \tag{9}$$

where the Fourier coefficients $LP[j; G, F] = \mathbb{E}[Leg_j \circ G(Y)]$.

For $G = \Phi$, Figure 2b displays the histogram of $U_i = \Phi(Y_i)$ for $i = 1, \ldots, n$. The corresponding comparison density estimate $\hat{d}(u; G, F) = 1 - 0.271 \, Leg_2(u) - 0.021 \, Leg_3(u) + 0.193 \, Leg_4(u)$ is shown with the blue curve, which reflects the fact that the distribution of daily return (i) has a sharp peaked (inverted "U" shape) and (ii) is negatively skewed with (iii) fatter tails than the Gaussian distribution. We can carry out a similar analysis by asking whether the t-distribution with two degrees of freedom provides a better fit. Figure 2c demonstrates the full analysis, where the estimated comparison density $\hat{d}(u; G, F) = 1 - 0.492 \, Leg_2(u) - 0.015 \, Leg_3(u) + 0.084 \, Leg_4(u)$ indicates that (iv) the t-distribution fits the data better than normal, especially in the tails, although not a fully-adequate model.

The shape of the comparison density (along with the histogram of $U_i = G(Y_i)$, $i = 1, \ldots, n$) captures and exposes the adequacy of the assumed model G for the true unknown F; thus acting as an exploratory, as well as confirmatory tool.

LP-Transformed Time Series

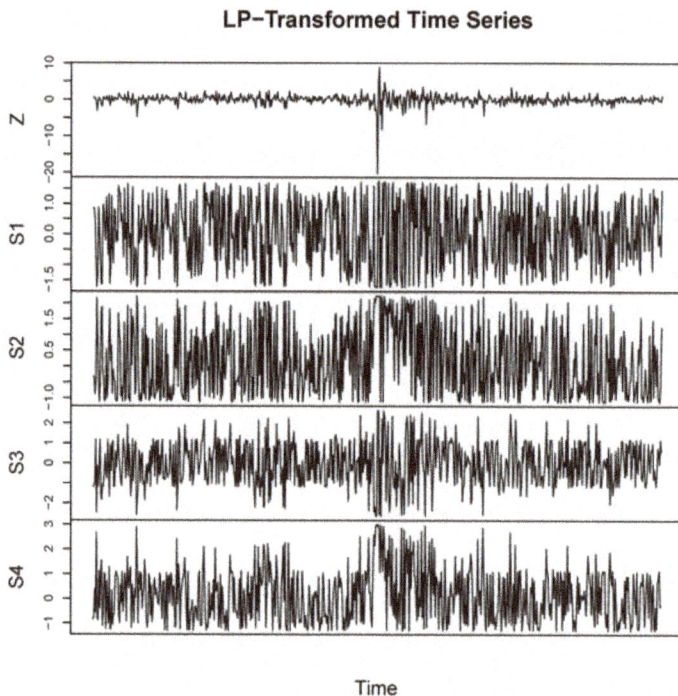

Figure 1. LP-transformed S&P 500 daily stock returns between October 1986 and October 1988. This is just a small part of the full time series from 2 January 1963–31 December 2009 (cf. Section 3.1).

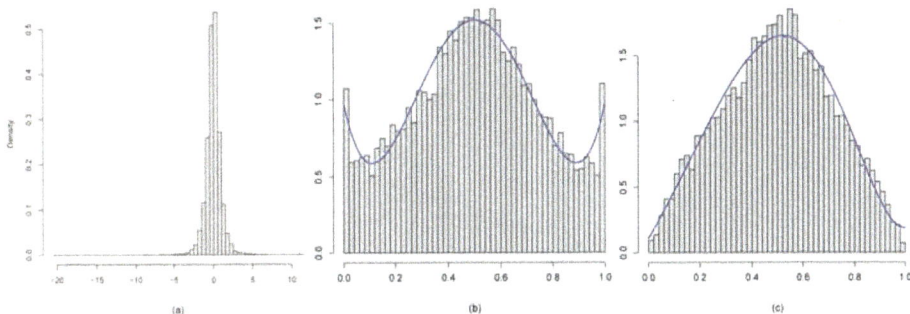

Figure 2. (a) The marginal distribution of daily returns; **(b)** plots the histogram of $\Phi(y_i)$ and display the LP-estimated comparison density curve. and **(c)** shows the associated comparison density estimate with G as t-distribution with 2 degrees of freedom.

3.3. Copula Dependence Modeling

Distinguishing uncorrelatedness and independence by properly quantifying association is an essential task in empirical nonlinear time series modeling.

3.3.1. Nonparametric Serial Copula

We display the nonparametrically-estimated smooth serial copula density $\text{cop}(u, v; Y(t), Y(t+h))$ to get a much finer understanding of the lagged interdependence structure of a stationary time series. For a continuous distribution, define the copula density for the pair $(Y(t), Y(t+h))$ as the joint density of $U = F(Y(t))$ and $V = F(Y(t+h))$, which is estimated by sample mid-distribution transform $\tilde{U} = \tilde{F}^{\text{mid}}(Y(t))$, $\tilde{V} = \tilde{F}^{\text{mid}}(Y(t+h))$. Following Mukhopadhyay and Parzen (2014) and Parzen and Mukhopadhyay (2012), we expand the copula density (square integrable) in a orthogonal series of product LP-basis functions as:

$$\text{cop}(u, v; Y(t), Y(t+h)) - 1 = \sum_{j,k} \text{LP}[j, k; Y(t), Y(t+h)] \, S_j(u; Y(t)) \, S_k(v; Y(t+h)), \qquad (10)$$

where $S_j(u; Y(t)) = \text{YS}_j(Q(u; Y(t)); Y(t))$. Equation (10) allows us to pictorially represent the information present in the LP-comoment matrix via copula density. The various "shapes" of the copula density give insight into the structure and dynamics of the time series.

Now, we apply this nonparametric copula estimation theory to model the temporal dependence structure of S&P return data. The copula density estimate $\widehat{\text{cop}}(u, v; Y(t), Y(t+1))$ based on the smooth LP-comoments is displayed in Figure 3. The shape of the copula density shows strong evidence of asymmetric tail dependence. Note that the dependence is only present in the extreme quantiles, another well-known stylized fact of economic and financial time series.

3.3.2. LP-Comoment of Lag h

Here, we will introduce the concept of the LP-comoment to get a complete understanding of the nature of the serial dependence present in the data. The LP-comoment of lag h is defined as the joint covariance of $\text{Vec}(\text{YS})(t)$ and $\text{Vec}(\text{YS})(t+h)$.

The lag one LP-comoment matrix for S&P 500 return data is displayed below:

$$\text{LP}\left[Y(t), Y(t+1)\right] = \begin{bmatrix} 0.0705^* & -0.0617^* & 0.0199 & 0.0113 \\ 0.0074 & 0.1542^* & 0.0077 & 0.0652^* \\ -0.0104 & -0.0071 & 0.0262 & -0.0355 \\ 0.0166 & 0.0438^* & 0.0113 & 0.0698^* \end{bmatrix} \qquad (11)$$

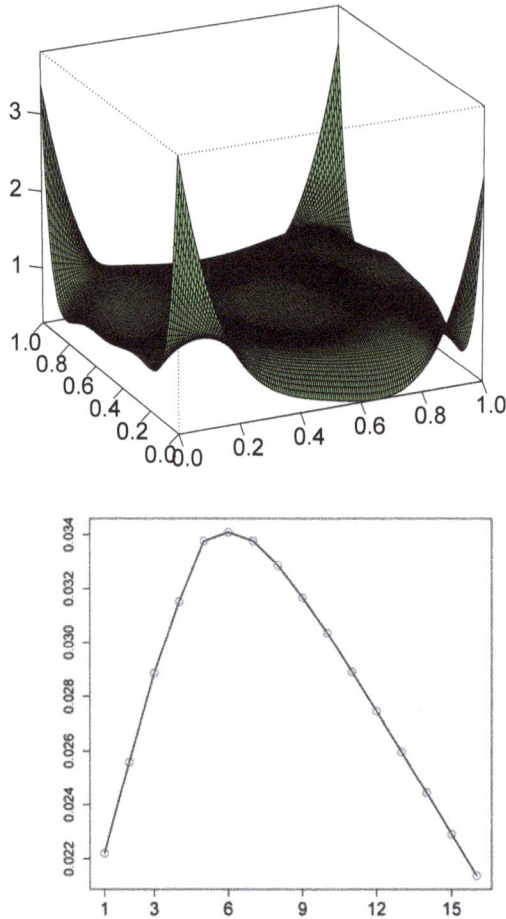

Figure 3. Top: Nonparametric smooth serial copula density (lag one) estimate of S&P return data. **Bottom**: BIC plot to select the significant LP-comoments computed in Equation (11).

To identify the significant elements, we first rank order the squared LP-comoments. Then, we take the penalized cumulative sum of m comoments using BIC criterion $2m \log(n)/n$, where n is the sample size, and choose the m for which the BIC is maximum. The complete BIC path for S&P 500 data is shown in Figure 3, which selects the top six comments, also denoted by $*$ in the LP-comoment matrix display (Equation (11)). By making all those uninteresting "small" comoments equal to zero, we get the "smooth" LP-comoment matrix denoted by $\widehat{LP}$. The linear auto-correlation is captured by the $LP[1, 1; Y(t), Y(t+1)] = \mathbb{E}[YS_1(t) YS_1(t+1)]$ term. The presence of higher order significant terms in the LP-comoment matrix indicates the possible nonlinearity. Another interesting point to note is that $CORR[Y(t), Y(t+1)] = 0.027$, whereas the auto-correlation between the mid-rank transformed data $CORR[F^{mid}(Y(t)), F^{mid}(Y(t+1))] = 0.071$, considerably larger and picked by the BIC criterion. This is an interesting fact as it indicates that the rank-transform time series $(YS_1(t))$ is much more predictable than the original raw time series $Y(t)$.

3.3.3. LP-Correlogram, Evidence and Source of Nonlinearity

We provide a nonparametric exploratory test for (non)linearity (the spectral domain test is given in Section 3.6). Plot the correlogram of $YS_1(t), \ldots, YS_4(t)$: (a) diagnose possible nonlinearity; and (b) identify possible sources. This constitutes an important building block for methods of model identification. The LP-correlogram generalizes the classical sample Autocorrelation Function (ACF). Applying the acf() R function on Vec(YS)(t) generates the graphical display of our proposed LP-correlogram plot.

Figure 4 shows the LP-correlogram of S&P stock return data. Panel A shows the absence of linear autocorrelation, which is known as an efficient market hypothesis in finance literature. A prominent auto-correlation pattern for the series $YS_2(t)$ (top right panel of Figure 4) is the source of nonlinearity. This fact is known as "volatility clustering", which says that a large price fluctuation is more likely to be followed by large price fluctuations. Furthermore, the slow decay of the autocorrelation of the series $YS_2(t)$ can be interpreted as an indication of the long-memory volatility structure.

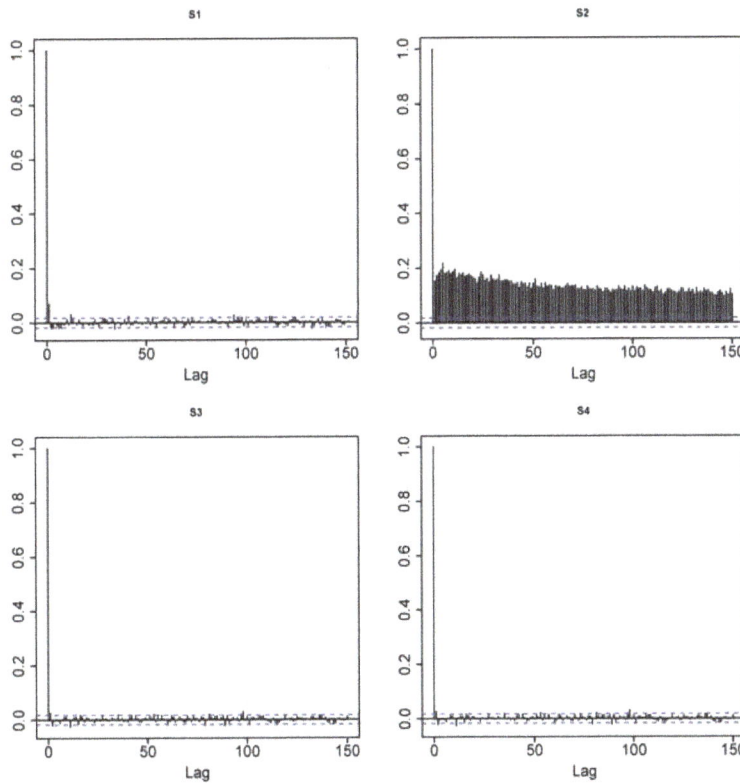

Figure 4. LP-correlogram: Sample autocorrelations of LP-transformed time series. The decay rate of the sample autocorrelations of $YS_2(t)$ appears to be much slower than the exponential decay of the ARMA process, implying possible long-memory behavior.

3.3.4. AutoLPinfor: Nonlinear Correlation Measure

We display the sample AutoLPinforplot, a diagnostic tool for nonlinear autocorrelation. We define the lag h AutoLPinfor as the squared Frobenius norm of the smooth-LP-comoment matrix of lag h,

$$\text{AutoLPinfor}(h) = \sum_{j,k} | \text{LP}[j, k; Y(t), Y(t+h)] |^2, \tag{12}$$

where the sum is over BIC selected j, k for which LP-comoments are significantly non-zero.

Our robust nonparametric measure can be viewed as capturing the deviation of the copula density from uniformity:

$$\text{AutoLPinfor}(h) = \iint \text{cop}^2[u, v; Y(t), Y(t+h)] \, du \, dv - 1, \tag{13}$$

which is closely related to the entropy measure of association proposed in Granger and Lin (1994):

$$\text{Granger–Lin}(h) = \iint \text{cop}[u, v; Y(t), Y(t+h)] \, \log \text{cop}[u, v; Y(t), Y(t+h)] \, du \, dv. \tag{14}$$

It can be shown using Taylor series expansion that asymptotically:

$$\text{AutoLPinfor}(h) \approx 2 \times \text{Granger–Lin}(h). \tag{15}$$

An excellent discussion of the role of information theory methods for unified time series analysis is given in Parzen (1992) and Brillinger (2004). For an extensive survey of tests of independence for nonlinear processes, see Chapter 7.7 of Terasvirta et al. (2010). AutoLPinfor is a new information theoretic nonlinear autocorrelation measure, which detects generic association and serial dependence present in a time series. Contrast the AutoLPinfor plot for S&P 500 return data shown in Figure 5 with the ACF plot (left panel). This underlies the need for building a nonlinear time series model, which we will be discussing next.

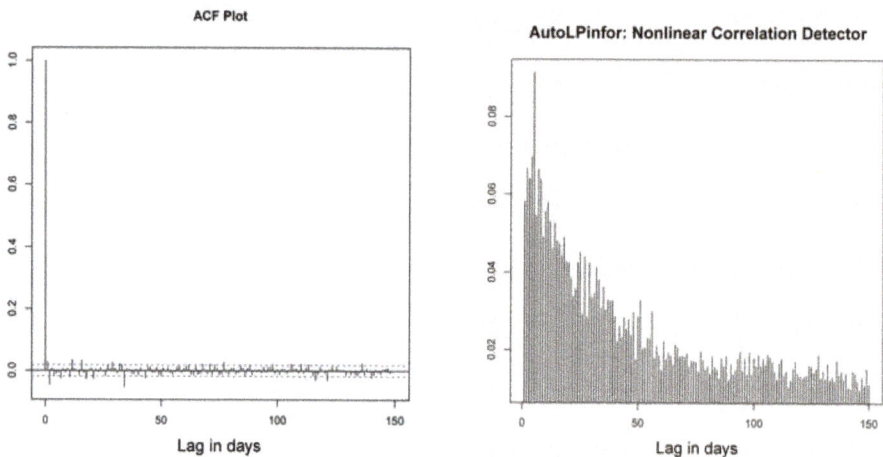

Figure 5. **Left**: ACF plot of S&P 500 data. **Right**: AutoLPinforPlot up to lag 150.

3.3.5. Nonparametric Estimation of Blomqvist's Beta

Estimate the Blomqvist's β (also known as the medial correlation coefficient) of lag h by using the LP-copula estimate in the following equation,

$$\widehat{\beta}_{\text{LP}}(h; Y(t)) := -1 + 4 \int_0^{1/2} \int_0^{1/2} \widehat{\text{cop}}[u, v; Y(t), Y(t+h)] \, du \, dv \tag{16}$$

The β values $-1, 0$ and 1 are interpreted as reverse correlation, independence and perfect correlation, respectively. Note that,

Blomqvist's β : Normalized distance of copula distribution $\text{Cop}(u, v)$ from independence copula uv
AutoLPinfor   : Distance of copula density $\text{cop}(u, v)$ from uniformity 1.

For S&P 500 return data, we compute the following dependence numbers,

$$\hat{\beta}_{LP}(1; Y(t)) = 0.0528$$
$$\hat{\beta}_{LP}(1; YS_1(t)) = 0.0528$$
$$\hat{\beta}_{LP}(1; YS_2(t)) = 0.0729$$
$$\hat{\beta}_{LP}(1; YS_3(t)) = 0.0$$
$$\hat{\beta}_{LP}(1; YS_4(t)) = 0.003.$$

3.3.6. Nonstationarity Diagnosis, LP-Comoment Approach

Viewing the time index $T = 1, \ldots, n$ as the covariate, we propose a nonstationarity diagnosis based on LP-comoments of $Y(t)$ and the time index variable T. Our treatment has the ability to detect the time-varying nature of mean, variance, skewness, and so on, represented by various custom-made LP-transformed time series.

For S&P data, we computed the following LP-comoment matrix to investigate the nonstationarity:

$$LP\left[T, Y(t)\right] = \begin{bmatrix} 0.012 & 0.180^* & -0.010 & 0.058^* \\ -0.005 & -0.034 & -0.036 & 0.080^* \\ -0.016 & 0.115^* & 0.001 & -0.001 \\ 0.024 & -0.040 & -0.010 & 0.049^* \end{bmatrix} \tag{17}$$

This indicates the presence of the slight non-stationarity behavior of variance or volatility ($YS_2(t)$) and the kurtosis of tail-thickness ($YS_4(t)$). Similar to AutoLPinfor, we propose the following statistic for detecting nonstationarity:

$$LPinfor[Y(t), T] = \sum_{j,k} |LP[j, k; T, Y(t)]|^2. \tag{18}$$

We can also generate the corresponding smooth copula density of $(T, Y(t))$ based on the smooth $LP\left[T, Y(t)\right]$ matr

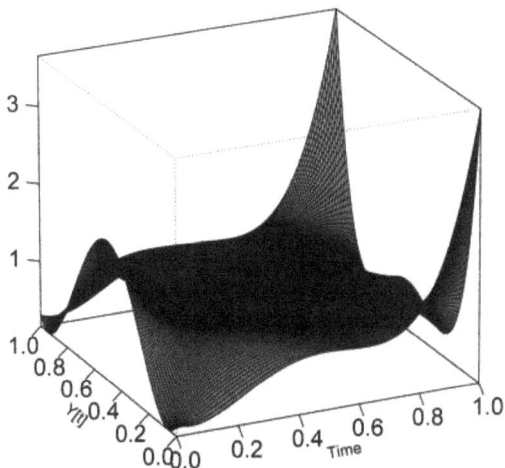

Figure 6. LP copula diagnostic for detecting non-stationarity in S&P 500 return data.

3.4. Local Dependence Modeling

3.4.1. Quantile Correlation Plot and Test for Asymmetry

We display the quantile correlation plot, a copula distribution-based graphical diagnostic to visually examine the asymmetry of dependence. The goal is to get more insight into the nature of tail-correlation.

Motivated by the concept of the lower and upper tail dependence coefficient, we define the quantile correlation function (QCF) as the following in terms of the copula distribution function of $(Y(t), Y(t+h))$ denoted by $\mathrm{Cop}(u, v; Y(t), Y(t+h)) := \mathrm{Cop}(u, v; h)$,

$$\lambda[u; Y(t), Y(t+h)] := \frac{\mathrm{Cop}(u, u; h)}{u} \mathbb{I}_{\{u \leq 0.5\}} + \frac{1 - 2u + \mathrm{Cop}(u, u; h)}{1 - u} \mathbb{I}_{\{u > 0.5\}}, \tag{19}$$

Our nonparametric estimate of the quantile correlation function is based on the LP-copula density, which we denote as $\hat{\lambda}_{\mathrm{LP}}[u; Y(t), Y(t+h)]$. Figure 7 shows the corresponding quantile correlation plot for S&P 500 data. The dotted line represents QCF under the independence assumption. Deviation from this line helps us to better understand the nature of asymmetry. We compute $\hat{\lambda}_G[u; Y(t), Y(t+h)]$ using the fitted Gaussian copula:

$$\widehat{\mathrm{Cop}}_G(u, v; Y(t), Y(t+h)) = \Phi(\Phi^{-1}(u), \Phi^{-1}(v); \hat{\Sigma} = S) \tag{20}$$

where S is the sample covariance matrix. The dark green line in Figure 7 shows the corresponding curve, which is almost identical to the "no dependence" curve, albeit misleading. The reason is the Gaussian copula is characterized by linear correlation, while S&P data are highly nonlinear in nature. As the linear auto-correlation of a stock return is almost zero, we have approximately $\Phi(\Phi^{-1}(u), \Phi^{-1}(u); \hat{\Sigma} = S) \approx \Phi(\Phi^{-1}(u))\Phi(\Phi^{-1}(u)) = u^2$. Similar to the Gaussian copula, there are several other parametric copula families, which can give similar misleading conclusions. This simple illustration reminds us of the pernicious effect of not "looking into the data".

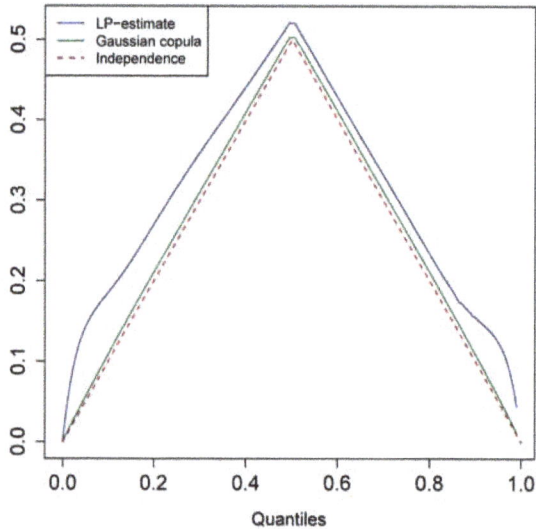

Figure 7. Estimated Quantile Correlation Function (QCF) $\hat{\lambda}_{\mathrm{LP}}[u; Y(t), Y(t+1)]$. It detects asymmetry in the tail dependence between the lower-left quadrant and upper-right quadrant for S&P 500 return data. The red dotted line denotes the quantile correlation function under dependence. The dark green line shows the quantile correlation curve for the fitted Gaussian copula.

3.4.2. Conditional LPinfor Dependence Measure

For more transparent and clear insight into the asymmetric nature of the tail dependence, we need to introduce the concept of conditional dependence. In what follows, we propose a conditional LPinfor function LPinfor$(Y(t+h)|Y(t) = Q(u; Y(t)))$, a quantile-based diagnostic for tracking how the dependence of $Y(t+h)$ on $Y(t)$ changes at various quantiles.

To quantify the conditional dependence, we seek to estimate $f(y; Y(t+h)|Y(t))/f(y; Y(t+h))$. A brute force approach estimates separately the conditional distribution and the unconditional distribution and takes the ratio to estimate this arbitrary function. An alternative elegant way is to recognize that by "going to the quantile domain" (i.e., $Y(t+h) = Q(v; Y(t+v))$ and $Y(t) = Q(u; Y(t))$), we can interpret the ratio as "slices" of the copula density, which we call the conditional comparison density:

$$d[v; Y(t+h), Y(t+h)|Y(t) = Q(u; Y(t))] = 1 + \sum_j LP[j; h, u] \, S_j(v; Y(t+h)), \tag{21}$$

where the LP-Fourier orthogonal coefficients LP$[j; h]$ are given by:

$$LP[j; h, u] = \sum_k LP[j, k; Y(t), Y(t+h)] \, S_k(u; Y(t)).$$

Define the conditional LPinfor as:

$$LPinfor\left[Y(t+h)|Y(t) = Q(u; Y(t))\right] = \sum_j |LP[j; h, u]|^2. \tag{22}$$

We use this theory to investigate the conditional dependency structure of S&P 500 return data. Figure 8a traces out the complete path of the estimated LPinfor$[Y(t+h) \mid Y(t) = Q(u; Y(t)]$ function, which indicates the high asymmetric tail correlation. These conditional correlation curves can be viewed as a "local" dependence measure. An excellent discussion on this topic is given in Section 3.3.8 of Terasvirta et al. (2010).

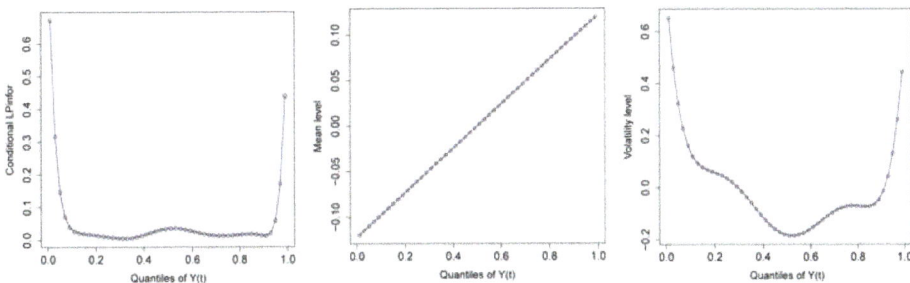

Figure 8. (**a**) The conditional LPinfor curve is shown for the pair $[Y(t), Y(t+1)]$. The asymmetric dependence in the tails is clearly shown, and almost nothing is going on in between. (**b,c**) Display of how the mean and volatility levels of conditional distribution $f[y; Y(t+1)|Y(t) = Q(u; Y(t))]$ change with respect to the unconditional marginal distribution $f(y; Y(t))$ at different quantiles.

At this point, we can legitimately ask: What aspects of the conditional distributions are changing most? Figure 8b,c displays only the two coefficients LP$[1; h, u]$ and LP$[2; h, u]$ for the S&P 500 return data for the pairs $(Y(t), Y(t+1))$. These two coefficients represent how the mean and the volatility levels of the conditional density change with respect to the unconditional reference distribution. The typical asymmetric shape of conditional volatility shown in the right panel of Figure 8b,c indicates what is known as the "leverage effect"; future stock volatility negatively correlated with past stock return, i.e., stock volatility tends to increase when stock prices drop.

3.5. Non-Crossing Conditional Quantile Modeling

We display the nonparametrically-estimated conditional quantile curves of $Y(t+h)$ given $Y(t)$. Our new modeling approach uses the estimated conditional comparison density $\hat{d}(v; h, u)$ to simulate from $F[y; Y(t+h)|Y(t) = Q(u; Y(t))]$ by utilizing the given sample $\tilde{Q}(u; Y(t))$ via an accept-reject rule to arrive at the "smooth" nonparametric model for $\hat{Q}[v; Y(t+h)|Y(t) = Q(u; Y(t))]$. See Parzen and Mukhopadhyay (2013b) for details about the method. Our proposed algorithm generates "large" additional simulated samples from the conditional distribution, which allows us to accurately estimate the conditional quantiles (especially the extreme quantiles). By construction, our method is guaranteed to produce non-crossing quantile curves; thus tackling a challenging practical problem.

For S&P 500 data, we first nonparametrically estimate the conditional comparison densities $\hat{d}(v; h, u)$ shown in the left panel of Figure 9 for $F(y; Y(t)) = 0.01, 0.5$ and 0.99, which can be thought of as a "weighting function" for an unconditional marginal distribution to produce the conditional distributions:

$$\hat{f}[y; Y(t+h)|Y(t) = Q(u; Y(t))] = f(y; Y(t)) \times \hat{d}[F(y; Y(t+h)); h, u]. \tag{23}$$

This density estimation technique belongs to the skew-G modeling class (Mukhopadhyay 2016). We simulate $n = 10,000$ samples from $\hat{f}(y; Y(t+h)|Y(t))$ by accept-reject sampling from $\hat{d}(v; h, u)$, $u = \{0.01, 0.5, 0.99\}$. The histograms and the smooth conditional densities are shown in the right panel of Figure 9. It shows some typical shapes in terms of long-tailedness.

Next, we proceed to estimate the nonparametric conditional quantiles $\hat{Q}(v; Y(t+h)|Y(t))$, for $v = 0.001, 0.25, 0.5, 0.75, 0.999$, from the simulated data. Figure 10 shows the estimated conditional quantiles. The extreme conditional quantiles have a special significance in the context of financial time series. They are sometimes popularly known as Conditional Value at Risk (CoVaR), currently the most popular quantitative risk management tool (see Adrian and Brunnermeier (2011); Engle and Manganelli (2004)). The red solid line in Figure 10 is $\hat{Q}[0.001; Y(t+1) \mid Y(t) = Q(u; Y(t))]$, which is known as the 0.1% CoVaR function for a one-day holding period for S&P 500 daily return data. Although the upper conditional quantile curve $\hat{Q}(0.999; Y(t+1)|Y(t))$ (blue solid line) shows symmetric behavior around $F(y; Y(t)) = 0.5$, the lower quantile has a prominent asymmetric shape. These conditional quantiles give the ultimate description of the auto-regressive dependence of S&P 500 return movement in the tail region.

3.6. Nonlinear Spectrum Analysis

Here, we extend the concept of spectral density for nonlinear processes. We display the LPSpectrum -Autoregressive (AR) spectral density estimates of $YS_1(t), \ldots, YS_4(t)$. The spectral density for each LP-transformed series is defined as:

$$\begin{aligned}
f(\omega; YS_j) &= \sum_h LP[j, j; Y(t), Y(t+h)] e^{-i2\pi h\omega}, & -1/2 < \omega < 1/2 \\
&= \sum_h Cov[YS_j(t), YS_j(t+h)] e^{-i2\pi h\omega}, & -1/2 < \omega < 1/2. \tag{24}
\end{aligned}$$

We separately fit the univariate AR model for the components of $Vec(YS)(t)$ and use the BIC order selection criterion to select the "best" parsimonious parametrization using the Burg method.

Finally, we use the estimated model coefficients to produce the "smooth" estimate of the spectral density function (see Equation (2)). The copula spectral density is defined as:

$$f(\omega; u, v) = \sum_h cop(u, v; h) e^{-i2\pi h\omega}, \qquad -1/2 < \omega < 1/2. \tag{25}$$

To estimate the copula spectral density, we use the LP-comoment-based nonparametric copula density estimate. Note that both the serial copula (3.12) and the corresponding spectral density (3.25) capture the same amount of information for the serial dependence of $\{Y(t)\}$. For that reason, we recommend computing AutoLPinfor as a general dependence measure for non-Gaussian nonlinear processes.

The application of our LPSpectral tool on S&P 500 return data is shown in Figure 11. A few interesting observations are: (i) the conventional spectral density (black solid line) provides no insight into the (complex) serial dependency present in the data; (ii) the nonlinearity in the series is captured by the interesting shapes of our specially-designed times series $YS_2(t)$ and $YS_4(t)$, which classical (linear) correlogram-based spectra cannot account for; (iii) the shape of the spectra of $\mathcal{Z}(Y(t))$ and the rank-transformed time series $YS_1(t)$ look very similar; and a (iv) pronounced singularity near zero of the spectrum of $YS_2(t)$ hints at some kind of "long-memory" behavior. This phenomena is also known as regular variation representation at frequency $\omega = 0$ (Granger and Joyeux 1980).

A quick diagnostic measure for screening significant spectrums can be computed via the information number $2 \int_0^{1/2} \log \widehat{f}(\omega; S_j)\ d\omega$. The LPSpectrum methodology is highly robust and, thus, can tackle the heavy-tailed S&P data quite successfully.

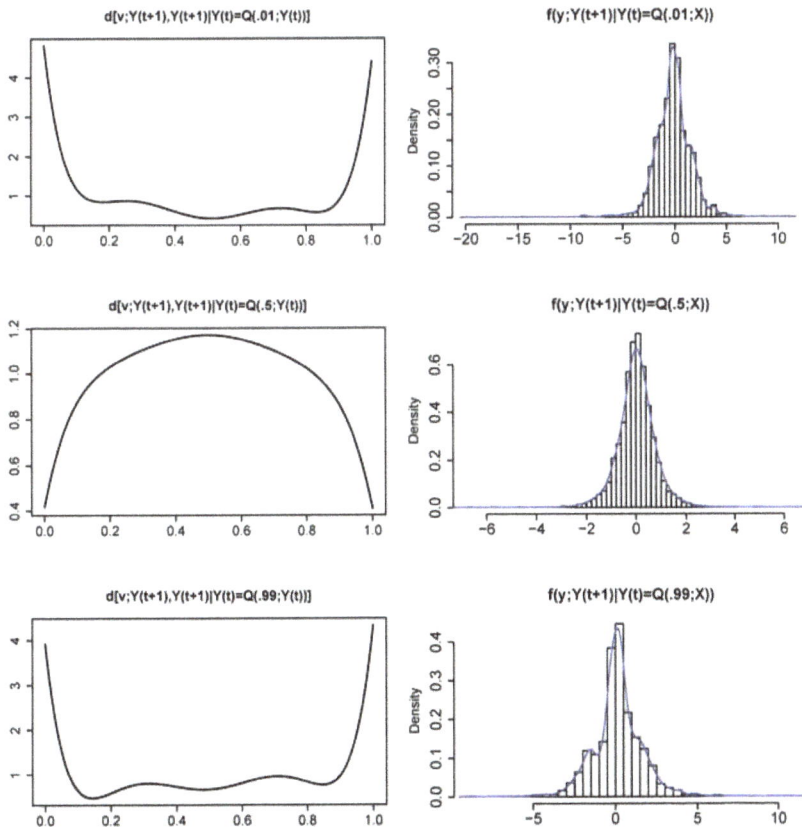

Figure 9. Each row displays the estimated conditional comparison density and the corresponding conditional distribution for $u = 0.01, 0.5, 0.99$.

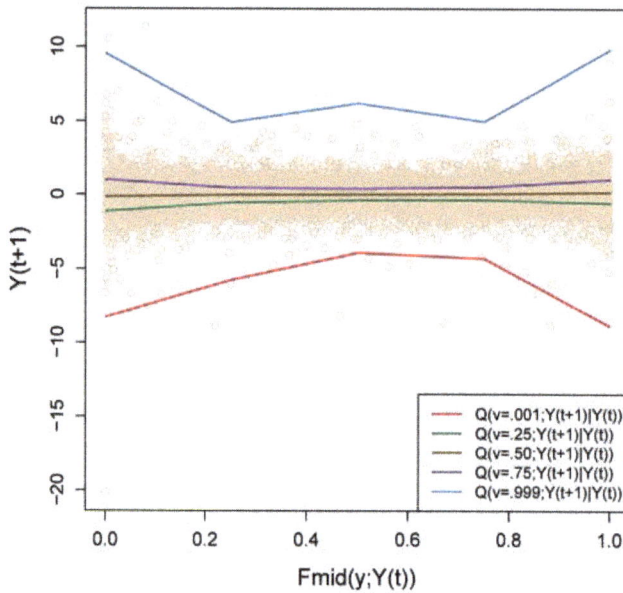

Figure 10. The figure shows estimated non-parametric conditional quantile curves for S&p 500 return data. The red solid line, which represents $\hat{Q}(0.001; Y(t+1)|Y(t))$, is popularly known as the one-day 0.1% Conditional Value at Risk measure (CoVaR).

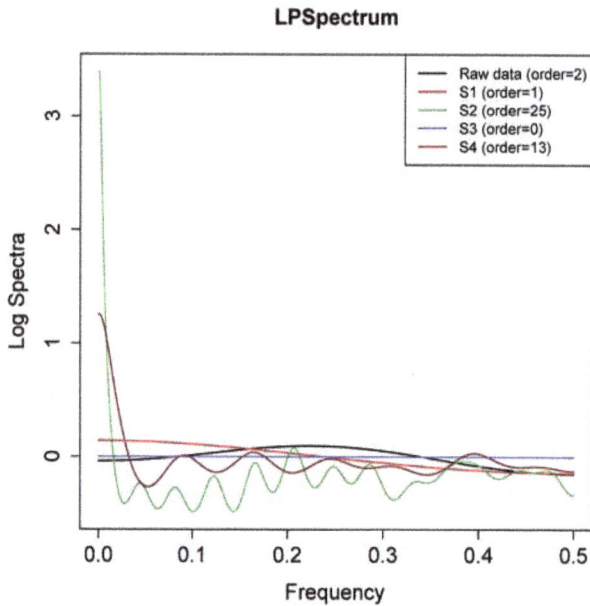

Figure 11. LPSpectrum: AR spectral density estimate for S&P 500 return data. Order selected by the BIC method. This provides a diagnostic tool for providing evidence of hidden periodicities in non-Gaussian nonlinear time series.

3.7. Nonparametric Model Specification

The ultimate goal of empirical time series analysis is nonparametric model identification. To model the univariate stationary nonlinear process, we specify the multiple autoregressive model based on $\text{Vec}(YS)(t) = [YS_1(t), \ldots, YS_k(t)]^T$ of the form:

$$\text{Vec}(YS)(t) = \sum_{k=1}^{m} A(k; m)\, \text{Vec}(YS)(t - k) + \epsilon(t). \tag{26}$$

where $\epsilon(t)$ is multivariate mean zero Gaussian white noise with covariance Σ_m. This system of equations jointly describes the dynamics of the nonlinear process and how it evolves over time. We use the BIC criterion to select the model order m, which minimizes:

$$\text{BIC}(m) = \log |\hat{\Sigma}_m| + mk^2 \frac{\log T}{T}. \tag{27}$$

We carry out this step for our S&P 500 return data. We estimate our multiple AR model based on $\text{Vec}(YS)(t) = [YS_1(t), YS_2(t), YS_4(t)]^T$. We discard $YS_3(t)$ due to its flat spectrum (see Figure 11). BIC selects "best" order eight. Although the complete description of the estimated model is clearly cumbersome, we provide below the approximate structure by selecting a few large coefficients from the actual matrix equation. The goal is to interpret the coefficients (statistical parameters) of the estimated model and relate them to economic theory (scientific parameters/theory). This multiple AR LP-model (LPVAR) is given by:

$$
\begin{aligned}
YS_1(t) &\approx 0.071\, YS_1(t-1) - 0.024\, YS_1(t-2) + \epsilon_1(t) \\
YS_2(t) &\approx -0.063\, YS_1(t-1) - 0.075\, YS_1(t-2) + 0.06\, YS_2(t-2) + 0.123\, YS_2(t-5) + 0.04\, YS_4(t-2) + \epsilon_2(t) \quad (28) \\
YS_4(t) &\approx 0.04\, YS_4(t-1) + 0.038\, YS_4(t-2) + 0.04\, YS_2(t-3) + \epsilon_4(t).
\end{aligned}
$$

and the residual covariance matrix is:

$$
\hat{\Sigma}_8 = \begin{bmatrix} 0.993 & -0.001 & -0.002 \\ -0.001 & 0.853 & -0.058 \\ -0.002 & -0.058 & 0.964 \end{bmatrix}
$$

The autoregressive model of $YS_2(t)$ can be considered as a robust stock return volatility model (LPVolatility modeling), which is less affected by unusually large extreme events. The model for $YS_2(t)$ automatically discovers many known facts: (a) the sign of the coefficient linking volatility and return is negative, confirming the "leverage effect"; (b) $YS_2(t)$ is positively autocorrelated, known as volatility clustering; (c) the positive interaction with lagged $YS_4(t)$ accounts for the "excess kurtosis".

4. Conclusions

This article provides a pragmatic and comprehensive framework for nonlinear time series modeling that is easier to use, more versatile and has a strong theoretical foundation based on the recently-developed theory of unified algorithms of data science via LP modeling (Mukhopadhyay 2016, 2017; Mukhopadhyay and Fletcher 2018; Mukhopadhyay and Parzen 2014; Parzen and Mukhopadhyay 2012, 2013a, 2013b). The summary and broader implications of the proposed research are:

- From the theoretical standpoint, the unique aspect of our proposal lies in its ability to simultaneously embrace and employ the spectral domain, time domain, quantile domain and information domain analyses for enhanced insights, which to the best of our knowledge has not appeared in the nonlinear time series literature before.
- From a practical angle, the novelty of our technique is that it permits us to use the techniques from linear Gaussian time series to create non-Gaussian nonlinear time series models with highly interpretable parameters. This aspect makes LPTime computationally extremely attractive for data

scientists, as they can now borrow all the standard time series analysis machinery from R libraries for implementation purposes.

- From the pedagogical side, we believe that these concepts and methods can easily be augmented with the standard time series analysis course to modernize the current curriculum so that students can handle complex time series modeling problems (McNeil et al. 2010) using the tools with which they are already familiar.

The main thrust of this article is to describe and interpret the steps of LPTime technology to create a realistic general-purpose algorithm for empirical time series modeling. In addition, many new theoretical results and diagnostic measures were presented, which laid the foundation for the algorithmic implementation of LPTime. We showed how LPTime can systematically explore the data to discover empirical facts hidden in time series. For example, LPTime empirical modeling of S&P 500 return data reproduces the 'stylized facts'—(a) heavy tails; (b) non-Gaussian; (c) nonlinear serial dependence; (d) tail correlation; (e) asymmetric dependence; (f) volatility clustering; (g) long-memory volatility structure; (h) efficient market hypothesis; (i) leverage effect; (j) excess kurtosis—in a coherent manner under a single general unified framework. We have emphasized how the statistical parameters of our model can be interpreted in light of established economic theory.

We have recently applied this theory for large-scale eye-movement pattern discovery problem, which came out as the winner (among 82 competing algorithms) of the 2014 IEEE International Biometric Eye Movements Verification and Identification Competition (Mukhopadhyay and Nandi 2017). The proposed algorithm is implemented in the R package LPTime (Mukhopadhyay and Nandi 2015), which is available on CRAN.

We conclude with some general references: a few popular articles: Brillinger (1977, 2004); Engle (1982); Granger and Lin (1994); Granger (1993, 2003); Parzen (1967, 1979); Salmon (2012); Tukey (1980); books: Guo et al. (2017); Terasvirta et al. (2010); Tsay (2010); Woodward et al. (2011); and review articles: Granger (1998); Hendry (2011).

Author Contributions: Conceptualization, S.M. and E.P.; Methodology, S.M. and E.P.; Formal Analysis, S.M.; Computation, S.M.; Writing-Review & Editing, S.M.

Funding: This research received no external funding.

Conflicts of Interest: The authors declare no conflict of interest.

References

Adrian, Tobias, and Markus K Brunnermeier. 2011. *Covar*. Technical Report. Cambridge: National Bureau of Economic Research.

Brillinger, David R. 1977. The identification of a particular nonlinear time series system. *Biometrika* 64: 509–15. [CrossRef]

Brillinger, David R. 2004. Some data analyses using mutual information. *Brazilian Journal of Probability and Statistics* 18: 163–83.

Engle, Robert F. 1982. Autoregressive conditional heteroscedasticity with estimates of the variance of united kingdom inflation. *Econometrica: Journal of the Econometric Society* 50: 987–1007. [CrossRef]

Engle, Robert F., and Simone Manganelli. 2004. Caviar: Conditional autoregressive value at risk by regression quantiles. *Journal of Business & Economic Statistics* 22: 367–81.

Granger, Clive, and Jin-Lung Lin. 1994. Using the mutual information coefficient to identify lags in nonlinear models. *Journal of Time Series Analysis* 15: 371–84. [CrossRef]

Granger, Clive W. J. 1993. Strategies for modelling nonlinear time-series relationships. *Economic Record* 69: 233–38. [CrossRef]

Granger, Clive W. J. 1998. Overview of nonlinear time series specification in economics. Paper presented at the NSF Symposium on Nonlinear Time Series Models, University of California, Berkeley, CA, USA, 22 May 1998.

Granger, Clive W. J. 2003. Time series concepts for conditional distributions. *Oxford Bulletin of Economics and Statistics* 65: 689–701. [CrossRef]

Granger, Clive W. J., and Roselyne Joyeux. 1980. An introduction to long-memory time series models and fractional differencing. *Journal of Time Series Analysis* 1: 15–29. [CrossRef]

Guo, Xin, Howard Shek, Tze Leung Lai, and Samuel Po-Shing Wong. 2017. *Quantitative Trading: Algorithms, Analytics, Data, Models, Optimization.* New York: Chapman and Hall/CRC.

Hendry, David F. 2011. Empirical economic model discovery and theory evaluation. *Rationality, Markets and Morals* 2: 115–45.

McNeil, Alexander J., Rüdiger Frey, and Paul Embrechts. 2010. *Quantitative Risk Management: Concepts, Techniques, and Tools.* Princeton: Princeton University Press.

Mukhopadhyay, Subhadeep. 2016. Large scale signal detection: A unifying view. *Biometrics* 72: 325–34. [CrossRef] [PubMed]

Mukhopadhyay, Subhadeep. 2017. Large-scale mode identification and data-driven sciences. *Electronic Journal of Statistics* 11: 215–40, doi:10.1214/17-EJS1229. [CrossRef]

Mukhopadhyay, Subhadeep, and Douglas Fletcher. 2018. Generalized Empirical Bayes Modeling via Frequentist Goodness-of-Fit. *Nature Scientific Reports* 8: 1–15. [CrossRef] [PubMed]

Mukhopadhyay, Subhadeep, and Shinjini Nandi. 2015. *LPTime: LP Nonparametric Approach to Non-Gaussian Non-Linear Time Series Modelling.* CRAN, R Package Version 1.0-2. Ithaca: Cornell University Library.

Mukhopadhyay, Subhadeep, and Shinjini Nandi. 2017. LPiTrack: Eye movement pattern recognition algorithm and application to biometric identification. *Machine Learning.* [CrossRef]

Mukhopadhyay, Subhadeep, and Emanuel Parzen. 2014. LP approach to statistical modeling. *arXiv.* arXiv:1405.2601.

Parzen, Emanuel. 1967. On empirical multiple time series analysis. In *Statistics, Proceedings of the Fifth Berkeley Symposium on Mathematical Statistics and Probability.* Berkeley: University of California Press, vol. 1, pp. 305–40.

Parzen, Emanuel. 1979. Nonparametric statistical data modeling (with discussion). *Journal of the American Statistical Association* 74: 105–31. [CrossRef]

Parzen, Emanuel. 1992. Time series, statistics, and information. In *New Directions in Time Series Analysis.* Edited by Emanuel Parzen, Murad Taqqu, David R. Brillinger, Peter Caines, John Geweke and Murray Rosenblatt. New York: Springer Verlag, pp. 265–86.

Parzen, Emanuel. 1997. Comparison distributions and quantile limit theorems. Paper presented at the International Conference on Asymptotic Methods in Probability and Statistics, Carleton University, Ottawa, ON, Canada, July 8–13.

Parzen, Emanuel, and Subhadeep Mukhopadhyay. 2012. Modeling, Dependence, Classification, United Statistical Science, Many Cultures. *arXiv.* arXiv:1204.4699.

Parzen, Emanuel, and Subhadeep Mukhopadhyay. 2013a. United Statistical Algorithms, LP comoment, Copula Density, Nonparametric Modeling. Paper presented at the 59th ISI World Statistics Congress (WSC) of the International Statistical Institute, Hong Kong, China, August 25–30.

Parzen, Emanuel, and Subhadeep Mukhopadhyay. 2013b. United Statistical Algorithms, Small and Big Data, Future of Statisticians. *arXiv.* arXiv:1308.0641.

Salmon, Felix. 2012. The formula that killed wall street. *Significance* 9: 16–20. [CrossRef]

Terasvirta, Timo, Dag Tjøstheim, and Clive W. J. Granger. 2010. *Modelling Nonlinear Economic Time Series.* Kettering: OUP Catalogue.

Tsay, Ruey S. 2010. *Analysis of Financial Time Series.* Hoboken: Wiley.

Tukey, John. 1980. Can we predict where "time series" should go next. In *Directions in Times Series.* Hayward: IMS, pp. 1–31.

Woodward, Wayne A., Henry L. Gray, and Alan C. Elliott. 2011. *Applied Time Series Analysis.* Boca Raton: CRC Press.

Journal of
Risk and Financial Management

MDPI

Article

How Informative Are Earnings Forecasts? †

Bert de Bruijn and Philip Hans Franses *

Econometric Institute, Erasmus School of Economics, Erasmus University Rotterdam, P.O. Box 1738,
NL-3000 DR Rotterdam, The Netherlands; lpdebruin@gmail.com
*   Correspondence: franses@ese.eur.nl; Tel.: +31-10-4081273; Fax: +31-10-4089162
†   Wharton Research Data Services (WRDS) was used in preparing this paper. This service and the
    data available thereon constitute valuable intellectual property and trade secrets of WRDS and/or
    its third-party suppliers.

Received: 28 May 2018; Accepted: 26 June 2018; Published: 1 July 2018

Abstract: We constructed forecasts of earnings forecasts using data on 406 firms and forecasts made
by 5419 individuals with on average 25 forecasts per individual. We verified previously found
predictors, which are the average of the most recent available forecast for each forecaster and the
difference between the average and the forecast that this forecaster previously made. We extended
the knowledge base by analyzing the unpredictable component of the earnings forecast. We found
that for some forecasters the unpredictable component can be used to improve upon the predictable
forecast, but we also found that this property is not persistent over time. Hence, a user of the forecasts
cannot trust that the forecaster will remain to be of forecasting value. We found that, in general,
the larger is the unpredictable component, the larger is the forecast error, while small unpredictable
components can lead to gains in forecast accuracy. Based on our results, we formulate the following
practical guidelines for investors: (i) for earnings analysts themselves, it seems to be the safest to not
make large adjustments to the predictable forecast, unless one is very confident about the additional
information; and (ii) for users of earnings forecasts, it seems best to only use those forecasts that do
not differ much from their predicted values.

Keywords: earnings forecasts; earnings announcements; financial markets; financial analysts

JEL Classification: G17; G24; M41.

---

1. Introduction

Earnings forecasts can provide useful information for investors. When investors in part rely on
such forecasts, it is important to have more insights into how such earnings forecasts are created. A key
research subject therefore concerns the drivers of the forecasts of earnings analysts. Such knowledge is
relevant as the part that can be predicted from factors that are also observable to the end user of the
forecast might not be the most interesting part of an earnings forecast. Indeed, it is the unpredictable
component of the earnings forecast that amounts to the forecaster's true added value, based on latent
expertise and domain-specific knowledge. Consequently, in our perspective, the evaluation of the
quality of earnings forecasts should mainly focus on that unpredictable part, as that is truly the added
value of the professional forecaster.

There is much literature on the properties and accuracy of earnings forecasts, but there is no
research that focuses on the prediction of such forecasts. Which variables are the most relevant drivers
of earnings forecasts? Can we use the unpredictable part of the forecast to improve forecasts? In this
paperm we answer these questions using appropriate models. We applied these models to the earnings
forecasts for a large number of firms which constitute the S&P500. Using this large sample of firms,
we are confident to draw a few generalizing conclusions.

A key predictor of the earnings forecasts appears to be the average of all available earnings forecasts concerning the same forecast event. As an example, consider a forecaster who has produced his most recent forecast some time ago. If in the meantime information has been provided on the firm that has driven the forecasts of all (other) forecasters down, this forecaster will also on average produce a lower-valued forecast than before. A second predictor is the most recent difference between the individual forecaster's forecast and the average of the available contemporaneous forecasts. For example, a forecaster who previously was more optimistic about the earnings of a particular firm can be expected to persist in quoting above-average values. Other important conclusions that we draw from the data are that more unpredictable forecasts tend to be less accurate, and that the unpredictable component of the forecast can be used to improve the forecast. Overall, we document that earnings forecasts are quite predictable from data that are also available to the end user.

The outline of our paper is as follows. In Section 2, we develop several hypotheses to guide our empirical analysis, and we base these hypotheses on available studies, reviewed in Section 2. In Section 3, we discuss the data and, in Sections 4 and 5, we present our results. Section 6 concludes and provides various avenues for further research.

2. Literature Review

Earnings forecasts have been the topic of interest for many researchers. For an extensive discussion of research on earnings forecasts in the period 1992–2007, see Ramnath et al. (2008). For earlier overviews, we refer to Schipper (1991) and Brown (1993).

One stream of earnings forecasts research has focused on relationships between forecast performance and forecaster characteristics. Performance can be measured by forecast accuracy and forecast impact on stock market fluctuations. The characteristics of these performance measurements have been related to timeliness (Cooper et al. 2001; Kim et al. 2011), the number of firms that the analyst follows (Bolliger 2004; Kim et al. 2011), the firm-specific experience of the analyst (Bolliger 2004), age (Bolliger 2004), the size of the firm being followed and of the firm at which the analyst works (Bolliger 2004; Kim et al. 2011), and whether the analyst works individually or in a team (Brown and Hugon 2009).

Another stream of research concerns the value of an earnings forecast and how it is related to what other analysts do. In particular, herding behavior is considered, which occurs when forecasters produce forecasts that converge towards the average of those of the other forecasters. There has been an effort to categorize earnings forecasters into two groups, corresponding to leaders and followers or to innovators and herders (Clement and Tse 2005; Jegadeesh and Woojin 2010). This is interesting as different types of forecasters might consult different amounts of information which in turn can be useful for investors to incorporate into their investment decisions. A leading or innovating forecaster might on average be more useful to follow than a herding forecaster. This does not directly imply that leading forecasts are also more accurate, as accuracy and the type of forecast are not necessarily related. In fact, it has been documented that aggregation of leading forecasts is a fruitful tactic to produce accurate forecasts (Kim et al. 2011).

Recently, Clement et al. (2011) studied the effect of stock returns and other analysts' forecasts on what analysts do. In contrast to Jegadeesh and Woojin (2010) and Clement and Tse (2005), Clement et al. (2011) did not consider categorizing the forecasters into different groups. Instead, they considered how the first forecast revision after a forecast announcement is affected by how the stock market and other analysts have reacted to that forecast announcement. Landsman et al. (2012) also looked at how earnings announcements affect the stock market, focusing on how mandatory IFRS adoption has influenced this effect. Sheng and Thevenot (2012) proposed a new earnings forecast uncertainty measure, which they use to demonstrate that forecasters focus more on the information in the earnings announcement if there is high uncertainty in the available set of earnings forecasts.

In sum, earnings forecasts have been studied concerning their performance and a few of their potential drivers. In this paper, we extend the knowledge base by considering many more drivers of earnings forecasts, while we pay specific attention to the value of the unpredictable component of earnings forecasts.

3. Data and Sample Selection

Data were collected from WRDS[1], using the I/B/E/S database for the analyst forecasts and the CRSP data for the stock prices and returns.

Concerning the earnings forecasts, we collected data for all firms which have been part of the S&P500 during the period 1995–2011. This amounts to 658 firms due to mergers, name changes and entry and exit of firms. We focused on the within-year yearly earnings forecasts, that is, the forecasts that are produced to forecast the earnings of the current year. The structure of the data is characterized in Figure 1. This figure shows a cross for the moment an analyst makes a forecast available, which is not at the same moment or with the same frequency for all analysts. Next, this figure shows that there are variables which we measured at the highest frequency. As an example, the returns are shown, which we measured daily. Finally, this figure shows vertical lines depicting the moment of the earnings announcement, at which point the realization occurs of the variable that is to be forecasted by the analysts. We only used within-year earnings forecasts, which means that we only included forecasts that are forecasting the variable announced at the next upcoming yearly earnings announcement.

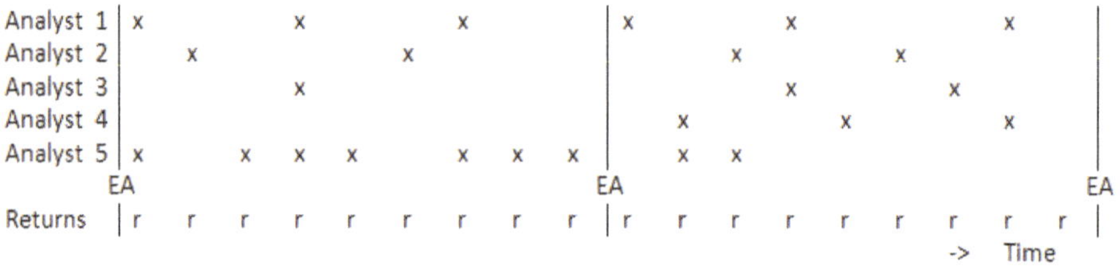

Figure 1. An example of the data format, with x indicating an earnings forecast and EA indicating when a new yearly earnings announcement takes place. This figure shows for five forecasters for two years a variety of hypothetical patterns of forecasts, including analysts that follow a very regular forecasting pattern, or the opposite, and including forecasters that quit producing forecasts or that joined a later year.

For several reasons, we had to omit some of the data at different parts of the rest of the paper. For example, we linked the earnings data to the stock data where possible, but for some firms this link could not be established. In addition, we had a threshold for the number of observations that we wanted at minimum for each regression or correlation. For these reasons and other, smaller reasons, the initial sample was cut down to 316 firms. Some descriptives of the remaining sample are shown in Table 1. The large drop in number of forecasters and forecasts in Sections 5.2 and 5.3 are due to the fact that we used forecaster-specific regressions and correlations in these sections, meaning that the majority of forecasters (those with only a few observations) dropped out.

Table 1. The number of firms, forecasters and forecasts for each upcoming section and subsection. The number of forecasts is shown separately for the estimation sample, which is up until 2005, and the evaluation sample, which is from 2006 onwards.

	Number of Firms	Number of Forecasters	Number of Forecasts	
			Estimation Sample	Evaluation Sample
Sections 4 and 5.1	316	18,338	146,319	126,651
Section 5.2	316	1835	52,236	36,403
Section 5.3	316	4541	90,190	28,000

---

[1] http://wrds-web.wharton.upenn.edu/wrds/.

4. Predicting Earnings Forecasts

In this section, we put forward a model to predict earnings forecasts using information available up until the day before the publication of the earnings forecast. First, we introduce the prediction equation that we used to predict the earnings forecast, and the variables that were included, for which we give estimation results. Next, we also discuss and apply a correction to account for the firms with a low number of observations.

4.1. The Prediction Equation, the Choice of Predictors and Estimation Results

For predicting the earnings forecast, we utilized a linear equation. In contrast to Stickel (1990), we were not interested in the change in the earnings forecast compared to the previous forecast, but focused on the earnings forecast directly. The set of predictors consists of several variables that were also used by Stickel (1990), as well as others. The full list of predictors can be found in Table 2.

First, we expected forecasters to produce similar forecasts at similar times, both because they use roughly the same information to form the forecast and because they might even look at the values of competing forecasters. Thus, we used as predictor the average of all most recent forecasts per individual forecaster, in which we only included forecasts that have been made for the same year.

We also included several variables that are related to the average forecast. First, the average forecast might contain more information if it is based on a larger number of forecasters. To see whether this holds, we also include a cross product of the average forecast with an indicator function, that is 1 if the number of forecasters is below 10 and 0 otherwise. The average forecast might also be more relevant the closer we are to the announcement of the true value of the earnings. For this, we add a cross product with an indicator function for the last two weeks before the announcement. The final predictor related to the average forecast is the day-to-day growth. If the average forecast has risen on one day, that might cause individual forecasters to extrapolate this growth to the next day.

We also included several variables that are related to the stock market. First, we included the stock index of the firm for which these earnings are predicted, because stock market value might be related to earnings expectations, and this might not be entirely represented by the average forecast yet. In addition, recent increases in the stock market value might be a expected to continue according to an individual forecaster, so we also included stock market returns. We included two different returns: the daily return and the return relative to the previous time that individual produced a forecast. Next to these three firm-related stock market variables, we also included similar variables based on the entire S&P500 index.

Finally, we included two variables that are determined by the previous forecast of this forecaster. The first of these two is this previous forecast itself, and the other is the difference between this previous forecast and the average forecast at that time. These two variables allow for persistence in the opinion of the forecaster, for example if this forecaster is systematically more optimistic or pessimistic.

We estimated the prediction equation using Ordinary Least Squares for all firms, and aggregated estimation results across firms are shown in Table 3. The first five columns show results on the aggregated raw estimate, including the mean, the median and the standard deviation of the estimates across all firms and also the 5% and 95% percentiles. The next two columns depict the aggregated standardized estimates, which are the estimates that are found if the variables are first all standardized. This measure can be helpful for comparing contribution to fit, as shown in the final column.

Table 2. The variables that were used to forecast the earnings forecast. These variables enter a linear model. They all use one-day lagged information. Several variables are based on historic analyst behaviour, while others are based on stock market data.

	Variable	Description
	Intercept	
Analyst variables	Average Forecast	The average of all most recent forecasts of every forecaster, until the previous day *Average Forecast is also included in a multiplication with two indicator variables:*
		1. Whether the number of forecasters is lower than 10 or not
		2. Whether the time until the announcement of the earnings is more than two weeks or not
	Δ Average Forecast	First difference in Average Active Forecast
	Δ Previous Forecast	The difference between the previous forecast of the forecaster, and the average active forecast at that time
	Previous Forecast	The previous forecast of the individual forecaster
Stock variables	Stock Index Firm	The stock market index of the firm for which the earnings are forecasted
	Stock Returns Firm	The stock market daily returns of the firm for which the earnings are forecasted
	Cumulative Stock Returns Firm	Stock market returns of the firm since the day of the previous forecast by this forecaster
	Stock Index S&P500	The stock market index of the S&P500 index
	Stock Returns S&P500	The stock market daily returns of the S&P500 index
	Cumulative Stock Returns S&P500	Stock market returns of the S&P500 index since the day of the previous forecast by this forecaster

Table 3. A summary of estimation results of forecasting earnings forecasts. Results are for the estimation sample, which amounts to 316 firms, 18.338 forecasters and 146.319 forecasts (on average slightly more than 463 forecasts per firm). As variable to be explained, we used the earnings forecasts by the analysts. As explanatory variables, we included the variables mentioned in Table 2. The regression was run individually for each firm, and the table shows statistics which summarize these results. The first five columns contain summary results on the regular parameter estimates (average, median, standard deviation and bounds of a 90% interval). The last three columns show summarized results for the standardized estimate, which is included to compare contributions to fit. The standardized estimate is defined as the estimate that would have been obtained had the regressor been standardized beforehand (which is a transformation to having an average of zero and a standard deviation of one).

	Estimate					Standardized Estimate		
	Average	Median	Standard Deviation	Bounds of 90% Interval		Median	Median of Absolute	Contribution to Total Fit
Intercept	−0.028	−0.026	0.278	−0.395	0.229			
Analyst-based								
Average Forecast	1.050	1.077	0.384	0.557	1.483	0.490	0.491	96.9%
Average Forecast $\times$ $I[nrF < 10]$	0.018	0.005	0.172	−0.053	0.078	0.001	0.004	0.0%
Average Forecast $\times$ $I[TUA > 14]$	−0.038	−0.034	0.292	−0.212	0.058	−0.017	0.025	0.3%
Δ Average Forecast	0.765	0.607	1.053	−0.526	2.438	0.005	0.006	0.0%
Δ Previous Forecast	0.498	0.548	0.359	−0.151	1.051	0.029	0.030	0.4%
Previous Forecast	−0.046	−0.078	0.273	−0.388	0.375	−0.028	0.076	2.3%
Stock market								
Stock Index Firm	0.002	0.001	0.004	−0.001	0.007	0.009	0.013	0.1%
Stock Returns Firm	0.302	0.150	1.039	−0.264	1.291	0.005	0.007	0.0%
Cumulative Stock Returns Firm	0.054	0.018	0.206	−0.092	0.285	0.003	0.005	0.0%
Stock Index S&P500	0.000	0.000	0.002	−0.001	0.002	0.001	0.009	0.0%
Stock Returns S&P500	−0.214	−0.096	1.226	−2.155	1.421	−0.001	0.004	0.0%
Cumulative Stock Returns S&P500	−0.032	−0.006	0.238	−0.408	0.256	0.000	0.005	0.0%

The results show that, on average, the coefficient of the average forecast is about 1, which can be interpreted as a partial random walk (partial, because the new forecast is only one of the many forecasts on which the average is based). The distribution of this effect across firms indicates that the sign of the effect is consistently positive. None of the other variables have this property. In addition, looking at the contribution to the fit, it is clear that the average forecast triumphs all, with the previous forecast and its difference to the average forecast as distant second and third.

Next, Table 4 shows statistics on the *t*-Statistic. This table shows that all variables are significant for at least 20% of the firms, but it also repeats the finding that most of the variables are not consistent in the sign of their effect (and thus, the sign of their *t*-Statistic). Again, the average forecast performs very well, having the highest significance percentage, the highest median value of the *t*-Statistic and also being consistent in the sign of the *t*-Statistic. Next to this variable, the difference of the previous forecast to the average also stands out with a higher percentage significant and a high median value of the *t*-Statistic.

Table 4. A summary of *t*-Statistics when forecasting earnings forecasts. Results are for the estimation sample, which amounts to 316 firms, 18,338 forecasters and 146,319 forecasts (on average slightly more than 463 forecasts per firm). As variable to be explained, we used the earnings forecasts by the analysts. As explanatory variables, we included the variables mentioned in Table 2. The regression was run individually for each firm, and the table shows statistics which summarize these results.

		Median *t*-Statistic	Median Absolute of *t*-Statistic	Percentage Significant at 5% Level
	Intercept	−0.986	1.920	48.4%
Analyst-based	Average Forecast	9.865	9.865	96.4%
	Average Forecast × $I[nrF < 10]$	0.530	1.118	27.9%
	Average Forecast × $I[TUA > 14]$	−1.662	2.212	51.6%
	Δ Average Forecast	1.680	1.766	47.2%
	Δ Previous Forecast	4.794	4.794	78.0%
	Previous Forecast	−0.804	1.599	38,6%
Stock market	Stock Index Firm	1.928	2.402	55.8%
	Stock Returns Firm	1.378	1.653	40.1%
	Cumulative Stock Returns Firm	0.730	1.329	32.9%
	Stock Index S&P500	0.151	1.928	49.3%
	Stock Returns S&P500	−0.395	1.192	24.9%
	Cumulative Stock Returns S&P500	−0.110	1.196	26.7%

4.2. Correction for Sampling Error in Case of a Low Number of Observations

In the previous subsection, we show that several variables are inconsistent in the sign of their effect. The most straightforward explanation for this result is of course that this finding is true and that, for example, for some firms, the value of the stock index has a positive effect on the earnings forecast of a forecaster, while for other firms this effect is negative. The latter relation seems counter-intuitive, and for some of the other variables one of the signs is also counter-intuitive, so in this subsection we investigate a different cause for this disparity.

One other explanation for having a few estimates with a unexpected sign might be that these estimates do not correspond to the true value, but that the estimates has been distorted by sampling bias more than other estimates have. This will be the case for firms for which we have only a few observations (just above our cut-off point of 10 valid data points). For these firms, the accuracy of the estimated variables might not be high. We could discard them, but then these firms would also not be a part of the analyses in the next section. Instead, we corrected the estimates for the firms with a low number of observations in such a way that the estimates for firms with a high number of observations will not be affected.

To do this, we assumed that the collection of firm-specific (population) parameters for one of the variables corresponds to a normal distribution. For now, assume that we know the values of mu and sigma. The effect of this is that there are two sources of information on the value of each individual β_i: first, the estimated least squares coefficient, but next to that also this common distribution. The optimal choice is a weighted average of these two values, with weights determined by the standard error of the estimated coefficient and the standard deviation in the underlying distribution. For firms with only a few observations, the weight for the estimated coefficient will be low, and the best estimate will be relatively close to the mean of the common distribution, which we can then use in the rest of the paper. On the other hand, for firms with many observations, the weight of the estimated coefficient will be high and the best estimate will not deviate much from the OLS estimation.

In application, we do not know the values of mu and sigma. For this, we applied an iterative process. First, these values were initialized on the sample mean and standard deviation of all OLS estimates. Then, we adjusted the estimates using the previously discussed weights. After adjustment, we used the weighted mean and weighted standard deviation to construct a new value of mu and sigma, with weights that are equal to the reciprocal of the estimated standard error. This was again followed by a new adjustment of the estimated parameters, and then again the calculation of a new set of mu and sigma. We did this until convergence.

After applying the above discussed correction, we ended up with the aggregated results in Table 5. Comparing this table with Table 3, we can see that (as can be expected) the average and median values have not changed much. The standard deviation and the width of the 90% interval on the other hand have clearly decreased. There are now more variables that are (almost) consistent in their estimated sign, and among them is the previously discussed parameter of the stock market index (both firm-specific and S&P500). On the other hand, the contribution to the fit has stayed about the same.

Table 5. A summary of estimation results of forecasting earnings forecasts, after using the correction method to account for small-sample error. Results are for the estimation sample, which amounts to 316 firms, 18,338 forecasters and 146,319 forecasts (on average slightly more than 463 forecasts per firm). As variable to be explained, we used the earnings forecasts by the analysts. As explanatory variables, we included the variables mentioned in Table 2. The regression was run individually for each firm, and the table shows statistics which summarize these results. The first five columns contain summary results on the regular parameter estimates (average, median, standard deviation and bounds of a 90% interval). The last three columns show summarized results for the standardized estimate, which is included to compare contributions to fit. The standardized estimate is defined as the estimate that would have been obtained had the regressor been standardized beforehand (which is a transformation to having an average of zero and a standard deviation of one). The correction method is based on the assumption of an underlying distribution out of which each variable (for the different firms) is drawn. This provides additional information on the firm-specific estimate especially in the case when the firm has only a few observations.

	Estimate			Bounds of 90% Interval		Standardized Estimate		
	Average	Median	Standard Deviation			Median	Median of Absolute	Contribution to Total Fit
Analyst-based								
Intercept	−0.019	−0.021	0.051	−0.113	0.068			
Average Forecast	1.097	1.094	0.134	0.880	1.287	0.479	0.479	98.5%
Average Forecast × $I[nrF < 10]$	0.003	0.004	0.011	−0.012	0.019	0.001	0.002	0.0%
Average Forecast × $I[TUA > 14]$	−0.048	−0.040	0.063	−0.161	0.018	−0.019	0.022	0.2%
Δ Average Forecast	0.741	0.687	0.409	0.148	1.444	0.005	0.005	0.0%
Δ Previous Forecast	0.553	0.564	0.192	0.206	0.865	0.029	0.029	0.4%
Previous Forecast	−0.081	−0.087	0.120	−0.253	0.117	−0.031	0.044	0.8%
Stock market								
Stock Index Firm	0.001	0.001	0.001	0.000	0.002	0.009	0.009	0.0%
Stock Returns Firm	0.160	0.120	0.175	−0.043	0.508	0.005	0.005	0.0%
Cumulative Stock Returns Firm	0.016	0.013	0.022	−0.013	0.055	0.002	0.003	0.0%
Stock Index S&P500	0.000	0.000	0.000	0.000	0.000	0.000	0.005	0.0%
Stock Returns S&P500	−0.087	−0.081	0.214	−0.410	0.251	−0.001	0.001	0.0%
Cumulative Stock Returns S&P500	−0.002	−0.002	0.036	−0.065	0.060	0.000	0.002	0.0%

5. Using the Predictable and Unpredictable Component

In this section, we analyze the use of both the predictable and unpredictable component. We do this first for all forecasts in general, then in a way in which we can compare forecasters, and finally in a way in which we can compare a single forecast compared to other forecasts by the same forecaster.

5.1. Comparison in General

In this subsection, we look at the use of the predictable and unpredictable component in general over all firms. First, we compare the performance of the analyst forecasts (which are equal to the sum of the predictable and unpredictable component) with the model forecasts (which are just the predictable component). Next, we look at the performance of large unpredictable components in comparison to smaller ones. Finally, we look at whether we can use the unpredictable component in a better way than just adding it to the predictable component, such as by using different weights.

5.1.1. Do the Analyst Forecasts Perform Better than the Model?

Table 6 shows statistics on the median ratio of squared analyst forecast error over squared model forecast error per firm, where the model forecast is equal to the predictable component. The difference between these two sets of forecasts is the unpredictable component, so, if this performance ratio is different from 1 in either direction, that is due to this unpredictable component. The table shows this median ratio for both the estimation sample and the evaluation sample, and also for individual years. In the evaluation sample, we reused the model parameters that have been estimated using the estimation sample.

Table 6. A summary of results on median $\frac{FE^2}{PCE^2}$, the median ratio of squared analyst forecast error over squared predictable component error. The analyst forecast is the earnings forecast that is reported by an analyst, while the predictable component error is the error made if we use the part of the earnings forecast that we can predict beforehand as forecast. This ratio shows us whether the inclusion of the unpredictable component results in an improvement. We show results for 18,338 forecasters across 316 firms, separated for the estimation (146,319 forecasts) and evaluation (126,651 forecasts) samples. We take the median ratio per firm to not let a few situations in which the denominator is almost zero influence the measure much.

Period	Estimation Sample	Evaluation Sample
Average	0.609	0.638
Median	0.655	0.631
Standard Deviation	0.304	0.571
5% percentile	0.071	0.061
95% percentile	1.031	1.207

First, the performance ratio is for most firms below 1, which indicates that in general using the unpredictable component (in other words: the analyst forecast) improves the accuracy compared to using just the predictable component. Second, the spread is larger in the evaluation sample, which is not surprising given that the predictable component also in the evaluation sample is based on the model parameter estimates from the estimation sample, and the relation between this effect in both sample sets might differ for different firms.

Next, Table 7 shows the same ratio, but now for different segments of the year. The borders of these segments have been determined manually by looking at a daily graph over the year, and they correspond to the four periods between quarterly announcements and the three periods surrounding the quarterly announcements (except for the quarterly announcement that coincides with the yearly announcement that we are interested in). This table shows that the performance ratio increases throughout the year, which indicates that the unpredictable component has less positive influence late in the year than in the beginning. This might be due to an increase in the accuracy of the predictable component in the latter part of the year, since the predictable component is then based on the highest number of observations. Another reason might be that, at that point, most of the year has already happened, so there is not much left for a judgemental interpretation that could be incorporated in the unpredictable component.

Table 7. A summary of results on median $\frac{FE^2}{PCE^2}$, the median ratio of squared analyst forecast error over squared predictable component error. The analyst forecast is the earnings forecast that is reported by an analyst, while the predictable component error is the error made if we use the part of the earnings forecast that we can predict beforehand as forecast. This ratio shows us whether the inclusion of the unpredictable component results in an improvement or not. We show results for 18,338 forecasters across 316 firms, for a total number of 272,970 observations spread over seven periods in the year leading up to the earnings announcement. The seven periods roughly correspond to the periods around the quarterly earnings announcement (excluding the fourth quarter, which coincides with the announcement of the earnings of interest) and the four periods in-between. We take the median ratio per firm to not let a few situations in which the denominator is almost zero influence the measure much.

	During Q1	Announcement Q1	During Q2	Announcement Q2	During Q3	Announcement Q3	During Q4
Average	0.455	0.414	0.632	0.613	0.797	0.789	0.921
Median	0.335	0.350	0.640	0.625	0.808	0.750	0.887
Standard Deviation	0.464	0.329	0.351	0.379	0.411	0.683	0.552
5% percentile	0.020	0.025	0.077	0.088	0.166	0.180	0.266
95% percentile	1.170	1.032	1.136	1.209	1.463	1.378	1.581

5.1.2. Are There Properties of the Unpredictable Component That Are Associated with a Better Performance?

We also investigated whether there are characteristics of the unpredictable component that we find more frequent with a better performance. For this, we regressed the squared analyst forecast error on a constant, the unpredictable component and the squared unpredictable component. We did this directly as well as after the first applying one of two different standardization approaches. Standardization might be necessary because of differences in how predictable or unstable earnings of a particular firm might be, which would have an effect on both the squared analyst forecast error and the unpredictable components. The first standardization uses the variance of the predictable component for the firm, the second uses the variance of the unpredictable component. Results are shown in Table 8.

The left column of Table 8 shows the unstandardized results, while the other two column show both standardized results. In all cases, and for both the estimation and evaluation samples, the implied result for UC^2 is the same: the larger the squared unpredictable component, the larger the squared forecast error of the analyst forecast. In general, forecasts that are close to the predictable component perform better.

The story for whether a forecast is better off being higher or lower than the predictable component is not so clear. Using no standardization or the first standardization suggests that negative unpredictable components perform better, but the second standardization method gives no relationship (in the estimation sample) or the opposite relationship (in the evaluation sample).

Table 8. Regression of squared forecast error of the analyst earnings forecasts on the unpredictable component and its square: $FE^2 = \beta_0 + \beta_1 UC + \beta_2 UC^2$. We did this for all 316 firms and 18,338 forecasters simultaneously in two regressions, one for the estimation sample ($n = 146{,}319$) and one for the evaluation sample ($n = 126{,}651$). Next to the normal least-squares estimation of the above linear model, we also used two standardization methods to account for firm differences in the size of earnings and the uncertainty of earnings. Standardization 1 uses the variance of the predictable component per firm. Standardization 2 uses the variance of the unpredictable component per firm. Standard errors are in parentheses. Short summary: The parameter of UC^2 is in each case positive and around 1, which indicates that in general forecasts with a large unpredictable component are less accurate. The parameter of UC is not consistent for the different samples and standardization methods, which shows that there is no clear sign of larger errors for either higher-than-predicted or lower-than-predicted forecasts.

		No Standardization		Standardization 1		Standardization 2	
	intercept	0.116	(0.003)	0.079	(0.002)	0.419	(0.005)
Estimation sample	UC	0.539	(0.020)	0.257	(0.012)	−0.001	(0.012)
	UC^2	0.891	(0.011)	0.940	(0.008)	1.043	(0.004)
	R^2	0.044		0.085		0.346	
	intercept	0.777	(0.024)	0.163	(0.004)	1.052	(0.012)
Evaluation sample	UC	0.292	(0.054)	0.250	(0.015)	−0.947	(0.013)
	UC^2	0.980	(0.002)	1.006	(0.001)	1.006	(0.001)
	R^2	0.625		0.810		0.838	

5.1.3. Is There Additional Information in the Unpredictable Component That Can Be Used?

Table 9 shows estimation results of the regression of the actuals on different functions of the predictable and unpredictable component. We included cross terms with the number of forecasts, since the predictable component might be more accurate if it is based on a higher number of forecasts. We also included cross terms with the time until the announcement, since forecasts just before the announcement might have all information already incorporated into the predictable component with not much room for extra information left for the unpredictable part.

Several results from the table are interesting. First, the estimated parameters for just the predictable and the unpredictable component in the estimation sample seem to suggest that they need to be made more important than in the actual forecast (which is similar to the situation where both parameters are 1), but in actuality this is countered by the cross terms with the number of forecasts and the time until announcement, which are both strictly positive and have an associated negative parameter estimate. In fact, Figure 2 shows the effective parameters for both components throughout the year, both in the estimation and in the evaluation sample, and this figure demonstrates that the optimal contribution is always below 1 for both components. For the predictable component, the contribution is relatively stable throughout the year, while for the unpredictable component the contribution is highest in the beginning of the year.

Another result from Table 9 is that the predictable component parameters are all estimated more accurately than their unpredictable component counterparts, and the estimation results are more accurate in the estimation sample than in the evaluation sample.

Thus, this shows that the optimal contribution of the unpredictable component might be less than 1, in other words, less than what the analyst actually do. However, that does not mean that the unpredictable component does not contribute at all. Table 10 shows results on the F-test for the joint significance of the four parameter estimates related to the unpredictable component. In both sample periods, the median F-statistic is larger than 20, and the F-test rejects no significant effect at all in more than 90% of the cases. There are clear signs that the unpredictable component does add information.

Table 9. A summary of results of the regression of the actual earnings on predictable and unpredictable component variables: $Actual = \alpha + \beta PCV + \gamma UCV$. PCV not only includes the predictable component itself, but also multiplications of the predictable component with logNF, the logarithm of the number of forecasts on which Average Forecast is based at that moment, and, with logTUA, the logarithm of the number of days until the announcement. In a similar way, UCV is based on the unpredictable component and multiplications of unpredictable component with logNF and logTUA. We performed these regressions for each firm separately (of the 316 firms) but pooled the results of all 18,338 forecasters. The total number of observations in the regressions across all firms is 146,319 in the estimation sample and 126,651 in the evaluation sample. We show as summary of the results several statistics (average, median, standard deviation, and 90% interval) on the estimated parameters and also the average and median of the standard error of the parameters.

		Estimated Coefficient					Standard Error	
		Average	Median	Standard Deviation	Bounds of 90% Interval		Average	Median
Estimation sample	intercept	0.067	0.021	0.348	−0.243	0.509	0.034	0.020
	PC	1.060	1.099	3.815	−3.274	4.489	0.663	0.444
	PC*logNF	−0.018	−0.019	1.176	−0.980	1.240	0.233	0.152
	PC*logTUA	−0.020	−0.016	0.704	−0.582	0.834	0.122	0.081
	PC*logNF*logTUA	0.004	0.004	0.215	−0.249	0.182	0.043	0.027
	UC	2.400	1.506	24.167	−34.384	40.469	11.212	10.087
	UC*logNF	−0.663	−0.456	8.279	−13.757	12.491	4.005	3.460
	UC*logTUA	−0.198	0.028	4.458	−7.161	6.155	2.068	1.836
	UC*logNF*logTUA	0.082	0.029	1.543	-2.411	2.530	0.744	0.646
Evaluation sample	intercept	0.394	0.278	0.972	−0.498	1.704	0.067	0.046
	PC	0.054	0.711	5.900	−8.086	5.740	0.950	0.506
	PC*logNF	0.242	0.068	1.888	−1.590	2.451	0.326	0.174
	PC*logTUA	0.084	0.027	0.988	−0.959	1.272	0.172	0.095
	PC*logNF*logTUA	−0.024	−0.006	0.321	−0.367	0.343	0.059	0.033
	UC	−2.370	−2.213	43.991	−52.879	50.791	13.371	9.822
	UC*logNF	0.712	0.793	14.559	−18.921	16.258	4.661	3.402
	UC*logTUA	0.811	0.655	7.789	−9.058	9.518	2.435	1.832
	UC*logNF*logTUA	−0.224	−0.229	2.584	−3.003	3.002	0.853	0.631

Table 10. A summary of results on the comparison between the regressions: of (1) $Actual = \alpha + \beta PC$, the actual earnings on only predictable component variables; and (2) $Actual = \alpha + \beta PCV + \gamma UC$, the actual earnings on both the predictable and unpredictable component variables. We performed these regressions for each firm separately (of the 316 firms) but pooled the results of all 18,338 forecasters. The total number of observations in the regressions across all firms is 146,319 in the estimation sample and 126,651 in the evaluation sample. The F-Statistic is based on the test for the joint significance of γ, the parameters of the unpredictable component variables, and the results for the associated P-value are shown in the column labeled P-value. The summarized results for the R^2 values for both the restricted and the unrestricted model are also shown.

	Estimation Sample				Evaluation Sample			
	F-Statistic	P-Value	R^2 without UC	R^2 with UC	F-Statistic	P-Value	R^2 without UC	R^2 with UC
Average	33.776	0.015	0.868	0.893	29.292	0.039	0.817	0.850
Median	21.554	0.000	0.918	0.935	20.794	0.000	0.878	0.901
Standard Deviation	44.568	0.103	0.155	0.129	30.484	0.164	0.180	0.155
5% percentile	3.066	0.000	0.554	0.610	1.442	0.000	0.422	0.508
95% percentile	101.095	0.032	0.997	0.997	85.891	0.233	0.988	0.993
Significant at 5% level	96.2%				91.8%			

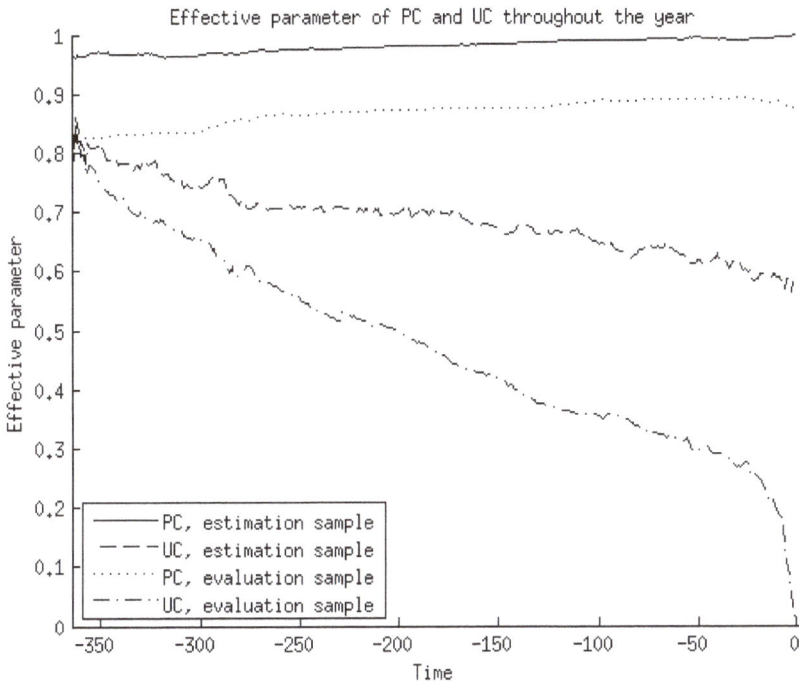

Figure 2. The effective parameter of the predictable and unpredictable component in forecasting the actual earnings throughout the year (with earnings announcement at $t = 0$), after filling in average actual values for the number of forecasts and time until announcement across all firms and all years in the estimation or evaluation sample.

Now that we know that the unpredictable component does contribute, we can take a look at how much it contributes. Table 10 also shows the R^2 both when just using the predictable component variables and when also including the unpredictable component variables, for both sample periods. The increase in median R^2 is about 2–3%, which is not much, while the median R^2 using just the predictable variables is already around 90% so there is not much left to be explained.

Finally, we look at the comparison of the accuracy of this optimal forecast to the analyst forecast and model forecast, as shown in Table 11. What can be seen is that the ratios that include the error of the optimal forecast are smaller than 1 for the samples for which the optimal relation has been determined (so when using estimation sample parameters for the estimation sample data, or evaluation sample parameters for the evaluation sample data). On the other hand, when we reuse the estimation sample parameters for the evaluation sample data, the ratio is larger than 1 compared to both the model forecast and the analyst forecast, indicating that the optimal relation is not stable over time and needs to be re-estimated regularly.

Table 11. A summary of results on the median ratios between two squared errors. Used are combinations of the following: FE^2, the squared analyst forecast error; PCE^2, the squared error of using the predictable component as forecast; and OE^2, the squared error of the optimal combination of the predictable component and unpredictable component variables. We calculated these median ratios for each firm separately (of the 316 firms) but pooled the ratios of all 18,338 forecasters. The total number of observations across all firms is 146,319 in the estimation sample and 126,651 in the evaluation sample. We calculated some ratios in the evaluation sample twice: once with the weights (used in the construction of the optimal forecast) as estimated in the estimation sample, and once using weights based on the evaluation sample itself.

	Estimation Sample with Estimation Sample Weights			Evaluation Sample with Estimation Sample Weights			Evaluation Sample with Evaluation Sample Weights	
	$\dfrac{FE^2}{PCE^2}$	$\dfrac{OE^2}{PCE^2}$	$\dfrac{OE^2}{FE^2}$	$\dfrac{FE^2}{PCE^2}$	$\dfrac{OE^2}{PCE^2}$	$\dfrac{OE^2}{FE^2}$	$\dfrac{OE^2}{PCE^2}$	$\dfrac{OE^2}{FE^2}$
Average	0.609	0.669	1.499	0.638	2.878	7.463	0.570	1.123
Median	0.655	0.532	0.877	0.631	1.107	2.165	0.311	0.591
Standard Deviation	0.304	1.206	4.425	0.571	5.703	18.399	3.097	5.330
5% percentile	0.071	0.059	0.279	0.061	0.142	0.642	0.031	0.164
95% percentile	1.031	1.371	3.437	1.207	10.102	33.621	0.943	1.757

5.2. Comparison Across Forecasters

In this subsection, we aspire to find estimation sample properties of forecasters that are linked with a superior performance or a more informative unpredictable component in the evaluation sample.

5.2.1. Is It Possible to Select Forecasters Who Can Be Predicted to Outperform the Model?

First, we look at the performance of individual forecasters. A first idea might be to use again the median ratio of squared analyst forecast error to squared model forecast error as measure. This leads to a low number of forecasts on which each individual median ratio is based. In fact, it occasionally happens that the median ratio is dominated by a few observations for which either of the squared errors is almost zero. We instead want to have a more confined measure that results in a smaller interval of numbers, but that still maintains the property that a lower number means a better performance. For this, we use the balanced relative difference: $BRD(A, M) = \dfrac{AFE^2 - MFE^2}{AFE^2 + MFE^2}$.

Table 12 depicts the regression of the balanced relative difference between the analyst and model forecasts in the evaluation sample on an intercept, the ratio of the squared unpredictable component to the squared predictable component in the estimation sample and three balanced relative differences in the estimation sample: the $BRD(A, M)$ itself, but also $BRD(U, M) = \dfrac{UC^2 - MFE^2}{UC^2 + MFE^2}$ and $BRD(O, M) = \dfrac{OFE^2 - MFE^2}{OFE^2 + MFE^2}$. Three variables show significant results: first, $BRD(A, M)$ in the evaluation sample is significantly related to its previous value in the estimation sample, and, second, it is related to the previous value of the relative size of the unpredictable component to the predictable component and to the previous value of BRD(U,M). The results show that the forecasters that will predict best in the evaluation sample are those that have predicted best in the estimation sample, that have a small unpredictable component relative to the predictable component and that have a small unpredictable component relative to the error of the predictable component. Of these, the autoregressive type variable has the result that has the most statistical significance.

Table 12. The results for the regressions to predict better analysts in the evaluation sample using variables in the evaluation sample. This is based on 1835 forecasters (since we only include forecasters with a minimum of 10 observations in both sample periods) with a total of 52,236 forecasts in the estimation sample and 36,403 forecasts in the evaluation sample. We put the data across all firms in one regression. We used two interpretations for what a better analyst is: an analyst that has a smaller forecast error compared to the predicted component ("better performing") and an analyst whose associated optimally constructed forecasts have smaller forecast errors compared to the predicted component error ("having more information"). These might overlap if the forecasters with more information also used them well (so if the optimal forecast is similar to the analyst forecast), but there could also be forecasters that do not use their information well, which is why we separate these measures. In these regressions we used the balanced relative difference: $BRD(x, y) = \frac{x-y}{x+y}$ with x and y being combinations of A (for the analyst forecast error, FE^2), P (for the predictable component error, PCE^2), O (for the optimal forecast error, OE^2) and U (for the squared unpredictable component, UC^2). As performance variable, we used $BRD(A, P)$, while we used $BRD(O, P)$ as information variable. The variables to be explained were measured in the evaluation sample, while the regressors were measured in the estimation sample. Standard errors are shown in parentheses. Short conclusion: (1) Better performing forecasters (low value of $BRD(A, P)$) can be predicted by looking at historically better performing forecasters and at forecasters that have relatively small unpredictable components (compared to PC^2); and (2) forecasters that have more usable information (low value of $BRD(O, P)$) can be predicted by looking at forecasters that historically have more information and forecasters that performed better.

	Variable to Explain			
	$BRD(A, P)$		$BRD(O, P)$	
intercept	−0.174	(0.020)	−0.003	(0.022)
$\frac{UC^2}{PC^2}$	1.152	(0.398)	0.244	(0.440)
BRD(U,P)	−0.098	(0.029)	−0.148	(0.032)
BRD(A,P)	0.407	(0.035)	0.302	(0.038)
BRD(O,P)	0.042	(0.026)	0.266	(0.029)

We can use the above regression to produce forecasts of the median balanced relative difference of each forecaster, and then compare the actual errors of the half that has the best performance prediction to the half that is predicted to perform worst. The ratio of the median squared error of the best 50% to the median squared error of the worst 50% is 0.600. In addition, the predicted probabilities of having a negative balanced relative difference (in other words: the probabilities of outperforming the model) are, on average, 80.8% and 61.9% for the best and worst half, respectively. This shows that it is possible to select a subset of all forecasters that will perform better in future that the entire set does.

5.2.2. Is It Possible to Select Forecasters Who Can Be Predicted to Have More Information in Their Unpredictable Component?

Next, we used a similar approach to investigate whether it is possible to select forecasters that have more useful information in their unpredictable component, in other words, for which the optimal forecast performs best. For this, we used again a balanced relative difference, for the same reasons as above. We again used a regression and we reused the regressors. The variable to be explained in this case was $BRD(O, M)$ in the evaluation sample. The results are also shown in Table 12.

Similar to the previous regression, again the autoregressive type variable is statistically most significant. The other two significant regressors are the other two balanced relative differences: $BRD(U, M)$ and $BRD(A, M)$. The forecasters with the most useful information (low $BRD(O, M)$) in the evaluation sample are those with the most useful information in the estimation sample that are most accurate in the estimation sample and, surprisingly, that have a large unpredictable component compared to the model error. We can again do as before, and compare the actual optimal forecast errors of two groups that are predicted to have the most and the least information. The relative median squared optimal forecast error is 0.566. It is possible to select a subset of the forecasters that contains those that have more informative unpredictable components.

5.2.3. Are the Informative Forecasters and the Performant Forecasters the Same?

One might wonder whether there is a significant overlap between the informative and the best-performant forecasters. To investigate this, we calculated the hit rate: the percentage of cases in which a forecaster is categorized in the same group for both measures. This hit rate is 85.4%, showing that there is definitely a pattern that the better forecasters also tend to have more information in their unpredictable components.

5.3. Comparison within Forecasters

In this subsection, we look at individual forecasts and compare their properties to other forecasts by the same forecaster. For example, the same large unpredictable component might be much more surprising if produced by someone who always has small unpredictable components than if produced by someone else who tends to produce large unpredictable components regularly. In the former case, this might indicate that this individual forecast is based on unique and important information, but it might also mean that the forecaster just has an off-day. Which of those two is true in different situations is what we investigate in this section.

First, we restricted ourselves to just the evaluation sample. The situation of comparing forecasts to other forecasts by the same forecasters meant that we often had only a few observations to compare against, and this limited us in what we can do. We did the following: we calculated for just the forecasts of one forecaster the correlation of the size of the unpredictable component with balanced relative difference variables: $BRD(A, M)$, $BRD(O, M)$ and $BRD(O, A)$, of which the latter is defined as $BRD(O, A) = \dfrac{OFE^2 - AFE^2}{OFE^2 + AFE^2}$. As measures for the size of the unpredictable component we used both $|UC|$ and UC^2. Aggregate results across all forecasters are shown in Table 13.

Table 13. A summary of results on the correlation between three balanced relative difference variables and two unpredictable component variables, calculated per individual forecaster. This is based on 4541 forecasters, with 90,190 forecasts in the estimation sample and 28,000 in the evaluation sample. We calculated the correlation of the UC-variables with three balanced relative difference variables, with the definition $BRD(x, y) = \frac{x-y}{x+y}$ with x and y being combinations of A (for the analyst forecast error, FE^2), P (for the predictable component error, PCE^2) and O (for the optimal forecast error, OE^2).

		Correlation with $|UC|$			Correlation with UC^2		
		$BRD(A,P)$	$BRD(O,P)$	$BRD(O,A)$	$BRD(A,P)$	$BRD(O,P)$	$BRD(O,A)$
Estimation sample	Average	−0.096	−0.185	−0.116	−0.069	−0.166	−0.121
	Median	−0.125	−0.214	−0.133	−0.124	−0.210	−0.146
	Standard Deviation	0.322	0.279	0.273	0.335	0.278	0.272
	5% percentile	−0.582	−0.598	−0.535	−0.559	−0.556	−0.526
	95% percentile	0.454	0.324	0.359	0.506	0.354	0.358
Evaluation sample	Average	−0.146	−0.122	0.033	−0.125	−0.105	0.030
	Median	−0.173	−0.129	0.049	−0.177	−0.116	0.046
	Standard Deviation	0.477	0.490	0.472	0.481	0.487	0.468
	5% percentile	−0.953	−0.967	−0.877	−0.954	−0.963	−0.863
	95% percentile	0.790	0.852	0.909	0.816	0.835	0.892

Table 13 shows, after summarizing, only negative correlations are found, which have varying interpretations. The negative correlations between the size variables of UC and $BRD(A, M)$ shows that large unpredictable components for that particular forecaster are associated with a better performance compared to the model which has no unpredictable component. Similarly, the negative correlations with $BRD(O, M)$ show that large unpredictable components are associated with more information in that unpredictable component. Finally, the negative correlations with $BRD(O, A)$ show that large unpredictable components are associated with a better optimal forecast than the actual analyst forecast, and thus with less optimal use of the unpredictable component by the analyst.

Table 13 also extends the discussion to the situation in the evaluation sample. In this case, not all correlations are again negative. The ones that are (the correlations with $BRD(A, M)$ and $BRD(O, M)$) result in the same conclusion as before: large unpredictable components are associated with a better performance and more information than smaller unpredictable components produced by the same forecaster. The positive correlation of $BRD(O, A)$ with the size of the unpredictable component indicates that, in this case, on aggregate, large unpredictable components tend to coincide with less room to optimize the use of the unpredictable component compared to the analyst forecast. This difference in result compared to the estimation sample might be due to a structural change over time in how forecaster behave, but a more plausible explanation might be that the parameter estimates that are used in the construction of the optimal forecast are not stable over time, which is what we have found in Section 5.1.3.

6. Conclusions

- Earnings forecasts are an important factor in the decision making process of investors. In this paper we have shown that earnings forecasts can be predicted, which allows investors to already incorporate the predictable part in their investment decision. Furthermore, we also show that the unpredictable part of an earnings forecast can be used. One way to use it, is to improve the forecast based on just the predictable part. This is especially beneficial in the beginning of the year. Another use of the predictable and unpredictable components concerns the selection of earnings forecasters, which can be relevant if an investor wants to ignore the forecasters with a poor track record. We have shown that there is persistence in the performance of forecasters compared to the predictable component, that is, earnings forecasters who perform better in our estimation sample, also perform better, on average, in the evaluation sample. Similarly, the information in the unpredictable component, that can be used to improve the optimal forecast, is also persistent, that is, earnings forecasters whose unpredictable components are more useful in the estimation sample also have this property in the evaluation sample.
- In general, large unpredictable components seem to be a bad sign, as they are associated with large relative forecast errors. This is not the case if the earnings forecaster normally produces small unpredictable components. In that case, a large unpredictable component is a sign of both good performance and more useful information in this unpredictable component.

Author Contributions: B.d.B. and P.H.F. desiged the data collection and research project. B.d.B. performed the computations. B.d.B. and P.H.F. jointly wrote the paper.

Acknowledgments: We thank Marno Verbeek, Bert de Groot, Peter Boswijk and three anonymous reviewers for helpful comments.

Conflicts of Interest: The authors declare no conflict of interest.

Appendix A

We conjecture that individual earnings forecasts can be forecasted using: (1) the average of the available forecasts; and (2) the difference between the previous forecast of the analyst and the average forecast at that time. We tested this hypothesis by regressing the earnings forecast on several explanatory variables, and we expected the regression coefficients to be positive and significant for both these variables. These two variables are depicted in the top panel of Table 2, along with other variables that we included in the regression (bottom panel), as discussed below. We describe the regression by using the notation:

$$y_{i,j,t} = X_{i,j,t}\beta_j + \varepsilon_{i,j,t},$$ (A1)

with subscript i denoting the individual forecaster, j the firm for which the earnings are forecasted and t the day on which the forecast is produced. The parameter coefficients are denoted by β_j, which is a vector consisting of $\beta_{j,k}$ for $k = 1, ..., K$, one parameter for each variable in $X_{i,j,t}$. We let the vector of parameter coefficients differ per firm, but not per individual nor for different time periods. In addition, the error variance $\sigma_{\varepsilon,j}^2$ differs per firm.

In addition to the two above-mentioned variables, we also included the first difference in the average of the active forecasts. Forecasters tend to herd (Clement and Tse 2005; Jegadeesh and Woojin 2010), but not every forecaster will respond during the same day, so that led us to suspect that some forecasters will respond one day later. We expect these herders to follow the trend and move in the same direction as the change in the previous day, so we expect the associated parameter to be positive.

Next, we also included the previous forecast, on top of already including the difference between the previous forecast and the average forecast at that time. Some forecasters might not be as influenced by what other forecasters do. Therefore, we do not want their relative forecast (compared to the average forecast), but the forecast itself as an additional predictor.

Finally, we also included some information about the stock market. If the stock market in general, or the market for the firm-specific stocks, is healthy, forecasters might be more positive on the future than if the situation is unhealthy. This also holds in the short-term case, which is why we expected the forecasts to be higher if the daily returns have been higher. This implies that we expected all associated signs to be positive.

For estimating this regression, we started with the standard Ordinary Least Squares (OLS). There might be some firms for which the results will differ greatly from the other firms due to outliers, especially if the number of forecasts for such a firm is not high. Extreme cases were left out of the sample, for which we used the criterion that none of the regression estimates should be more than four times the standard deviation away from the mean of that parameter. In addition, firms with fewer than 50 data points in the regression were left out. If we included these firms (with estimates based on a low number of data points, or with very outlying estimates), we would add noise to our results.

For the remaining firms, we introduced a latent variable model for β_j. We used this latent variable model to correct estimates that were estimated with just over 50 data points and thus were less accurate and more prone to outliers. These estimates could be adjusted towards the overall mean of that respective parameter, and we did that in such a way that estimates based on more than one thousand observations were hardly affected. As necessary assumption for this model, we used:

$$\beta_j \sim N(\beta^*, \Sigma_\beta) \tag{A2}$$

which means that the latent parameter vector β_j (the estimated parameters for firm j) is related to the overall mean parameter vector β^*. For simplicity, we assumed the covariance matrix Σ_β to be diagonal. Then, we employed the following steps:

1. The elements of β^* and Σ_β were estimated by taking the weighted average and weighted variance of all individual estimates.
2. We updated each individual estimate by taking a weighted average:

$$\beta_{j,k}^{(u)} = w_{j,k}\beta_k^* + (1 - w_{j,k})\beta_{j,k} \tag{A3}$$

$$w_{j,k} = \frac{\frac{1}{\sigma_{\beta,k}}}{\frac{1}{\sigma_{\beta,k}} + \frac{n_k}{\sigma_{\varepsilon,j}}} \tag{A4}$$

The weights were calculated using the inverses of the latent variable standard deviation and the standard error of the regression, as these determine how accurate both sources of information on the $\beta_{j,k}$ estimate are.

We repeat Equations (A3) and (A4) until convergence.

References

Bolliger, Guido. 2004. The characteristics of individual analysts' forecasts in Europe. *Journal of Banking & Finance* 28: 2283–309. [CrossRef]

Brown, Lawrence D. 1993. Earnings forecasting research: its implications for capital markets research. *International Journal of Forecasting* 9: 295–320. [CrossRef]

Brown, Lawrence D., and Artur Hugon. 2009. Team earnings forecasting. *Review of Accounting Studies* 14: 587–607. [CrossRef]

Clement, Michael B., Jeffrey Hales, and Yanfeng Xue. 2011. Understanding analysts' use of stock returns and other analysts' revisions when forecasting earnings. *Journal of Accounting and Economics* 51: 279–99. [CrossRef]

Clement, Michael B., and Senyo Y. Tse. 2005. Financial analyst characteristics and herding behavior in forecasting. *The Journal of Finance* 60: 307–41. [CrossRef]

Cooper, Rick A., Theodore E. Day, and Craig M. Lewis. 2001. Following the leader: A study of individual analysts' earnings forecasts. *Journal of Financial Economics* 61: 383–416. [CrossRef]

Jegadeesh, Narasimhan, and Kim Woojin. 2010. Do analysts herd? An analysis of recommendations and market reactions. *Review of Financial Studies* 23: 901–37. [CrossRef]

Kim, Yongtae, Gerald J. Lobo, and Minsup Song. 2011. Analyst characteristics, timing of forecast revisions, and analyst forecasting ability. *Journal of Banking & Finance* 35: 2158–68.

Landsman, Wayne R., Edward L. Maydew, and Jacob R. Thornock. 2012. The information content of annual earnings announcements and mandatory adoption of IFRS. *Journal of Accounting and Economics* 53: 34–54. [CrossRef]

Ramnath, Sundaresh, Steve Rock, and Philip Shane. 2008. The financial analyst forecasting literature: A taxonomy with suggestions for further research. *International Journal of Forecasting* 24: 34–75. [CrossRef]

Schipper, Katherine. 1991. Analysts' forecasts. *Accounting Horizons* 5: 105–21.

Sheng, Xuguang, and Maya Thevenot. 2012. A new measure of earnings forecast uncertainty. *Journal of Accounting and Economics* 53: 21–33. [CrossRef]

Stickel, Scott E. 1990. Predicting Individual Analyst Earnings Forecasts. *Journal of Accounting Research* 53: 409–17. [CrossRef]

Journal of
*Risk and Financial
Management*

MDPI

Article

FHA Loans in Foreclosure Proceedings: Distinguishing Sources of Interdependence in Competing Risks

Ran Deng [†] and Shermineh Haghani *,[†]

Office of the Comptroller of the Currency, 400 7th Street S.W., Washington, DC 20219, USA;
ran.deng@occ.treas.gov
* Correspondence: shermineh.haghani@occ.treas.gov; Tel.: +1-202-649-6296
† The views in this paper are those of the authors and do not necessarily reflect those of the Office of the Comptroller of the Currency or the Department of Treasury.

Received: 31 October 2017; Accepted: 18 December 2017; Published: 28 December 2017

Abstract: A mortgage borrower has several options once a foreclosure proceedings is initiated, mainly default and prepayment. Using a sample of FHA mortgage loans, we develop a dependent competing risks framework to examine the determinants of time to default and time to prepayment once the foreclosure proceedings is initiated. More importantly, we examine the interdependence between default and prepayment, through both the correlation of the unobserved heterogeneity terms and the preventive behavior of the individual mortgage borrowers. We find that time to default and time to prepayment are affected by several factors, such as the Loan-To-Value ratio (LTV), FICO score and unemployment rate. In addition, we find strong evidence that supports the existence of interdependence between the default and prepayment hazards through both the correlation of the unobserved heterogeneity terms and the preventive behavior of individual mortgage borrowers. We show that neglecting the interdependence through the preventive behavior of the individual mortgage borrowers can lead to biased estimates and misleading inference.

Keywords: FHA loan; home mortgage; foreclosure; default and prepayment; unobserved heterogeneity; duration models; competing risks

JEL Classification: C23; C24; C41; G21

1. Introduction

A mortgage borrower is technically delinquent once a monthly mortgage payment due date is missed. Most lenders, however, give the borrower a substantial period of time (typically 90 days, but varying by lender) to bring the loan into current status by making up all the missed payments plus the associated late fees. If the borrower is still delinquent after a certain time period, the lender initiates a foreclosure proceedings. Loans that are in foreclosure proceedings are not fully terminated. In fact, some of these loans can be reinstated, prepaid or modified (extended term or other alterations to lower the monthly payment), or have other alternative outcomes. These outcomes can be considered as competing risks. In this paper, we examine the lifetime of an FHA mortgage loan from the onset of foreclosure until one of the main types of outcomes is observed. In particular, we examine the probability that an FHA mortgage loan in a foreclosure proceedings will eventually be prepaid or defaulted to Real Estate Owned (REO).[1]

---

[1]   It is the U.S. Department of Housing and Urban Development (HUD) that takes ownership of any properties that complete the foreclosure process for FHA mortgage loans.

There is an extensive literature on mortgage terminations. The focus of most of the early studies was on mortgage terminations either due to prepayment (e.g., Green and Shoven 1986; Schwartz and Torous 1989; Quigley and Van Order 1990) or due to default (e.g., Cunningham and Hendershott 1984; Quigley and Van Order 1995), but not both. A number of theoretical papers emphasized the importance of jointly estimating default and prepayment (e.g., Kau and Keenan 1996; Titman and Torous 1989). The work in Foster and Van Order (1985) was among the first papers that simultaneously estimated both default and prepayment for FHA loans. The work in Schwartz and Torous (1993) applies Poisson regression to jointly estimate hazards for default and prepayment. The works in Deng et al. (1996) and Deng (1997) examine default and prepayment jointly using a competing risks model. The works in Deng et al. (2000) and Pennington-Cross (2006) also use a competing risks model, where they account for one possible type of interdependence between the default and prepayment hazards. This was through the correlation of associated unobserved heterogeneity terms for the purpose of capturing the unobservable loan-specific characteristics (such as the effect of borrowers' intentions and strategies) that affect both default and prepayment hazards. Such unobserved heterogeneity terms might induce either negative or positive interdependence between the default and prepayment hazards.

This paper adds to the existing literature by accounting for another possible type of interdependence between the default and prepayment hazards. This interdependence stems from the fact that the motives behind prepayments in the case of a mortgage for which the foreclosure proceedings is initiated are distinct from the traditional motives for prepayment. In particular, prepayments of a mortgage for which the foreclosure proceedings is initiated can be viewed as "distressed prepayments"[2] in which borrowers want to sell their homes to avoid a default outcome.[3] The reason to avoid default is its significant costs, such as legal fees and a negative credit report, that make prepayment a more attractive option to borrowers in foreclosure proceedings. Thus, if borrowers are in foreclosure proceedings and foresee themselves facing a high risk of default, they might increase their intensity to sell their homes to prepay, in order to avoid default. Such a kind of behavior by borrowers implies that higher risks of default might lead to higher probability of prepayment. This induces a positive correlation between the default and prepayment hazards.

In this paper, we specify a dependent competing risks framework to examine the interdependence between the default and prepayment hazards through both the correlation of the unobserved heterogeneity terms associated with each risk and the preventive behavior of individual mortgage borrowers. The interdependence between the hazards through the preventive behavior of individuals is referred to as the "structural" dependence in the literature (e.g., Rosholm and Svarer 2001). While the interdependence between the hazards through the correlation of the unobserved heterogeneity terms is a common practice, to our knowledge, there are no empirical studies that have examined the structural dependence in the mortgage literature. Not accounting for the structural dependence can bias the correlation; for example, if the structural dependence is not counted in the model, we might fail to detect any correlation, since the distinct driving forces of the interdependence between the default and prepayment hazards might cancel each other out. To allow for the structural dependence, we allow the default hazard, both the observable and the unobservable parts, to directly affect the prepayment hazard.

The most important finding of this paper is that default and prepayment hazards are interdependent in two distinct ways. First, we find a significant positive correlation between the unobserved heterogeneity terms. This finding suggests that there are some unobservable loan-specific characteristics that affect both default and prepayment hazards in the same direction. Second, we find a significant positive structural dependence, suggesting that higher risk of default leads to higher probability of prepayment. We show that neglecting the interdependence through both the correlation

---

2   This terminology is used by Danis and Pennington-Cross (2005).
3   The Federal Housing Administration (FHA) has a program called "Pre-Foreclosure Sales" that allows borrowers who are in foreclosure proceedings to sell their homes and to use the sales proceeds to satisfy the mortgage debt. Under this program, the debt is satisfied even if the sales proceeds are less than the loan balance owed.

of the unobserved heterogeneity terms and the preventive behavior of the individual mortgage borrowers can lead to biased estimates and misleading inference. As for the effects of covariates on the likelihood of default and prepayment, we find that loans with the following characteristics have a higher probability of default: more equity, low FICO score, high unemployment rate in the borrower's geographical area, short delinquency spells, nonjudicial states and positive interest rate spread. In addition, we find that loans with the following characteristics have higher probability to prepay: more equity, high FICO score, high unemployment rate, short delinquency spells, nonjudicial states and negative interest rate spread.

The remainder of this paper is organized as follows. Section 2 presents the data and some descriptive statistics. Section 3 presents the model. Section 4 reports the empirical results. Section 5 concludes.

2. Data Description and Summary Statistics

We use a panel dataset of first-lien residential mortgage loans obtained from the OCCMortgage Metrics data (OCCMM). OCCMM includes loans serviced by seven large banks and covers monthly loan performance from January 2008 until March 2016. The dataset consists of more than 21.1 million first-lien mortgage loans with $3.6 trillion in unpaid principal balances, which make up about 38 percent of all first-lien residential mortgage debt outstanding in the U.S.[4]

For the purposes of this paper, we focus on FHA loans[5] for which the foreclosure proceedings were initiated. There is a total of 231,800 of these loans in our sample of 3,359,573 FHA loans.[6] In our analysis, we exclude loans for which: (i) foreclosure proceedings end for reasons other than default and prepayment; (ii) servicing was transferred to different servicers; and (iii) values for explanatory variables are missing. Following the outlined exclusion criteria, our final sample size is 107,627, out of which 8974 are prepaid, 84,012 are defaulted and 14,641 are still in foreclosure proceedings as of March 2016.

We measure the lifetime of an FHA loan as the number of months from the onset of foreclosure until the loan is either defaulted or prepaid. We denote a loan that is still in a foreclosure proceedings at the end of the observation period as right censored and measure its lifetime as the number of months from the onset of foreclosure until March 2016. Table 1 presents descriptive statistics of the lifetime by status. The mean lifetime of a loan is about 15 months, which is higher than that reported by Pennington-Cross (2006) for subprime loans. The mean lifetime for prepaid loans is higher than for defaulted loans. This result suggests interdependence between default and prepayment. In other words, if default and prepayment were independent, presumably no loans would make it through to prepay, as they would on average reach the default option at 14 months before the prepay at 18 months. Thus, it might be misleading to consider independency between default and prepayment.

To examine how default and prepayment rates change with age, Figure 1 shows the smooth nonparametric estimation of the hazard function.[7] The figure shows that the probability of default increases during the first 18 months after foreclosure proceedings are initiated and then rapidly decreases. In addition, the figure shows that the probability of prepayment increases as foreclosure proceedings lengthen.

---

[4] See the quarterly OCC/OTSMortgage Metrics Reports for further details on the dataset.
[5] FHA loans are mortgage loans on which the lender is insured against loss by the Federal Housing Administration, with the borrower paying the mortgage insurance premiums. These loans offer low down payments and generous credit score and debt to income requirements.
[6] Ninety three percent of the FHA loans in our sample are 30-year fixed rate loans.
[7] The estimation is based on the Nelson–Aalen estimator.

Table 1. Statistics for lifetimes of individual FHA loans by status.

Status	Mean	Median	Std.Dev.	Min	Max	Qu. (25%)	Qu. (75%)
All Loans	15.21	10.00	14.11	1.00	78.00	5.00	21.00
Defaulted Loans	14.00	9.00	12.25	2.00	78.00	5.00	19.00
Prepaid Loans	18.27	12.00	16.36	2.00	78.00	5.00	28.00

The table provides the descriptive statistics of lifetimes (in months) of all FHA loans from January 2008 to March 2016. The descriptive statistics include the mean, median, standard deviation, minimum, maximum, 25% quartile and 75% quartile. All loans refer to all defaulted, prepaid and right censored loans in the sample.

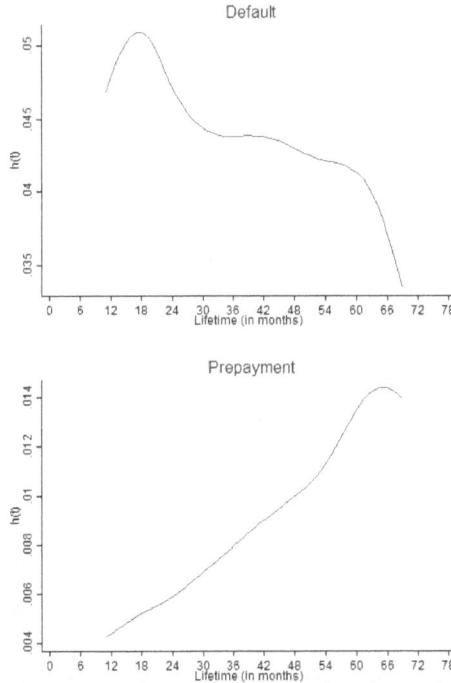

Figure 1. Smoothed nonparametric hazard Function. The figures display the smooth nonparametric estimation of default and prepayment hazard functions. The estimate is based on the Nelson–Aalen estimator. To smooth the Nelson–Aalen estimator, we specify an Epanechnikov kernel function with the default bandwidth in STATA.

The following explanatory variables are used to examine the determinants of default and prepayment hazards and their interdependence:

- LTV: To measure equity remaining in the property, we calculate Loan-To-Value ratio (LTV) using the current balance of the loan in each month and the estimated property value.[8]
- FICO score: To proxy for the overall borrower's creditworthiness, we use the borrower's FICO score in each month.
- Unemployment rate: To proxy for financial instability, we use the seasonally-adjusted monthly unemployment rate lagged by six months in the state where the property is located.[9]

---

[8] The estimated property value is obtained from the Lender Processing Services (LPS) Home Price Index (HPI).
[9] The seasonally-adjusted monthly unemployment rate is obtained from the Bureau of Labor Statistics (BLS).

- Delinquency spell: To measure delinquency behavior, we calculate the fraction of months in delinquency prior to the beginning of a foreclosure proceedings.
- Judicial status: To examine state foreclosure laws, we use an indicator variable equal to one if the state is a judicial foreclosure state, and zero otherwise.[10]
- Interest rate spread: To measure the change in the market interest rate, we use an indicator variable equal to one if the current interest rate is higher than the current 30-year fixed rate, and zero otherwise.[11,12].

Table 2 provides summary statistics of the explanatory variables. A quick comparison shows that the average characteristics are different between default and prepayment. In particular, on average, defaulted loans have less equity, lower FICO score and higher unemployment rate.

Table 2. Statistics of the explanatory variables by status. LTV, Loan-To-Value ratio.

	LTV			
Status	**Mean**	**Std.Dev.**	**Min**	**Max**
All Loans	95.48	6.14	80.91	100.58
Defaulted Loans	99.47	4.40	88.97	103.51
Prepaid Loans	75.71	27.17	5.38	91.64

	FICO Score			
Status	**Mean**	**Std.Dev.**	**Min**	**Max**
All Loans	540.20	18.31	516.51	567.38
Defaulted Loans	538.76	17.57	516.54	564.87
Prepaid Loans	556.64	23.27	523.40	590.85

	Unemployment Rate			
Status	**Mean**	**Std.Dev.**	**Min**	**Max**
All Loans	7.84	0.56	6.97	8.74
Defaulted Loans	8.20	0.54	7.38	9.06
Prepaid Loans	7.70	0.62	6.70	8.72

	Delinquency Spell			
Status	**Mean**	**Std.Dev.**	**Min**	**Max**
All Loans	0.41	0.23	0.02	1
Defaulted Loans	0.41	0.23	0.02	1
Prepaid Loans	0.40	0.22	0.03	1

	Judicial Status			
Status	**Mean**	**Std.Dev.**	**Min**	**Max**
All Loans	0.41	0.49	0	1
Defaulted Loans	0.37	0.48	0	1
Prepaid Loans	0.37	0.48	0	1

	Interest Rate Spread			
Status	**Mean**	**Std.Dev.**	**Min**	**Max**
All Loans	0.94	0.04	0.88	0.97
Defaulted Loans	0.95	0.03	0.91	0.98
Prepaid Loans	0.89	0.07	0.79	0.96

The table provides the descriptive statistics for LTV, FICO score, unemployment rate, delinquency spell, judicial states, and interest rate spread from January 2008 to March 2016. The descriptive statistics include the mean, standard deviation, minimum and maximum. The reported descriptive statistics for time-dependent variables are averaged over loans. All loans refer to all defaulted, prepaid and right censored loans in the sample.

---

[10] We identified judicial states using RealtyTrac.com and FindLaw.com.
[11] The 30-year fixed rate is obtained from primary mortgage market survey.
[12] About 94 percent of the loans are 30-year fixed rate mortgages.

3. Econometric Methodology

In this section, we propose a dependent competing risks duration model that is capable of incorporating time-varying covariates and censored observations easily. More importantly, the model controls for unobserved covariates, allows for estimating the default and prepayment hazards jointly and accounts for the interdependence of these hazards through both the correlation of the unobserved heterogeneity terms and the preventive behavior of individual mortgage borrowers. We first describe the specification of the model and then derive the likelihood function.

3.1. Model Specification

There are two main options available to the mortgage borrowers once foreclosure proceedings are initiated; namely, default (D) and prepayment (P). The prepayment (P) option can be viewed as "distressed prepayments" since borrowers in the foreclosure proceedings want to sell their homes to avoid a default outcome. Suppose that nonnegative random variables T_D and T_P are the potential lifetimes from the onset of foreclosure until default (D) and prepayment (P), respectively. In the competing risks framework, only the shortest lifetime is actually observed; that is $T = \min[T_D, T_P]$ and the corresponding actual event type, $J \in \{D, P\}$. Let $x(t)$ be a vector of observable covariates at time t and $v = (v_D, v_P)$ be a vector of unobservable covariates. The advantage of introducing two unobservable covariates (also called unobserved heterogeneity terms or frailties) is the possibility of exploring the dependence between the default and prepayment hazards, whenever v_D and v_P are positively or negatively correlated. In particular, this specification avoids using a restrictive one-factor model (e.g., Flinn and Heckman 1982; Clayton and Cuzick 1985; Heckman and Walker 1990) and so does not restrict the sign of dependence when a sufficiently flexible class of joint distributions is chosen for the unobserved heterogeneity terms.

Before elaborating the model specification, we list the regularity assumptions where index $i, i = 1, \ldots, n$, denotes individual mortgage loans:

Assumption 1. *(a) The unobserved heterogeneity terms are time invariant and depend on the individual mortgage loans i. (b) The individual heterogeneities $(v_{iD}, v_{iP}), i = 1, \ldots, n$, are independent and have the same distribution $G(v_D, v_P)$.*[13]

Assumption 2. *The potential lifetimes T_{iD} and $T_{iP}, i = 1, \ldots, n$, are independent conditional on the observable covariate histories $X_i = \{x_i(t), t \in \mathcal{N}\}, i = 1, \ldots, n$, and on heterogeneities $(v_{iD}, v_{iP}), i = 1, \ldots, n$.*

Assumption 3. *The individual heterogeneities are independent of the covariate histories.*

Assumption 4. *The variables T_{iD} (resp. $T_{iP}), i = 1, \ldots, n$, have identical conditional distributions given the individual covariate histories and the individual unobserved heterogeneities.*[14]

Assumption 5. *The type-specific hazard functions conditional on $(x_i(t), v_{iD}, v_{iP}), i = 1, \ldots, n$, are mixed proportional hazard functions:*

$$h_D(t; x(t), v_D) = h_{0D}(t) \exp(x(t)'\beta_D) \exp(v_D),$$
$$h_P(t; x(t), v_P, v_D) = h_{0P}(t) \exp(x(t)'\beta_P) \exp(v_P) \exp(\gamma . \log(h_D(t; x(t), v_D))). \quad (1)$$

---

[13] This assumption is commonly imposed in microeconomic studies, and it indicates that the focus of the analysis is on individual omitted heterogeneity. It implies that individual heterogeneities that depend on both individual loans and time are excluded. This allows us to assume away the moral hazard phenomena (e.g., Gourieroux and Jasiak 2004) and the omitted dynamic variables. The omitted time-dependent variables could be loan-specific or common to all loans. The analysis of these unobserved variables is left for further research.

[14] Assumptions 2 to 4 are standard.

where β_D and β_P are type-specific regression coefficients' vectors and h_{0D} and h_{0P} are the type-specific baseline hazard functions. The parameter γ captures the structural dependence of the prepayment hazard rate on the default probability.

Equation (1) accounts for interdependence between default and prepayment hazards in two ways, through: (1) the correlation of the unobserved heterogeneity terms; default and prepayment hazards might share similar or distinctive unobserved loan-specific characteristics that are identified by the negative or positive correlation of v_D and v_P; and (2) the structural dependence; borrowers who are in foreclosure proceedings and foresee themselves facing a high risk of default might increase their intensity to sell their homes to prepay in order to avoid default. If this hypothesis is true, we should expect γ to be significant and positive.

The model defined by Equation (1) nests three restricted models that are generally used in applied studies. The first restriction can be imposed to the general model by specifying $\gamma = 0$, which eliminates the structural dependence of the default and prepayment hazards and allows the interdependence between the hazards only through unobserved heterogeneity terms. The next restriction can be applied by assuming that the unobserved heterogeneity terms v_D and v_P are independent (i.e., $v_D \perp v_P$). This is a common assumption in empirical competing risks studies.[15] The last restriction can completely ignore unobserved heterogeneity terms. To illustrate the advantage of the model defined by Equation (1) and the potential bias of the restricted models, all four models are estimated.

Assumption 6. *The baseline hazard functions follow an expo-power distribution:*

$$h_{0j}(t) = \alpha_j t^{\alpha_j-1} exp(\theta_j t^{\alpha_j}), \tag{2}$$

where $j = D, P, \alpha_j > 0, -\infty < \theta_j < +\infty$.

This parametric specification was introduced by Saha and Hilton (1997). It can represent a variety of patterns of the hazard function, including constant, monotonically increasing, monotonically decreasing, U-shaped, inverted U-shaped or display humps. It includes as a special case the Weibull hazard function for $\theta = 0$, which is monotone. For $\theta \neq 0$, the hazard function has a turning point at $[(1-\alpha_j)/(\alpha_j\theta_j)]^{1/\alpha_j}$.

Conditional on the observable covariate histories, the distributions of the uncensored and right censored observations are characterized by the probabilities $Pr(t \leq T < t + \Delta t, J = j|X(t))$ and $Pr(T > c|X(c))$, respectively. These probabilities are obtained by integrating out v_D and v_P:

---

[15] One of the main reasons for these studies to make the independence assumption, in addition to computational convenience, is the common misunderstanding that dependent competing risks' specifications are not identifiable. This non-identifiability property is studied in detail by Tsiatis (1975), who proves that for any joint survival function with arbitrary dependence between the competing risks, one can find a different joint survival function with independent competing risks. If that is the case, then there is no point in complicating the model with the dependence assumption because the data cannot test for it anyway. However, Tsiatis's argument is valid only if the sample is homogenous. Thus, the problem of non-identifiability can be resolved by introducing heterogeneity through the variation of the observed covariates, as discussed at length by Heckman and Honore (1989), Abbring and Van den Berg (2003) and Colby and Rilstone (2004).

$$Pr(t \leq T < t + \Delta t, J = j | X(t)) = \int_{v_D} \int_{v_P} Pr(t \leq T < t + \Delta t, J = j | X(t), v_D, v_P) dG(v_D, v_P)$$

where $j = D, P$

and $Pr(t \leq T < t + \Delta t, J = D | X(t), v_D, v_P)$

$$= h_D(t; x(t), v_D) \exp\left(-\int_0^t h_D(u; x(u), v_D) du\right) \exp\left(-\int_0^t h_P(u; x(u), v_P, v_D) du\right) \Delta t.$$

and $Pr(t \leq T < t + \Delta t, J = P | X(t), v_D, v_P)$

$$= h_P(t; x(t), v_P, v_D) \exp\left(-\int_0^t h_D(u; x(u), v_D) du\right) \exp\left(-\int_0^t h_P(u; x(u), v_P, v_D) du\right) \Delta t. \qquad (3)$$

This quantity depends on the covariate histories up to time t only. In addition, we have:

$$Pr(T > c | X(c)) = \int_{v_D} \int_{v_P} Pr(T > c | X(c), v_D, v_P) dG(v_D, v_P),$$

where $Pr(T > c | X(c), v_D, v_P) = \exp\left(-\int_0^c h_D(u; x(u), v_D) du\right) \exp\left(-\int_0^c h_P(u; x(u), v_P, v_D) du\right). \quad (4)$

This quantity depends on the covariate history up to time c only.

In practice, the model has to be completed by specifying the joint distribution of the unobserved heterogeneity terms. In this subsection, we use an extension of the approach of Heckman and Singer (1984) (see also Nickell 1979; Van den Berg et al. 2004) and assume the following:

Assumption 7. *The joint distribution of the unobserved heterogeneity terms is bivariate discrete in which* v_D *and* v_P *can only take two values. Let* v_D^1 *and* v_D^2 *denote the values of* v_D *and* v_P^1 *and* v_P^2 *denote the values of* v_P. *Conditional on covariate histories, the set of individual mortgage loans can be divided into four classes that correspond to* $(v_D^1, v_P^1), (v_D^1, v_P^2), (v_D^2, v_P^1)$ *and* (v_D^2, v_P^2), *respectively. The sizes of these classes are unknown a priori and will be approximated by means of their associated probability estimates. Under Assumption 7, the joint distribution of* v_D, v_P *is characterized by the following elementary probabilities:*

$$Pr(v_D = v_D^1, v_P = v_P^1) = p_{11}, \quad Pr(v_D = v_D^1, v_P = v_P^2) = p_{12},$$
$$Pr(v_D = v_D^2, v_P = v_P^1) = p_{21}, \quad Pr(v_D = v_D^2, v_P = v_P^2) = p_{22}.$$

with $0 \leq p_{kl} \leq 1$ *and* $\sum_{k=1}^2 \sum_{l=1}^2 p_{kl} = 1$ *for* $k, l = 1, 2$.[16,17]

Under Assumption 7, the characteristics of the uncensored and right censored distributions become:

$$Pr(t \leq T < t + \Delta t, J = j | X(t)) = \sum_{k=1}^2 \sum_{l=1}^2 Pr(t \leq T < t + \Delta t, J = j | X(t), v_D^k, v_P^l) p_{kl}, \qquad (5)$$

---

[16] To ensure that the probabilities lie between $[0, 1]$ and sum up to one, we apply the logistic transformation, i.e.,

$$p_{kl} = \frac{\exp(q_{kl})}{\sum_{k=1}^2 \sum_{l=1}^2 \exp(q_{kl})}.$$

where $-\infty < q_{kl} < +\infty$, for $k, l = 1, 2$.

[17] The covariance of v_D and v_P can be derived as (see Van den Berg et al. 1994): $Cov(v_D, v_P) = (p_{11}p_{22} - p_{12}p_{21})(v_D^1 - v_D^2)(v_P^1 - v_P^2)$. Therefore, the correlation between v_D and v_P becomes:

$$\rho(v_D, v_P) = \frac{p_{11}p_{22} - p_{12}p_{21}}{\sqrt{(p_{11} + p_{12})(p_{11} + p_{21})(p_{22} + p_{12})(p_{22} + p_{21})}}.$$

Variables v_D and v_P will be perfectly correlated if either $p_{12} = p_{21} = 0$, or $p_{11} = p_{22} = 0$. Further, v_D and v_P are independent if and only if $p_{11}p_{22} - p_{12}p_{21} = 0$.

and

$$Pr(T > c|X(c)) = \sum_{k=1}^{2} \sum_{l=1}^{2} Pr(T > c|X(c), v_D^k, v_P^l) p_{kl}. \tag{6}$$

3.2. The Likelihood Function

We derive the likelihood function as follows:

$$\ell \; (\beta, \alpha, \theta, v, p, \gamma)$$

$$\propto \prod_{i \in W_{11}} \left[\sum_{k=1}^{2} \sum_{l=1}^{2} (h_D(t_i; x_i(t_i), v_D^k) \exp\left(-\int_0^{t_i} h_D(u; x_i(u), v_D^k) du\right) \exp\left(-\int_0^{t_i} h_P(u; x_i(u), v_P^l, v_D^k) du\right) p_{kl} \right]$$

$$\times \prod_{i \in W_{12}} \left[\sum_{k=1}^{2} \sum_{l=1}^{2} (h_P(u; x_i(u), v_P^l, v_D^k) \exp\left(-\int_0^{t_i} h_D(u; x_i(u), v_D^k) du\right) \exp\left(-\int_0^{t_i} h_P(u; x_i(u), v_P^l, v_D^k) du\right) p_{kl} \right] \tag{7}$$

$$\times \prod_{i \in W_{2}} \left[\sum_{k=1}^{2} \sum_{l=1}^{2} \exp\left(-\int_0^{c_i} h_D(u; x_i(u), v_D^k) du\right) \exp\left(-\int_0^{c_i} h_P(u; x_i(u), v_P^l, v_P^k) du\right) p_{kl} \right]$$

where W_{11} is the set of 84,012 uncensored loans that are defaulted (D), W_{12} is the set of 8974 loans that are prepaid (P) and W_2 is the set of 14,641 right-censored loans that are still in foreclosure proceedings as of March 2016.

There are three important points that should be noted about the likelihood function: (1) In order to avoid identification problems, we assume no constant covariates; that is, no intercept in the proportionality term. The levels of the intensities are captured by means of the values $v_D^1, v_D^2, v_P^1, v_P^2$, which are left unconstrained; (2) The likelihood function is valid when the covariates are continuously observed since the foreclosure proceedings is initiated. This condition is automatically satisfied by covariates x_i, which depend on individuals only. However, the covariates that depend on time are usually observed in discrete time. In this case, the likelihood function has to be approximated by assuming that the covariates are constant between two consecutive observation dates; (3) There is no closed-form expression for the integration of the prepayment hazard function. Thus, the integral is evaluated using the trapezoidal rule.[18]

4. Empirical Analysis

Here, we report and discuss the maximum likelihood estimates of the general model and its associated nested models. The general model, Model (1), is the unrestricted model introduced in the previous section. Model (2) is the model in which there is no structural dependence between the default and prepayment hazards, i.e., $\gamma = 0$. Model (3) is the model in which the unobserved heterogeneity terms v_D and v_P are assumed independent. This independence assumption is equivalent to the condition $p_{11}p_{22} - p_{12}p_{21} = 0$, whenever $v_D^1 \neq v_D^2$ and $v_P^1 \neq v_P^2$. Under Model (3), the two competing risks are independent conditional on the observed covariates. Finally, Model (4) is the model without unobserved heterogeneity terms. Tables 3 and 4 provide estimation results for Model (1), Model (2), Model (3) and Model (4), respectively.[19] The intercepts are set equal to zero in all models with unobserved heterogeneity terms (that is Models (1), (2) and (3)) since the intercepts cannot be distinguished from multiplicative constants in unobserved heterogeneities.

Based on the likelihood ratio tests, all the restricted models are rejected in favor of Model (1) (see Appendix A for details on comparing Models (1), (2), (3) and (4) based on the likelihood ratio tests). Thus, it can be concluded that unobserved dependent heterogeneities, as well as the structural dependence of the prepayment hazard rate on the default probability exist. In particular, the results confirm that neglecting the structural dependence can lead to overestimation of the correlation of the

---

[18] The mathematical details of the estimation of the likelihood function will be provided upon request.
[19] The numbers in parentheses are the standard errors for the estimated coefficients. *, ** and *** indicate that the coefficients are statistically significant at the 10%, 5% and 1% levels, respectively. The standard errors reported for the $p = (p_{11}, p_{12}, p_{21}, p_{22})$ and ρ are estimated using the delta method. The mathematical details of the estimation will be provided upon request.

unobserved heterogeneity terms. This can be seen by comparing Model (1) to Model (2), where the magnitude of the correlation parameter, ρ, decreased, but remained significant, and the coefficient of the structural dependence, γ, is positive and statistically significant.

Table 3. Dependent competing risks' estimates: Models (1) and (2).

	Model (1)				Model (2)			
	Default		Prepayment		Default		Prepayment	
LTV	−0.205	*	−3.223	***	−0.183		−3.373	***
	(0.108)		(0.182)		(0.122)		(0.274)	
FICO Score	−0.181	***	0.299	***	−0.194	***	0.131	
	(0.046)		(0.082)		(0.043)		(0.086)	
Unemployment Rate	1.038	***	0.369	**	1.024	***	0.818	***
	(0.116)		(0.162)		(0.145)		(0.212)	
Delinquency Spell	−0.753	***	−0.671	***	−0.755	***	−1.28	***
	(0.063)		(0.187)		(0.071)		(0.136)	
Judicial States	−0.859	***	−0.430	***	−0.86	***	−0.43	***
	(0.030)		(0.030)		(0.025)		(0.025)	
Interest Rate Spread	0.366	**	−0.530	**	0.307	***	−0.424	***
	(0.167)		(0.211)		(0.080)		(0.071)	
α	2.956	***	1.109	***	2.974	***	2.617	***
	(0.059)		(0.098)		(0.058)		(0.179)	
θ	−7.595	***	−1.139	***	−8.349	***	1.288	***
	(0.523)		(0.081)		(0.029)		(0.029)	
v_D^1	6.553	***			6.709	***		
	(0.137)				(0.063)			
v_D^2	0.911	***			1.069	***		
	(0.146)				(0.057)			
v_P^1	0.524	***			5.899	***		
	(0.172)				(0.228)			
v_P^2	−0.404	***			0.665	***		
	(0.067)				(0.257)			
P_{11}	0.353	***			0.427	***		
	(0.013)				(0.014)			
P_{12}	0.216	***			0.046	***		
	(0.010)				(0.012)			
P_{21}	0.000	***			0.002	***		
	(0.000)				(1.91×10^{-4})			
P_{22}	0.430	***			0.525	***		
	(0.015)				(0.171)			
ρ	0.624	***			0.907	***		
	(0.013)				(0.017)			
γ	0.421	***						
	(0.055)							
Log-Likelihood	−107,855.160				−108,080.63			

The table provides the maximum likelihood estimates for Model (1) and Model (2). Model (1) is the model with dependent unobserved heterogeneities and structural dependence, and Model (2) is the model with dependent unobserved heterogeneities. The numbers in parentheses are the standard errors for the estimated coefficients. *, ** and *** indicate that the coefficients are statistically significant at the 10%, 5% and 1% levels, respectively.

Table 4. Independent competing risks' estimates: Models (3) and (4).

	Model (3)		Model (4)	
	Default	Prepayment	Default	Prepayment
Constant			0.373 (0.330)	−1.053 (0.788)
LTV	−0.236 (0.188)	−2.444 *** (0.341)	−0.542 *** (0.145)	−3.663 *** (0.272)
FICO Score	−0.196 *** (0.050)	0.261 (0.170)	−0.153 *** (0.049)	0.112 (0.091)
Unemployment Rate	1.050 *** (0.234)	0.481 (0.671)	0.763 *** (0.179)	1.041 ** (0.473)
Delinquency Spell	−0.696 *** (0.203)	−1.491 ** (0.656)	−1.331 *** (0.159)	−1.749 *** (0.229)
Judicial States	−0.858 *** (0.030)	−0.433 *** (0.030)	−0.87 *** (0.023)	−0.42 *** (0.023)
Interest Rate Spread	0.321 * (0.194)	−0.599 (0.365)	0.525 *** (0.149)	−0.256 (0.304)
α	2.977 *** (0.076)	2.681 *** (0.277)	1.231 *** (0.031)	0.925 *** (0.214)
θ	−8.400 *** (0.800)	1.218 *** (0.275)	−1.829 *** (0.113)	3.328 *** (0.018)
v_D^1	6.749 (0.209)			
v_D^2	1.073 (0.190)			
v_P^1	6.756 (0.493)			
v_P^2	−0.283 (0.343)			
P_{11}	0.039 (0.008)			
P_{12}	0.511 (0.018)			
P_{21}	0.032 (0.006)			
P_{22}	0.418 (0.018)			
Log−Likelihood	−109,291.210		−192,769.690	

The table provides the maximum likelihood estimates for Model (3) and Model (4). Model (3) is the model with independent unobserved heterogeneities, and Model (4) is the model with no unobserved heterogeneities. The numbers in parentheses are the standard errors for the estimated coefficients. *, ** and *** indicate that the coefficients are statistically significant at the 10%, 5% and 1% levels, respectively.

In the following, we focus on the results of Model (1) to analyze the effects of covariates. The results in Table 3 show that the higher the equity in the property (evidenced by LTV), the higher the probabilities of default and prepayment. These results suggest that lenders seek to own properties that have more equity to lower their loss rate, and borrowers like to sell the properties that have more equity to lower their mortgage debt. In terms of credit scores, the results indicate that loans with higher FICO scores are less likely to default and more likely to prepay. Unemployment rate is used as a proxy for financial instability and suggests that a higher unemployment rate increases the probabilities of default and prepayment. The share of months in which the loan was delinquent prior to a foreclosure proceedings affects the likelihood of default and prepayment. In particular, loans with long delinquency spells are less likely to default and to prepay. Judicial states have lower probabilities of default and prepayment than nonjudicial states, suggesting that the foreclosure process lasts longer for states in which foreclosure is processed through the state court system. In terms of interest rates, an increase in the interest rate spread increases the probability of default and decreases the probability of prepayment.

Table 3 also lists the estimated parameters of expo-power distribution. Using these estimates from Model (1), Figure 2 presents the baseline hazards for default and prepayment. As shown in Figure 2, the baseline hazard for default appears to be inverted U-shaped. That is, the likelihood of default increases in the first months, reaches a peak and then decreases. The baseline hazard for prepayment features an initial increase followed by a gradual decrease. Note that at all time points, the baseline hazard for prepayment is higher than the baseline hazard for default. This means that, in the absence of covariates, the chance of prepayment for loans in foreclosure proceedings is higher than the chance of default.

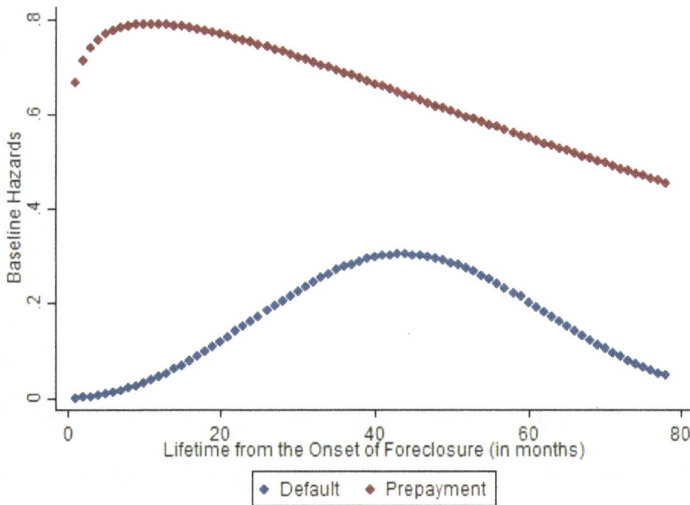

Figure 2. Baseline hazards for default and prepayment. The figure displays the estimates of the baseline hazards for default and prepayment. The estimate of the baseline hazards for event type j ($j = D, P$) is obtained using the maximum likelihood estimates of α_j and θ_j ($j = D, P$) from Model (1) and the lifetimes of loans from the onset of foreclosure.

$\rho(v_D, v_B)$ and γ in Table 3 denote interdependence between the default and prepayment hazards through the correlation of the unobserved heterogeneity terms and through the preventive behavior of individual mortgage borrowers, respectively. The positive and significant sign of the estimated correlation between the unobserved heterogeneity terms suggests that there are some unobservable loan-specific characteristics that affect both default and prepayment hazards in the same direction. The positive and significant sign of γ implies that the higher risk of default leads to a higher probability of prepayment. The result supports the hypothesis of structural dependence induced by the preventive behavior of individual mortgage borrowers.

5. Conclusions

Using a panel data of FHA mortgage loans, we specify a dependent competing risks framework to examine the determinants of the default and prepayment hazards once the foreclosure proceedings is initiated. More importantly, we examine the interdependence between default and prepayment, through both the correlation of the unobserved heterogeneity terms and the preventive behavior of the individual mortgage borrowers. We incorporate interdependence between the default and prepayment hazards through both the correlation of the unobserved heterogeneity terms associated with each risk and the preventive behavior of individual mortgage borrowers.

Our most important empirical finding here is that default and prepayment hazards are interdependent in two distinct ways. First, we find a significant positive correlation between the unobserved heterogeneity terms. This finding suggests that there are some unobservable loan-specific characteristics that affect both default and prepayment hazards in the same direction. Second, we find a significant positive structural dependence, suggesting that higher risk of default leads to higher probability of prepayment. We show that neglecting the interdependence through the correlation of the unobserved heterogeneity terms and through the preventive behavior of the individual mortgage borrowers can lead to biased estimates and misleading inference. As for the effects of covariates, we find that equity, FICO score, unemployment rate, delinquency spells, judicial states and interest rate spread are affecting the default and prepayment hazards.

Author Contributions: All authors have contributed in this paper. All authors have read and approved the final paper.

Conflicts of Interest: The authors declare no conflict of interest.

Appendix A. Comparing Models (1), (2), (3) and (4) Based on the Likelihood Ratio Tests

By comparing Models (3) and (4), we can assess whether unobserved independent heterogeneity terms exist in the default and prepayment hazards. The test statistics for the presence of v_D and v_P are independent under the null since the likelihood function can be factorized into the product of likelihood functions for default and prepayment. However, the likelihood ratio test for the null hypothesis $H_{0D} = \{v_D^1 = v_D^2\}$ and for the null hypothesis $H_{0P} = \{v_P^1 = v_P^2\}$ are nonstandard, since fewer parameters are identified under the null hypothesis than under the alternative. For instance, the probabilities p_{11}, p_{12}, p_{21} and p_{21} are not identifiable if $v_D^1 = v_D^2$ and $v_P^1 = v_P^2$. A careful analysis of this problem is out of the scope of our analysis and would require either assumptions on the local alternatives of interest or some prior restrictions on the parameter domain to avoid difficulties (e.g., Andrews and Ploberger 1994). It has been widely assumed in the literature that the critical value of the chi-square distribution with two degrees of freedom is a conservative test to use. Thus, in our analysis, we compare the likelihood ratio test with the critical value of the χ_2^2 distribution. For Model (3), the log-likelihood values for default and prepayment are $-61,931.37$ and $-28,668.87$, respectively; and for Model (4), the log-likelihood values for default and prepayment are $-135,705.99$ and $-35,007.83$, respectively. The calculated values of the likelihood ratio test are larger than the critical value of χ_2^2 at the five percent level. Thus, a significant improvement of Model (3) over Model (4) is concluded.

By comparing Models (2) and (3), we can test whether the unobserved heterogeneity terms are dependent. Testing for independence between v_D and v_P is equivalent to testing the null hypothesis $H_0 = \{p_{11}p_{22} - p_{12}p_{21} = 0\} = \{\rho = 0\}$. Under the null hypothesis, the likelihood ratio test is distributed as a chi-square with one degree of freedom. The calculated value of the likelihood ratio test is larger than the critical value of χ_1^2 at the five percent level. Hence, we conclude that the unobserved heterogeneity terms are dependent, and Model (2) is improved significantly over Model (3). Equivalently, we can consider the significance of the maximum likelihood estimate of correlation ρ. We reject the null hypothesis that the estimate of the correlation parameter, ρ, equals zero.

By comparing Models (1) and (2), we can test whether the structural dependence of the prepayment hazard rate on the default probability exists or not. The calculated value of the likelihood ratio test is larger than the critical value of χ_1^2 at the five percent level, which supports the existence of interdependence between the default and prepayment hazards through both the correlation of the unobserved heterogeneities and the preventive behavior of individual mortgage borrowers.

References

Abbring, Jaap H., and Gerard J. Van den Berg. 2003. The Identifiability of the Mixed Proportional Hazards Competing Risks Model. *Journal of the Royal Statistical Society: Series B (Statistical Methodology)* 65: 701–10.

Andrews, Donald W. K., and Werner Ploberger. 1994. Optimal Tests When a Nuisance Parameter is Present Only Under the Alternative. *Econometrica* 62: 1383–414.

Clayton, David, and Jack Cuzick. 1985. Multivariate Generalization of the Proportional Hazards Model. *Journal of Royal Statistical Society Series A* 148: 82–117.

Colby, Gordana, and Paul Rilstone. 2004. Nonparametric Identification of Latent Competing Risks Models. *Econometric Theory* 20: 883–90.

Cunningham, Donald F., and Patric Hendershott. 1984. Pricing FHA Mortgage Default Insurance. *Housing Finance Review* 13: 373–92.

Danis, Michelle A., and Anthony Pennington-Cross. 2005. *A Dynamic Look at Subprime Loan Performance*; Working paper; St. Louis: Federal Reserve Bank of St. Louis.

Deng, Yongheng. 1997. Mortgage Termination: An Empirical Hazard Model with Stochastic Term Structure. *The Journal of Real Estate Finance and Economics* 14: 309–31.

Deng, Yongheng, John M. Quigley, Robert Van Order, and Freddie Mac. 1996. Mortgage Default and Low Down-payment Loans: The Cost of Public Subsidy. *Regional Science and Urban Economics* 26: 263–85.

Deng, Yongheng, John M. Quigley, and Robert Van Order. 2000. Mortgage Terminations, Heterogeneity and the Exercise of Mortgage Options. *Econometrica* 68: 275–307.

Flinn, Christopher, and James Heckman. 1982. New Methods for Analyzing Structural Models of Labor Force Dynamics. *Journal of Econometrics* 18: 115–68.

Foster, Chester, and Robert Van Order. 1985. FHA Terminations: A Prelude to Rational Mortgage Pricing. *Journal of the American Real Estate and Urban Economics Association* 13: 273–91.

Green, Jerry R., and John B. Shoven. 1986. The Effect of Interest Rates on Mortgage Prepayments. *Journal of Money, Credit and Banking* 18: 41–50.

Gourieroux, Christian, and Joann Jasiak. 2004. Heterogeneous INAR(1) Model with Application to Car Insurance. *Insurance: Mathematics and Economics* 34: 177–92.

Heckman, James J., and Bo E. Honore. 1989. The Identifiability of the Competing Risks Model. *Biometrika* 76: 325–30.

Heckman, James, and Burton Singer. 1984. A Method for Minimizing the Impact of Distributional Assumptions in Econometric Models for Duration Data. *Econometrica* 52: 271–320.

Heckman, James J., and James R. Walker. 1990. Estimating Fecundability from Data on Waiting Times to First Conception. *Journal of American Statistical Association* 85: 283–94.

Kau, James B., and Donald C. Keenan, 1996. *Patterns of Rational Default*; Working paper; Athens: The University of Georgia.

Nickell, Stephen. 1979. Estimating the Probability of Leaving Unemployment. *Econometrica* 47: 1249–66.

Pennington-Cross, A. 2006. *The Duration of Foreclosure on the Subprime Mortgage Market: A Competing Risks Model with Mixing*; Working paper; St. Louis: Federal Reserve Bank of St. Louis.

Quigley, John M., and Robert Van Order. 1990. Efficiency in the Mortgage Market: The Borrower's Perspective. *Journal of the American Real Estate and Urban Association* 18: 237–52.

Quigley, John M., and Robert Van Order. 1995. Explicit Tests of Contingent Claims Models of Mortgage Default. *The Journal of Real Estate Finance and Economics* 11: 99–117.

Rosholm, Michael, and Michael Svarer. 2001. Structurally Dependent Competing Risks. *Economic Letters* 73: 169–73.

Saha, Atanu, and Lynette Hilton. 1997. Expo-power: A Flexible Hazard Function for Duration Data Models. *Economics Letters* 54: 227–33.

Schwartz, Eduardo S., and Walter N. Torous. 1989. Prepayment and the Valuation of Mortgage-Backed Securities. *The Journal of Finance* 44: 375–92.

Schwartz, Eduardo S., and Walter N. Torous. 1993. Mortgage Prepayment and Default Decisions: A Poisson Reegression Approach. *Journal of the American Real Estate and Urban Economics Association* 21: 431–49.

Titman, Sheridan, and Walter Torous. 1989. Valuing Commercial Mortages: An Empirical Investigation of the Contingent Claims Approach to Pricing Risky Debt. *The Journal of Finance* 44: 345–73.

Tsiatis, Anastasios. 1975. A Nonidentifiability Aspect of the Problem of Competing Risks. *Proceedings of the National Academy of Sciences* 72: 20–22.

Van den Berg, Gerard J., Marten Lindeboom, and Geert Ridder. 1994. Attrition in Longitudinal Panel Data and the Empirical Analysis of Dynamic Labour Market Behaviour. *Journal of Applied Econometrics* 9: 421–35.

Van den Berg, Gerard J., Bas Van der Klaauw, and Jan C. Van Ours. 2004. Punitive Sanctions and the Transition Rate from Welfare to Work. *Journal of Labor Economics* 22: 211–41.

Journal of
*Risk and Financial
Management*

MDPI

Article

Recovering Historical Inflation Data from Postage Stamps Prices

Philip Hans Franses * and Eva Janssens

Econometric Institute, Erasmus School of Economics, Burgemeester Oudlaan 50, 3062PA Rotterdam,
The Netherlands; janssens@ese.eur.nl
* Correspondence: franses@ese.eur.nl; Tel.: +31-10-4081273

Received: 17 October 2017; Accepted: 9 November 2017; Published: 14 November 2017

Abstract: For many developing countries, historical inflation figures are rarely available. We propose a simple method that aims to recover such figures of inflation using prices of postage stamps issued in earlier years. We illustrate our method for Suriname, where annual inflation rates are available for 1961 until 2015, and where fluctuations in inflation rates are prominent. We estimate the inflation rates for the sample 1873 to 1960. Our main finding is that high inflation periods usually last no longer than 2 or 3 years. An Exponential Generalized Autoregressive Conditional Heteroscedasticity (EGARCH) model for the recent sample and for the full sample with the recovered inflation rates shows the relevance of adding the recovered data.

Keywords: inflation; postage stamps; price recovery; historical time series; EGARCH

JEL Classification: E31; N10; N16

---

1. Introduction and Motivation

The World Bank collects annual inflation rates for all countries in the world. For developed countries, such data can be available for a long span of time, also because statistical bureaus for the countries exist for a long time.[1] For many developing countries, matters can be different. For example, Benin's first available inflation figure concerns 1993, whereas Ethiopia's first quote concerns 1966. There may be various causes for this lack of data, which can relate to a lack of institutions and the effects of decolonization.

For various reasons, one may want to have some impression of historical figures. One would perhaps want to know if a current high inflation period, which indicates a period with risky economic fluctuations, has occurred before and which measures were taken to reduce inflation. Alternatively, one may want to compare inflation patterns across countries to discern similarities or specific differences. In addition, one may want to compute historical data on real GDP, real wages, and purchasing power parity, which all involve price levels. Preferably, one would also want to have annual data without missing data in between.

Recovering historical price levels can be difficult because of lack of information on the prices of many goods and because good and services may have changed substantially over the years. Various recent studies present discussions of methods to recover historical data and the reliability of those historical statistics, see Allen et al. (2011), Bolt and Zanden (2014), Cendejas Bueno and Font de Villanueva (2015), Deaton and Heston (2010), Frankema and Waijenburg (2012), and Jerven (2009).

In the present paper, we present a new and very simple method that aims to reconstruct historical inflation rates. We seek to alleviate the issue of changing products over time by considering a product

---

[1] See Franses and Legerstee (2014) for a table with dates for 106 countries when statistical bureaus were founded.

that has not much changed over time and for which prices are immediately available. This product concerns postage stamps. First, postage stamps have been issued in many countries for a long time. Next, the type of product and its use did not change much over the years. In addition, evidently, the price of the stamp is printed on the stamp; see for example Figure 1, where we present a few stamps for Suriname.

Figure 1. A few stamps issued in 1996 in Suriname (with exceptionally high prices).

In the present paper, and only for illustrative purposes, we consider the historical prices of this South American country, which borders Guyana and Brazil. The World Bank can provide us with annual inflation rates starting in 1961. The first stamps in Suriname were issued in 1873, and hence we aim to retrieve annual inflation rates since that year. We chose Suriname as the estimation sample because it is reasonably large, ranging from, 1961 to and including 2015, as there were many stamps issued per year, and also as there is substantial variation in the inflation figures over time. It also so happens that, at the time of writing this paper in 2016, inflation is again very high, and people may wonder how long high inflation periods typically last.

The outline of our paper is as follows. Section 2 deals with the inflation rates data and with the stamps data, and provides some characteristics. Section 3 deals with two types of models to see if (changes in) postal stamps prices have explanatory value for inflation. One model is a simple regression model, while the other is a MIDAS regression, which fits annual inflation rates to quarterly stamps prices.[2] Both models suggest strong predictive power of the stamps prices. Section 4 deals with the backward extrapolation and identifies a few historical periods with excessive inflation rates and their potential causes. Section 5 concludes.

---

[2] Important references to MIDAS regression are Andreou et al. (2010), Clements and Galvao (2008), Ghysels et al. (2004), and Ghysels et al. (2007).

2. The Data

The annual inflation rates for 1961 to 2015 for Suriname are retrieved from the World Bank. Table 1 presents the data, and Figure 2 visualizes the data. Clearly, the data show periods with high inflation, and 1994 stands out with an inflation rate of 368.5 per cent. This number associates with approximately 1.6 per cent per day. Periods with high inflation are 1993 to 1995 and 1999 to 2001, while 1987 was also an exceptional year. The International Monetary Fund provides a review of the potential causes for the high inflation rates in the nineties.[3]

Table 1. Inflation data. All items index annual average (source: World Bank).

1961	1.7	1971	0.2	1981	8.8
1962	2.1	1972	3.2	1982	7.3
1963	2.1	1973	12.9	1983	4.4
1964	4.2	1974	16.9	1984	3.7
1965	1.9	1975	8.4	1985	10.9
1966	4.7	1976	10.1	1986	18.7
1967	10.7	1977	9.7	1987	53.4
1968	0.2	1978	8.8	1988	7.3
1969	11.3	1979	14.8	1989	0.8
1970	2.6	1980	14.1	1990	21.7
1991	26	2001	38.6	2011	17.7
1992	43.7	2002	15.5	2012	5
1993	143.5	2003	23	2013	2
1994	368.5	2004	10	2014	3.3
1995	235.6	2005	9.9	2015	6.9
1996	−0.7	2006	11.3		
1997	7.1	2007	6.4		
1998	19	2008	14.7		
1999	98.8	2009	−0.2		
2000	59.4	2010	6.9		

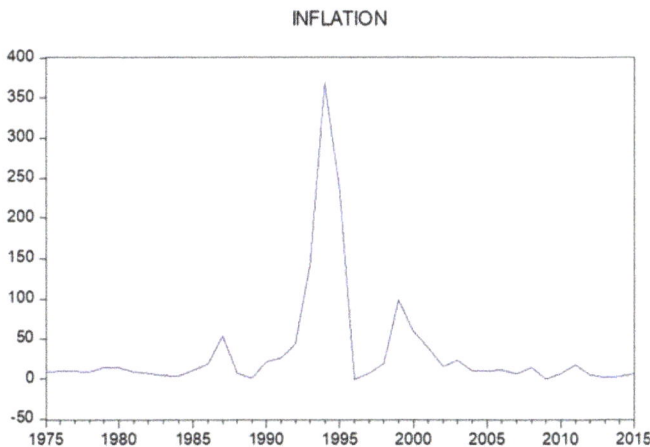

Figure 2. Inflation (in yearly percentages) in Suriname.

Table 2 presents the data on the postage stamps, also for the period 1961 to 2015. We consulted two catalogues, and retrieved the median prices of all the stamps in each year. The first catalogue

---

3   http://www.imf.org/external/np/sec/pn/1999/PN9980.HTM.

runs until 12 November 1975, a few weeks before Suriname became an independent country on 25 November 1975. Before independence, Suriname was a colony of the Netherlands since the 17th century. The first postage stamp in Suriname was issued in 1873.

Table 2. Percentage changes in the median stamp price per year (sources: for the data until and including 12 November 1975, "Speciale catalogus 2002, Postzegels van Nederland en overzeese rijksdelen" NVPH, Amsterdam, Joh Enschede, and for the data since 25 November 1975, "Officiele postzegelcatalogus," Suriname, 31ste Editie 2016, Guernsey, Uitgeverij Zonnebloem).

1961	33.33	1971	8.7	1981	50
1962	−30	1972	20	1982	−16.67
1963	0	1973	0	1983	−50
1964	3.57	1974	0	1984	33.33
1965	3.45	1975	0	1985	10
1966	33.33	1976	16.67	1986	−9.09
1967	25	1977	42.86	1987	120
1968	0	1978	0	1988	0
1969	0	1979	−10	1989	0
1970	−8	1980	33.33	1990	0
1991	0	2001	−60	2011	−12.5
1992	40.91	2002	70	2012	28.57
1993	30.65	2003	−41.18	2013	13.89
1994	4220.99	2004	−20	2014	7.32
1995	471.43	2005	−43.75	2015	6.82
1996	−61	2006	277.78		
1997	15.38	2007	17.65		
1998	61.11	2008	50		
1999	148.28	2009	0		
2000	177.78	2010	33.33		

The data in Table 2 show that, like inflation, the percentage changes in postal stamp prices can be substantial. The observation in 1994 stands out with a value of 4220.99 per cent. In various years, we also see that price changes were equal to zero.

Figures 3 and 4 provide scatters of inflation versus the percentage changes in stamps prices. The first scatter covers all data, whereas Figure 4 concerns the data except 1994. A first impression is that there may exist a positive relationship between the two series.

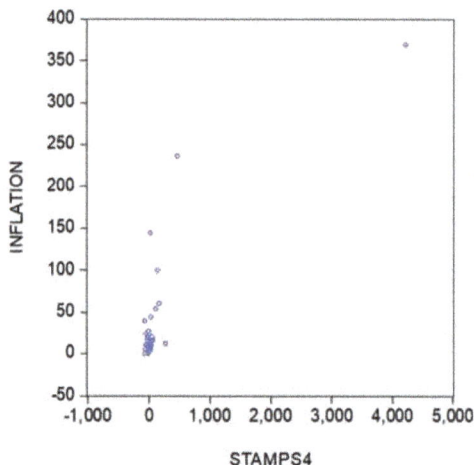

Figure 3. Scatter of inflation versus percentage changes in stamps prices (all observations).

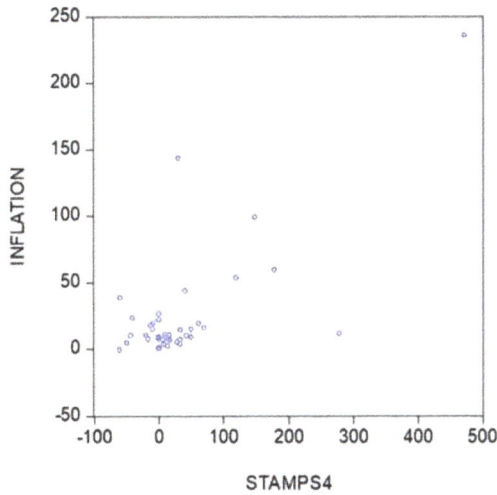

Figure 4. Scatter of inflation versus percentage changes in stamps prices (excluding 1994).

3. Two Econometric Models

In this section, we consider two econometric models to link inflation with changes in stamp prices. We denote annual inflation as Y_T and the annual changes in stamps prices as X_T. For inflation, we have only annual data, but for the stamps prices, we can also construct quarterly data. Each year, a range of stamps was issued, and this allows us to construct quarterly percentage changes, as the catalogues give the exact dates (day, month, and year) of issue. There are now two ways to compute these changes in postal stamps prices. The first refer a current quarter with the previous quarter—that is, the first-order differences. We denote these as $X^1_{q,T}$, where T again corresponds with years and q with the quarters 1, 2, 3, and 4. The data appear in Figure 5. The second type of percentage changes concern the differences between a current quarter and the same quarter the year before. We denote these as $X^4_{q,T}$, as these concern fourth-order differences. The data are depicted in Figure 6.

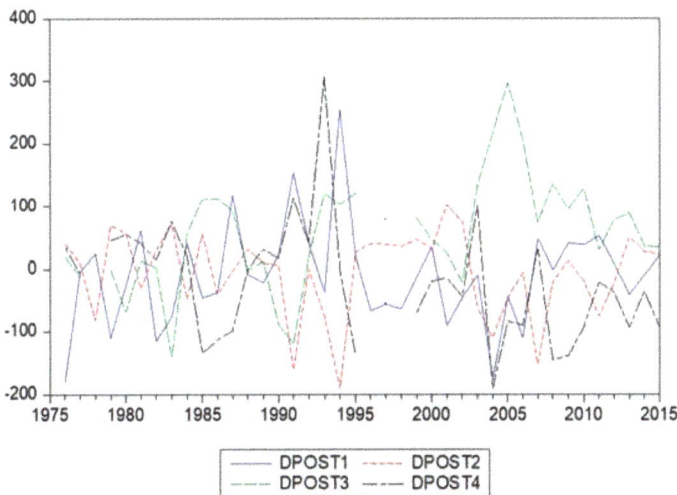

Figure 5. Quarter-to-quarter changes in stamps prices for MIDAS regression.

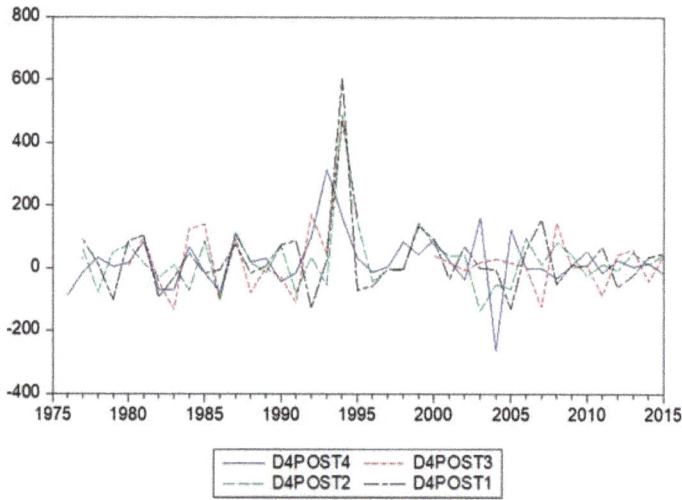

Figure 6. Annual changes in stamps prices, observed per quarter, for MIDAS regression.

At first, we allow for potential differences across models for the periods before and after the date of independence, and we thus start with the following regression model for the data from 1975 onwards, that is

$$Y_T = \mu + \alpha_0 X_T + \alpha_1 X_{T-1} + \rho Y_{T-1} + \varepsilon_T$$

where Y_T is annual inflation and as X_T are the annual changes in stamps prices. The estimation results for the sample 1975 to 2015 appear in the first panel of Table 3. The parameters are estimated using Ordinary Least Squares (OLS), with Newey-West adjusted standard errors. The tests for normality and first-order residual autocorrelation indicate that the model can be improved. A closer look at the residuals reveals that there are (at least) two very large residuals, concerning 1993 and 1999. The second panel of Table 3 displays the estimation results for the case where lagged inflation is deleted (as it was not significant) and where the observations in 1993 and 1999 are not included. The test results now suggest that the model is appropriately specified. The last panel of Table 3 presents the results for the same model, but now for the sample starting in 1961. Even though the tests do diagnose some problems with the errors (which are due to some modest outliers), the parameter estimates for current and lagged changes in stamps prices are remarkably constant across models and samples.

Table 3. Estimation results for various regression models relating inflation with lagged inflation and current and lagged percentage changes in stamps prices. Estimated Newey-West adjusted standard errors are in parentheses.

Variable	Sample 1975–2015	Sample 1975–2015 (without 1993, 1999)	Sample 1961–2015 (without 1993, 1999)
Intercept	15.683 (5.398)	11.032 (2.796)	9.288 (2.171)
Y_{T-1}	0.026 (0.162)		
X_T	0.083 (0.005)	0.085 (0.001)	0.085 (0.001)
X_{T-1}	0.040 (0.013)	0.043 (0.001)	0.044 (0.001)
R^2	0.858	0.967	0.964
p value tests			
Normality	0.000	0.131	0.000
Autocorrelation	0.010	0.037	0.008

To see if data that are more detailed can lead to better models, we consider two MIDAS models. The first model is

$$Y_T = \mu + \rho Y_{T-1} + \beta_0 X^1_{4,T} + \beta_1 X^1_{3,T} + \beta_2 X^1_{2,T} + \beta_3 X^1_{1,T} + \beta_4 X^1_{4,T-1} + \beta_5 X^1_{3,T-1} + \varepsilon_T$$

where $X^1_{q,T}$ is the first-order differenced median stamps prices, where T again corresponds with years and q with the quarters 1, 2, 3, and 4. The OLS estimation results, with Newey-West adjusted standard errors, for this model are given in the left panel of Table 4. The diagnostic tests for normality and first-order residual autocorrelation suggest that this model is adequately specified.

Table 4. Estimation results for the (unrestricted) MIDAS regression models, sample runs from 1975 to and including 2015. Estimated Newey-West adjusted standard errors are in parentheses. $X^1_{q,T}$ are the first-order differenced median stamps prices, where T again corresponds with years and q with the quarters 1, 2, 3, and 4, and differenced median stamps price. $X^4_{q,T}$ are the fourth-order differenced median stamps prices.

Variable	Version 1		Variable	Version 2	
Intercept	1.828	(3.240)	Intercept	0.315	(2.811)
Y_{T-1}	0.554	(0.037)	Y_{T-1}	0.893	(0.134)
$X^1_{4,T}$	0.240	(0.066)	$X^4_{4,T}$	0.190	(0.065)
$X^1_{3,T}$	0.209	(0.060)	$X^4_{3,T}$	0.051	(0.099)
$X^1_{2,T}$	0.190	(0.085)	$X^4_{2,T}$	−0.023	(0.078)
$X^1_{1,T}$	0.402	(0.068)	$X^4_{1,T}$	0.232	(0.061)
$X^1_{4,T-1}$	0.430	(0.073)	$X^4_{4,T-1}$	0.049	(0.050)
$X^1_{3,T-1}$	0.319	(0.100)	$X^4_{3,T-1}$	0.084	(0.050)
			$X^4_{2,T-1}$	−0.264	(0.098)
R^2	0.932			0.944	
p value tests					
Normality	0.184			0.645	
Autocorrelation	0.149			0.740	
RMSPE, in sample	19.305			18.363	

The second MIDAS model is

$$Y_T = \mu + \rho Y_{T-1} + \beta_0 X^4_{4,T} + \beta_1 X^4_{3,T} + \beta_2 X^4_{2,T} + \beta_3 X^4_{1,T} + \beta_4 X^4_{4,T-1} + \beta_5 X^4_{3,T-1} + \beta_6 X^4_{2,T-1} + \varepsilon_T$$

where $X^4_{q,T}$ are the fourth-order differenced median stamps prices, where T again corresponds with years and q with the quarters 1, 2, 3 and 4. The OLS estimation results, with Newey-West adjusted standard errors, are in the second panel of Table 4. This MIDAS model also seems to fit the data well. When we compare the in-sample prediction errors, we see that the difference in accuracy is small. Given that the diagnostic tests indicate appropriate models, we learn that adding higher frequency terms to the regression models leads to more accuracy.

Overall, the estimation results in this section show that inflation and changes in stamps prices are strongly connected, at least here for the case of Suriname. Because the frequency of publication of the postal stamps before 1975 is lower, the MIDAS models however are not useful for the purpose we have in mind, namely recovering historical inflation rates, despite the increased accuracy they offered.

4. Recovery of Historical Inflation Rates

Given that, a suitable model for annual inflation rates appears to be

$$Y_T = \mu + \alpha_0 X_T + \alpha_1 X_{T-1} + \varepsilon_T$$

we will use the parameter estimates in the final panel of Table 3 to make backward predictions for inflation. That is, for the sample 1873 to 1960, we compute

$$\hat{Y}_T = 9.288 + 0.085X_T + 0.044X_{T-1} \tag{1}$$

Figure 7 displays the observations on the changes in the postal stamps prices for these years, which were collected from the first mentioned catalogue in Table 2. In addition, Figure 8 displays the estimated historical inflation observations.

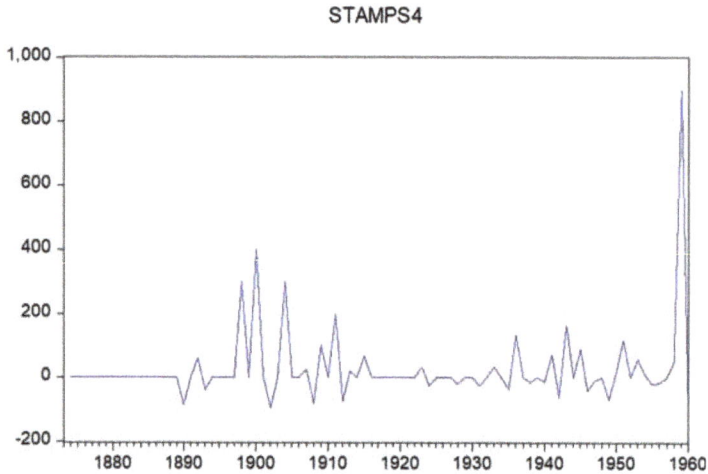

Figure 7. Percentage changes in postal stamps prices, 1873–1960.

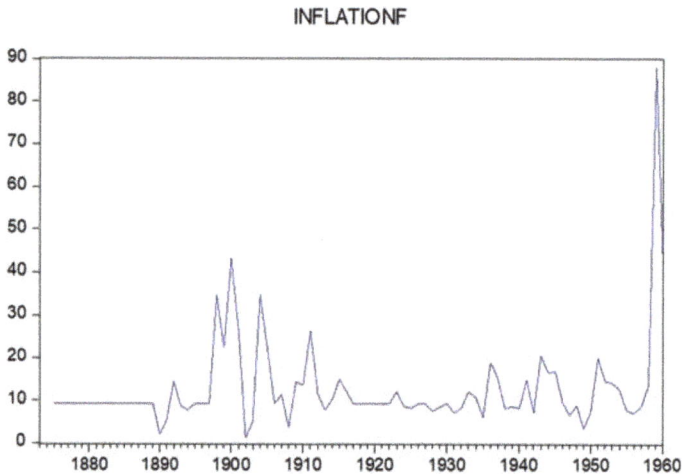

Figure 8. Predictions of inflation rates for 1873 to 1960.

We see that high inflation periods each time last for usually one or one years, and at most four years (Figure 9). Specifically, if we define a high inflation period as a period with inflation higher than 10 per cent, the average length of such a period is 1.45 using the fitted sample from 1873–2015.

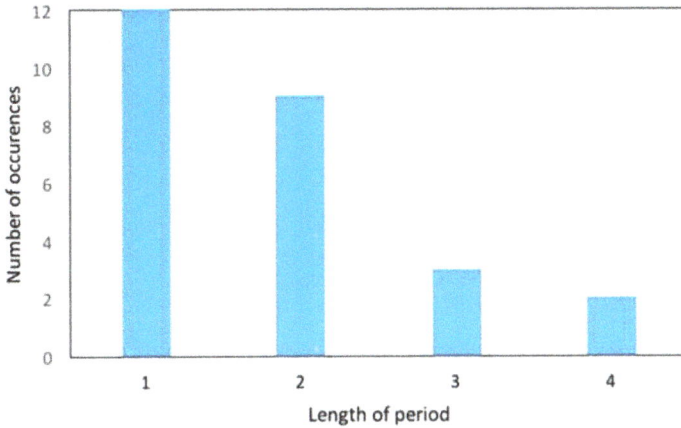

Figure 9. Length of periods with high inflation rates (inflation above 10 per cent) and their frequency of occurrence, based on fitted sample of 1873–2015.

Figure 10 displays the actual data from 1961 onward and the estimated data back to 1873 in one single graph. Clearly, the data in the nineties are exceptional. Postal stamps experienced enormous price changes during the 1990s. This period exactly coincides with the hyperinflation that Suriname experienced during that time.

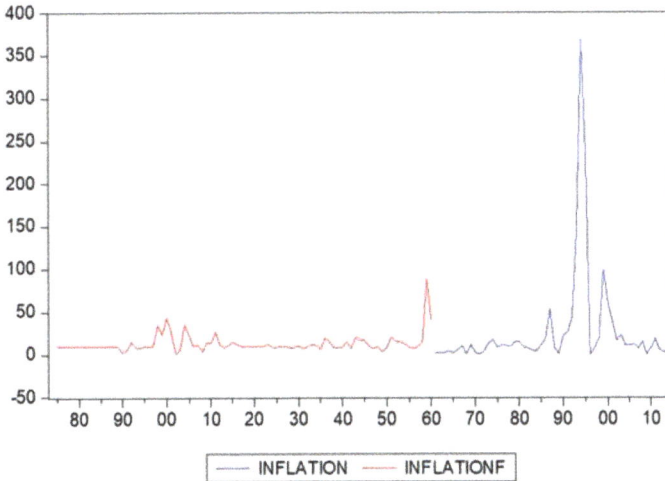

Figure 10. True and estimated inflation rates.

However, various other periods in our forecasting sample are characterized by high inflation rates. Consider for example the 1900s, 1930s, 1940s, and 1950s (specifically 1957). In Table 5, more details on these periods are discussed. The high inflation rates around 1900 coincides with the gold rush at the same time at the Lawa River in Suriname, which amounted to higher tariffs for transportation (see Van Velzen and Hoogbergen (2013)). The higher inflation rates in the 1930s can be related to a period of economic decline and austerity measures, causing social upheaval (Hoefte 2013). The developments in 1940s can be most likely attributed to the consequences of the Second World War. The very high inflation rates as indicated by the peak at 1957 occur in the same year as the establishment of the central bank of Suriname,[4] but certainly coincides with the so-called Eisenhower recession.

Table 5. Estimated historical episodes with high inflation.

Years	Potential Causes
1900s	Gold rush (Lawa railway construction)
1930s	Economic decline, social upheaval in the form of riots
1940s	WW II
1957	Establishment of the Central Bank of Suriname, Brokopondo-agreement with Alcoa and Eisenhower Recession

Finally, Table 6 presents the estimation results of an EGARCH model, measuring risk.[5] The model reads as

$$\log\left(Inflation_t + 1\right) = \mu + \rho\log\left(Inflation_{t-1} + 1\right) + z_t\sqrt{h_t}$$

where $Inflation_t$ covers the full sample from 1873 to 2015, with

$$\log\left(h_t\right) = \omega + \alpha_1|z_{t-1}| + \alpha_2 z_{t-1} + \alpha_3\log\left(h_{t-1}\right)$$

in addition, z_t is a standard normally distributed variable. We need to add 1 to where $Inflation_t$ to make sure that all observations are positive. The estimation results (with Bollerslev-Wooldridge robust standard errors in parentheses) for the sample 1961–2015 and the full sample (1873–2015) with the recovered data shows reasonably similar parameter estimates and much smaller estimated standard errors in the latter case. This seems to support the quality of the recovered inflation figures.

$$\log\left(Inflation_t + 1\right) = \mu + \rho\log\left(Inflation_{t-1} + 1\right) + z_t\sqrt{h_t}$$

with

$$\log\left(h_t\right) = \omega + \alpha_1|z_{t-1}| + \alpha_2 z_{t-1} + \alpha_3\log\left(h_{t-1}\right)$$

Estimated using Eviews package 8.0. To reduce the effect of outliers, the data are transformed as indicated. Bollerslev-Wooldridge robust standard errors are in parentheses.

Table 6. Estimated parameters and associated standard errors in the EGARCH model.

Parameters	Sample			
	1961–2015		1873–2015	
μ	1.457	(0.200)	1.595	(0.219)
ρ	0.327	(0.089)	0.314	(0.096)
ω	−0.939	(0.249)	−0.311	(0.103)
α_1	1.073	(0.308)	0.311	(0.113)
α_2	0.711	(0.182)	0.208	(0.095)
α_3	0.659	(0.146)	0.855	(0.048)

5. Conclusions

We proposed a simple method to estimate annual historical data on inflation using changes in postal stamps prices. The method seems to work, at least for Suriname. A next step would be to

---

4   https://www.cbvs.sr/about-cbvs/history.
5   See Chang and McAleer (2017) and McAleer and Hafner (2014) for two recent studies on this very useful model.

reconstruct historical figures for other countries. If possible, we would want to match our estimates with actually observed inflation rates, should those data be available.

Author Contributions: Philip Hans Franses and Eva Janssens collected the data, performed the analysis and Philip Hans Franses and Eva Janssens wrote the paper.

Conflicts of Interest: The authors declare no conflict of interest.

References

Allen, Robert C., Jean-Pascal Bassino, Debin Ma, Christine Moll-Murata, and Jan Luiten van Zanden. 2011. Wages, prices, and living standards in China, 1738–1925: In comparison with Europe, Japan, and India. *Economic History Review* 64: 8–38. [CrossRef]

Andreou, Elena, Eric Ghysels, and Andros Kourtellos. 2010. Regression models with mixed sampling frequencies. *Journal of Econometrics* 158: 246–61. [CrossRef]

Bolt, Jutta, and Jan Luiten van Zanden. 2014. The Maddison Project: Collaborative research on historical national accounts. *Economic History Review* 67: 627–51. [CrossRef]

Cendejas Bueno, Jose Luis, and Cecilia Font de Villanueva. 2015. Convergence of inflation with a common cycle: Estimating and modelling Spanish historical inflation from the 16th to the 18th centuries. *Empirical Economics* 48: 1643–65. [CrossRef]

Chang, Chia-Lin, and Michael McAleer. 2017. The correct regularity condition and interpretation of asymmetry in EGARCH. *Economics Letters* 161: 52–55. [CrossRef]

Clements, Michael P., and Anna B. Galvao. 2008. Macroeconomic forecasting with mixed-frequency data. *Journal of Business and Economic Statistics* 26: 546–54. [CrossRef]

Deaton, Angus, and Alan Heston. 2010. Understanding PPPs and PPP-based national accounts. *American Economic Journal: Macroeconomics* 2: 1–35. [CrossRef]

Frankema, Ewout H. P., and Marlous van Waijenburg. 2012. Structural impediments to African growth? New evidence from real wages in British Africa, 1880–1965. *Journal of Economic History* 72: 895–926. [CrossRef]

Franses, Philip Hans, and Rianne Legerstee. 2014. Statistical institutes and economic prosperity. *Quality and Quantity* 48: 507–20. [CrossRef]

Ghysels, Eric, Pedro Santa-Clara, and Rossen Valkanov. 2004. The MIDAS Touch: Mixed Data Sampling Regression Models. CIRANO Working Paper 2004s-20. Montreal, QC, Canada: CIRANO.

Ghysels, Eric, Arthur Sinko, and Rossen Valkanov. 2007. Midas regressions: Further results and new directions. *Econometric Reviews* 26: 53–90. [CrossRef]

Hoefte, Rosemarijn. 2013. *Suriname in the Long Twentieth Century: Domination, Contestation, Globalization*. Berlin: Springer.

Jerven, Morten. 2009. The relativity of poverty and income: How reliable are African economic statistics? *African Affairs* 109: 77–96. [CrossRef]

McAleer, Michael, and Christiaan Hafner. 2014. A one line derivation of EGARCH. *Econometrics* 2: 92–97. [CrossRef]

Van Velzen, Thoden, and Wim Hoogbergen. 2013. *Een Zwarte Vrijstaat in Suriname (Deel 2): De Okaanse Samenleving in de Negentiende en Twintigste Eeuw*. Leiden: Brill.

MDPI

St. Alban-Anlage 66

4052 Basel

Switzerland

Tel. +41 61 683 77 34

Fax +41 61 302 89 18

www.mdpi.com

Journal of Risk and Financial Management Editorial Office

E-mail: jrfm@mdpi.com

www.mdpi.com/journal/jrfm

www.ingramcontent.com/pod-product-compliance
Lightning Source LLC
Chambersburg PA
CBHW051841210326
41597CB00033B/5736